Alive at the Core

Alive at the Core

Exemplary Approaches to General Education in the Humanities

Michael Nelson and Associates

JOSSEY-BASS
A Wiley Company
San Francisco

Jossey-Bass books and products are available through most bookstores. To contact Jossey-Bass directly, call (888) 378–2537, fax to (800) 605–2665, or visit our website at www.josseybass.com.

Substantial discounts on bulk quantities of Jossey-Bass books are available to corporations, professional associations, and other organizations. For details and discount information, contact the special sales department at Jossey-Bass.

 Manufactured in the United States of America on Lyons Falls Turin Book. This paper is acid-free and 100 percent totally chlorine-free.

Library of Congress Cataloging-in-Publication Data
Alive at the core: exemplary approaches to general education in the humanities / Michael Nelson and associates.
    p. cm.—(The Jossey-Bass higher and adult education series)
Includes bibliographical references and index.
  ISBN 0-7879-4760-1 (alk. paper)
    1. Humanities—Study and teaching (Higher)—United States. I. Nelson, Michael, 1949– II. Series.
AZ183.U5 A45   2000
001.3'071'173—dc21   00-008253

FIRST EDITION
HB Printing 10 9 8 7 6 5 4 3 2 1

**The Jossey-Bass
Higher and Adult Education Series**

For my sons, Michael Nelson, Jr., and Sam Nelson

When wisdom entereth into thine heart,
and knowledge is pleasant unto thy soul;
Discretion shall preserve thee,
and understanding shall keep thee.

—Proverbs 2:10–11

Contents

Foreword

Martha C. Nussbaum

How should a liberal education prepare students to be citizens of an increasingly complex and interlocking world? This is, as it should be, a central question in contemporary debates about the college curriculum. Most other countries of the world treat higher education as primarily a preparation for a career. Students typically study just one subject from the beginning, such as law or philosophy or chemistry. They do not get together across disciplines in shared courses in the humanities, social sciences, and natural sciences. Higher education in the United States, by contrast, has typically followed a different tradition. We believe that a college or university education, while it offers specialized training in a major subject, should also offer a general preparation for life and citizenship, what has come to be called a "liberal education." But we have deep disagreements about what a liberal education should do.

There is broad agreement that liberal education should offer a general enrichment of life that is also in some way connected with building democratic citizens, people who can deliberate well about pressing issues that they will need to face, whether as jurors or voters or simply as neighbors and friends. But as the chapter authors in this book show, there are deep disagreements about how to promote these goals. Sometimes these disagreements are only apparent, reflecting intelligent responses to real differences of student preparation or attitude. Any single approach to liberal education in the United States indicts itself by its very singleness, since our country contains a tremendous diversity of students and institutions. But some of the differences are deeper, reflecting long-standing debates concerning what education is all about. In thinking about these deeper issues we are helped by turning to Seneca, who gave us the concept of "liberal education" in a famous letter he wrote on the topic in A.D 64.

Should a liberal education be an acculturation into the time-honored values of one's own culture? Or should it follow Socrates, arguing that "the examined life" is the best preparation for citizenship? This is the question Seneca still poses to modern readers. Seneca was a wealthy and powerful member of Rome's elite, regent of the empire during the youth of Nero. He had received a traditional Roman education, which emphasized a rather uncritical reception of tradition through study of the "great books" of his culture. But Seneca inhabited a diverse multicultural society, in which political deliberation had to bring together people from many different ethnic, national, and religious groups in a search for the common good. Rome of the first century contained Jews, Christians, followers of traditional Roman religion, and adherents of a wide range of sects and cults. It contained men and women. It contained differences of ethnic and national origin. (Seneca himself was born in Spain; he was vividly aware of his own outsider status, and his thinking was probably colored by this experience.) So it is not idly that he poses the question: Should an education for citizenship in this complex world follow the traditional model or the example of Socrates? He sets out to defend the latter.

Seneca begins his letter by describing the traditional style of education, noting that it is called "liberal" (*liberalis*) because it is understood to be an education for well-brought-up young gentlemen, who were called the *liberales,* meaning the "free born." Traditional education, he makes clear, produced people who were sometimes good at dealing with what they knew, but not very good at reflecting under their own steam about the difficult challenges created by new events. Nor were they very good at respecting the human worth of people who did not belong to their elite group. He makes it clear that excessive reverence for tradition frequently impedes the recognition of humanity.

Seneca himself, he now announces, would use the term *liberal* in a very different way. In his view, an education is truly liberal (that is, connected to freedom) only if it "liberates" the student's mind, encouraging him or her to take charge of his or her own thinking, leading the Socratic "examined life" and becoming a reflective critic of traditional practices. (I say "him or her" not only out of contemporary political correctness. Stoics of the first century A.D. wrote eloquently about the equal education of women, defending the view that women as much as men should lead the "examined life.") Seneca goes on to argue that only this sort of education will develop each person's capacity to be fully human, by which he means self-aware, self-governing, and capable of recognizing and respecting the humanity of all our fellow human beings, no matter where they are born, no matter what social class they inhabit, no matter what their gender or ethnic origin. "Soon we shall breathe our last," he concludes in his related treatise, *On Anger.* "Meanwhile, while we live, while we are among human beings, let us cultivate our humanity."

Liberal Education in the United States: The Three Abilities

What would it mean to cultivate our humanity through a liberal education in the contemporary United States? The chapters in this book provide a wide range of answers to that question. Not all of them agree with Seneca's preference for Socratic questioning over traditional acculturation, although most do. Among those who follow the Senecan idea, we find a wide range of approaches to the construction of basic curricular requirements. In all cases, however, we see that the humanities, often scorned as useless in an increasingly specialized world, are providing essential ingredients for citizenship. Most of the curricula described here turn to literature and philosophy to foster a type of Socratic self-examination and a sense of citizenship that is reflective and deliberative rather than simply the trading of claims and counterclaims. If there is just one general conclusion to draw from this book, it is that we must continue to support the humanities if we want citizens who have the kind of mental self-command and responsiveness to the claims of others that Seneca describes. If we should ever become a nation of narrowly specialized professionals, with little general humanistic learning, we will have lost crucial opportunities for deliberation and fellowship with one another.

In my own writing on liberal education (Nussbaum, 1997), I have argued that three abilities are essential to the cultivation of humanity in today's world. First is the capacity for critical examination of oneself and one's own traditions—for what Socrates called the examined life. This means a life that accepts no belief as authoritative because it has been transmitted by tradition or habit, a life that questions all beliefs and accepts only those that survive reason's demand for arguments and explanations.

Second is the ability to think of oneself as what Stoic philosophers called a "citizen of the world," rather than merely of some region or group. Our world is inescapably international. Issues from agriculture to human rights to the relief of famine require our minds to venture beyond local affiliations and consider the reality of distant lives. To attain this ability, however, students need to learn a great deal more than students in previous generations typically did about the history and culture of non-Western people, and of ethnic and racial minorities within their own culture; about the achievements and experiences of women; and about the variety of human sexuality.

Finally is the ability that I call the "narrative imagination": the ability to try to understand what it might be like to experience life from a position other than one's own, to be an intelligent reader of other life stories—and also to understand how difficult it is to be an intelligent reader. This ability is cultivated, above all, by courses in literature and the arts.

Liberal Education and Great Books

Should the proponent of a Senecan liberal education, with its emphasis on these three abilities, approve of curricula that center on a "great books" course? The Greek and Roman philosophers had a number of concerns about an education that relies on a list of great books of the tradition, concerns that apply to our debates today.

First, such courses frequently encourage passivity in students. They teach them that education is all about deference to authority, and they may even prevent them from developing their own ideas. Seneca imagines a pupil who says, "Zeno said this." He replies: "What do *you* say? How long will you march under someone else's banner? . . . Now bring out something of your own."

Second, such lists of traditional books are frequently unresponsive to the diversity of students and their intellectual needs. Our country contains institutions large and small, state and private, four year and two year, religious and secular. It is unreasonable to think that a single list will be best at cultivating the three abilities in all of these students.

Third, curricula based on "great books" often encourage what Plato called the "false conceit of wisdom." The Roman Stoic philosopher Epictetus imagines a young man who proudly proclaims that he has memorized a treatise of Chrysippus. His reply: You are just like an athlete who boasts that he has got a brand new set of training weights, and thinks he is a great athlete because of this. Books are like training weights in the mind. You have to show what you yourself can do with them, or they are nothing but useless paraphernalia.

Finally, tradition-based lists are likely to have a narrow frame of reference, because they will very likely deal with our own history, leaving out much that we urgently need to understand. That problem, acute even in first-century Rome, is especially acute today, given the enormous diversity of nations and groups with which modern citizens must be prepared to interact.

I shall now add a concern of my own that is not represented in ancient debates. Great books curricula are based on books, rather than musical works, or works of visual art, or the study of social history. This is unfair to these other arts, and it also extracts the books from their historical setting in ways that can distort their meaning. I am particularly troubled by the tendency of many of these curricula to include the Bible alongside Plato and Aristotle as among the great books of the Western tradition. In a nation still not free of anti-Semitism, it is particularly important to remind students that, as Leopold Bloom says in *Ulysses* to the incredulous anti-Semites in Barney Kiernan's bar, "Christ was a Jew like me." Jesus was the heir of a long Jewish tradition, not in the least "Western," that had only around Seneca's time (also the time of Saint Paul) developed any links with Greek culture. We should study the Bible as a part of the Jewish tradition, and only after that study the links between that tradition and the Greco-Roman traditions.

Most of the colleges and universities represented in this book have chosen a great books approach. How might someone with educational views like mine defend that choice? Obviously I do not want to defend it altogether. But there are also some things that a Senecan should say in favor of such courses.

Let me return to the metaphor of training weights: the great books of our tradition are among the best ways of training the mind to ponder deep issues of morality and truth. Students often come alive when they read the works of Plato or Sophocles or Kant. These works are not called "great" for nothing: they really do have a marvelous ability to deepen and challenge our thought. For many students, they supply a type of excitement and intellectual depth that was previously lacking in their lives, and that might well remain lacking in the absence of courses requiring such readings. Grouped together, they provide a wide array of positions, thus stimulating students to debate and self-examination.

How might one teach such a course so as to avoid, as much as possible, the pitfalls I have identified? Deference to authority can be avoided if the instructor constantly challenges the students as Seneca challenged his: What do *you* say? What criticisms would *you* make here? Is this a good argument or not? What I saw of Rhodes College's Search course (The Search for Values in the Light of Western History and Religion) convinced me that it was grappling well with this question, treating books as the basis for constructing good arguments rather than as a final authority.

Nonresponsiveness to the diverse needs of students is best addressed by choosing the list after careful thought about one's own students and what they need—and by insisting on small sections in large lecture courses, where students can encounter a more Socratic type of teaching. Writing assignments that are carefully graded, with lots of individualized comments, are also of the greatest importance.

The false conceit of wisdom is best addressed by arguing with the texts, not letting any text have the last word, as if it represented the final statement on any serious matter. Here again the Rhodes Search course does well, in the way in which it represents texts as the "training weights" students will use to search for their own truth. Students initially shocked by this treatment, for example, of the Bible eventually find the approach valuable, conducive to a more thoughtful style of religious life, in which one takes more responsibility for one's own conduct.

Narrowness of range can best be addressed by other curricular requirements outside the great books course. It seems counterproductive to sandwich one or two Asian or African works into an already packed list of Western texts: this just ensures that no systematic understanding of a non-Western culture will emerge. On the other hand, if one does not begin from a list of Western books at all, one may fruitfully approach this problem in other ways. For example, Stanford has paired books from different traditions in ways that illuminate both issues and cultures.

Finally, students desperately need to understand that literature and philosophy do not exist in a historic vacuum. Difficult though it may be, historic background about the era of each text must be included in any responsible great books course. As for the other arts, some of the curricula described in this book have incorporated musical and visual works with good results. Often, however, students—and faculty—are too ill prepared in music and visual art for such approaches to be fruitful. This is an issue that needs much more attention than it has so far received.

Whatever we conclude about general education courses in the humanities, we should insist that the abilities they seek to cultivate are at the very heart of a strong democracy. If we allow our curricula to be dominated by courses that have an immediate "cash value," we will all be the poorer for it, and the hope for genuine deliberation in public life will be faint indeed.

Reference

Nussbaum, M. C. *Cultivating Humanity: A Classical Defense of Reform in Liberal Education.* Cambridge, Mass.: Harvard University Press, 1997.

Preface: From Rhetoric to Reality

Michael Nelson

In the broad swath of academe that encompasses the humanities, the final decades of the twentieth century were marked by endless, sometimes bitter, and often highly public controversies about the content, strategies, and methods of general education that are appropriate for colleges and universities.

These controversies marked both a departure from and a continuity with the experiences of earlier decades. From the 1920s through the 1940s, general education in the humanities usually meant "Western Civ," sometimes in the form of close study of the "great books." The two world wars had brought the United States into alliance with Great Britain and other European nations, reminding Americans of their Old World roots, both intellectual and personal. The wars also had aroused concerns in educational circles that Americans needed to be immersed in the ideals for which they were fighting on the battlefield.

The cold war had a different effect. The combination of the Soviet explosion of a hydrogen bomb in 1953 and the *Sputnik* launch in 1957 provoked such widespread anxiety about American science education as to prompt a hasty turn away from general education in the humanities and toward academic specialization. In addition, the global rivalry with the Soviets in the emerging nations of the Third World diverted scholarly attention from Europe to Asia, Africa, and South America. Responding to these changes, many colleges and universities ceased to require general

Western civilization courses of their students. "When compulsion stopped," the historian Gilbert Allardyce (1982) found, "enrollment dwindled, and across the nation, one after another, Western Civ courses were decommissioned like old battleships."

Allardyce's study was published in 1982. In 1984 National Endowment for the Humanities chair William J. Bennett (1984) offered a different explanation for the declining interest in Western civilization and other humanities courses, one grounded in the anti-Western and libertarian pressures that had been aroused by the campus protest movements of the 1960s. Bennett began his widely publicized report, *To Reclaim a Legacy,* by declaring that educators "too often have given up the great task of transmitting a culture to its rightful heirs." Blaming "a collective loss of nerve and faith on the part of both faculty and academic administrators during the late 1960s and early 1970s [that] was undeniably destructive of the curriculum," Bennett issued a wide-ranging indictment: of colleges and universities for failing to require more humanities courses of their students; of humanities departments for assigning the teaching of general education courses to inexperienced or part-time faculty; and of politically radical humanities scholars for labeling the traditional teaching of their subjects as, alternately, "handmaidens of ideology" and devoid of "inherent meaning because all meaning is subjective." What students needed, Bennett concluded, was "access to the best that [Western] tradition has to offer." Specifically, he listed "such principles as justice, liberty, government with the consent of the governed, and equality under the law," all of them "descended directly from great epochs of Western civilization—Enlightenment England and France, Renaissance Florence, and Periclean Athens."

Bennett's report struck a responsive chord among editorial writers and other opinion leaders, as did Allan Bloom's *The Closing of the American Mind* (1987), a polemic on the subject of (to quote its subtitle) "How Higher Education Has Failed Democracy and Impoverished the Souls of Today's Students" that led the nonfiction best-seller lists for more than six months in 1987. Bloom, a philosopher, argued that colleges and universities had embraced relativism and abandoned their responsibility to give students "the good old Great Books approach, in which a liberal education means reading certain generally recognized classic texts, just reading them, letting them dictate what the questions are and the methods of approaching them." Like Bennett, Bloom laid much of the blame for the decline in general education on a 1960s-spawned combination of political pressure from faculty activists on the humanistic left and acquiescence from timid colleagues and administrators in the middle.

Supporters of Bennett and Bloom (known to their critics as the "Killer Bs") seemed to find grist for their mill everywhere they looked. In 1988 conservatives jeered when Stanford University revised its Western civilization requirement to ensure that a wider range of authors would be studied and that "substantial attention" would be given to "the issues of race, gender, and class." Two years later "P.C." entered the national vocabulary as shorthand for a congeries of "politically correct" opinions and practices that supposedly had become the new academic orthodoxy concerning cultural matters.

Defenders of the changes that were taking place in the humanities were slow to respond to their critics. As the literary scholar Gerald Graff (1992), who identified himself as one of the "academic radicals" he describes, noted, "Having trained themselves for two decades to speak in voices that would be resistant to cooptation by the dominant discourses, academic radicals find themselves almost without an idiom in which to contest the misrepresentations being made of them. . . . Thus the right has been able to coopt the rhetoric of democracy and populism, and turn labels like 'elitist' and 'authoritarian' against the academic left."

Graff was right: the jargon-ridden, self-referential responses of academic radicals to conservative critics in pamphlets such as the American Council of Learned Societies' *Speaking for the Humanities* (Levine and others, 1989) and anthologies such as *The Politics of Liberal Education,* edited by Darryl J. Gless and Barbara Herrnstein Smith (1992), reached the general public mainly through the critiques of conservative writers like Roger Kimball (1990) and Dinesh D'Souza (1991). Yet the radicals remained influential within the humanities community itself. Their argument, loosely translated, generally went something like this: the history of the West is in large measure a history of oppression—of women who have been degraded; of ethnic, racial, and cultural minorities who have been enslaved or exploited; and of non-Western peoples, who have been made subject to imperialism and colonialism. White males have been the main villains in this historical drama, and the so-called great books of Western civilization (almost all of them authored by white males) have been, in the philosopher John Searle's (1990) ironic phrase, "the official publications of their system of oppression." Bennett, Bloom, and other conservatives wanted general education in the humanities to serve as a vehicle to "transmit" (a word that Bennett, in particular, used a lot) this system to future generations of students, thereby "assuring assent to a political and economic establishment." Instead, the radicals argued, education should liberate students by unmasking the oppressors and lifting up the voices of the oppressed.

Distressingly, given the importance of the issue, this debate was highly unsatisfactory, consisting almost entirely of polemical arguments ungrounded in evidence about what particular colleges and universities actually had been doing in the realm of general education in the humanities. Yet deciding what to do is precisely the challenge that every college and university is required to face. This challenge is best met not with ideological manifestos but with specific courses, reading lists, assignments, and instructors.

Fortunately, some progress has recently been made. In 1996, Vanderbilt University Press published *Celebrating the Humanities: A Half Century of the Search Course at Rhodes College* (Nelson, 1996). The book described, in a nonpolemical way, Rhodes's long experience in offering most of its students a twelve-credit course of study on the history, religion, philosophy, literature, and politics of the West. At about the same time, Simon and Schuster published David Denby's *Great Books* (1996), a widely discussed journalistic account of Columbia University's core curriculum. The advantage of both books was that they descended from the airy precincts of rhetorical position taking and described what particular schools actually were doing in the realm of general education.

In 1997, as a way of building on this progress, Rhodes commissioned thirteen papers from scholars around the country who teach in general education humanities programs at their respective institutions. (Those papers are now published in this book.) The programs were chosen for their excellence and variety. Some of the programs are old; some are fairly new. Some are centered on the West; others are global in scope. Some regard themselves as traditional, some as nontraditional. The schools whose programs are represented also are varied: small and large, public and private, church affiliated and secular, urban and small town, liberal art colleges and universities, North, South, and all other points on the compass. The papers formed the basis for a well-attended national conference, "Teaching the Humanities," that took place on Rhodes's campus in Memphis, Tennessee, in November 1998 as part of the college's sesquicentennial celebration.

To provide thematic and organizational coherence to the papers, each author was charged to tell the story of the program at his or her school by addressing the following concerns:

- How the program began: its founding philosophy, content, and approaches
- How the program has evolved, with an emphasis on changes and landmark events
- How the program functions today: its place in the curriculum and culture of the institution, the support it receives from the administration, and so on
- How students have responded to the program over the years
- How faculty are recruited and integrated into the program, along with the attitudes of other faculty members to the program
- The effects of national controversies and developments in the humanities on the program, with particular attention to feminism and postmodernism
- The place of biblical and other sacred works in the program
- The place of non-Western studies in the program
- The place of nonwritten works, such as music and art, in the program
- The use of computer-based educational technologies in the program
- Issues that the program will need or want to address in the years to come

Martha Nussbaum and Roger Shattuck, two of the leading humanities scholars in the United States, attended every session of the conference, read all the papers, and offered synthesizing contributions to this book. Their essays serve as bookends to the chapters that follow about the programs, which are arranged in the order of their creation.

This book is intended to reach a broad audience in higher education circles. Academic administrators immersed in matters of curriculum, along with members of faculty curriculum committees, will be interested to learn how other colleges and universities deal with issues of general education. So, perhaps most of all, will the many faculty members who teach in programs such as the ones represented in this book. Faculty grapple constantly with the same issues of course design, faculty recruitment, pedagogy, and student satisfaction that their colleagues in these programs grapple with. Learning from others who have been there before us is something we teach our students to do. This book offers an opportunity to benefit from that lesson ourselves.

As with the courses this book chronicles, so with the book itself: many hands contributed to its making, and all have my great thanks—Rhodes College's sesquicentennial committee for generously funding the commissioning of the chapters, Gale Erlandson of Jossey-Bass for her enthusiasm and efforts on behalf of the book, Carolyn Uno of Tigris Productions, Bev Miller, and Tom Finnegan for their skillful editing and production, and above all the chapter authors for the excellent contributions.

References

Allardyce, G. "The Rise and Fall of the Western Civilization Course." *American Historical Review*, 1982, *87*, 695–725.

Bennett, W. J. *To Reclaim a Legacy: A Report on the Humanities in Higher Education*. Washington, D.C.: National Endowment for the Humanities, 1984.

Bloom, A. *The Closing of the American Mind: How Higher Education Has Failed Democracy and Impoverished the Souls of Today's Students*. New York: Simon & Schuster, 1987.

Denby, D. *Great Books: My Adventures with Homer, Rousseau, Woolf, and Other Indestructible Writers of the Western World*. New York: Simon & Schuster, 1996.

D'Souza, D. *Illiberal Education: The Politics of Race and Sex on Campus*. New York: Free Press, 1991.

Gless, D. J., and Herrnstein, B. S. *The Politics of Liberal Education*. Durham, N.C.: Duke University Press, 1992.

Graff, G. "Academic Writing and the Uses of Bad Publicity." *South Atlantic Quarterly,* 1992, *51,* pp. 5–17.

Kimball, R. *Tenured Radicals: How Politics Has Corrupted Our Higher Education.* New York: HarperCollins, 1990.

Levine, G., and others. *Speaking for the Humanities.* Washington, D.C.: American Council of Learned Societies, 1989.

Nelson, M. *Celebrating the Humanities: A Half-Century of the Search Course at Rhodes College.* Nashville, Tenn.: Vanderbilt University Press, 1996.

Searle, J. "Storm over the University." *New York Review of Books,* Dec. 6, 1990, pp. 34–42.

The Authors

Michael Nelson is professor of political science at Rhodes College. A former editor of the *Washington Monthly,* he is the author, coauthor, or editor of several books on the American presidency and presidential elections, including *Presidents, Politics, and Policy* (1984), *A Heartbeat Away* (1988), *The Elections of 1996* (1997), *The American Presidency: Origins and Development, 1776–1998* (1999), and *The Presidency and the Political System* (2000). In the field of higher education, he is the editor and coauthor of *Celebrating the Humanities: A Half-Century of the Search Course at Rhodes College.* He has won national awards for articles on classical music and baseball, and more than forty of his articles have been reprinted in anthologies of political science, history, and English composition. He is currently writing *The Politics of Gambling in the South: Case Studies of State Policy Innovation* (with John Lyman Mason).

Lloyd W. Chapin is vice president and dean of faculty of Eckerd College, where he also holds the rank of professor of philosophy and religion. Before becoming Eckerd's chief academic officer in 1979, he was associate dean of Emory College of Emory University for a decade and, before that, assistant professor of philosophy and religion and assistant dean of faculty at Colgate University. He is a past chair of the board of directors of the American Conference of Academic Deans and served for three years as chair of the board of directors of the Florida Humanities Council.

John Churchill is vice president for academic affairs, dean of the college, and professor of philosophy at Hendrix College. Churchill has published extensively on the philosophy of Ludwig Wittgenstein and in the philosophies of language and religion. His chief research interests deal with Wittgenstein's relevance to the philosophy of religion. He has published articles on liberal education, the humanities, pedagogy, and ethics. A member of the board of directors of the American Conference of Academic Deans, Churchill teaches first-year students in the Western Intellectual Traditions course at Hendrix.

Margaret J. Downes is the director of the Humanities Program and National Endowment for the Humanities Distinguished Teaching Professor in Humanities at the University of North Carolina at Asheville. She is also a professor in the Department of Literature and Language. Her research and publications concentrate on interdisciplinary studies and the writings and art of William Blake.

Harry J. Elam, Jr., is Christensen Professor for the Humanities, director of the Introduction to the Humanities Program, director of graduate studies in drama, and director of the Committee on Black Performing Arts at Stanford University. He is author of *Taking It to the Streets: The Social Protest Theater of Luis Valdez and Amiri Baraka* (1997) and coeditor of *Colored Contradictions: An Anthology of Contemporary African American Drama* (1996) and the forthcoming critical anthology *Performing Blackness: African American Performance and Theatre History: A Critical Reader.* He has published articles in *Theatre Journal, Text and Performance Quarterly,* and *American Drama* as well as several critical anthologies.

Mera J. Flaumenhaft has taught at St. John's College in Annapolis, Maryland, since 1977. She is the author of *The Civic Spectacle: Essays in Drama and Community* (1994) and has translated Machiavelli's *Mandragola* (1981). She has published articles on Homer, Aeschylus, Euripides, Machiavelli, Shakespeare, and Twain, and occasional film and theater reviews. Her interests include literature and politics, popular entertainment, and civic life.

Margaret Heller is a past director of the Foundation Year Programme (1994–1997) at the University of King's College, Halifax, Nova Scotia. She first taught in Foundation Year in 1982 as a junior fellow and is now a lecturer at King's in humanities and social sciences. Heller's research interest is historical narrative and how an understanding of the past shapes the curriculum. She has contributed to a number of conferences on education in the humanities, has served on the Council of the Liberal Studies Association of Canada, and is serving on the Board of the Association for Core Texts and Courses.

James V. Mirollo is the Parr Professor Emeritus of English and Comparative Literature at Columbia University, where he taught full time between 1967 and 1987. He has directed both the Literature Humanities course at Columbia College and its associated orientation and guidance program for new instructors in the course, a program that he established. He has taught in the course for twenty-five years and continues to teach it since retirement from full-time teaching in December 1996.

Martha C. Nussbaum is the Ernst Freud Distinguished Service Professor of Law and Ethics at the University of Chicago. Over the years, she has held appointments in classics, philosophy, comparative literature, and political science at Brown University, Princeton University, Harvard University, Stanford University, Oxford University, Wellesley College, and the University of Oslo. Her books include *The Fragility of Goodness: Luck and Ethics in Greek Tragedy and Philosophy* (1986), *Poetics of Therapy* (1991), *Love's Knowledge: Essays on Philosophy and Literature* (1992), *Cultivating Humanity: A Classical Defense of Reform in Liberal Education* (1998), and *Sex and Social Justice* (1999).

W. Brown Patterson is professor of history at the University of the South in Sewanee, Tennessee, and has served as dean of the college. Since 1993 he has taught in the interdisciplinary humanities program Tradition and Criticism in Western Culture. He is the author of twenty articles in professional journals and collections of essays and a book, *King James VI and I and the Reunion of Christendom* (1997), which was awarded the Albert C. Outler Prize in Ecumenical Church History by the American Society of Church History.

Cheri Ross is associate director of the Introduction to the Humanities Program at Stanford University. She has written on Shakespeare, Jonson, Milton, and Woolf, as well as the semiotics of natural history museums. She is currently working on the development of core courses in the United States and their social context.

W. Charles Sallis is professor of history and former chair of the department at Millsaps College. He has also taught in and directed the Heritage Program, an interdisciplinary humanities course for freshmen. Named Millsaps's Distinguished Professor in 1973, he is coauthor *of Mississippi: Conflict and Change,* which won the Southern Regional Council's Lillian Smith Award in 1975 as the outstanding work in southern history. Sallis is Millsaps's 1999–2000 recipient of the Mississippi Humanities Council award for outstanding contributions to the humanities.

Roger Shattuck is University Professor Emeritus of Modern Languages and Literature at Boston University. A founder and former president of the Association of Literary Scholars and Critics, he won the National Book Award in biography for *Marcel Proust* (1974). His other books include *The Banquet Years* (1979), *Forbidden Knowledge: From Prometheus to Pornography* (1996), *Candor and Perversion: Literature, Education, and the Arts* (1999), and, most recently, *Proust's Way: A Full Guide to "In Search of Lost Time."*

Brian J. Shaw is the 1999–2001 E. Craig Wall, Jr., Distinguished Teaching Professor of Humanities at Davidson College. Shaw's research interests have focused on twentieth-century continental political philosophy, especially the writings of Max Horkheimer, Georg Lukacs, and Jürgen Habermas. His articles have appeared in the *Journal of Politics, Philosophical Forum, History of Political Thought, Political Theory,* and other journals.

Katherine Trow is a clinical psychologist and a research fellow at the Center for Studies in Higher Education at the University of California, Berkeley. She taught for many years in the San Francisco State University Graduate Clinical/School Psychology Program and has held research positions at the Fels Research Institute for Human Development at Antioch College and the Survey Research Center at the University of California, Berkeley. Her recent book, *Habits of Mind: The Experimental College Program at*

Berkeley (1998), reports a study of the long-term effects of that program on the lives of its students.

Stephen Zelnick is director of Temple University's Intellectual Heritage Program and has served as director of writing programs and as special assistant to the president of the university. He specializes in Victorian literature and has published on Defoe, Carlyle, Melville, Conrad, Fitzgerald, Darwin, and numerous educational topics. Coeditor of *A Student's Introduction to Charles Darwin,* he will soon publish a teaching edition of *The Communist Manifesto* and two anthologies of great books materials. Zelnick is also executive director of the Association for Core Texts and Courses, a national association of colleges and universities that sponsor great books studies.

Alive at the Core

Chapter One

Alive at the Core: Programs and Issues

Michael Nelson

At King's College, the general education program in the humanities, Foundation Year Programme, is for freshmen only, as its name implies. At Eckerd, the program begins with the entering class but culminates in a senior capstone course, Quest for Meaning. The University of North Carolina at Asheville's Humanities Program is required of all students; indeed, it is the campus's flagship program. At Davidson College, the Humanities Program (Humes) is an option for fulfilling distribution requirements that is now available to less than one-fourth of the freshman class.

Almost every humanities program mixes lectures with discussions, but at Columbia University, lectures are expressly forbidden in Masterpieces of Western Literature (Lit. Hum.). Millsaps College requires that students in its Heritage program attend off-campus artistic and cultural events, and at St. John's College, students not only study music as part of the core curriculum but also sing. Rhodes College initially included music and art in its Search course but quickly abandoned them for the sake of closer study of written works. Temple University's Intellectual Heritage (IH) program does not shy away from its original conception as a great books course; instead, it unabashedly urges students to "think in agreement" with each work as they read it, relying on subsequent primary texts to supply differing perspectives. The

University of the South's contrasting approach is embodied in the name of its program: Tradition and Criticism in Western Culture. At Stanford University, every course in the IHUM program (Introduction to the Humanities) is required to have at least one "non-canonical" work on the syllabus.

The four-year curriculum at St. John's is entirely Western, the college's main justification being that the West has been the well-spring of modern science, philosophy, and liberalism. At Hendrix College, each unit of Western Intellectual Traditions includes study of a corresponding non-Western culture: ancient Greece with Persia, seventeenth-century Europe with Africa, and so on. Most programs are comprehensively chronological, but the Experimental College Program at the University of California at Berkeley focused on just four periods, ranging from fifth-century Greece to the contemporary United States. Although the founding vision of many general education programs in the humanities included close study of the Bible, at Columbia the Bible was left out deliberately until late in the history of the core curriculum

Some of the differences among the humanities programs represented in this book were matters of original design. Others have come about through continuing innovation in the face of new challenges, insights, and opportunities. Rhodes's Search course, for example, directly influenced the creation of humanities programs at several other colleges, including Davidson, Eckerd, Millsaps, and the University of the South. Yet its fifty-five-year history has been marked by frequent innovations, such as a smorgasbord of week-long special-topics seminars by individual instructors that happily interrupts the otherwise lockstep progress of the course's first year, and a "track" system for sophomores that enables them to leaven the common syllabus with a particular emphasis on literature, philosophy, religion, history, or politics.

General education in the humanities, as practiced today in American higher education, is clearly marked by great variety. Yet all, or nearly all, of these programs share certain vital characteristics. The most important of these is the premise that college students, before becoming immersed in their major subjects, should participate in a multiterm program that spurs them to reflect from a variety of perspectives on the great issues that have occupied humankind, especially in the West, through all of history. Some label this kind of program multidisciplinary, and others call it interdisciplinary or nondisciplinary. The idea in all cases is to transcend the specialized approach to knowledge that will characterize students' later studies as advanced undergraduates and graduate students.

All of the programs that are represented in this book agree that college students should be guided in their general education by faculty members from a variety of disciplines, sometimes reaching beyond the humanities into the natural and social sciences. None of these faculty docents, of course, will be expert in every aspect of the course. Perhaps for this reason, the faculty of each program gathers regularly during the academic year, the summer, or both to plan and discuss the assigned works. A consensus also exists on the centrality of primary texts as the main, and in some cases the exclusive, source of reading assignments. Finally, although one could imagine a general education program in the humanities that was organized around issues such as justice and order, some form of chronological organization is the nearly universal practice.

The Programs

Columbia's core curriculum is the grandmother of general education in the humanities. Its two-semester Introduction to Contemporary Civilization course (CC), which entered the curriculum in 1919, was the first tangible expression of the then-popular great books movement. This movement, whose leaders were Robert Hutchins and Mortimer Adler of the University of Chicago, Alexander Meiklejohn of the University of Wisconsin, Stringfellow Barr of the University of Virginia, and Columbia's own John Erskine, was born in reaction to the segmentation and specialization of the undergraduate curriculum that characterized the increasingly common free electives system of higher education. Columbia added another year-long great books course, Masterpieces of Western Literature (Lit. Hum.) to its core in 1937, followed a decade later by Masterpieces of Western Art and Masterpieces of Western Music, each of them a semester course. For nearly a century, all Columbia freshmen and sophomores have met in small classes to discuss important works from the Western tradition with a faculty member (or, increasingly, an advanced graduate student) from one of the humanities departments.

Great books education has constituted the entire curriculum of St. John's College since 1937, when Stringfellow Barr became president. The heart of the curriculum is the seminar, a twice-weekly gathering of students that meets all four years for the purpose of discussing landmark Western writings. Each seminar consists of eighteen students and is led by two faculty members. In addition, all students spend four years studying Greek, French, and English in the language tutorial; four years working their way chronologically from Euclid to Einstein in the mathematics tutorial; and three years studying the historical progression of the sciences in the laboratory. The two-year music tutorial combines singing with musical elements from the other tutorials, such as rhetoric, poetry, number, and ratio. St. John's has no departments, and every faculty member teaches throughout the curriculum.

Rhodes College, previously known as Southwestern at Memphis, inaugurated its twelve-credit Search course in 1945. Influenced by the great books movement, President Charles Diehl decried the national trend toward specialization in undergraduate education and regarded a common, nondisciplinary grounding in the humanities as an essential part of a college education. Departing from that avowedly secular movement, Diehl also believed that scholarly study of the Bible was an essential part of such an education. Thus, the avowed purpose of The Search for Values in the Light of Western History and Religion (known until 1986 as Man in the Light of History and Religion) was to "recover the understanding, exemplified by Socrates' 'Know thyself' and Jesus' 'Perfect thyself,' that man is a rational animal with a spark of the divine in him." The Search course today, which a majority of Rhodes freshmen and sophomores take, is a discussion-based survey of primary texts of Western literature, history, religion, philosophy, and politics from the ancient world to the present. Its faculty in recent years has been drawn from fourteen departments, several of them outside the humanities.

An interdisciplinary core curriculum that extended over four years and was focused on values questions was part of the founding vision of Eckerd College (né Florida Presbyterian College) in 1960. The foundation course in the program was a required two-year sequence, Western Civilization and Its Christian Heritage, which combined lectures and discussions, was chronologically organized and based on primary texts, and merged the social and natural sciences with the humanities. The name of today's one-year freshman version of the course—Western Heritage in a Global Context—indicates its shift in thematic emphasis from Christianity to a mixture of Western and non-Western topics. Although Eckerd's curriculum now allows students more opportunity to specialize in a major than was the case when the college was founded, seniors still must take the values-focused Quest for Meaning capstone course.

Davidson College's Humanities (Humes) Program was founded in 1962 by Daniel Rhodes, who had been recruited from Rhodes College to introduce a version of the Search course to the Davidson curriculum. Like the Search course, Humes integrated biblical study into a great books program and offered students an alternative way of satisfying several distribution requirements in the humanities. The program has changed very little over the years, and although it remains popular with students and administrators, most faculty members in the college's humanities departments now dislike it. Their objections range from hostility to having aspects of their subjects taught by nonspecialists to a postmodern disdain for the course's assumption, largely unaltered over the years, that an organic narrative unity underlies the Western tradition.

The Humanities Program at the University of North Carolina at Asheville was created in 1964. Originally a chronologically organized, four-course, great books sequence required of freshmen and sophomores, the program now extends across all four years and, although it is still grounded in primary texts, has adopted a more critical and cross-cultural approach to the Western experience. In addition, the program includes an "Arts and Ideas" course that involves music, art, drama, and creative writing and pays more attention to the natural and social sciences. A mix of lectures and discussions, the Humanities Program draws on faculty from a wide range of departments.

In 1965, under the leadership of Joseph Tussman, a student of Meiklejohn, the University of California at Berkeley launched the Experimental College Program, which constituted nearly the entire freshman and sophomore curriculum for the students who elected to take it. A semester each was devoted to fifth-century Greece, seventeenth-century England, Federalist America, and contemporary America in a thematic study of the challenges confronting democracy. Frequent lectures, discussions, and tutorials took the place of normal courses. Inadequate faculty and administration support doomed the experiment after four years, however. Members of the Berkeley faculty were unwilling to forsake their departments to devote themselves to Tussman's program, and the administration would not authorize him to offer permanent positions to prospective faculty members from elsewhere.

Millsaps College's Cultural Heritage of the West program was created in 1968. It was modeled on Rhodes College's Search course but placed additional emphasis on music and art. The Heritage program, a year-long course that meets for seven hours each week, provides students an alternative means to fulfill several distribution requirements. It combines lectures and discussions with cocurricular cultural events. In 1992 the program was renamed Heritage of the West in a World Perspective to reflect its new "global and multicultural perspective."

The Foundation Year Programme at King's College was founded in 1972 at a time when the college was in danger of being absorbed by Dalhousie University. An unusual faculty alliance of "traditionalists," whose main concern was to introduce a great books program into the curriculum, and "radicals," who wanted to create a distinct identity for King's that would enable it to fend off the Dalhousie "megaversity," formed to create Foundation Year. The program's avowed purpose is to overcome "the fragmentation of knowledge of the contemporary university curriculum." It provides the entire course of study for freshmen at King's, proceeding chronologically from the ancient world to the modern West and relying on lectures, discussions, and common reading of primary works. Traditionalists and radicals still contend over whether the program's overarching narrative should be Hegelian or Marxist.

Temple University created the Intellectual Heritage Program in 1979 as a required year-long course for freshmen in the College of Arts and Sciences; seven years later, IH was required of all Temple freshmen. Like most other general education programs in the humanities, it is chronologically organized, Western in emphasis, and uses only "excellent, time-tested works." Each section of the course is taught by one faculty member, with no common lectures. Unfortunately, administration support for IH has declined over the years, and Temple's recent emphasis has been on satisfying a perceived student demand for career-related courses. Thus, the university's initial commitment to have 80 percent of all IH sections taught by permanent members of the faculty has been attenuated to the point that 80 percent of the sections are taught by part-time and adjunct faculty.

Tradition and Criticism in Western Culture, a four-course sequence for freshmen and sophomores at the University of the South that was created in 1992, offers an alternative way of fulfilling several distribution requirements and enrolls around one-fourth of the student body. Its four semester-long courses are "Ancient World," "Medieval World," "Early Modern World," and "Modern World." Each course is taught by a four-member faculty team drawn from the humanities departments, including the fine arts. Although traditional Christian writings constitute an important part of the syllabus, so does explicit attention to issues of feminism, multiculturalism, moral relativism, deconstruction, race, and gender.

Hendrix College created Western Intellectual Traditions in 1993 as a year-long course that all freshmen must take. Primary texts, including works of music and art, are used, along with a faculty-published book that contains introductory essays, time lines, and other aids to study. Several so-called "Big Questions" (for example, What is a good person? What is beauty and why is it important?) animate the program, which proceeds chronologically through four major periods in Western history. Each unit includes a major non-Western culture with which the West was interacting at that time.

Stanford University's Area One Program, called Introduction to the Humanities, or IHUM, could as easily be grouped with the older programs as with the younger ones. For many years, Stanford required that all freshmen take a year-long, multidisciplinary Western civilization course. In 1988, in a move that enflamed many conservatives around the country, Stanford replaced Western Civ with Cultures, Ideas, and Values (CIV), a variety of courses that "confront[ed] issues relating to class, ethnicity, race, religion, gender, and sexual orientation." CIV's replacement by IHUM in 1997 marked a change less in content than in pedagogy, with a new emphasis on disciplinary tools and methods. IHUM requires all freshmen to choose two courses. The fall term courses are taught by at least two faculty lecturers from different departments, whose task is to compare the ways in which each of their disciplines approaches several identical works. The winter and spring terms courses are more departmental. They must be organized chronologically and cover a span of at least two centuries. Postdoctoral fellows lead the discussion sections in all IHUM classes.

Issues Confronting the Programs

Although most of the general education programs in the humanities chronicled in this book appear to be thriving, all confront difficult issues. Some of these issues involve people, notably students, faculty, and administrators. Others involve curriculum, such as the prominence of sacred works on the syllabus, the place of non-Western studies, and the inclusion of music, art, and other nonwritten works. Still others are issues of pedagogy: What use can be profitably made of computer-based educational technologies? What is the proper balance between breadth and depth of coverage? between expert and broad-gauged teaching?

Student and Alumni Response

General education programs in the humanities consist of courses that students must take, either as an explicit requirement or as one means of meeting a set of distribution requirements. The great majority of these students do not plan careers or even majors in the humanities. Not surprisingly, many resent being required to take the courses and are convinced that the humanities will be of no value in their preparation for a career. Once enrolled, a large number of them find the primary texts to be difficult and overwhelming ("I have yet to meet the dynamo for whom this program was intended," one King's student lamented) and the lectures to be "boring."

Most humanities programs use a variety of methods to solicit student assessments of their experience in these courses. Multiple choice–style course evaluation forms are standard, and focus groups are widely used. At Rhodes, the best students in first-year Search are invited at year's end to join the Search Advisory Council and critique the course. Each section of the Foundation Year Programme at King's elects a student to discuss the program with the director. Millsaps provides Heritage students with a suggestion box.

Surprisingly, perhaps, these evaluation instruments find students' opinions of their experience in humanities programs to be generally positive. They like the small discussion sections. They enjoy the esprit de corps that develops from sharing a common experience with many, and sometimes all, of their fellow undergraduates. As they become accustomed to studying primary texts, they revel in their ability to read and discuss great books. Most students, for example, have read Martin Luther King's "Letter from the Birmingham Jail" in high school. But, Stephen Zelnick observes, at Temple, "One of the delights of the second course of the IH sequence is to teach King's 'Letter' and to show students how King himself made excellent use of his own 'IH' education . . . the Greeks, the Scriptures, the natural rights tradition, and Gandhi."

Several programs have found that the more students know about the humanities requirement before they matriculate, the more likely they are to embrace their experience. At St. John's, Rhodes, Columbia, and the University of North Carolina at Asheville, the information that prospective students receive from admissions offices and commercial college guides tends to herald these institutions' programs. In contrast, when the University of the South did a poor job informing incoming freshmen about Tradition and Criticism during the early years of the program, writes Brown Patterson, "Many students seemed to feel that they were guinea pigs in an ill-designed experiment." Since then, entering students have been amply informed in advance about what to expect in Tradition and Criticism, with significant and positive effects on their opinion of the program.

Alumni memories of their general education courses in the humanities tend to be uniformly positive—so much so that, as at Columbia, the alumni can be fiercely protective of the program when changes are discussed. Lloyd Chapin offers two reasons that Eckerd alumni ("especially those who have been out several years") remember their experience so fondly: the link that the courses

provide "to their classmates, to the faculty, and to other generations of alumni" and the realization, as they grow older, that "the
texts and themes of these courses are often the texts and themes
that are central to their lives." Katherine Trow's interviews of
alumni of Berkeley's Experimental College Program uncovered an
interesting gender difference in their assessments of the program's
effects. Women appreciated the process of learning fostered by the
program, especially the small group discussions and tutorials. Men
were more likely to remember the content of the program—the
ideas that had stayed with them through the years.

Faculty Recruitment and Retention

The generally positive response of students to their experience in
humanities programs is hard won. It depends to a great extent on
the quality of the teaching they receive. Yet except at St. John's, no
program is staffed entirely, or even substantially, by its own faculty.
Instead, the faculty for these nondisciplinary programs must be
recruited from the ranks of each college's discipline-based departments. Recruiting talented and committed teachers may be the
greatest challenge that humanities programs face.

With rare exception, faculty members cite the opportunity to
work with colleagues from other disciplines as one of the great sat-
isfactions of participating in a humanities program. The Lit. Hum.
staff at Columbia, for example, meets every Monday to discuss the
text being taught that week. "Unlike any other university event,"
reports James Mirollo, "instructors of different rank and experience can talk with each other about books without departmental
pressure." Other programs gather their faculty for summer workshops, which often include studying a work or an author in common as well as planning for the year to come. "But the most
important consequence of bringing the faculty together for an
extended period of time," writes Michael Nelson about Rhodes's
annual Douglass Seminar, "may be the renewing of social and intellectual bonds, along with the initiation of new instructors into the
collegial norms of the course."

A related pleasure for discipline-based faculty members is the
opportunity to improve their own education. Participation in the
Millsaps Heritage Program allowed him to "continue with the

unfinished business of being educated," wrote one faculty participant quoted by Charles Sallis. As Hendrix's John Churchill notes,
to teach in a humanities program involves a willingness to say, "'I,
from philosophy, am willing to lead students in discussions of
Greek statuary and seventeenth-century opera,' or 'I, from the
music department, am willing to teach Plato and Descartes.'"
Churchill also contends that to "read and reread the same texts
annually over a period of years, sharing them with a body of students who are always the same age," is "an important part of my
own self-discovery."

Yet teaching outside one's discipline is a terrifying prospect to
many faculty members. It requires that "faculty become students
themselves," writes Zelnick, "and until they have taught the course
several times, they will feel out of their depth." However satisfying
it may be to master unfamiliar works from unfamiliar disciplines,
much of the time spent doing so is time diverted from making
progress in one's own discipline. At Davidson, Brian Shaw found,
"junior faculty already teaching in Humes or contemplating joining it harbored real concerns about the adverse consequences of
participation for their scholarly productivity and professional security. Teaching outside their normal competence in such a time-consuming enterprise did little, after all, to enhance their status in an
increasingly precarious job market."

A further obstacle to teaching in a humanities program may
be the attitudes of a faculty member's departmental colleagues. At
Temple, as at several other colleges, every student in IH is
regarded by the departments as a student *not* enrolled in their
introductory survey courses. Faculty critics at Columbia disdain the
core curriculum as superficial, nonexpertly taught, a distraction
from the department-based majors, and Eurocentric. The humanities programs at Rhodes and the University of the South were
nearly smothered in their cradles by departments that resented
having members of their faculty siphoned off.

Most colleges have developed ways to strengthen the appeal of
teaching in humanities programs. These begin with faculty hiring.
Unless the chair of the program is involved in the interviewing
process and candidates for positions in individual humanities
departments are told that general education courses are part of
the job, then teaching in the program may well be regarded as an

unfairly imposed burden. At Eckerd, "announcements of faculty positions include a reference to 'willingness to participate in the college's values-oriented interdisciplinary general education program,'" notes Chapin, and "search committees weigh heavily the thoughtfulness and enthusiasm of each candidate's response." Tangible support from the institution to help instructors make up for time away from the discipline is also important: a reduction in teaching load, an additional semester leave, a summer stipend, and, most important, favorable attention from academic administrators when tenure and promotion decisions are made. Less tangible support from program colleagues is also helpful. The IH program at Temple, for example, operates a faculty listserv that, according to Zelnick, "allows experienced and newer faculty to discuss problems in understanding the books and in teaching them." Finally, a certain degree of instructor autonomy in course design may make participation in the program more appealing. Rhodes's Search course follows a common syllabus for the first year, but instructors in the second year of the course are granted considerable flexibility in deciding which works to assign.

Curriculum

The curricula of all the general education humanities programs represented in this book share several common elements: a chronological organization spanning many centuries, the assignment of primary texts from several genres (for example, poetry, philosophy, history), and a strong emphasis on the Western tradition. Previously neglected works of distinction by women have entered the reading lists of every program, along with greater attention to female characters and concerns in traditional works.

The programs' approaches to other curricular matters are more varied. Should music and art be woven into the curriculum? Should the Bible and other sacred works be included? Should the curriculum be broadened to include non-Western texts?

Music and Art

In 1945–46, the first year that Rhodes offered its Search course, music and art were an important part of the syllabus. In 1946–47, they were not. The Search faculty decided to abandon music and art for two reasons. First, although historians were reasonably comfortable teaching the Bible and philosophers were willing to teach epic poetry, few faculty members felt they had the technical training to teach music and art. Second, the faculty felt that it was all they and their students could do to meet the demands of a syllabus already crowded with important written texts.

A number of programs have followed the word-centered Rhodes approach to humanities education, and for essentially the same reasons. Two—Columbia and the University of North Carolina at Asheville—have adopted what might be called a "Rhodes-plus" approach: a main group of courses centered on written texts, and one or two additional required courses on music and art. Still others, such as King's and Millsaps, bring in faculty from the music and art departments to lecture on these subjects in the main course.

The programs at Stanford, Hendrix, and the University of the South do not attempt to cover the entire sweep of Western history. For this reason, they have more time in their courses to give sustained treatment to the art and music of the periods their students study. Each of these programs has taken advantage of the breathing room that a noncomprehensive program allows.

Sacred Works

"The Bible appears on the syllabus alongside other books," writes Churchill about Hendrix's Western Intellectual Traditions program. "But as everyone who has tried it knows, it is difficult to approach the Bible as one among the books." For students who view the Bible as the revealed word of God, "their capacity to read the text and to ask what it means in a scholarly setting is occluded by a reverential trance." Other students, "disabled by scorn, . . . are certain that everything in the Bible is either rank superstition or manipulative lie."

In part because students find it so hard to discuss biblical works in a scholarly way and in part because of the primacy assigned to reason over revelation by early great books advocates such as Hutchins and Adler, the Bible was a late entry to Columbia's core curriculum. Mirollo's comparison of the 1937–38 and 1986–87 Lit. Hum. reading lists reveals no books from the Bible on the earlier list and five—Genesis, Exodus, Isaiah, Matthew, and Romans—on the later one. (By his count, eight other books from the Bible have been on the syllabus at various times.) The faculty finally realized, he writes, that "the course is essentially about tradition and response, and that the Bible constitutes one of those traditions, without which a good deal of the [reading] list, especially the post-classical works, makes little sense." The challenge of discussing the Bible in the face of students' preconceptions is simply a challenge that instructors must meet. Zelnick writes of Temple's program, "Most students know some of these [biblical] materials, but in a juvenile way. The aim in IH is to present the biblical materials as worthy of mature study."

Many programs have arrived at the same place as Columbia and Temple in their treatment of the Bible, but from a different direction. At church-related colleges such as Rhodes, Eckerd, and Davidson, the original humanities programs were infused with a strongly Christian ethos, primarily that of liberal Protestantism. The Bible has always featured prominently in these programs, and it still does. But as the colleges' broader curricula have grown more secular, so has their approach to biblical study. In addition, several of the humanities programs at both secular and church-related colleges have come to include sacred works from other traditions in their courses, such as the Qur'an, the West African Sundiata, and a variety of Eastern writings.

Non-Western Content

Nearly every program that was established before the 1990s was exclusively Western, and around half still are. At Columbia, Rhodes, St. John's, Davidson, Berkeley, and King's—all of whose programs originated more than a quarter of a century ago—virtually every assigned work on the syllabus is Western in origin. The other older programs, although still predominantly Western, recently have woven in Asian, African, and Latin American materials to one degree or another. Some of the name changes in these programs capture the spirit of this modification. Millsaps's Cultural Heritage of the West program is now Heritage of the West in a World Perspective, for example, and Eckerd's Western Heritage program has become Western Heritage in a Global Context. The programs created in the 1990s at Hendrix, Stanford, and the University of the South were all designed to include at least some non-Western works.

Programs that have remained Western have not done so mind-lessly. Students need to understand their own cultural traditions, these programs' advocates argue; indeed one cannot adequately appreciate other traditions unless one is firmly grounded in one's own. Further, the philosophy, literature, history, religion, art, and music of the West are so extensive and varied as to require all the time and attention—indeed, quite a bit more time and attention—than humanities programs usually have. Faculty members, already stretched far beyond their professional training in a multidiscipli-nary Western course, would be impossibly burdened if they had to master the diverse and extensive cultural traditions of the East and South. Finally, with the exception of St. John's, where the entire four-year curriculum is Western, students are urged or even required to take non-Western courses offered by the departments. As Margaret Heller writes of the King's Foundation Year Programme, "We always need to say to ourselves, 'It's only a first-year course!'"

Other programs argue that one cannot understand the West-ern, much less the human, experience in a purely Western course. For one thing, through most of its history, the West has been defined in part by its encounters with non-Western civilizations. Thus, to study ancient Greece apart from Persia, or medieval Europe apart from Islam, is to study them inadequately. In addition, some familiarity with other cultures can give students an additional vantage point from which to understand their own. Reading the Sundiata, for example, helps Temple students "to think about 'West-ern,'" argues Zelnick. "A list might include the objectification of nature, demystification (even in a prescientific time), literacy (Sun-diata is defiantly antiliteracy), and the authority of justice distinct from mere power. Sometimes one discovers more looking in from outside the windows than from the view inside a familiar room."

Pedagogy

Universal agreement exists among the programs represented in this book about several pedagogical issues. Even in programs that are heavy with lectures, small group discussions are regarded as the setting in which the most important teaching and learning take place. Instructors in the Rhodes Search course, for example, believe that each student's personal "search for values" is as impor-tant a part of the program as the West's historical search for values.

The latter search may be facilitated by occasional lectures, but the former requires extensive time for discussion. In addition, all of the programs last at least one year and are offered primarily to freshmen and sophomores. The rationale seems to be not only that students will benefit from taking general education courses in the humanities before entering their majors, but also that they are more likely to appreciate these courses during the early years of college than the later ones. The exception in this regard may demonstrate the rule. Eckerd's required capstone humanities course for seniors, Quest for Meaning, is resisted by some students who, according to Chapin, "are at the stage in their education when they want to focus on their individual interests and enjoy maximum freedom."

Other pedagogical questions are more disputed. Among the most difficult issues that programs are currently dealing with is a new one—the use of computer-based educational technologies—and a perennial one—how to strike the right balances between competing educational goods.

Computers

"As with almost all new technologies," writes Nelson, "the advantages computers offer are instantly apparent, the costs subtle and hard to discern." Several programs now operate web sites, although more for the purpose of making syllabi, lecture outlines, and some other course materials available electronically than to give students access to additional resources. Several programs also have created listservs for each course so that students can pose questions or offer opinions to their classmates and instructors on-line. Temple, whose IH faculty is so large and far-flung as to make regular meetings difficult, operates a listserv in which instructors can seek advice from their colleagues about teaching difficult works.

Although enthusiasm for electronic pedagogy is the norm among humanities programs, it is far from universal. One expects humanists to be sensitive to the hidden consequences of technological change, and some are. "In Foundation Year," writes Heller, "the book, the human voice, and face-to-face teaching are still central, and there is a strong aversion to any suggestion of accessing texts through the Internet, [or] of submitting and responding to papers via computer." (Indeed, the King's program's recent decision to provide lecturers with a microphone was controversial.) The language tutorial at St. John's resists the use of electronic dictionaries, Mera Flaumenhaft suggests, because "the laborious investigation of words in the lexicon, and the time-consuming generation of multiple translations seem more conducive to the speculative, communal learning of the language class." Concerning listservs, Nelson is concerned that students may be "encouraged to think that transmitting messages from the solitude of their terminals [is] an adequate substitute for joining discussion in the company of their fellows." He also worries that "electronic bells and whistles" may distract students from "the hard work of reading and thinking deeply about serious and complex works and expressing themselves in intelligent, evidence-based arguments."

Trade-offs

General educational programs in the humanities inevitably involve trade-offs between competing goals, all of which are meritorious. The age-old depth versus breadth controversy is perhaps the most familiar dilemma. Given the hundreds of works worth studying, is it better to sample many of them—hoping that a few will stick in students' minds but risking that none will—or to study a few of them at length, with all the dangers of narrowness of perspective that a short reading list entails? What about the competing claims of coherence and comprehensiveness? Organizing a program around certain big questions, as at Hendrix, or along a narrative line, as at King's, helps students to put the many pieces of a general education program together, but what about the pieces that are left out simply because they do not fit the theme?

The competing claims of the generalist and the expert vex several of the programs examined in this book. General education requires that faculty members teach outside their training: no one has graduate degrees in literature, classics, religion, history, philosophy, and politics. In doing so, instructors model for their students the idea that the good life encompasses lifelong learning, which does not end with the receiving of academic credentials. The concerns and questions of generalists may also be closer to those of students than the concerns and questions of their expert colleagues. At Rhodes, for example, members of the Search faculty were discouraged for many years from lecturing in their discipline, for fear that the aspects of a work that would interest them might be far removed from those that students needed to hear about. Yet one can readily understand the frustration of discipline-based departments on these issues. Davidson's religion department, for example, recently requested that Humes students not be granted credit toward the college's graduation requirement in religion.

The list of trade-offs is hardly a short one. Should the syllabus of a general education course be the same for all sections, or should instructors be granted a certain measure of individual autonomy? The latter approach would please instructors more, but would it excessively dilute the benefit that students derive from participating in a common experience? Should students remain in the same discussion section all year, maximizing the possibility that mutual trust and community will develop, or should they be rotated from instructor to instructor so that they will be exposed to different approaches? Many of the assigned works in a humanities program deal with issues that are important to students. How much time should be spent discussing the assigned works in a scholarly way, and how much opportunity should students have to engage the material personally?

Conclusion

The reading list for literary scholar John Erskine's General Honors seminar at Columbia consisted of sixty great books from the Western tradition—a book a week for two academic years. Because, in Erskine's view, the mark of these books was that they continued to speak to successive generations of readers centuries after they had been written, no textbooks or other secondary readings were used. Because the books would shed light on the students' own lives (or so Erskine hoped), the class would discuss them, not hear lectures from the professor. And because the books were universally illuminating, leadership of the class would not rotate from specialist to specialist in literature, the classics, philosophy, and so on, but would remain with one instructor, an amateur in the best sense of the word, who would be the students' fellow seeker as well as their guide in the search for truth and meaning.

Contemporary visitors to almost any of the humanities programs chronicled in this book would notice some differences from the Erskine seminars of nearly a century ago. Works by women and issues of concern to women are much more likely to be discussed. (The same is true of works by non-Westerners.) A more critical stance toward the works might well characterize the discussion. The term *great books* would less likely be used, in favor of *time-tested works* or *enduring texts*. Music might be heard, or art viewed. References might be made to downloading a reading or a lecture outline from the Internet.

Yet Erskine's seminars were the roots from which modern general education programs in the humanities have grown, and even today, the branch has not grown so far from the tree as to be unrecognizable. Students still gather around seminar tables in the courses that constitute these programs, and they do so for more than one semester. They still read and discuss primary texts, many of them the same works that Erskine's students read and discussed. Discussions are still led by professors who, most of the time, are teaching outside their specialty. Most important, perhaps, students continue to find these programs to be crucibles in which the beliefs and attitudes that will shape their lives are forged.

Chapter Two

The Humanities in the Core Curriculum at Columbia College

James V. Mirollo

As I begin to write, the 1997–98 academic year has just come to an end at Columbia University, and I have just completed my twenty-fifth year of teaching a Humanities component of the Columbia College Core Curriculum. That I continue to do so two years after retiring from full-time teaching indicates that mine will be the testimony of a believing witness, if not a giddy celebrant. I aim here at objectivity, even though teaching in our core has been the most rewarding part of a long professional career. Perhaps "tough love" would be the best way to describe my approach.

The story of Columbia's adventure in general education, because of its pioneering status and long endurance, has been told many times by both outsiders and insiders (Cross, 1995; Gray 1985; Mirollo, 1987, 1993; Nelson, 1996; Columbia College, 1988, 1993). Especially during the past decade, we have told it to ourselves quite often, with an equal mix of pride and anxiety. One reason that we seem to need reassurance is our awareness that if the adventure were to start afresh today, it would flounder. Its antiquity assures us that even with the problems and challenges I will delineate, one does not easily end a program that dates back to 1919, before most of us were born. At the same time, that venerable status invites instant suspicion of sclerosis. And it does not help that ideologues of the right and the left, both on and off campus, constantly praise or damn us out of ignorance or for the wrong reasons—unaware, of course, that their predictable squabbles are by now thoroughly boring and certainly irrelevant to the daily struggles to keep a historic enterprise alive and well.

Where We Are and How We Got There

The Core Curriculum of Columbia College consists of a group of required courses and other requirements that involve options, all of which take up the first two years of study.

The "core" of the Core consists of four "historic" courses (the dates in parentheses mark their official entry into required status):

Contemporary Civilization C1101–C1102: Introduction to Contemporary Civilization (1919). A year-long course earning four credits, meeting four hours a week, taught by an interdepartmental staff. Selected readings in the history of social and political thought. Known as CC.

Humanities C1001–C1002: Masterpieces of Western Literature and Philosophy (1937). A year-long course earning four credits, meeting four hours a week, taught by an interdepartmental staff. Known as Literature Humanities because of the predominance of literary texts in the syllabus. Students call it "Lit. Hum."; veteran faculty nostalgically still call it by its original name, Humanities A.

Humanities C1121: Masterpieces of Western Art (1947). A semester course earning three credits, meeting for three hours a week, taught by the faculty of the department of art history and archeology. Known as Art Humanities or "Art Hum."

Humanities C1123: Masterpieces of Western Music (1947). A semester course earning three credits, meeting for three hours a week (including a "listening hour"), taught by the faculty of the department of music. Known as Music Humanities or "Music Hum."

In addition, the Core includes a two-course major cultures requirement (chosen from designated courses in the cultures and civilizations of Asia, Africa, Latin America), a three-course science requirement, a semester of composition ("logic and rhetoric"), a foreign language requirement, and a physical education requirement.

The Core Curriculum has been described as (and I quote myself) "an oasis of order and purpose" (Columbia College, 1993, p. 24). Since the order may be more apparent than the purpose, it may be helpful to define that purpose in a general way while reserving specifics for discussion below. The Core, and particularly the Humanities components, attempts to prepare students to inhabit multiple communities or worlds in the future while offering to them the opportunity to stretch their minds and enhance their sensitivities to those experiences that make for a full and rich life. In sum, both civic and personal enrichment are aimed at.

Literature Humanities is now the most popular course in the Core with students and faculty (Mirollo, 1987). It began in 1937 with twenty sections taught by such luminaries as Jacques Barzun, Lionel Trilling, Mark Van Doren, and Moses Hadas. If anything, their original syllabus of important books was far too optimistic about students' capacity and hence had to be cut down fairly soon. But following on such predecessors as John Erskine's Honors Course and a variant of it, Colloquium on Important Books, the new course featured small classes, discussion of primary texts, quizzes and papers, and a common final exam. The Lit. Hum. staff agreed from the start that its syllabus would stress commonality: all sections reading the same texts on the same schedule each week. The staff met weekly, as it still does, to discuss the text to be taught that week. Given the demise of the Latin and Greek requirements at Columbia, as at other colleges, and the gathering storm clouds of World War II, the focus on the classical tradition and a Western literary canon may well reflect a sense in the founders that something precious needed to be preserved as a resource for a besieged humanity.

Exhibit 2.1 compares the reading lists of 1937–38 and 1986–87, a half-century later. Some of the differences between the two lists can be attributed to the arrival of women at Columbia College in the fall of 1983. Those of us who had fought for this change were extremely concerned that these new students should feel welcome,

Exhibit 2.1. Lit. Hum. Reading Lists, Columbia College, 1937–38 and 1986–87.

Fall 1937	*Fall 1986*
Homer, *Iliad*	Homer, *Iliad*
Aeschylus, *Oresteia*	Sappho, *Poems*
Sophocles, *Oedipus the King; Antigone*	Anonymous, *Hymn to Demeter*
	Aeschylus, *Oresteia*
Euripides, *Electra; Iphigenia in Tauris; Medea*	Sophocles, *Oedipus the King; Oedipus at Colonus; Antigone*
Aristophanes, *Frogs*	Thucydides, *Peloponnesian Wars*
Plato, *Apology; Symposium; Republic*	Euripides, *Medea; Bacchae*
Aristotle, *Ethics; Poetics*	Aristophanes, *Frogs*
Lucretius, *On the Nature of the Universe*	Plato, *Apology; Symposium; Republic*
Aurelius, *Meditations*	Aristotle, *Ethics; Poetics*
Virgil, *Aeneid*	Virgil, *Aeneid*

Spring 1938	*Spring 1987*
Augustine, *Confessions*	Old Testament: Genesis, Exodus, Isaiah
Dante, *Inferno*	
Machiavelli, *The Prince*	New Testament: Matthew, Romans
Rabelais, *Gargantua and Pantagruel,* Books I and II	Augustine, *Confessions*
	Dante, *Inferno*
Montaigne, *Essays*	Boccaccio, *Decameron*
Shakespeare, *Henry IV, Parts I and II; Twelfth Night; Hamlet; King Lear*	Montaigne, *Essays*
	Shakespeare, *King Lear*
Cervantes, *Don Quixote*	Descartes, *Meditations*
Milton, *Paradise Lost*	de Lafayette, *The Princess of Cleves*
Spinoza, *Ethics*	Goethe, *Faust,* Part I
Molière, *The Physician in Spite of Himself; Tartuffe; Misanthrope*	Austen, *Pride and Prejudice*
Swift, *Gulliver's Travels*	An optional text, preferably a nineteenth- or twentieth-century novel, to be read in the final week and a half
Fielding, *Tom Jones*	
Rousseau, *Confessions*	
Voltaire, *Candide*	
Goethe, *Faust*	

and those of us involved with Lit. Hum. (I was chair at that time) scrutinized our reading list to determine if any of its works could be deemed guilty of textual harassment. At the same time we were being pressed by some of our young colleagues to revise and reform the course as a whole in order to remedy its perceived biases: in favor of the Western tradition, dead white males, and the canonical texts, and its exclusion of other voices. Whatever changes we made, and from whatever pure or impure motives, we ended up doing the right thing since, according to surveys, our current list is exceedingly satisfactory to both students and faculty.

Those of us who endured the restlessness of the late 1960s and again of the late 1980s were bound to find the lull of the 1990s both soothing and surprising. It reminds us that in academic matters generally, and specifically in curricular skirmishes, one has to take the long view. The Lit. Hum. syllabus for 1997–98, for example, has only a few changes from the fiftieth anniversary model of 1986–87. In the interval we made Sappho optional, restored Herodotus, and gave Aristophanes a well-deserved vacation (although he returned in 1998–99 thanks to some persistent clamoring from his supporters). In the spring we now teach Woolf's *To the Lighthouse,* which has replaced *The Princess of Cleves.* More significant, we have added Hebrew Bible and the New Testament selections to the fall semester by giving Plato's *Republic* exclusively to the CC syllabus and moving Virgil's *Aeneid* to the spring. The spring now begins with the Latin tradition, Virgil, the *Golden Ass* of Apuleius or Ovid's *Art of Love,* and Augustine. The other significant change lies in the range of nineteenth- and twentieth-century texts now chosen by individual instructors to be taught in the final weeks of the term. These include, in more sections than a decade ago, Morrison's *Beloved,* Hurston's *Their Eyes Were Watching God,* Achebe's *Things Fall Apart,* Garcia Marquez's *One Hundred Years of Solitude,* and the more recent *Omeros* of Derek Walcott. *Omeros* is catching on as a superb way to end the course, since it is an epic of the Caribbean that uses and contests Homer, Virgil, and Dante. But the older favorite end-of-the-termer, *Crime and Punishment,* still has its advocates, although they have not emphasized that, as far as contestation goes, the character Svidgigailov, in a final, loud salute to Hebraism and Hellenism, shoots himself in front of a Jewish gatekeeper wearing an Achilles helmet instead of going to America!

Not only have there been no bitter complaints against the nature or existence of the course, but the "monumental" move of the Bible to the fall, to join the Greeks, was argued and approved on the grounds of pedagogical sense (not to break up the juxtaposition of fall Hellenism and spring Hebraism or Judeo-Christian tradition), and the need to make the spring list more flexible and hospitable to experiment and change. Indeed, the most vexing issue raised among faculty in the spring of 1998 had to do with depth versus breadth—the possibility of teaching fewer books in greater detail. Much time too has been spent on the perennial problem of what to do about the truly "big" books, like *Don Quixote,* which needs to be excerpted (how, and how much?), and potential gate crashers like *Brothers Karamazov.*

When word that these changes were being discussed got about and with no final decisions yet made, we were immediately plagued by student reporters asking if it were true that we were going to "go Stanford," or P.C., by junking *Faust* or the *Decameron.* Clearly students, in their combat readiness, are more querulous than faculty are. My own class swore that if we removed the *Decameron* they would protest or take over buildings. Obviously this echo of Columbia's "troubles" in the late 1960s could be disconcerting, but certainly it would be a first for students to storm the campus over a favorite text.

Alumni, out of nostalgia but also serious concern, occasionally query us about favorite texts not on the current list of Lit. Hum. I reply by pointing out that since 1937, nearly 150 different texts have been read in Lit. Hum., that only a handful have never been off the list (*Iliad, Oresteia, Oedipus Rex, Inferno*), and that others have regularly been given vacations from us and we from them. If this is a canon, it is (as a local wag put it) a loose one.

Being Columbia University in the City of New York is a mixed blessing when it comes to curricular history and change. The *New York Times,* keeps a sharp eye on Columbia's affairs, and since 1968, it has been preternaturally alert to any rumblings of dissent on campus. Generally, if change occurs elsewhere, say Stanford, Columbia's *not* changing (however untrue) is juxtaposed, with appropriate comments from conservatives and their opposites. For example, on April 12, 1987, the *Times* devoted a front-page story to Columbia's fiftieth anniversary celebration of Lit. Hum., including a sidebar of the 1937 and 1987 syllabi and suitable quotations from me and others. But the story was told within the larger news story that colleges were adding required courses to their curricula and turning against student choice—that is, they were catching up to Columbia, which had become avant garde by staying still.

The Non-Western Component

Multiculturalism came to Columbia in 1948 with the beginning of the Oriental Studies program. In the Columbia tradition, the founders of this program produced syllabi, outlines, guides, collections of translated primary materials, and translations of individual works—all duly used elsewhere by the inaugurators of similar programs. But since that time, as courses have proliferated and the riches thereby available have reached a remarkable level, it has become clear that the Core humanities model is not what everyone at Columbia—and elsewhere—means by "multiculturalism." The focus on the civilizations of Asia, Africa, and Latin America, while laudably global and expansively non-Western, is not what some mean who speak of "Eurocentrism," or "hegemony," or "colonialism." The semantic field of "multiculturalism" includes prominently for many critics the ethnic cultures of the United States; hence identity politics have complicated the debate that was once focused on incorporating non-Western civilizations into the curriculum. The availability of lots of courses that meet these different needs has not satisfied the desire to see these courses as part of the required Core, given its historic prestige and influence.

A move in that direction was taken in 1988 when six credits were freed up in the Core for what was then called the Extended Core. The very name, "extended core," must have seemed to its inventors to foretell an ideal solution. Alas, the idea of "extended" (meaning merely an "extension") would not do, and so "Cultures and Issues" was tried, but it too did not satisfy—hence the current Major Cultures, which promises what is actually delivered.

The preliminary statement of purpose in the college bulletin emphasizes that "the effect of the Core as a whole should be to reveal connections, influences, parallels, and blurry boundaries between cultures as much as to show their partial distinctness." It then goes on to say:

But the Core requirements do recognize that cultures and civilizations in different parts of the world have developed across long periods as partly independent traditions with histories of their own, and that the wide variety of important things that have been thought, said, and written in the world, many of which still help shape human actions in our own time, cannot be adequately understood or appreciated if torn from those traditions and histories. The Major Cultures requirement, founded on this recognition, promotes learning and thought about the variety of traditions that have formed the world and continue to interact in it today. [Columbia College, 1997–98]

Obviously these noble aims cannot be accomplished with six credits of course work, but they do require students to make a beginning and encourage them to continue beyond that, provided the major requirements and other distractions of the third and fourth years do not intervene.

Under the A (or introductory) list, students can choose from two courses in African civilization; seven in Asian civilizations and humanities; six in Latin American civilization, literature, and humanities; and six in Middle East languages and cultures. The distinctions between *civilizations* and *humanities* in the titles and content of these courses are intended to reinforce parallels and complementarity of these courses with CC and Lit. Hum. A similar number of courses, more advanced and specialized, are available under these same rubrics for List B, including the arts, religion, and contemporary societies.

List C, manifestations of major cultures in the United States, offers fifteen courses in African American studies, seven in Asian American studies, two in the Latino and Chicano experience, and five general courses that take up issues of ethnicity, race, and the immigrant experience. These courses, along with the others listed under B and C, are made available by departments, centers, and programs. Decisions as to their suitability to fulfill the major cultures requirement and under which list they should be placed are made by a standing committee of the college faculty on the core curriculum, established in 1988 to oversee such matters. It consists of chairs of Core courses and programs along with college administrators who meet regularly to take the pulse of the Core and determine its general health as well as to deal with particular issues such as course candidates submitted for the major cultures requirement.

The Place of the Bible

In Lit. Hum., Job made its entry in 1940, followed by the Gospel of Matthew in 1948. Since then, the Lit. Hum. staff has chosen at different times to include Genesis, Amos, Ecclesiastes, Exodus, Isaiah, and Hosea. From the New Testament, in addition to Matthew we have read Luke, John, I Corinthians, Revelation, and Romans. Some of these were tried just once (Hosea) or twice (Revelation), then banished for good (thus far). Others have spent many years on the list, taken a vacation, then returned. Thus there is no canon of these canonical texts, and if it were possible to have recordings of staff conversations since 1937, it would be fascinating to hear why some texts were added and others banished. As to whether the Bible should be read at all in a secular university, the current staff seems to have accepted, if only intuitively, that the course is essentially about tradition and response, and that the Bible constitutes one of those traditions, without which a good deal of the list, especially the postclassical works, makes little sense.

Indeed, we have lately discussed the imbalance between the Greek grip on the fall reading list and the biblical hold on only about one-third of it. Arguing as he has in his recent book *contra* Allan Bloom (1987), David Damrosch (1995) has contended that the Hebrew Bible and its Middle Eastern sources and analogues are getting short shrift in the Core, despite the living importance of the Bible as a whole for many students.

In 1977, the student editors of *Perspectives,* a magazine produced by the Jewish Student Union, asked in a series of essays how students of faith responded to the secular examination of the Bible as a "great book." Despite some difficulties, such as having the instructor reject Bible class meanings and rabbinic interpretations, none of the respondents suggested removing the Bible. Indeed, one student averred that her first real encounter with the Bible had come through Lit. Hum. and made it seem more significant to her as a Jew than it had been earlier. Another student concluded that the Columbia College faculty had decided that these texts are among the foremost that the Western world has produced, and had backed up this feeling by including the texts in the Core—a difficult "lineup" to break into.

Not all of our encounters with believing students are as heart-warming—and flattering—as the one just quoted. I have had my struggles with both Jewish and Christian students, as well as Muslims and Buddhists, not to mention very young atheists, over my literary interpretation of the Bible. Indeed, I can never forget one "born again" Christian student who sat in the back of the room with a huge Bible opened as I spoke, checking furiously everything I said, ready to pounce on any dubious statement I made. At the end of our Bible study, when I asked him how I did, and he replied that I had done okay, I was relieved and pleased to see that one could walk on eggs after all, testing but not crushing anyone's beliefs.

How Literature Humanities Works

There are approximately fifty sections of Lit. Hum., a required course for new students, with CC normally reserved for the year. In addition to Columbia College students, there are enrollees from the Engineering School who have chosen the course in order to fulfill a requirement. Each section is limited to twenty-two to twenty-four students. Incoming students have been told to read the first six books of the *Iliad* for the first class meeting.

Because Lit. Hum. is interdepartmentally staffed, it has a faculty chair drawn from one of the participating departments and appointed by the dean. The chair receives compensation from an endowed professorship that he or she holds during tenure in office. Normally the chair has taught and continues to teach the course. The chair is assisted by an administrative director who presides over the CC-Humanities office and staff, the latter serving in place of the usual departmental office and staff. The chair and the director handle the logistics: textbooks, meetings of the staff, student problems, and liaison with other administrative officials and offices of the college and university. Given that there are some one hundred sections of CC and Lit. Hum. to deal with, the process of keeping the two courses functioning smoothly is complex and requires the presence of an extraordinarily effective administrative director. Without such direction of the office operation, no faculty member could be persuaded to assume the chair for the usual three-year term.

The staff of Lit. Hum. meets every Monday for a two-hour brown bag luncheon to discuss the text being taught that week. A guest speaker who is a specialist in the text starts the meeting, followed by what is usually a lively exchange. Because the staff includes senior professors, nontenured professors and fellows, and graduate student preceptors and because the meeting is nondepartmental, the Monday meetings (dating to 1937) are unique. Unlike any other university event, instructors of different rank and experience can talk with each other about books without departmental pressure. The setting for the meetings, the Heyman Center for the Humanities, is itself an oasis, as hospitable a setting for intellectual exchange as can be imagined.

On the previous Friday afternoon there is a meeting of the chair and the newcomers—preceptors mostly, although beginning professors are welcome. Part of a teaching apprentice program, these required propaedeutic seminars enable the new Lit. Hum. teachers to discuss with the chair and each other strategies for teaching the following week's text. The teaching apprentice program includes recruitment, preliminary orientation and training, and subsequent monitoring and evaluation of classroom performance. Normally preceptors teach for two years only, because of concern about the progress of graduate study given the difficulties of teaching the course with its often-unfamiliar texts. The teaching apprentice activity has largely overcome those concerns.

The staff teaches the same texts on schedule until the final week of the year, when there is a choice of a modern work. Although each instructor makes up his or her own midterm exam and paper assignments, there is a common final exam prepared by the staff. In addition, approximately every two years, the staff engages in a thorough review of the syllabus with an eye to continuing, excluding, or adding texts, editions, and translations.

In order to assist new assistant professors to teach the course while establishing their scholarly credentials for tenure consideration, those who teach the course for three years are given a semester leave with pay (the so-called Chamberlain leaves), along with a university development grant of a second semester leave with pay.

Student and Alumni Response to the Core

At the end of each semester, students evaluate the course by responding to a questionnaire provided by the office of the vice president for arts and sciences. The questions ask the students to rate content and teaching on a scale from excellent to poor. The second part of the questionnaire allows students to respond in several paragraphs to questions about how the course and teaching can be improved. The instructor is required to leave the room after handing out the materials and assigning a student to collect the completed anonymous answer sheets and take them to the Core office. After final grades are handed in, instructors can consult the answer sheets. The responses may be used as evidence of teaching performance by departmental and central administration officers and committees in matters of tenure and promotion. To date, the college has not developed a systematic method of polling alumni reaction soon after or many years later than graduation, relying instead on anecdotal evidence.

Perhaps because students choose Columbia knowing about the Core, or because they enjoy the course, they have generally expressed enthusiastic approval. Among the reasons they give are the small classes and discussion format (lecturing in the classroom is not only discouraged but forbidden), the challenging syllabus, and the teaching, which is the single greatest source of myth and legend in the Columbia College experience. Obviously there is grumbling, whether about less-than-legendary teaching, the "Eurocentric" focus, or the impediment offered by the Core to early professional preparation. But these laments have been in the minority and in any event are not easily countered. We would certainly wish to have legendary teachers in all fifty sections, and we would, if we could, have every culture represented, and we know that many students are under pressure from departments to fulfill preprofessional and major requirements as early as possible. Discouraged at times by our inability to satisfy these wishes, we are suddenly and unexpectedly jolted into joy by an essay published in the student newspaper:

> One returns after a summer break to Columbia's second year to
> an introduction to Contemporary Civilization, Columbia's oldest

tradition. Again, one's entire class is engulfed, this time by some heavy philosophy. Much as Lit. Hum. had the year before, CC provides a link between nearly all College students here, guaranteeing each student has a minimum of experience in common with everyone else in his class. As well, these classes offer intellectual freedom from practical concerns. . . .

Leaving the Core behind prods me to think that perhaps I and others did not appreciate what we had until we were ready to leave it. There is a carefree spirit to thinking for thinking's sake, without a grad school or a job in mind. The Core is unstrategic in that it has no ultimate end in mind. One does not graduate CC and head for Wall Street. What is sad is that many of us will never recapture this intellectual innocence once the Core is behind us.

Equally encouraging has been the support of the alumni. Indeed, they have been not only staunch supporters of the Core but also eager guardians of its purity, ready to pounce on any assumed deviation. All the reasons were given by alumnus Eric D. Witkin in 1988:

For most alumni of the College, the Core is the center of their common experience of Columbia College, an experience more important and more central to their experience of the College than the Columbia Lion, the King's Crown, the football team and certainly the experience of dormitory life. . . . The common experience of the Core Curriculum is synonymous with a Columbia College education, the thing that College alumni are proudest of when they compare their undergraduate experiences with those of graduates of other institutions. . . . In addition they give money because they feel an obligation to future generations, to make available to those young people what they, the alumni, thought was precious to their own experience. [Columbia College, 1988]

There have been two other concrete manifestations of alumni enthusiasm and support in recent years. The first occurred in November 1994 on the occasion of the seventy-fifth anniversary of the inauguration of the Core with the CC course. Alumni awarded to Jacques Barzun on our behalf, as well as to each of us, a special medal honoring teachers of the Core. In addition, the alumni commissioned a new and updated history of the Core (Cross, 1995).

The second has been the response of alumni to the Alumni Colloquia, which are based on Colloquium, the successor course to Erskine's Honors program and the predecessor to Lit. Hum., which is still being offered. The colloquium model involves two instructors discussing with a seminar a series of texts chosen or agreed on by the students themselves. Beginning in 1987–88, some faculty began offering colloquia under the general rubric of "revisiting the Core" to interested alumni. The idea of returning to campus and reencountering Core works from past syllabi (verbal, visual, and audio)—and not to mention new works—after twenty, thirty, forty, even fifty years proved irresistible. The appetite for this experience, as evidenced by David Denby's book (1996) on the subject, has swamped us into a much larger program than we ever envisioned, and more interest than we can easily satisfy.

Problems and Issues

There is continuing controversy about what a core curriculum is and does. In the past, the claims of liberal education were pitted against those of preprofessional training. As a small college in a large university whoring after the German model of professional schooling, Columbia's experiment with general education was always embattled. Until recently, it was the tail that never wagged the dog, and unlike undergraduate colleges elsewhere, especially in the Ivy League, it was not the apple of the university's eye. The paradox was that being small, it could do a core curriculum of its kind, but at the same time, it was not large enough to have clout. That Barnard College was and remains an autonomous women's college only affiliated contractually with Columbia meant that until women were admitted in 1983, the college was a small male-only place. Then, under the presidency of George Rupp, a move was made a few years ago to make the college central to the university. Although the recent attractiveness of the Core has made this move possible, it has also meant that an educational approach originally intended for a small college is now being stretched and strained (twenty sections of Lit. Hum. then, more than fifty now), especially with regard to faculty and maintaining small classes.

The result has been the resurfacing of some old and familiar arguments against general education and its embodiment in a core curriculum: that it is superficial, requires instructors to teach other than what they know, takes up too much of the student's college years against the needs of specialization, and is generally too expensive to maintain, especially in a large college where a distribution system would work better. It has also been suggested, externally as well as internally, that a core curriculum is synonymous with "reverential canonization of 'great books of the Western tradition'" (Oakley, 1991). The Core's past success answers the early complaints. I will focus here on a misunderstanding about what core curriculum is.

It is sometimes said that a core program works because of content and great (or at least committed) teaching. But the books we teach are taught elsewhere, and there are outstanding teachers elsewhere too. So I conclude that the idea of a core curriculum refers to the container or packaging, not the contents, which in any event are constantly changing. Granted that the container and the contents influence each other, the crucial elements in the packaging are commonality and small classes.

The advantage of commonality for students is the ability to talk together outside class about the same books. For faculty, it is the opportunity to talk to each other about books and ideas and teaching rather than only campus politics, departmental tensions, and administrative bungling.

The rationale for small classes goes back at least as far as Plato's *Symposium* and *Apology*. We see in them a vivid contrast between Socrates addressing (brilliantly) a small circle of disciples and Socrates on trial, who is fairly helpless in dealing with a mob. The method of Socratic dialogue, with questions and answers, opinions and beliefs, energetically exchanged, is a model, though not the only one, of progressive learning in a setting of smallness. Much of the power of Denby's account in *Great Books* of his return visit to the Core derives from what I call the culture of the small class. Indeed one might say his book could not have been written had he been obliged to sit in on large lecture classes—with no interaction between instructor and students, or between students and students, or between Denby and both. The dynamics of the small class are the key to the success of the Columbia College core and, I suspect, that of any other core program.

Another feature of the small class that merits attention is the bond of intellectual intimacy that develops between teacher and students, especially when they stay together for a whole academic year. In an atmosphere of affectionate possessiveness, interlopers are scorned, references are made to "my kids," and warm feelings are stirred and remembered. Twenty years later a teacher may receive a telephone call or letter from a former student who wants to continue an early debate with a new insight.

Canon Debates

I would gladly banish the terms *canon* and *canonical*. They belong to the discourse of sacred texts and can only do mischief when applied to novels, plays, and poems, not to mention treatises and tractates. But they have been used often in attacks on Western domination of curricula, just as *multiculturalism* has been a banner raised to propose what should take its place.

Although the Core at Columbia has been under constant siege, there were two particularly tense, if not defining, moments in the struggle. The first occurred during the Columbia "troubles," when targets marked for extinction included the Core, and more particularly the required, common reading list of Lit. Hum. In fact, for a few years the reading list was drastically reduced so that instructors could have room to include other, formerly excluded texts having different ideological bearings. By 1970, too, a faculty commission had actually recommended that CC and Lit. Hum. be made optional. When the college faculty voted down such a change, continuation of a totally required Core was assured, though some dissent has persisted. Cross (1995, pp. 83–84) notes that "after fifty years, it is perhaps surprising that the College's core curriculum was so close to complete collapse."

The next tense moment occurred in the late 1980s, when the Commission of the Core Curriculum reexamined the Core. A group of young colleagues teaching the course appealed for greater flexibility in order to allow different cultures, issues of gender, and the voices of the historically marginalized to be heard. Not all younger members of the staff shared these views. Nor did others share the feeling that being compelled to teach the course for three years in order to earn paid leave time was a burden. There were defenders not only of the syllabus as a whole but also of individual authors who might have to be retired or deemphasized.

With conservatives, young and old, arguing for no change and reformers wanting a radical adjustment, compromise was not possible. A divided staff could not summon a majority in support of either position, so the status quo prevailed. At the time, and since (more recently preaching largely to the converted), I have pointed out that the goals of the reformers had to be met, were indeed being met, by the curriculum as a whole—in fact, more so now than years ago. It could not be possible for a single course, even a year-long course, to include every desirable text without courting incoherence, tokenism, and faculty disaffection. Even my colleague Edward Said, no enemy of the reformers, asserted at the time that the texts in the current syllabus spoke to each other, as intended by its structure, and that the conversation should not be interrupted by the insertion of other texts. I added that if the purpose of such insertions was to challenge alleged representations of a hegemonic Western tradition, the texts in the current syllabus did that themselves, each challenging its predecessors on ideological grounds, not only out of Harold Bloom's anxiety of influence.

Put as the students themselves would, and have, put it, we should choose texts that rattle their brains and knock their socks off and that resonate with each other. We should be wary of depriving students of the cultural riches their predecessors have cherished and praised.

Faculty Recruitment and Incentives and Administrative Support

Although there is enough faculty support to ensure the continuity of the Core, especially given the enthusiasm of the alumni, this support is mixed and certainly not as fervid as it was in the early years of the founders. One reason is that the Columbia faculty is no longer as inbred as it once was, so that graduates of the college no longer dominate faculty ranks. Coming from elsewhere, lacking the Columbia College religion, and feeling that they thrived in their undergraduate institutions under distribution systems rather than core curricula, they are unsympathetic, if not hostile. Another motive, particularly among many members of the science faculty, is to have their majors start earlier, before the third year.

The usual problems of inadequate budgetary resources, faculty shortages, and overcrowded classes, all exacerbated by the expansion of the college, have taken their toll on support. Yet it is clearly unthinkable that Columbia College would abandon its Core Curriculum or even enlarge its class sizes to make it more economical. Apart from the issue of alumni support, there is the truth that the Core so completely identifies the college that there is a real question why anyone would wish to test the thesis. The lack of support among the scientists and most of the social scientists (excluding historians) has meant their effective withdrawal from teaching the Core and their unwillingness to create and teach courses of their own in the mode of general education.

But since other faculty are also reluctant to do so out of motives ranging from ideological objections to departmental priorities to career considerations, there has been a struggle to staff the Core. The report of the Commission of the Core Curriculum (1988) confirmed the goal of having the four major courses staffed by a combination of professors, nontenured professors, and trained preceptors. Although this does not match the claim that Columbia College students encounter professors in basic courses, many of them do, and certainly more than elsewhere in the Ivy League.

There have been several administrative efforts to support the Core's material and staffing needs. The most promising thus far is the effort of the current dean of the college, Austin Quigley, to promote endowed support for the Core. He also has stressed that currently there is no inducement for many faculty to teach the Core, regardless of their ideological or practical concerns, since professional rewards come from other activities, such as scholarly publishing. Consequently he is planning to offer research stipends and other means of rewarding those who are engaged. There also is an award from the Heyman Center for the Humanities for outstanding service to the Core and several collegiate chairs, named after their donors or distinguished past teachers, that are awarded to teachers of the Core.

In addition, the vice president for arts and sciences has stressed and enforced the faculty's obligation to staff the Core as a matter of faculty advancement, beginning with hiring. In the past, especially when hiring tenured faculty, the possibility of teaching in the

Core was hardly mentioned. Even now, when assistant professors are hired, they are told about the Chamberlain Fellowships but not about the need or expectation that they will teach the Core thereafter. That the graduate programs of the Arts and Sciences have shrunk in response to the job market has allowed for the principle that faculty should teach a significant part of their load in undergraduate courses. The provost has maintained that the granting of tenure will include consideration of teaching commitment at the undergraduate level. Further help has come from the recently established Society of Senior Scholars at the Heyman Center. Underwritten in part by a Mellon grant, the Scholars are retired professors who continue to teach in the Core. (The Scholars are supplementary, taken on as needed, and paid less than preceptors, with whom they are not in competition.)

In the end, we cannot relish the idea of compulsory teaching, which can only be counterproductive. One has to love to teach the Core courses, as many of us do and I suspect many will in the future. I am reminded of the reason why this is and will be so when I recall a colleague no longer in my department who was reluctant to teach Lit. Hum. Knowing him to be a good teacher as well as a distinguished literary critic, I badgered him into giving it a try. A year later, when pressed, he told me that he still did not believe in such a course but that teaching it had been the best classroom experience of his life. I rested my case.

References

Barzun, J. "The Birth of the Humanities Course." *Columbia College Today,* Fall 1987, pp. 12–15.

Bloom, A. *The Closing of the American Mind: How Higher Education Has Failed Democracy and Impoverished the Souls of Today's Students.* New York: Simon & Schuster, 1987.

Columbia College. *Report of the Commission of the Core Curriculum.* New York: Columbia College, 1988.

Columbia College. *Report on the Future of Columbia College.* New York: Columbia College, 1993.

Columbia College. *Columbia College Bulletin.* New York: Columbia College, 1997–1998.

Cross, T. P. *An Oasis of Order: The Core at Columbia College.* New York: Columbia College, 1995.

Damrosch, D. *We Scholars: Changing the Culture of the University.* Cambridge, Mass.: Harvard University Press, 1995.

Denby, D. *Great Books: My Adventures with Homer, Rousseau, Woolf, and Other Indestructible Writers of the Western World.* New York: Simon & Schuster, 1996.

Gray, W. *Homer to Joyce.* New York: Macmillan, 1985.

Mirollo, J. V. "Happy Birthday Humanities A." *Columbia Magazine,* Apr. 1987, pp. 32–38.

Mirollo, J. V. "The Core Curriculum Idea." *Professional Scholar,* Mar. 1993, pp. 3–4.

Nelson, M. *Celebrating the Humanities: A Half-Century of the Search Course at Rhodes College.* Nashville, Tenn.: Vanderbilt University Press, 1996.

Oakley, F. "Against Nostalgia: Reflections on Our Present Discontents in Higher Education." *National Humanities Newsletter,* 1991, *12*(2), 1–14.

Yufe, J. *Perspectives,* Winter 1977, pp. 14–15.

Chapter Three

Freedom and Wholeness at St. John's College

Mera J. Flaumenhaft

The "New Program" of St. John's College is not so new: it has been in existence for sixty years. This itself is a sign of the soundness of its aims and its success in fulfilling many of them. The college seeks to shape inquiring human beings who wish to understand themselves and the world they live in, and to do this by reading and discussing great books. It is animated by the belief that inquiring human beings are the most truly free human beings. Its students freely elect an education that, paradoxically, does not leave them free to elect what they will study. But within the confines of the entirely prescribed curriculum, they are permitted—indeed required—to think as freely and as deeply as they can.

St. John's College differs from other undergraduate programs with a liberal arts or general education component in two decisive respects: the program constitutes the entire four-year education of every student, and science and mathematics are included among

From the beginning, St. John's College has continually sought to explain itself and its aims—both to itself and to outsiders. Characteristically, this has been a communal effort, and many of the formulations in this chapter are thus common property. I have not attempted to sort out who said what first, but anyone who turns to the References at the end of this chapter will see immediately how much I owe to others.

the humanities. From its beginnings, St. John's College has fostered inquiry into freedom and wholeness as features of the best human life.

Origins

In June 1937, Scott Buchanan and Stringfellow Barr walked into a bankrupt conventional college in Annapolis, Maryland, and revived it in an entirely new form. Closely associated with the work of John Erskine, Alexander Meiklejohn, Robert Hutchins, Mark Van Doren, and Mortimer Adler, the founders of the New Program at St. John's were determined to avoid the obstacles encountered by experimental liberal arts programs at Columbia, the University of Wisconsin, the University of Chicago and the University of Virginia. They abolished conventional departments, faculty titles, and salaries based on external reputation and publication, thus eliminating many of the divisions and turf fights that characterize most academic institutions. It would not have made sense to say that students should have a broad liberal arts education if their teachers had a narrow, specialized one. A faculty responsible for the whole curriculum would validate the whole endeavor. All faculty members would have the same title, "tutor," and be expected to teach throughout the program. The dean would be drawn from the faculty for a limited period (five years) of leadership and service, before returning to full teaching responsibilities. In the absence of traditional departments, there would be no organized resistance to the comprehensive new curriculum. The students would be full-time residents in a small community. Fraternities and intercollegiate athletics, which often fragment community and distract attention from academic programs, were eliminated. Unlike undergraduates eager to begin their majors or busy adults stealing time for enrichment, St. John's students would immerse themselves entirely in the work of the common program, to which all administrative energy and all financial resources would be devoted. The liberation of this program from the difficulties of being part of a wider institution is clearly one of the keys to its success.

The student body remained very small until after World War II. Over the next few decades it continued to grow, stabilizing finally at about 450 undergraduates. In 1964, St. John's opened a second campus of the same size in Santa Fe, New Mexico. Except for a few minor differences, the program in Santa Fe is the same as the one in Annapolis, allowing for some student transfer between campuses. (The following account of the life around the common curriculum restricts itself to the Annapolis campus.) In addition to the undergraduate program, both campuses now offer an interdisciplinary master's degree program in the Graduate Institute in Liberal Education.

A "complete" course of study cannot mean a perfect one. Nor can it include everything that is worth knowing. For example, St. John's does not have the resources to take on the study of non-Western books. Few would dispute the worth of such study. But time is limited, and the fact is that it is Western thought that has given rise to the concepts of philosophy, science, democracy, and liberalism as we know them—and to liberal education itself. So it makes sense to concentrate on the more coherent body of western writings in more accessible languages. (In the Graduate Program in Eastern Classics, a one-year master's program offered only on the Santa Fe campus, students read classic texts in the Chinese and Indian traditions and study some classical Chinese or Sanskrit.)

What "complete" does mean is that those who undertake such a program experience its parts as parts of a whole. Individual classes are not called "courses" because only when taken all together do they add up to a full "course" of study—a "curriculum." Any one class is related vertically to those preceding it; it assumes that the students have worked through related material in the tutorials, laboratories, and seminars of the previous years. Members of a seminar who are reading Machiavelli have some familiarity with Aristotle, Plato, and the Bible, as Machiavelli did, and those reading Newton have thought their way there, as he did, through Aristotle, Ptolemy, Copernicus, Kepler, and Galileo. Aside from minor changes, every older student has read what the younger ones are reading, so it is common to find students of different years engaged in serious discussions about the same books and questions—in dorm rooms, in the gym, and at lunch. Such discussions are on the table all the time. Nor, since each class is also related horizontally to other classes of the same year, is it unusual to find freshmen talking about Euclid's diction in their language class, or about things they have learned about embryology in the laboratory in a seminar on Aristotle's other writings. This utterly unbounded conversation is one of the features that makes the greatest impression on prospective students and other visitors to the college. The very restriction of students to the same classes is itself responsible for the deep freedom that characterizes the intellectual life of the place.

Even the arrangement of space and time at the college contributes to the sense of a common endeavor. The Annapolis campus is compact. All classes are taught in the same rooms in a few buildings. Blackboard work left from a freshman mathematics or language class often reminds those who have come to do junior mathematics of Euclid propositions or Greek passages studied in previous years. In the same way, younger students catch glimpses of Racine or Einstein long before they encounter them in their own classes. Even these casual reminders and introductions play a part in the sense of the whole that informs the curriculum. The round-the-clock schedule has the same effect. Buchanan (1962) spoke of the rhythms of a life organized throughout the hours of the day, like that of a Benedictine monastery. The hours are, in fact, rung out from the bell tower and can be heard around town. Students who live together, and attend classes every day and on two evenings, do not distinguish between work and play as sharply as those at many other colleges do. There is a seamless quality to life at St. John's.

Before turning to the curriculum itself, something should be said about the most important postfounding influence on the program. Jacob Klein arrived at St. John's in 1938, a Russian refugee unable to return to his work in Germany. A student of Plato, Heidegger, and Husserl and of Greek and post-Cartesian mathematics, Klein found the aims of the new program wonderfully close to his own. Like Barr and Buchanan, he was concerned with the need to liberate earlier—especially Greek—thinkers from the distorting "sedimentation" of scholarship, especially in the sciences, and to go to the roots of accumulated tradition. He differed from Buchanan, perhaps, in his sense that the radically differing views found in great books cannot always be reconciled by reformulation and analogy and that serious study might reveal fractures, even chasms, in the Western tradition studied as a whole. He became dean at a time when the new program was in danger of foundering for lack of effective leadership. From 1949 to 1958, he addressed the problem (still with the college today) of trying to read so much in so little time. Buchanan and his associates insisted that all books be read in their entirety. Klein was responsible for reducing the size of seminar assignments and for selecting parts of some books for study in tutorials, in order to help students achieve more mastery of, and to reflect better on, what they did read. He emphasized that diligent preparation was necessary, as well as enthusiastic conversation, and that although the program transcends conventional disciplines, it demands rigorous discipline on the part of the learner. He also recognized the importance of institutionalized means for faculty development. Under his leadership, the laboratory and music classes were refined. Klein lectured frequently and, like Buchanan, was a compelling teacher. His writings remain a rich resource for the college community and for others interested in liberal education.

Curriculum

The program has three components: tutorial (mathematics, language, and music), laboratory, and seminar, each embodying a different way of learning that complements and enriches the others. By translating and demonstrating at the blackboard, singing and analyzing music, observing and experimenting in the laboratory, and, above all, asking and exploring questions around a table, students begin to make the acquaintance of the thinkers who, for the most part, have made them what they are.

The primary activity in every part of the program is the study of great books. The promotional pamphlet that students applying to the college most often mention announces that "the following teachers will return to St. John's next year," and goes on to list the great writers of the Western tradition. The books are approached without mediation, so that they can speak directly to new readers today, as they have since they were written. No summarizing textbooks are used, nor are surveys or histories. Students may read whatever edition or translation they prefer, although guidance is available from tutors and information provided by the bookstore. Notes and commentaries are available in most good editions, and scholarly works are available in the bookstore and library. But the best secondary works on the books are thought to be works by the authors of other great books. So the books assigned for seminars and other classes are not prepackaged in scholarly interpretations or schemas, or read with premature conviction of the truth of particular authors, as some church-related colleges read Aristotle, the Bible, and Aquinas. Rather, first-time readers encounter the authors and their ideas in roughly chronological order. As far as is possible in a community that includes more and less experienced readers, all are encouraged to grapple with these books on their own rather than to repeat what they have read or been told. This way of proceeding means a deliberate decision to exclude historical context—and history in general—from the curriculum. Although this sometimes leads to obliviousness or misunderstandings, it seems a lesser, more easily remediable distortion than those resulting from passive reliance on more experienced readers, or the interpretation of all thought as the product of its peculiar time and place. Some knowledge of some of the languages in which the books are written is acquired by all, again in an effort to avoid having to agree on the use of any one authoritative translation.

The Seminar

The seminar is often said to be the heart of the St. John's curriculum. On Mondays and Thursdays, from eight to ten P.M., from the first class of freshman year to the last class of senior year, the entire college meets in groups of about eighteen students and two tutors. A master list shows at a glance what book or portion of a book students of any year will be discussing for any session. The reading might be the first six books of the *Iliad,* speeches by Frederick Douglass, a chapter from Hegel, or a novel by Jane Austen. The seminar is an entirely communal event. A table brings its members together, face to face; their attention is always on the books and each other. No extended presentations are made, and blackboards are rarely used. Most students dress informally, but some still dress up for seminars, and the nighttime makes the event feel special. It seems to foster speculation, and allows the official discussion to continue longer than scheduled, and informal ones to continue deep into the night.

One of the tutors begins with a question, and the discussion proceeds freely for the next two hours. No one is called on; no one asks permission to speak. The intimacy of the small group and of friendships in a small community is offset by the custom, here and in all other classes, of students and tutors addressing each other by "Mr." and "Ms." and last names. The formality elevates the tone and impresses young people with their responsibility to speak maturely, politely, and on the same level as their elders. The more experienced readers tell young students what they must read, but leave them entirely free in their responses to these readings. Often the best way to generate discussion is to refrain from helping too soon. When students realize that they themselves are responsible, they cease to rely on the tutors. The sharing of responsibility is also fostered by having two discussion leaders. Their job is not to supply information, lengthy explanations, or interpretations, although they too offer their ideas and ask questions. Their primary function is to help guide the discussion: to keep it moving, raise helpful objections, and draw attention to the relations among contributions. Tutors can often be most helpful when they ask *why* someone else thinks something, what the speaker means by a particular word, or how two things fit together.

Because students address each other, not just the tutors, and because anyone may initiate a new question or line of thought, a seminar can degenerate into a series of answers to the opening question or into interesting, but unrelated, observations. Students must learn to keep to the topic, choose their words with care, and adjust the mode of discussion to the kind of reading. Poetry and philosophy, and, indeed, different kinds of poetry and philosophy, may require different approaches. Those who previously have been encouraged to debate or zealously defend their own opinions are now encouraged to try to understand the positions of others, see the complexities and problems in their own positions, and refer directly to passages in the readings. They develop the habit of asking each other and themselves questions and become, as a result, both better members of the communal discussion and better thinkers when they are alone.

Sometimes it takes months for a group to learn to work well together. Most tutors agree that there are major questions and passages that readers should attend to. But different groups may focus on different questions or approach them in different ways, and there is no assurance, as there is in a lecture or a tightly guided discussion, that every important issue will get its due. The discussion may focus on a key word or passage, the title, the relation of one author to another, or an example from current affairs. The only rules are that all opinions be seriously held and seriously explored and that they be expressed rationally and courteously.

The direction of such discussions is not predictable. There are always unexpected connections, thoughtful musings, and interesting sidelines. There are also distracting digressions, stubborn refusals to give up an opinion, and promising remarks that are ignored. In short, the seminar is just what its name says it is: a "seeding" ground. Some ideas are generated and flower then and there. Others bloom later that night in the coffee shop or in the dormitory. Some lie dormant until a student has had some further experience, read something else, or written a paper with the guidance of another tutor. And others die and are forgotten because they are weak, or because no one recognized their depth and importance.

In seminar, students begin to think through the questions that have occupied most thinkers in the Western tradition: questions about nature and convention, about human nature and the rest of the natural world, about time and history, about human life in families and wider political communities, about science and technology, about becoming and being, and about whether there is anything above human beings and the natural world they live in. Along with these questions, students find themselves thinking about what thinking itself is, about learning and knowing. There is no received doctrine about such questions. Two questions, perhaps, can be said to assume special importance: "What is a good life for a human being?" and "Is there a consistent contrast between ancient and modern thought: about nature, mathematics, ethics, politics, and knowledge?" The latter question, articulated repeatedly by Jacob Klein, arises in mathematics and language tutorials and in laboratories as well. This is the first time that many students have been asked to give a reasoned account of what they think to others who may not share their opinions. The time spent on the Bible in sophomore seminar, for example, is often a particularly charged time. Despite its inherited name,

St. John's is an entirely secular institution; it has no religious affiliation whatsoever. Seminar discussions raise the most radical questions about reason and revelation, as they explore the stories of the Hebrew Bible, the Gospels, Paul's letters, and later theological writings. This is a rare and precious opportunity, sometimes exhilarating, sometimes embarrassing. Such discussions may have great or little immediate consequences, or they may influence a student's thinking for years to come.

Although there are now fewer books and shorter assignments than in the past, the list of seminar readings has remained fairly stable since the founding of the New Program. There is continual tinkering with the selections from books not read in their entirety. Some substitutions have been made, and some additions. And there is perennial discussion about whether there should be more political Plato and Aristotle, about when to read Virgil and other Roman authors, and about the placement of the Bible readings. Two considerations are always paramount: the college cannot and does not claim to read every great book, and whenever a reading is added, another must be removed. These are practical questions. The main principle—that there are some books that are deeper and more important to read than others—is acknowledged by all who choose this program. This principle frees them from debilitating debates about the canon, postmodernism, feminism, and the new historicism. In fact, such "isms" are rarely debated at St. John's, where the books themselves are the gateways to thinking about men and women, nature, and thinking itself.

For seven weeks in the middle of the year, the junior and senior seminars are redistributed into preceptorials. Offered by the tutors of that year's junior and senior seminars, these smaller classes—the only "electives" in the program—concentrate on one work or one subject. Preceptorials are usually on "program" books, but may sometimes be on something not studied by everyone in the common program. Recent preceptorials have included ones on *The Republic*, the *Odyssey*, Spinoza, the *St. Matthew Passion*, Faraday, *The Brothers Karamazov*, linguistics, *The Tale of Genji*, and medical ethics. In connection with these closer readings, students write papers, prepare presentations, and make more use of the blackboard than they do in seminars.

In the spring term of the first three years, each student submits an annual essay. This is not a research paper, but an opportunity for the student to speak about a book or theme that has been important to him or her that year. Here again, the free choice of the individual grows out of experience and growth in the prescribed common curriculum. The essay is discussed in an "oral" with the two tutors. The sophomore annual essay is especially important, since it helps to determine whether the student is ready to continue with the work of the next two years and to write an adequate senior essay in January of the senior year, when all senior classes are suspended and the student, under the supervision of a faculty adviser, devotes full attention to it. After a committee of three other faculty members accepts a senior essay, it is scheduled for an hour-long "oral." The participants wear academic regalia, and the session is open to all members of the community. This event is not called a "defense." It is intended to be a genuine, open discussion about the essay.

It is a serious mistake to think that seminar, as the heart of the program, is the most important part, or that its mode of discussion is the only one practiced at St. John's. Students who enroll under the illusion that their classwork will consist entirely of freewheeling discussions about literature and philosophy discover that they are much mistaken. One reason for emphasizing the importance of a campus visit by prospective students is to make vivid the way in which the seminar relates to the tutorial and laboratory components of the program.

The Language Tutorial

The language tutorial reflects on the relations of language to thought, of correct to persuasive speech, of logic to grammar, and of languages to each other. It corresponds roughly to the trivium of the traditional liberal arts: grammar, logic, and rhetoric. It is a tutorial in the elements of language rather than a course in particular languages, because it aims to reflect on all aspects of language—morphology, etymology, syntax, rhetoric, and style—in the context of the reading and thinking that students are doing in other parts of the program. There, the readings are done mostly in English translations. In language classes, students acquire the ability to enrich their readings of English translations with the original Greek or French.

In the early days of the program, the language curriculum consisted of one year each of Greek, Latin, German, and French. It was soon thought preferable to study two languages more intensively and to include extended study of literary works in English as well. The liberal arts of language liberate the learner from the constrictions and assumptions of his or her own language, the distortions of vernacular and scholarly usage over the centuries, and dependence on translations that may distort the original meaning of an author. Few students continue to study Greek or French after they leave St. John's. But most remain avid readers of books not always written in their own language. The language tutorial accustoms them to choose translations intelligently and to use bilingual texts. It also gives a remarkable number of alumni the courage to tackle new languages. This courage in learning new things—*any* new things—is often remarked on by those who meet St. John's students and alumni.

The tutorials are smaller classes of about fifteen students. They are taught by one tutor who is responsible for moving the group through the material to be covered and for guiding discussion, assigning written work, and ensuring that students achieve an adequate understanding of the readings. In contrast to the rapid, free exchanges in seminar and other discussions, the art of translation in the language tutorial is slow work, often painstakingly so, in its attempt to be both accurate and elegant. The longer one looks at and talks about the same thing, the more one sees. This is true also of the animal, the painting, or the geometrical proposition examined in other classes. The careful analysis of a sentence or argument often reveals its logic or rhetoric. A class may diagram a sentence, list all forms of the same verb along with its roots and cognates, or compare two accurate but different translations. In tutorials, students look not only at the book and at each other, but together at the blackboard. Computer programs and electronic dictionaries might be effective aids in learning grammar and vocabulary and in improving speed and accuracy in translating, but they are rarely used at St. John's. The laborious investigation of words in the lexicon and the time-consuming generation of multiple translations seem more conducive to the speculative, communal learning of the language class. Electronic aids, used carefully outside class, might make more time for such learning. But resistance to speed and efficiency is often a healthy antidote to the dominant intellectual tendencies of our time.

The language tutorial also aims to make students more attentive to clarity in their own use of language. Classes are largely communal efforts in which students help each other to demonstrate mathematical propositions, translate sentences, and think through the implications of an argument. In their own writing, students have the opportunity to make an extended statement without help—or interruptions—from well-meaning others. Although many students write very well, some do not. Some have had inadequate previous instruction. Some find that keeping up with the heavy class preparation leaves too little time. Some even claim that the emphasis on conversation gets in the way of their ability to sustain an argument in writing—that they are poor writers because they are good talkers. That should not be so. There are required papers in all classes, including mathematics, but language tutors attend closely to structure, diction, and style, as well as to the content of papers. Many students do grow as a result of paper conferences, guided rewriting, and the help of writing assistants. Nevertheless, the faculty frequently reconsiders what more can be done in this area.

The freshman language tutorial begins with ancient Greek because it is the fixed and literary language of most of the first year's readings. In contrast to English, it is highly inflected, but English nevertheless owes much to it. The Greek text used in this class was written especially for St. John's, but it is fully usable by those outside the college who would like to learn Greek on their own. It gives a good sense of the spirit of the language tutorials, stressing the universality and intelligibility of grammatical distinctions, an emphasis that is helpful in promoting class discussion and reflection. Classes spend the first semester and part of the second on the Greek text, and, almost from the start, students translate original Greek sentences and passages from seminar readings. By March, students have acquired enough Greek to be able to translate passages from Aristotle's *Physics* and *Ethics* and an extended section of Plato's *Meno*.

A word should be said about the *Meno*. It is the first Platonic dialogue freshmen read in seminar. That discussion is often confused and perplexing; it is their introduction to Socrates, to Greek rhetoric, to a "what-is" question, and to the idea of "Ideas." By the time they reconsider this dialogue, now in its original language, they have read many more works by Plato and other Greek authors, and are ready to study it more closely. In exposing competitive argument as debased speech, associating human virtue with the desire and effort to learn, and focusing on the learner rather than the teacher, the *Meno* is a central and formative text at St. John's. It is fitting that it occupies such a prominent place in the first year of a program devoted to liberal learning.

The sophomore language tutorial reaps the reward of diligent work on the elements of Greek prose in freshman language. The class spends the entire first semester slowly translating portions of a Greek tragedy (or, occasionally, of Homer) and discussing its structure, diction, and thought. Although most classes follow the same plan, there is room for variety, depending on the students' interests and the tutor's judgment. Some classes take time at the end of the semester to read some New Testament Greek in connection with the Bible readings of the sophomore seminar.

Second term begins with the remnant of the logic component of the traditional trivium. It contains readings by Aristotle, Aquinas, and others and a small manual on the elements of traditional formal logical analysis. Students then return to their own language in a play by Shakespeare, which they read with the same careful attention given to the Greek works. The year ends with English poems (Shakespeare, Wyatt, Donne, Marvell, Vaughan, and others), many with themes explored in sophomore seminar readings. Here, too, the pace is leisurely, with time for both meticulous analysis of language and speculative discussion of thought in the poems. The return to English in the second semester is a high point for many students. Even those for whom the Greek has been a great struggle find themselves exhilarated by their capacity to read more attentively and to see more than they did less than two years before.

The junior language tutorial begins with a brief, intensive study of French grammar. As juniors are reading Descartes and Pascal in translation in seminar, they are learning to read short passages from these authors and others in their original language. By the end of the first semester, some classes translate the first part of Descartes' *Discourse on Method*. The second semester is devoted to the reading of two masterpieces of French classical drama, Racine's *Phèdre* and Molière's *Misanthrope* (or *Tartuffe*). Here, too, students write essays and translations in connection with the works studied.

The senior language tutorial begins with modern French poems by Malherbe, Ronsard, Lamartine, Rimbaud, Valéry, and others. The emphasis is not on historical development but on understanding each poem in its parts and as a whole. Discussions of Baudelaire focus on the sensibility and technique of the poems, the relation of language to the visual arts, the activity of the poet himself, and Paris. Some classes conclude the first semester with Valéry's *Le cimitière marin*. Others read *Madame Bovary* (in English with some passages in French) or passages from Proust. Flaubert is especially interesting in connection with questions about modernity, equality, enlightenment, cities, and men and women, which become prominent in the junior and senior years. He provides an opportunity to consider the novel as a characteristically modern genre and to think about it in connection with the ancient Greek and modern French tragedies studied earlier, especially *Hippolytus* and *Phèdre*.

Like second-term sophomores, second-term seniors return to their own language after the rigorous study of an alien one, reading poems by Keats, Wordsworth, Hopkins, Yeats, Eliot, Stevens, and others. Some read classic essays about poetry by some of these writers. Some read short stories or novels by Woolf, Flaubert, Camus, Faulkner, and Dinesen, and plays by Eliot, Shaw, and others, that return to themes and questions that have been important throughout the program. Finally, some classes look at paintings or listen to musical works in connection with their investigations of the arts of language.

The Mathematics Tutorial

The four-year required mathematics sequence at St. John's College is unique in American higher education. Only small parts of it have been adopted by a few of the liberal arts programs that have looked to St. John's in planning their own curricula. Buchanan's conviction that one must study poetry *and* mathematics was perhaps his greatest contribution to the idea of liberal education. Of the traditional liberal arts, four of the seven were mathematical: arithmetic, geometry, astronomy, and music. Although the arts of the trivium might be thought to be deeper and broader, those of the quadrivium were thought to concern the "learnable things" simply, and to be a necessary foundation for the study of many other subjects.

The word *mathematics* contains the Greek root for "learning" or "understanding" and suggests that the active study of mathematics is a way of thinking about what it means to learn or understand anything. Until modern times, the "humane sciences," or "humanities," were distinguished from the "divine sciences" as those having to do with human beings. They did not exclude the mathematics and science that many "liberally" educated Americans today assume either to be too difficult or to require too much previous preparation. When they are attempted, these subjects are often presented as history of mathematics or science, in brief summaries, or in watered-down versions like the "physics for poets" courses offered in many general education programs. Often they are just not thought to be interesting or accessible to the cultivated man or woman who enjoys Shakespeare and wants to know something about Plato, Machiavelli, or the Bible. But the world in which people make this distinction is pervaded with, even defined by, mathematics. Whether one thinks that human beings have been liberated and enhanced by modern science and its mathematical language, or enslaved and diminished by them, the liberal arts of the quadrivium aim to liberate one from the unexplored assumptions of one's own time and vocabulary. This can be done only by going back to the original thoughts that got us here and treating them not as historical information about what earlier people thought before they knew the truth, but as serious attempts to make sense of the world. Here, too, the books themselves present new and old ways of thinking: about geometry, number, ratio and proportion, trigonometry, the motion of celestial and terrestrial bodies, limits, infinity, completeness, and relativity. In short, the "humanities" at St. John's College include *all* the humanities.

Many students arrive at St. John's with some trepidation about the mathematics requirements. Four years seems like a big commitment, especially for some who think they ought to learn something about it but who never had much interest or success before. If it is different for them this time, there are two reasons. First, beyond the ordinary capacity to speak and count (the only skills required of Meno's slave), nothing is assumed of them. This approach means that no one is behind at the beginning. Mistakes can be made without embarrassment. The most elementary questions are asked: they often turn out to be not "dumb" intrusions, but the occasions for clearer articulations and interesting explorations. In the mathematics tutorials, demonstration serves some of the same purposes that translation serves in language classes. One student goes to the board to demonstrate a proposition—in Euclid, Apollonius, or Newton, for example. Slowly, with the aid of diagrams, he or she tries to articulate clearly the givens and the end, and to outline the strategy of the proof. Other students and the tutor ask questions, make corrections and suggestions, and often discover and share their own misunderstandings. The proof's relation to previous proofs is explored. Other ways of proving the same proposition may be suggested, provoking discussions about why the author prefers the given one. Students learn to read Euclid's *Elements* and Newton's *Principia* as coherent books with careful, even rhetorical, arguments that can be studied as they study political and philosophical treatises.

A second reason for newfound interest is that discussions often develop in which mathematical questions lead to issues raised in other classes. Students discover that their thinking about *reductio* proofs, numbers, ratios, and bodies in motion has something to do with their thinking about logical reasoning, infinity, beauty, and the divine. Differences between ancient and modern mathematics are seen to resemble those between ancient and modern politics, literature, and philosophy. The very language and vocabulary, whether in ordinary words or technical symbols, raise questions about the objects of our thought and how we are thinking about them. It is not surprising that with guidance and the support of a whole community, thoughtful human beings who are willing to try to learn get interested in this enterprise.

The freshman mathematics tutorial spends two-thirds of the year in the leisurely study of Euclid's *Elements*. Beginning with the first definitions, postulates, and common notions and ending with the construction of the five regular solids, it investigates many of the questions mentioned above, as well as the notions of deductive science and mathematical system in general. In the last third of the year, students begin Ptolemy's *Almagest,* his "hypotheses" explaining the "appearances" (the phenomena) of the motions of celestial bodies. This is the first attempt they encounter to use mathematics to give an account of the world as we see it.

The sophomore mathematics tutorial continues the study of Ptolemy on the motion of the sun and planets around the earth and then turns to the heliocentric alternative of Copernicus. Returning to Greek geometry, second-term sophomores read the *Conics* of Apollonius, exploring synthetically the different kinds of conic sections. Here, as elsewhere in the program, students begin with the definition of the words they are using, grounding their thinking about parabolas, hyperbolas, and ellipses in the very meaning of the names of these objects of thought. After thinking about them in this way, they turn to Descartes' analytic treatment of these same objects in the algebraic form familiar to many high school graduates. But to both those who took to them easily in high school and those who turned away in distaste or despair, the enterprise now makes more sense. The equations and formulas that some love and others hate are now understood as the outcome of previous thinking and the attempt to make this thinking universally useful in solving problems. Those who speak in symbols and equations will better understand the meaning of the words they use. And they will begin to think about the scientific, political, religious, and artistic thinking that may shift in response to the shift in mathematics. Here, too, the order is primarily chronological. Themes and interpretations are not imposed from the beginning, but arise from the material as the authors present it. Students who have studied much mathematics in their previous schooling are soon intrigued by the turn to the fundamental questions behind the sophisticated geometry, astronomy, algebra, and calculus they have previously been taught to take for granted. The aim is not to study history but to get to the roots and the truth.

The junior mathematics tutorial begins by reading some ancient and modern paradoxes about motion, infinity, and limits. The discussions about these passages from Zeno (via Aristotle) and

Galileo prepare students to study calculus, as Newton introduces it geometrically in the lemmas that begin his *Principia* and analytically in its more modern form. For the latter, students use a manual written for this tutorial, which grounds the study of calculus in Newton's thinking about areas under and tangents to curves. The derivations of standard formulas are presented, and students get some practice in solving representative problems. For those who have previously studied calculus, this is beginners' work in the best sense: it explores the elements and often elucidates operations that they performed mechanically before. Those for whom it is new do not develop much facility in using it (they get more practice in the junior laboratory). Although the range of abilities and experience among students can present problems, the principles of the subject do emerge. This literacy with respect to calculus—like that of analytic geometry in sophomore mathematics—is analogous to the reading knowledge of Greek and French that students acquire in the language tutorials.

For most of the second semester, students return to the *Principia,* with its generalized presentation of force laws and their particular manifestation in astronomical phenomena. The circular motion of the heavenly bodies is reinterpreted as a combination of straight-line motions. To the geometry of Ptolemy and Copernicus, Newton adds the study of dynamics. The orbits of the moon and planets are determined by the same laws of force that terrestrial bodies obey: with respect to motion at least, they must all share the same nature. The philosophical, theological, and political implications of Newton's great argument are wide reaching. They are explored here in the mathematics tutorial, junior laboratory and language, and seminar discussions of Descartes, Hobbes, Kant, Swift, and others.

The last few weeks are devoted to the reading of Dedekind's theory of real numbers, the reconsideration of numbers that the new science of calculus required, and the relation of these "new" numbers to the calculus. Discussions of Euclid's treatment of number, ratio, and proportion and of modern notions of number deepen the understanding of students who have referred easily, but without much thought, to the number line, fractions, zero, decimals, square roots, and negative and irrational numbers since they were children.

The senior mathematics tutorial begins by reflecting on the postulates of geometry, first discussed at the beginning of freshman year. Lobachevsky's treatise on "non-Euclidean" geometry raises questions about the nature of the study of geometry, about the relation of mathematical knowledge to the world, and about imagination, consistency, and completeness.

In the last semester of the mathematics program, students read Einstein's 1905 paper on the special theory of relativity and explore the relation between our knowledge of mathematics and our knowledge of physics. This question is pursued in further readings about gravitation. Although these senior readings are very difficult, students can gain some access to major themes in twentieth-century mathematical thought and their implications elsewhere. Some knowledge of these matters seems imperative, since they have influenced the way most educated people think about most things.

The Music Tutorial

Music at St. John's College is studied in the same spirit as the arts of language and mathematics. This makes sense, since the elements of music are the very elements investigated in the other tutorials: language, rhetoric, and poetry are here combined with number, ratio, and measure to produce a sensible product, which is both learnable and discussable. Music is not a special elective for those with extraordinary ability or previous training. Nor is it actively performed by some, while others passively appreciate. Rather, like language and mathematics, it is considered an appropriate activity for all thoughtful, cultivated human beings. All are "amateurs" in the truest sense of the word: they translate, demonstrate, and sing not for professional reasons, but because they love (or learn to love) it.

The freshmen meet for one long session a week for the entire year. They learn the elements of music—rhythm, meter, tonal order, pitch intervals, chords—in preparation for the study of great classical works in the sophomore year. And they sing, learning a number of compositions, which, like a memorized sonnet or Euclid's proof of the Pythagorean theorem, will be theirs forever. Sometimes they are joined by older students or tutors, who come to help out or just because they like it. Students must listen carefully to each other and compensate for each other's weaknesses. The beauty of the chants, chorales, and simple rounds and the pleasure of making something beautiful together affect their learning and attitudes toward learning throughout the program. At the end of the year, they sing for the rest of the community, most of whom have previously learned the same songs and can join them. At the end of their senior dinner before graduation, they share some of these same songs again.

Sophomore music investigates the relationship between discursive intellect and sensibility. Many people, especially the young, assume that art, especially music, is to be felt, not analyzed. They resist efforts to understand music or think about the relationship between music and mathematics, morality, or the visual arts. In the music tutorial, rhythm, melody, harmony, and counterpoint are liberal studies in their own right, and in connection with broader questions about their effects on human beings. Manuals, Schiller's *Letters on Aesthetic Education,* and Victor Zuckerkandl's *The Sense of Music* prepare students to listen to and "read" great original works: Bach inventions, Schubert songs, Palestrina masses, the *St. Matthew Passion,* and an opera by Mozart. The close study of the last two occupies most of second semester and resembles the study of a play by Sophocles or Shakespeare in sophomore language, or of Ptolemy's *Almagest* or Descartes' *Geometry* in sophomore mathematics. Students participate in discussions, demonstrate at the blackboard, and write essays. Many later report that, like the mathematics tutorials, the music tutorial introduced them to an art and a pleasure that they had not previously found accessible.

The Laboratory

The material and activities in the three years of laboratory differ from those of the tutorials and seminar in several ways, but are also integral parts of the same organic program. As its name indicates, the laboratory is a workshop. Students learn not only from reasoned discourse but from hands-on experience and experiments, tests, or trials deliberately arranged to make nature reveal itself to the investigator. Students look together at animals and plants, balanced weights, chemical reactions, and electrical phenomena.

Just as they learn to translate and demonstrate in tutorials, they learn in laboratory the arts of careful observation, dissection, measurement, and experimentation, as well as to record what they observe in drawings, symbols, and graphs. The laboratory may seem to be organized more by disciplines or topics than the other tutorials. But here too the emphasis is on themes and questions, the study of original texts, and the reenactment of classic experiments. Although science is in some ways inherently progressive, St. John's emphasizes elementary questions and explores fundamental assumptions so that when students finally reencounter the familiar science of the modern world, they will have some idea of the thinking that got them there. This is not history of science any more than other classes are history of literature, mathematics, or philosophy. Although the junior and senior laboratories speak the advanced language of modern science, they concentrate on fundamental questions about matter, life, growth, motion, electricity, and magnetism. They also continue to inquire about the activity of the scientist: What is a hypothesis? What are the criteria for naming or classifying nature? What is the difference between observation and experiment? Is the most complete understanding of the natural world mathematical? Is nature conquerable by those who understand it? and should it be?

Freshman laboratory is roughly divided into biology, physics, and chemistry sequences, but the natural sciences are conceived as parts of a coherent whole, not as separate disciplines. The year begins with the study of living bodies: what they are and how they come to be what they are. Students read Aristotle, Portmann, Harvey, Spemann, and Driesch as they do their own detailed observations and dissections. The careful looking and drawing they do in laboratory have the same results as close looking at a sentence by Heraclitus, a Shakespeare sonnet, or a Euclid proposition: the longer they look—and talk about—the parts, the more they see the whole. Discussions focus on plant and animal structure, form and function, and relations with other living organisms and the environment. Dissections are not directed by manuals that correctly identify "systems" and "parts." Rather, in the spirit of Aristotle's *Parts of Animals* and Harvey's *Movement of the Heart and Blood,* students are invited to think about the meaning of parts and wholes, and asked to decide themselves which cut and which "parts" will help them learn best what they want to learn about the organism. The embryology sequence investigates, through classic papers and observation, sea urchin, frog, and chick development.

The second main segment of the year studies mathematical properties in nonliving bodies. Measurement and equilibrium are considered with respect to weight, heat, hydrostatics, and air pressure by performing classic experiments and reading related works by Aristotle, Archimedes, Pascal, Black, and Gay-Lussac. Prominent here is the search for fundamental laws in nature and for the mathematical statement of such laws. The last part of the year's work is concerned with the constitution of all bodies, both living and nonliving. Students read Aristotle and Lavoisier on elemental substances and substantial change, and papers on the development of atomic-molecular theory by Dalton, Thomson, Gay-Lussac, Avogadro, Cannizzaro, and Mendeleev. Throughout the work of the physics and chemistry segments, discussions revisit issues raised in the biology segment, not the least of which is this very articulation of natural science into three specialized fields and modern attempts to reduce biology to chemistry and physics.

The laboratory consisted originally of four years. In 1976, the second year was dropped and the whole reorganized into a three-year sequence. Junior laboratory now deals with motion: uniform and accelerated, straight line and curved, and the periodic motion of pendulums, vibrating strings, and waves. Works by Aristotle, Galileo, Descartes, Huygens, Newton, and Leibniz inform and guide practical, hands-on work. This work is closely related to that of junior math, in which students are introduced to the rigorous mathematical methods necessary for the modern investigation of physics. The second semester is spent on optics and on electricity and magnetism. Fundamental phenomena are studied observationally and experimentally, and are formulated in mathematical terms. As students discover in junior seminar and language, modern mathematical physics had far-reaching implications for metaphysics, politics, and poetry. Students find the revolutionary ideas sometimes refreshing and sometimes repellent, but always exciting. All agree that junior year as a whole rivals freshman year in the way that its parts reflect on each other and constitute a whole.

The senior laboratory returns to many of the questions first confronted in freshman laboratory. The first semester reconsiders the nature of matter and the theory of atomism, taking into account electrical phenomena studied in junior laboratory. Practical and "thought" experiments are discussed with writings of the physicists (Planck, Einstein, Bohr, de Brogle, Heisenberg, and Schrödinger) who articulated and refined the concepts of atomic structure and particle and wave. In the second semester, seniors return to the consideration of living organisms, now observed over a longer time period and in a smaller spatial scale. Oriented by discussions of Schrödinger's *What Is Life?* they are introduced to theories of evolution by natural selection (Darwin), genetics (Mendel, Morgan, Sturtevant), intracellular processes (Boveri, Sutton), population genetics (Hardy, Chetverikov), and contemporary molecular biology (Beadle and Tatum, Watson and Crick, Jacob and Monod). Although the accompanying experiments are sophisticated and use modern equipment and techniques, the laboratory program ends where it begins: by asking whether the new discoveries in biology have fundamentally changed our understanding of what a living organism is, a question that is less likely to be answered—or even asked—in a curriculum divided into specialized science, philosophy, religion, and literature courses.

The Lecture

Seminars, tutorials, and laboratories are conducted entirely as small group discussions. In contrast, at Friday night lectures, the entire community gathers in a large auditorium. The lecturer may be a tutor or an invited scholar, public figure, poet, or artist. This occasion offers the opportunity to listen closely to an extended argument, a new interpretation, or a presentation about an unfamiliar subject. (Lectures are occasionally replaced by concerts or plays.) The lecture is followed by a coffee break and question period in the smaller "Conversation Room," a discussion that often continues for several hours, dwindling by the end to a few hardy souls. Lecturers, as well as audience, learn from these sessions, refining arguments and adjusting their own views. Visitors are always impressed by the respect given to the lecturer; the audience stands at the beginning and end, and no one walks out in the middle. The free questioning is relentless and recognizes no limits, but it is bound by habits of civility and a desire to learn that often is missing in contemporary academic exchanges. Also remarkable is the simple fact that on any ordinary Friday evening, dozens of young people and their teachers find it appropriate and pleasurable to gather together to learn in yet another setting.

"Extracurricular" Activities

The Friday night lecture suggests that, in a sense, there are no "extracurricular" activities at St. John's College. That is not to say that the students all have the same religious or political views, or that they are not high-spirited young men and women who like to have a good time and look forward to getting out of town from time to time. What it does mean is that their lives at the college are characterized by an extraordinary coherence and continuity.

Like students everywhere else, many work long hours to help pay for tuition and living expenses. But the spirit in which they pursue their other extracurricular activities bears a remarkable resemblance to that in which they pursue curricular ones. Manifest in both are wholeness, freedom, and a delight in learning. Outside of classes, too, St. John's students are "amateurs" who engage in activities, not for reward or glory, but for love of the activity itself. There are dozens of informal study groups of students, tutors, or both: people who want to translate Aristotle, or to read modern biological papers, Shakespeare plays, or the *Tao Te Ching*. If you want to learn German or the waltz, play soccer, make a pot, or sail a boat, there is always someone to teach you and others who will join you to learn. You need not be embarrassed—or talented; as Socrates tells Meno, and all tutors tell their classes, you just have to be willing to try.

There are a small chorus, a madrigal group, string quartets, and rock groups. A large number of men and women participate in an intramural athletics program that welcomes anyone who wants to play. Many faculty also play music and on teams. The college has a gym and a boathouse, and nearly every spring, the croquet team crushes challengers from the U.S. Naval Academy. Many students volunteer for community service. The King William Players produces several major plays each year. These are directed and produced entirely by students (faculty sometimes take part), none of whom is majoring in theater arts, although the directors of recent productions of *Measure for Measure* and *Troilus and Cressida* wrote their seminar essays on these works. Special seminars, as well as some language classes, often prepare both cast and audiences for these performances; a visitor might be hard put to tell the difference between the formal class and the extracurricular discussions.

All of these conventionally extracurricular activities are informed by the serious reading and thinking that occupies most of the students' time. One is rarely out of earshot of a lively discussion connecting what they have learned from old books to what they are doing in their daily lives. These discussions, like question periods, are remarkably civil. Freedom of speech is understood to entail listening to others. Students and faculty are interested in the issues discussed elsewhere. But the campus is not disrupted by strident fights over oppression, diversity, feminism, or libertarianism. From talk in the coffee shop to toasts at the senior dinner, it is clear that the same good books that these students live and breathe and share for four years inform much of their thinking. In sum, the college is small enough to enjoy the advantages of unified and visible communal life, yet rich enough to allow for the stimulation of difference and variety.

Faculty

The great books and the immortal authors are the teachers at St. John's College, but there is much to be said of the mortal tutors who serve as midwives and matchmakers. Some faculty members are graduates of the college, but most have been educated in more conventional institutions. Most have advanced degrees in specialized fields, but their interests and backgrounds include, and often combine, a number of disciplines. New faculty, like many students, come to St. John's because it articulates and practices a way of learning that attracts them. They are interested in the curriculum itself and the chance it offers them to extend their own education. Some have had experience in liberal arts programs at other institutions and are attracted by the facts that the required program does not constantly need to defend the worth of what it is doing and that it does not have to recruit its faculty from graduate students or from unfriendly departments. Every tutor is expected to teach throughout the program. Since everyone's primary affiliation is with the program as a whole, faculty do not worry—with respect to their status at the college—about spending time away from particular disciplines or about publishing frequently, although many do continue to write and speak for wider audiences.

The demands on the faculty are immense. One is always learning—and teaching—something new and difficult, under severe time constraints. New tutors soon learn that they are expected to be not expert "professors" of any subject but rather the most mature and hard-working learners in their classes. There are weekly meetings of tutors teaching the same classes, and some audit the classes of more experienced colleagues. Also helpful are study groups and occasional released time. The amount of time tutors spend with each other, as well as with students, contributes greatly to the sense of support all members of the community need as they work their way through the program. Because students know that tutors are often learning along with them, they take their own responsibilities to teach each other all the more seriously. An immense amount of such teaching goes on in the coffee shop, library, and dormitories.

In addition to coping with the pressures of learning new material, new tutors are understandably concerned about their futures. Reappointments and tenure decisions are made on the criteria of excellence of intellect and imagination, abilities as a teacher and colleague, and willingness and ability to teach in different parts of the program. The community is small, and decisions are based on careful consideration of information provided by colleagues and students. One unavoidable difficulty is that as they devote themselves to the program, new tutors are likely to be distancing themselves from their earlier professional lives. The lack of time to publish and to keep up with a field during the six years before the tenure decision may have great consequences for those who do not remain at St. John's. For those who do remain at the college, there are also interesting tensions. Years of discussions of seminar books with young students who are reading them rapidly for the first time can be frustrating for mature readers who wish to work on particular books more intensively. So can the continued sense of amateurism in areas in which one has not had sustained study. Summers and sabbatical leaves (after six years of full-time teaching) are precious times for tutors who wish to concentrate on some aspect of their own studies or to write. There are also some opportunities for released time for auditing and for faculty study groups. Faculty life, like student life, at the college can be both exhilarating and exhausting. It too is touched by all the features of a whole community designed to encourage reflection and a common conversation.

Assessment

How does one know whether college students are successfully learning what the institution wants them to learn? St. John's does not admit students on the basis of conventional tests, but by assessing the whole student's interests and likelihood of benefiting from the program. Unlike many other great books programs, which are intended for selected honors students, St. John's students are largely self-selected. They must write several long application essays and commit themselves to four years of difficult language, philosophy, mathematics, and science classes. SAT scores are not required of applicants, although most are high. Once they matriculate, there are few tests, although students must still pass an algebra test by the middle of sophomore year. Official transcripts bear grades, but tutors do not put them on daily classwork and papers. Students are discouraged from checking grades until they need to for external purposes. The reason is simple: students of varying abilities have chosen to enroll in a prescribed and difficult curriculum because they want to learn. Most cannot do equally well in all parts of the program; what the college expects is that they will do the best they can and that they will make progress.

Assessment is an integral part of the day-to-day work of tutors, who work closely with small groups and individuals and are always vigilant about the work being done in their classes. Many give diagnostic quizzes to monitor progress in tutorials. Students frequently meet with tutors for paper conferences or extra help or to continue conversations. At the end of each semester each student has a conference at which each tutor reports on the work in his or her class: the strongest and weakest aspects, the student's writing, contributions to discussions, and whether he or she has learned enough to continue. The student listens and then is asked to comment. A discussion follows about what, if anything, might be done differently. The conference deals with the whole student and with the work as a whole. The reports about other classes often reveal the conditions under which a student flourishes or flags. Most tutors and students communicate closely all the time, but this more formal occasion has an especially serious tone, which often produces significant improvements.

At the end of each school year, a special faculty meeting is devoted to a review of all sophomores to determine which students should continue at the college. Each student's work is considered in the individual classes and as a whole, and all tutors take part in the discussion. A similar meeting rules on the satisfactory completion of graduation requirements by seniors.

Graduates of St. John's go on to a great variety of careers: they become stockbrokers, film directors, teachers, farmers, graphic artists, and architects. They do well on Graduate Record, law, and medical exams, although they are understandably less prepared for specialized subject area exams, since they have had no majors. There is no sign that they have difficulty entering graduate or professional schools; an extraordinarily high number (70 percent) eventually earn graduate degrees. Many graduate departments and professional schools say that they are well disposed to those prepared by such a curriculum.

Most tutors and officials of the college are convinced that the best way to assess the success of the program is to ask what the lives of its graduates are like. The answer reveals that a remarkable number of them—whatever line of work they enter—remain avid readers and bold learners in many fields, including mathematics and the sciences. They like to prepare before seeing a play, movie, or opera and to have a discussion afterward. They are always rereading some program (or other) book, alone or with study groups of alumni and like-minded friends that they form wherever they may find themselves. They set up great books programs and tutorials in other colleges and high schools, and offer to lead junior great books groups for children. Many of their own children seek admission, eager to enter the world their parents have introduced them to. The passion for books and conversation about serious questions seems to mark St. John's alumni in whatever they do. This suggests success of the deepest sort in achieving the aims of the college.

Conclusion

On the seal of St. John's College seven books encircle a set of scales pictured at the center. Around the circumference is printed the Latin motto, *Facio liberos ex liberis libris, libraque,* a clever pun that means: "I make free men out of boys ["people out of children," if you prefer] by means of books and a balance." The circular whole, embracing the seven liberal arts, is a fine image for the college. It reflects the belief that whole and free human beings are best shaped by a freely chosen but entirely prescribed whole curriculum that frees the human intellect by habituating it to serious conversation and by exercising it in the verbal and mathematical arts. Students enter as children and emerge as adults, having learned more about themselves and the world they live in, and, even more important, having prepared to continue learning for the rest of their lives.

References

Brann, E.T.H. "The Elements of Science." *Palaestra,* Apr. 1968.

Brann, E.T.H. "What Are the Beliefs and Teachings of St. John's College?" Pamphlet. Mar. 1978.

Brann, E.T.H. "The Program of St. John's College." In *Towards a Restoration of the Liberal Arts Curriculum: A Rockefeller Foundation Conference.* New York: Rockefeller Foundation, 1979.

Buchanan, S. *Poetry and Mathematics.* Philadelphia: Lippincott, 1962.

Flaumenhaft, H. Foreword to D. L. Sepper, *Newton's Optical Writings: A Guided Study.* New Brunswick, N.J.: Rutgers University Press, 1994.

Flaumenhaft, H. "An Introductory Note on Apollonius." In D. Densmore (ed.), *Apollonius of Perga: Conics: Books I–III.* Santa Fe, N.M.: Green Lion Press, 1998.

Kass, A. A. "The Liberal Arts Movement: From Ideas to Practice." *College,* Oct. 1973, pp. 1–26.

Klein, J. *A Commentary on Plato's Meno.* Chapel Hill: University of North Carolina Press, 1965.

Klein, J. *Greek Mathematical Thought and the Origin of Algebra.* Cambridge, Mass.: MIT Press, 1968.

Klein, J. "History and the Liberal Arts," "The Idea of Liberal Education," "On Liberal Education." In R. Williamson and E. Zuckerman (eds.), *Essays and Lectures.* Annapolis, Md.: St. John's College Press, 1995.

Mollin, A., and Williamson, R.. *An Introduction to Ancient Greek.* Lanham, Md.: University Press of America, 1995.

Nelson, C. (ed.). *Scott Buchanan: A Centennial Appreciation of His Life and Work, 1895–1968, Recollections and Essays.* Annapolis, Md.: St. John's College Press, 1995.

Nelson, C. (ed.). *Stringfellow Barr: A Centennial Appreciation of His Life and Work, 1897–1982.* Annapolis, Md.: St. John's College Press, 1997.

St. John's College. *St. John's College Catalog: Statement of the St. John's Program.* Annapolis, Md.: St. John's College, 1997–1998.

St. John's College. "Self-Study: St. John's College." Unpublished report prepared for the Middle States Commission on Higher Education, 1993.

Smith, J. W. *A Search for the Liberal College: The Beginnings of the St. John's Program.* Annapolis, Md.: St. John's College Press, 1983.

Chapter Four

The Search Course at Rhodes College

Michael Nelson

The Search for Values in the Light of Western History and Religion, informally known as the Search course, is a foundational part of the curriculum at Rhodes College, a Presbyterian-affiliated liberal arts college in Memphis, Tennessee. The course, which was created for entering freshmen in 1945–46 under the name Man in the Light of History and Religion, is a two-year, twelve-credit, colloquium-intensive study of the history, literature, philosophy, politics, and religion of the West from *Gilgamesh* to the present. Its catalogue listings are Humanities 101, 102, 201, and 202, and it constitutes more than 10 percent of a student's credits toward graduation. During their first and second years at Rhodes, every student must take four semesters of Search, choose four courses from a list of offerings by the religious studies and philosophy departments called Life: Then and Now, or take a year each of Search and Life. The majority choose Search.

Middle age has been kind to the Search course. Its staff consists almost entirely of full-time professors and in recent years has been drawn from fourteen departments: art, biology, classics, English, French, German, history, music, philosophy, political science, psychology, religious studies, sociology, and Spanish. In their orientation to the humanities, they range from staunch traditionalists to feminists and postmodernists. What unites the faculty members who teach in Search is their commitment to the course: virtually all are volunteers or at least willing conscripts. Student evaluations of their teaching and of the course itself have never been higher. After graduation, many alumni attest that Search was the most enduringly important intellectual experience of their lives (Nelson, 1996a). National recognition of the course came in 1996 with the publication by Vanderbilt University Press of *Celebrating the Humanities: A Half-Century of the Search Course at Rhodes College* (Nelson, 1996b). Among other things, the book chronicled Search's direct influence on the core curricula of other southern colleges and universities, including Davidson College, the University of the South, Eckerd College, and Millsaps College (Vest, 1996).

Not surprisingly, during the past half-century the Search course has spent time in the valley as well as on the mountaintop, and challenges persist. These range from the content of the course, in an era when the nature of the humanities is much contested, to the techniques of teaching it, especially those that involve making intelligent use of new computer-based technologies, and the recruitment and assimilation of the specialized faculty who do the intrinsically general teaching. In some cases, the course has developed ways of addressing these challenges; in others it has not yet been able to do so.

Origins and Development

Southwestern at Memphis (as Rhodes was known until it changed its name in 1984) was a small, regionally prestigious, strongly Presbyterian liberal arts college when Man in the Light of History and Religion was first offered to entering freshmen in the fall of 1945.[1] The college's president, Charles E. Diehl, a Presbyterian minister with degrees from Johns Hopkins University and Princeton University, had clear ideas about higher education, many of them grounded in his admiration of Oxford and Cambridge universities. He instituted an Oxbridge-style tutorial system, in which students studied certain subjects in individual sessions with their professors. He also recruited more than a dozen faculty members from the ranks of Rhodes scholars and other Oxford-trained academics. When the college moved from Clarksville, Tennessee, to Memphis in 1925, Diehl insisted that every building on the new campus be built in the collegiate gothic style, a practice that all of his successors have followed (Morgan, 1989).

Diehl held strong beliefs about the substance as well as the manner and setting of higher education. He decried the bifurcation that was taking place among church-related colleges and universities during the first third of the twentieth century, with most becoming secular and others turning fundamentalist (Marsden, 1994). He also disliked the recent trend away from general education and toward a narrow, electives-based curriculum. Diehl wanted Southwestern to open a third way: education that was liberal and general, not professional and specialized, and avowedly Christian but not constricted and sectarian. The curriculum he admired most was the one that had prevailed in American higher education from the seventeenth century through the late nineteenth century: a fixed course of study resting on the twin pillars of Christianity and the classics (Veysey, 1965). To Diehl, this meant the adoption of what was coming to be called "great books" education, but with more emphasis on the Bible and its enduring influence than the leading great books advocates, such as University of Chicago president Robert Hutchins and his energetic assistant, Mortimer Adler, tended to place on it.

In 1944–45, at Diehl's urging, the Southwestern faculty organized a weekly lecture series, The Great Centuries, for the college and the broader Memphis community. The titles of each week's two-hour programs tended toward the celebratory—for example, "The Greek Miracle (5th Century B.C.)," "The Greatness That Was Rome (1st Century A.D.)," and "The Century of Hope (19th Century)." Two of the main premises of the symposium, offered in the middle of World War II, were that, intellectually and spiritually, the past was better than the present and that the way to make things better in the future was to restore the best ideas and beliefs of the past. According to the program booklet, "The world is intellectually and spiritually adrift. Long established standards of life and conduct are being swept away in a torrent of fluid history. . . . Perhaps if we can trace our heritage back to Israel, Greece, and Rome, we shall find those 'first principles' which order our lives" ("The Great Centuries," 1944).

An additional premise underlay the Great Centuries symposium: the importance of Christianity in sorting out the wheat in the Western tradition from the tares. "The cultural materials of a Nazi, a Dane, or an American do not essentially differ," wrote John Osman

(1945), a young philosophy professor and assistant to the president. "It is in the arrangement of these materials and the emphasis placed upon certain ones of them that the great difference lies. The Symposium strives to work the materials of our Western cultural heritage into an organic whole under a single integrating principle. Such an approach will give us an approach to knowledge in the light of the highest truth—the sovereignty of God."

Nineteen of the college's thirty faculty members took part in the Great Centuries, several of them on numerous occasions. Five of the most active participants—Osman, historians John Henry Davis and W. Raymond Cooper, philosopher Alexander P. Kelso, and biblical scholar Laurence F. Kinney—made the obvious suggestion after the symposium was over: Why not offer something like this to our students? They had invested a great deal of time preparing lectures, had enjoyed the experience of working and teaching in a common endeavor, and shared Diehl's strong views about the value of general education grounded in a Christian worldview.

Diehl, who had planted the seeds from which their suggestion grew, welcomed it. Planning began in early 1945, with considerable help from Princeton philosopher Theodore M. Greene, who served as a consultant at Diehl's invitation. After overcoming some faculty doubts ("As you well know . . . ," Diehl [1945] confided to Greene, "the idea of paying less attention to departments than to fields or divisions is not heartily welcomed"), Man in the Light of History and Religion entered the curriculum in the fall of 1945. The staff of the course, all of them liberal Protestants like Diehl, defined as an important objective of the course to "recover the understanding, exemplified by Socrates' 'know thyself' and Jesus' 'perfect thyself,' that man is a rational animal with a spark of the divine in him. Whenever Western civilization has ignored this heritage, it has fallen into low estate" (Cooper and others, 1945).

The Man course, as it was instantly dubbed, was a year-long, twelve-credit freshman course that met for an hour every morning: lectures Monday through Thursday and discussions on Friday and Saturday. For those freshmen who took the course (105 of an entering class of 250), Man served as a substitute for the otherwise required classes in Bible and history. Cooper, Davis, Kelso, Kinney, and Osman divided up the lecturing among them, taking on two dozen topics apiece. Each also led a discussion section, with the students in each colloquium rotating from professor to professor during the course of the year. "The historian or the philosopher must be prepared to discuss with his section the assigned books of the Bible," wrote Davis (1949), reflecting on one of the special challenges of the Man course, "and on predominantly historical or philosophical readings the Bible instructors must be prepared to conduct discussions in what formerly may have been considered alien subjects." Davis and his colleagues met weekly over lunch to teach each other the material.

The course brimmed over with topics and readings. The first week included lectures on "The Nature and Origins of Civilization" and "The Hebrew Cosmogony," a list of discussion topics that included "What Is the Origin of Art?" "Creation: Ultimate Explanation of Proximate Causes," and "The Meaning of History," along with reading assignments that covered 98 pages in an art textbook, 101 pages in a history textbook, all of Genesis, the *Epic of Gilgamesh,* selections from Herodotus, and a variety of other primary texts. The pace never slackened, especially because each week brought either a paper or a quiz. A week-long spring semester unit on the Puritans, for example, required students to read *Pilgrim's Progress,* the *Areopagitica,* and selections from Locke, Harrington, Jonathan Edwards, and others. A columnist in the student newspaper lamented: "And that Man course! Imagine my joy when I open the syllabus and find that the professors have neatly arranged for me to read for tomorrow's lecture the following: (1) The Old Testament, (2) Ancient Hebrew Relics and Their Origins, pages 10–898, and (3) The Encyclopedia Britannica, Volumes A–M" (Botsford, 1946).

In response to student requests that the workload be reduced from "the unimaginable to the merely impossible," the staff made some adjustments in preparation for the 1946–47 academic year. The art textbook was abandoned, along with most references in the course to architecture, music, painting, and sculpture. (The staff's thinking seemed to be that since they could not do the arts well, it would be better not to do them at all.) Nips and tucks were made in the remaining weekly assignments. Herodotus was removed from the first week's reading list, for example, and Edwards and much of Bunyan were excised from the unit on the

Puritans. Wednesdays now offered, in place of a fourth lecture, a third colloquium; in time, a weekly pattern of lecture-colloquium, lecture-colloquium, lecture-colloquium was instituted. The results were encouraging. When Dean A. Theodore Johnson surveyed 139 current and former Man students in 1950, 90 percent said the course was "more valuable" than "other elementary courses, and as a basic orientation for college work," and 63 percent checked "much more meaningful" when asked, "Did it succeed in making clearer your concept of the role of religion in life?" Summarizing the results, Johnson (1950) wrote, "A number of students said it was the best course they had ever taken." By 1958, with only Davis and Kinney remaining of the original staff, more than two-thirds of the entering class was enrolling in Man.

More students meant more and different staff members, with predictable consequences for the style and content of the course. The addition of philosophers such as W. Larry Lacy and James Jobes helped to bring a more reflective perspective to the syllabus. Beginning in 1965, the first week of the course focused on questions such as, "What is history?" "What is religion?" and even, "What is man?" Milton Brown, the first religion professor on the Man staff to be trained in the methods of higher biblical criticism, influenced the course's approach to the Bible. Another new religion professor, Darrell Doughty, was the first to challenge one of the basic assumptions of the course: that the biblical tradition had been a generally positive influence in Western history.

Doughty's skepticism about the virtues of Christianity and, more generally, the West embodied one of the challenges to courses such as Man that were arising around the country during the politically charged late 1960s (Allardyce, 1982). The staff responded in 1970 by adding a unit on Buddhism, along with an anthropological unit on human origins. Revealingly, the staff also changed the catalogue description of the Man course from "A study of the origins and development of Christianity and its role in world affairs integrated with a study of the history of Western Civilization" to "A study of the history of Western Civilization integrated with a study of the origins and development of Christianity and its role in world affairs."

Another challenge of the 1960s came from the calendar reform movement in higher education, which was born of student demands for more innovative curricula. In a variation on the 4–1–4 calendar that many colleges and universities adopted (two semesters with a course load of four courses and a one-course January term set aside for a nontraditional course), Southwestern adopted a 4–4–2 calendar, in which students took four courses in both of the twelve-week terms, then two new-style courses during the six-week short term. (Saturday classes were abolished.) The college reverted to a two-semester system in 1986, but in the meantime Man not only found itself jammed into the two long terms, but during those terms it constituted fully half of a student's course load. Enrollment in the course dropped 40 percent in 1969–70, the year the new calendar was implemented, especially among freshmen in the natural sciences, who needed to fill their schedules with foundational courses in their intended majors and in mathematics.

In addition to these challenges, Man was threatened by students' growing demand for fewer required survey courses and more freedom to design their own curricula. Southwestern responded in 1970 by diluting the status Man had enjoyed in fulfilling distribution requirements and by creating ten-student freshman colloquia designed to treat specialized, interdisciplinary topics in depth. Each freshman colloquium instructor also served as faculty adviser for those ten students.

Strong leadership emerged to deal with these challenges. In 1969, with the retirement of John Henry Davis, the last of the founders, church historian Fred Neal became the leader of the staff. During the course's first quarter-century, no one person had performed this role; virtually everything was done by a committee of the whole or by individual professors on a rotating basis. But with the growth of the staff and the increasing precariousness of the course in the college's curriculum, it seemed sensible for someone to serve as chief. Neal, who had been teaching Man since 1958 and was tireless in his energy and advocacy of the course, was the ideal person to fulfill this role. He did so as a volunteer, receiving no additional compensation, relief from other responsibilities, or formal title from the college's administration.

Neal recruited faculty to the Man staff assiduously and, although teaching in the course constituted an uncompensated overload and took professors outside their disciplines, was remarkably successful. Faculty critics of the course were invited to join the staff and reform it. A few did, but the rest had the wind taken out of their rhetorical sails by Neal's velvet-gloved version of "put up or shut up." Neal also adapted the course to the freshman colloquium program; in the end, most of the colloquia were sections of the Man course. (This necessitated one change: students in Man, instead of rotating from colloquium to colloquium, now remained with the same instructor the entire year so that he or she could serve as their faculty adviser.) When the new five-day class schedule removed one lecture-colloquium pairing from each week and left Fridays dangling, Neal encouraged staff members to offer three-Friday-long seminars devoted to specific topics, such as "Pottery and the Prophetic People" and "The Concept of Holy War," that otherwise would have been passed over lightly (if treated at all) in the syllabus. He oversaw the production of staff-produced anthologies of primary texts, including new translations of Dante, Marcus Aurelius, and others by members of the college's language departments, so that students would not have to rely on the library's reserve room and instead could mark up and bring to class their own copies of the assigned readings. It was Neal who sparked the addition of the Buddhism and anthropology units in 1970. When the new units did not work, mostly because of their poor fit with the rest of the Western, humanities-based course and the uncertain confidence of the staff in teaching them, it was Neal who convinced the staff to eliminate them.

Neal could be stubborn in small things. Not surprisingly, the rise of feminism during the 1970s had made the name of the course increasingly objectionable. Yet until the day of his retirement in 1985, Neal vigorously defended Man's inclusive character: "We use the word *Man* in its true generic sense as encompassing in one species both men and women." Neal's design of the 1984–85 syllabus displayed "M A N" on its cover in large block letters, each letter shaded in with dozens of repetitions of the sequence "MAN-WOMAN-MAN-WOMAN-MAN-WOMAN" in small type. In addition, for the first time, the title page included a subtitle for the course: "A Study of the Ways in Which Men and Women of the Western World Have Understood Themselves as Human Beings in the Light of Their Significant Experiences and Their Highest Hopes and Values." The addition of *Western* to the subtitle was designed to ward off another set of critics: those who charged that the name of the course implied that the Western tradition incorporated all that was worth knowing. In 1986, the year after Neal retired, the staff, advised by a group of students, renamed the course The Search for Values in the Light of Western History and Religion.

Neal's final years as course director were dominated by a crisis much larger than nomenclature. In 1978 the Bellingrath-Morse Foundation, a major source of Southwestern's endowment, sent the college an unwelcome notice: the faculty's loosening of curriculum requirements meant that Southwestern no longer complied with the foundation's stipulation that beneficiaries must require their students "to take a sound and comprehensive course in the Holy Bible of six semester hours during the first academic year and at least six semester hours in one other academic year." (In truth, the college had been out of compliance since 1970.) Because in years past the Man course had been judged to satisfy the Bellingrath-Morse stipulation, the faculty, under considerable pressure from the administration to find a way of complying, voted in January 1981 to make the course mandatory for all students: six hours during the freshman year and six hours as sophomores.

Although this decision restored the college to the foundation's good graces, it left bad feelings in its wake. In a poll conducted by the school newspaper, 90 percent of students said they wanted an alternative to the Man requirement ("90 percent of Students Surveyed Want Man Alternative," 1981). In 1982 the faculty provided such an alternative: a program called Life: Then and Now that required two biblical studies courses for freshmen and, in subsequent years, two additional Bible-related courses from a wide-ranging list of offerings by the religious studies and philosophy departments. Evidence that the students' unhappiness was not with the Man course but rather with anything that drastically circumscribed their freedom of choice came when a large majority enrolled in Man rather than Life.

Neal believed strongly in what a later member of the staff called Search's "amateur ideal": the idea that a professor's genuine love of learning and teaching important works was of greater value in a course like Search than disciplinary expertise (Nelson, 1996d). He thought that every member of the faculty should teach in the course at one time or another and recruited professors from departments as far-flung as biology, psychology, and sociology. At a liberal arts college, Neal argued, "Education is a moral endeavor whereby we're all joined together in the common pursuit of knowledge, and if you can do it around certain tasks, it gives you a real sense of community" ("Dr. Neal Says Farewell to Man," 1985). He was not inclined to let people lecture in their fields: "Lectures that are suitable in a specialized discipline are much too detailed, and the material is lost on the Man student." When enrollment in the course expanded rapidly in the wake of the Bellingrath-Morse controversy, Neal inaugurated an annual summer workshop to serve as a gateway into the course for new staff members.

Neal's parting gift to his colleagues was to persuade the administration both to recognize his successor, history professor Douglas Hatfield, as a department chair, with appropriate compensation, and to count involvement in the course as a full part of each faculty member's course load. His still greater gift to his students was his final lecture, delivered on the last day of class in the spring 1985 semester:

> The vocation of students . . . is channeled and expressed by those peculiar understandings and skills which their experience of study has given them and which they can contribute to the common life of mankind. They are the gifts of *mind,* and *heart,* and *spirit* which have been sharpened through years of trial in the community of learning. . . . By what values do you appraise yourself? As a man seeketh in his heart, so is he. . . . In the midst of the pluralism in which we live, where competing principles of truth and value confront each other daily, where all judgments seem to be relative and all values transitory and fleeting, there is hunger in mankind for some *unity* to experience . . . some ultimate meaning.
> [Llewellyn, 1996, p. 101]

Hatfield assumed the mantle of leadership at a propitious time for the college. In 1984 the board of trustees had renamed the college Rhodes as part of an ambitious plan to raise it from regional to national stature. That commitment was supported with dramatically expanded scholarships for students, ambitious faculty recruitment, new facilities (all in the collegiate gothic style), and aggressive fundraising. The student body was increased in size and selectivity: enrollment went from around 1,000 in 1985 to

1,450 in 1998, and in the same period, the entering class's average score on the Scholastic Aptitude Test rose from 1155 to 1280. The burgeoning college-rating industry took note of Rhodes's progress. In 1990, for example, *U.S. News and World Report* identified Rhodes as first on the list of "up-and-coming" national liberal arts colleges in the judgment of college presidents and deans. Five years later, the college reached the magazine's top category of colleges.

The times remained unpropitious, however, for courses such as Search. During the 1960s and 1970s, as the philosopher John Searle (1971, pp. 171, 175, 176) has noted, "We lost confidence in our traditional conception of a liberal education, but we have not yet found anything to replace it with." In the traditional conception, which had prevailed at Rhodes and most other liberal arts colleges, students devoted two years to acquiring a general education, mainly in Western civilization, before embarking on concentrated study in a discipline. "Over the years," Searle pointed out, "the excitement has drained out of these general courses," in part because faculty members' "intellectual interests have grown more specialized and professionalized." (The same could be said of many students' interests.) In the 1980s, conservative intellectuals such as William J. Bennett (1984) and Allan Bloom (1987) added conservative ideology to the diagnosis (as well as to the cure, their critics claimed) of the humanities' ills, charging that general education had been enfeebled by a new generation of "tenured radicals" who regarded oppression on the basis of race, class, and gender, not great books and noble ideals, as the hallmarks of the Western tradition.[2] For all the public attention their broadsides earned Bennett and Bloom, however, the tides of feminism and postmodernism continued to rise in college and university humanities departments.

Whiffs of these conflicts occasionally intruded on the Search course. In a series of essays by Search staff members, for example, political scientist Daniel E. Cullen (1996) expressed his frank admiration for the same "great books" that religious studies scholar Gail Corrington Streete (1996) avowed to teach through a "strategy of subversion." Philosophers Larry Lacy (1996) and Ellen Armour (1996) agreed that their students should study the Bible critically, but for Lacy it was the "New Testament critics' . . . naturalistic assumption that miracles do not occur" that needed to be scrutinized, while for Armour, it was the Bible's "diversity of viewpoint, its bumps and bruises, its political legacies."

Yet through all this, Search has thrived. The staff's talent, energy, and commitment, always high but seldom higher than in recent years, has served the course well. One measure of the Search faculty's success, however imperfect, is the students' formal end-of-term course evaluations. As recently as the late 1980s, in the evaluation form's summary question, students in Search rated "the quality of instruction in this course" four-tenths of a point below the quality of instruction in the college's other courses—3.9 (on a five-point scale) compared with 4.3. By 1995, the average score of the Search staff on that question had risen to 4.6, one-tenth of a point higher than the itself remarkable college-wide average of 4.5 for courses other than Search.

A large part of the explanation for the recent success of the Search course is that the staff generally has been persuaded of the enduring value of reading the classic works of history, literature, philosophy, politics, and religion while remaining critical of a rigid canon reverently taught (or, as Bennett would prefer it, "transmitted"). Equally important, opponents of a traditional great books approach have had a standing invitation to bring their concerns into the course by joining the staff, serving as a summer workshop leader, or acting in some other advisory capacity; no one has been left to rail outside the gate. The result is that nearly every one of Bennett's recommended authors—from Homer, Aristotle, and Sophocles to Marx, Nietzsche, and King—continues to appear on Search's list of required readings. Yet it was just after Bennett published his 1984 broadside (and just before Bloom published *The Closing of the American Mind* in 1987) that the Search staff, responding to feminist concerns but operating by consensus, changed the name of the course from Man to Search. Subsequently, and again by consensus, writings by women such as *The Martyrdom of Perpetua and Felicitas* and Christine de Pizan's *Book of the City of Ladies* joined the familiar works of male writers (and Simone de Beauvoir, herself a late addition) on the syllabus, and new excerpts from existing texts that feature important female characters, such as Book 3 of the *Iliad* and the Old Testament books of Ruth and Esther, were assigned. In addition, other writings were added to the syllabus to vivify some of the historic conflicts within the Western tradition. Gnostic and Arian writers took their place alongside the orthodox church fathers, for example, making the presentation of early church history seem less like the linear unfolding of Christianity and more like a struggle among competing Christianities.

Consensus decisions such as these were facilitated by Hatfield's style of leadership, which was to allow the faculty to discuss curricular matters until, often in response to his adroit effort to "summarize the discussion," the grounds for a compromise—or, more often, a creative synthesis—appeared. To be sure, Fred Neal's leadership style had served the course admirably in the 1960s and 1970s. As Neal often said, he invited discussion on all questions, but at the end of the day, he made the decisions. Such a style would not have seen Search through the potentially divisive issues that arose in the 1980s and 1990s. Too many faculty members felt too strongly about too many things for any one of them to decide important matters for the whole.

Hatfield was aided in his efforts by Dean Harmon Dunathan, a humanities-oriented chemist who arrived at Rhodes in 1987 from Hampshire College, where he also had served as dean. Dunathan was strongly committed to Search. "We bring students to Rhodes, telling them, 'The institution really believes in the Search requirement, to the point that you must spend more than 10 percent of your academic work in that course,'" he said. "Having made that statement of belief, we had an obligation to see that the course was taught exceptionally well" (Vest and Cullen, 1996, p. 118). Under Dunathan, several tenure-track positions on the faculty were expressly designed to include participation in Search, so that new professors would have no reason to regard the course as an unwelcome imposition on their disciplinary teaching. Interviews of invited candidates probed their enthusiasm and potential aptitude for general education in the humanities.

An additional way of making use of the talent, as well as the diversity, of the Search staff was to decentralize whatever decisions did not have to be made collectively. For example, the course, which has always been colloquium intensive, became even more so. During the past half-century, the proportion of class meetings devoted to common lectures has descended at an accelerating pace from two-thirds to one-half to one-third to one-fourth to one-sixth in the first year of the course and none in the second year. One consequence of this trend has been that common readings do not have to be taught in a common way, which in view of the staff's diversity would necessarily be an imposed way. Some Search professors continue to prefer Bloom's "good old Great Books approach, in which a liberal education means reading certain generally recognized classic texts, just reading them, letting them dictate what the questions are and the methods of approaching them." Others have tried to "get behind the texts" to the social and political interests that may have shaped them. Decentralization carried over to testing as well: in 1995, examinations common to all sections of the course gave way to colloquium-specific essay questions that could better reflect each instructor's approaches and emphases.

Perhaps the Search course's most dramatically decentralizing reform was the track system for the sophomore year. In 1988, the staff affirmed that first-year Search would retain a common calendar and reading list in its survey of the ancient Hebrews, Greeks, and Romans and the early Christians through Augustine. But the second year of the course, although dominated by an extensive common core of readings, would be organized into disciplinary tracks: history, literature, philosophy, religion, and, beginning in 1995, politics. Instructors in each track were encouraged to supplement the core with readings of special significance to their discipline and to move at their own pace from the Middle Ages to the present. For example, although the natural tendency of the religious studies faculty has been to work slowly through Aquinas, the literature faculty often has preferred to consider religious questions mainly through the prism of Dante. The philosophy track might assign an excerpt from *The Prince,* while the politics track required students to read the entire book. Necessarily, common lectures were a casualty of the uneven calendars of the different tracks.

The track system for second-year Search has had several good effects. It eased the task of faculty recruitment by granting each staff member an island of disciplinary security in a sea of often unfamiliar works. It created a set of laboratories in which instructors could experiment with different readings, then report the results to their colleagues. Did adding Rousseau's *Discourse on the Origin of Inequality* to the syllabus shed light on his notoriously difficult *Social Contract*? Was *No Exit* a better entree to Sartre's thought than "Existentialism Is a Humanism"? The tracks also satisfied the desires of sophomores, who were ready to commit to a major. In the past, around 20 percent of Search's first-year class had abandoned Search for Life as sophomores, preferring the greater range of course offerings that the alternative humanities requirement allowed, along with the absence of common lectures. The introduction of tracks arrested the decline in second-year Search enrollments overnight.

To be sure, something has been lost with decentralization. Freshman halls, for example, no longer are charged with the intellectual adrenaline that used to characterize examination eves when all Search students knew that they would be facing the same challenge come morning. But decentralization has given students closer ongoing contact with their Search instructors and more choice, even on matters as small as offering sections of the course at a variety of class hours instead of the traditional "one hour fits all." Decentralization also has enabled the staff to treat individually matters that otherwise would have to be resolved legislatively, thereby creating friction where none now exists and jeopardizing the staff's ability to deal amicably with the decisions it really does have to make as a body.

Those decisions almost always are made in the setting of what may be the Search course's most important centralizing institution: the annual summer workshop, now called the Douglass Seminar in honor of a donor's decision to endow it. The two weeks of daylong sessions—one week for the first-year staff and one week for the (partially overlapping) second-year staff, with each week preceded by the labors of small committees—afford the Search faculty ample time to share ideas and experiences and to sort through the issues of course content and design that need to be resolved for the coming year. In 1997, for example, the staff decided to draw from the course's well of historical experience by reviving the old practice (abandoned for reasons that no one could recall) of allowing students in first-year Search to choose from a list of weeklong seminars on specialized topics offered by each professor in the midst of the spring semester.

The Douglass Seminar also allows the staff to study something in common—five sessions on Islam's influence in the West, for example, or a couple of days on new approaches to Aristotle—and thus to partake of what they hope their students experience in Search. The most important consequence of bringing the faculty together for an extended period of time may be the renewing of social and intellectual bonds, along with the initiation of new instructors into the collegial norms of the course. Habits of civility and mutual respect are not formed easily in any working group, but once they are, the chances that whatever issues arise will be dealt with in an atmosphere free of suspicion, stereotyping, and acrimony increase exponentially. As James Vest and Daniel Cullen (1996, p. 134) concluded in their study of the Search's recent history, "The Search course avoided ossification during the 1980s and 1990s principally because of these seminars, which allowed its diverse faculty both to recollect and renew its unifying mission and, not least, its members' respect and affection for one another."

How Search Works

Successful faculty recruitment for the Search course is vital to its continuing success. Around one-sixth of the college's 112-member faculty teach in the course each year, and another one-sixth have done so in the past or are scheduled to in the near future. Nothing could be more demoralizing than if the Search staff included unwilling conscripts, or if senior members of the faculty regarded teaching in the course as an unpleasant duty to be shunted off on their untenured colleagues.

Candidates for faculty positions at Rhodes that may involve teaching in Search are interviewed by the director of the course; indeed, he usually serves on the hiring committees and later participates in third-year reviews and tenure and promotion decisions. Staff members from the continuing faculty are willingly supplied in fixed quantities by the various humanities departments, notably religious studies, history, philosophy, and English (willingly because participation in the Search course enables these departments to justify new positions or preserve existing ones). In some cases, notably the political science department, faculty members from outside the humanities volunteer to teach in the course, but

Hatfield has not recruited social and natural scientists as aggres-
sively as Neal did. As soon as someone is slated to teach in Search,
sometimes with two or three years notice, he or she is invited to
participate in the Douglass Seminar.

Although some members of the college faculty are unenthusi-
astic about the Search course, whether because of its Western character, its diffuse instructional expertise, its emphasis on the Bible,
or its prominence in the curriculum, no stigma is attached to service on the course staff. In a typical year, around two-thirds of the
staff are associate or full professors, about the same proportion as
in the faculty as a whole. Nearly 90 percent of these staff members
will have taught in the course before, most of them for several
years. Such stability lightens the burden of faculty recruitment and
makes it easier to assimilate new members into the work and the
norms of the course.

On the other hand, no tangible incentives, such as research or
study grants or a lightening of course load, accompany participation in Search. Indeed, some faculty members regard certain
aspects of the course as disincentives to participate. Teaching outside one's expertise, as every member of the Search staff necessarily does, takes time away from teaching and research in the
discipline and channels it into a course that, because it is required,
presumably includes some students who would much rather be
looking through a microscope or analyzing election returns. Yet
evaluations of each staff member's teaching in Search figure in the
calculation of annual salary increases, as well as in more significant
performance reviews.

Student recruitment is as important for the Search course as
faculty recruitment but is more haphazard. Few entering students
know much about Search: the college's admissions office does not
strongly emphasize the course in its publications, and only one or
two of the commercial college guides do. During the summer
before they enroll, rising first-year students receive a brief description of the Search and Life alternatives from the registrar as part
of their registration packets. If they have heard anything from
other Rhodes students or recent alumni, it is likely to be that
Search is better than Life but Life is easier than Search. A slim
majority usually choose Search.

Once enrolled, students are required to complete the entire first year of Search before being given the option of switching to Life to fulfill the remaining two courses of the college's humanities requirement. (Life students may also switch to Search at this point.) Since the introduction of the history, literature, philosophy, political science, and religion tracks in second-year Search, few have done so. Even fewer exercise their option to change instructors midway through first-year Search, and most of those who switch do so for scheduling reasons, usually because of a spring semester science lab. To the extent that students vote with their feet, they vote heavily for incumbents.

With faculty and students thus recruited, how does Search work during the academic year? In first-year Search, virtually all of the readings are primary texts, chosen by the staff during the Douglass Seminar. In 1999–2000 the readings included much of the Bible and some of the Apocrypha; the Mesopotamian *Epic of Gilgamesh*; half of the *Iliad*; selections from Herodotus's *Histories* and Thucydides' *History of the Peloponnesian Wars*; all of Sophocles' *Oedipus the King* and Plato's *Phaedo* and *Apology*; much of Aristotle's *Nicomachean Ethics*; selections from Livy and Polybius; a sizable portion of the *Aeneid;* selections from Sallust, Epicurus, Lucretius, Seneca, Origen, Athanasius, and Perpetua; and part of Augustine's *City of God*. Each of the reading assignments is accompanied by a staff-written study guide, which offers introductory material and questions for review and discussion. Colloquium leaders vary widely in their use of the study guide.

Thorough reconsideration of the reading list and study guide is undertaken by the first-year staff every three years. Committee work both precedes the Douglass Seminar, at which final decisions are made by the staff, and follows it, as new study guide pages are written for the new or reconfigured assignments. In 1997, for example, the first year of the course was reorganized, mostly to introduce two new units: one on foundational epics (Genesis and Exodus from the Bible, along with the *Iliad* and Hesiod from the ancient Greeks) and the other on Judaism's post-Alexander encounter with Hellenism. In 1998 and 1999, remodeling gave way to redecorating, as the staff fine-tuned the syllabus pending another thorough review in 2000.

Most of the first-year readings are assigned to the students in book form, but shorter texts are compiled in a staff-produced anthology. The latter also are available on-line at the course's web site (www.humanities.rhodes.edu). The site, which currently serves only the first year of the course, also includes audiotapes of the lectures (around fifteen per year, compared with sixty-five colloquia), copies of the writing assignments and grading policies, and information about each colloquium leader.

Partway into the second semester, first-year Search departs briefly from the common calendar and divides into specialized, one-week seminars. Students are assigned to one of their top three choices, the only proviso being that their seminar leader cannot be their regular instructor. In 1997–98, the first year the seminars were offered since the early 1980s, the topics (twelve in all) included "Our Bodies, Our Selves: Sexual Differences Past and Present," "Socrates on Trial: Guilty or Innocent as Charged?" "Anger at God: Further Explorations of the Book of Job," "What Happened to Oedipus?" and "The Life and Teachings of the Buddha." Although the seminars were successful, one problem developed: a noticeable decline from previous years in the quality of the students' second-semester papers, which in 1997–98 were attached to the seminar, were due a month after the seminar was over, were graded by the seminar leader rather than the student's colloquium leader, and counted 25 percent of the student's final grade. In 1998–99 the paper was separated from the seminar and replaced by a take-home examination counting 10 percent of the final grade.

Second-year Search, which spans the period from the Middle Ages to the present, has no common syllabus, study guide, lectures, or grading policy. Many, but not all, of its readings are drawn from a core list, but even the core allows for considerable variation. Each instructor must assign works by certain authors: Francis of Assisi, Aquinas, Dante, Luther, Calvin, Kant, Schleiermacher, Marx, Nietzsche, Kierkegaard, Sartre, and Niebuhr. (These authors are mentioned by name in the college catalogue's description of the course, which is intended in part to ensure its "Bible-related" character.) In other cases, which are determined by the second-year staff at the Douglass Seminar, works by an author or an "equivalent author" must be assigned: Benedict of Nursia, Christine de Pizan, Petrarca, Mirandola, Erasmus, Cellini, Rabelais, Shakespeare, Montaigne, Machiavelli, Sadolet, Copernicus, Galileo, Bacon,

Descartes, Hobbes, Locke, Voltaire, Rousseau, Smith, Wollstonecraft, Madison, Coleridge, Malthus, J. S. Mill, Darwin, Freud, Dostoevsky, Wiesel, King, de Beauvoir, Gandhi, and Gutierrez. Finally, in a third category of core readings, selections from a number of other authors are made available for assignment, including Anselm, Julian of Norwich, Rorty, and Foucault.

These core readings are supplemented by each instructor, depending on the track. To cite just a few examples, in recent years the literature track has included the *Song of Roland* and Mann's *Death in Venice*; the politics track has assigned de Tocqueville, along with Koestler's *Darkness at Noon* and Margaret Atwood's *The Handmaid's Tale*; the religion track has included Bede, George Eliot, and de Chardin; the history track has assigned Burke and Marco Polo; and the philosophy track has included works by Pascal and Wittgenstein.

Course evaluations of both first- and second-year Search take place at the end of the year, not, as with other Rhodes courses, at the end of the semester. The belief is that, for evaluation purposes at least, Search consists of two one-year courses. No effort is made to evaluate second-year Search as a whole; in order to assess the first year of the course, newly inducted members of the Search Advisory Council (essentially the best students in first-year Search) are brought together in informal, student- and faculty-led focus groups. Their comments are summarized in writing and then reviewed by the staff at the Douglass Seminar. "Too many lectures" is a stock complaint, one with which most of the staff disagrees but, over the years, has grudgingly accommodated. (The same is true of "too much reading.") Other requests are more surprising. For example, in 1997 several students said that the biblical units contained too much about who wrote what and too little about what they wrote. In addition to the focus groups, a written questionnaire for all students was used for a short time, but the logistics of administering it were awkward, and little was added to what was learned from the advisory council.

To evaluate the work of individual instructors in Search, a student questionnaire is used throughout the college. Some of the questions, especially those concerning course design, do not apply very well to Search, which has many collectively designed elements. This bias in the evaluation instrument feeds prospective staff members' apprehensions about teaching in Search.

Challenges for Search

For all its success, the future of the Search course is rich with challenges. Some of these are perennial, a cause for both the despair that accompanies inherently insoluble problems and the consolation that long experience of living with them offers. Other challenges are new and, for that reason, more difficult to recognize, much less address.

One perennial challenge is to strike an appropriate balance between the West's historical search for values and each student's personal search. Although it lasts four semesters, the Search course partakes of the same "if-it's-Wednesday-this-must-be-Aristotle" problem of all survey courses. Yet anyone who has taught in Search knows that the liveliest and most serious (as distinct from most grim) discussions take place when the question turns from, "What is Aristotle's understanding of how humans flourish?" to, "What can I learn from Aristotle about my life?" Finding the right balance is a task that deserves as much time as the Search staff can give it, and more than it now does.

A second challenge, similar to the first in both its perennial character and its origins in the limits of time, is what to include in—or more realistically, what to leave out of—the course. The sorts of questions Search faces are these:

- Should the course devote time and attention to Western art, architecture, music, and dance? The arts were, after all, part of the original conception of the course.
- Should the course include non-Western history, literature, philosophy, politics, and religion (and art, architecture, music, and dance, for that matter)? A recurring complaint of some students has been that Search includes nothing about Eastern religion, and the week-long seminar devoted to Buddhism in 1997–98 attracted many more applicants than any of the others. (The staff experimented with a unit on Buddhism in 1970–71 but abandoned it after one year.)
- Should the second year of the course, in keeping with the Western emphasis, incorporate study of Islam? The religious studies track has begun doing so, and five half-day sessions of the Douglass Seminar were devoted to Islam in 1998.

- How can adequate attention be given to the works of women and minorities in the course? "It's still the Man course, no matter what they call it," was the recent complaint of one woman student. Yet little sentiment exists among the staff to add works to the syllabus merely for reasons of representation.

All of these questions, with the exception of the last, have recurred throughout the history of the course, with discussion tending to founder on the shoals of time and expertise. The Buddhism unit, for example, was abandoned because to include it meant diluting other topics that already seemed to be stretched too thin; in addition, one Eastern unit seemed like tokenism of the worst sort. When the name of the course was changed in 1986, "history and religion" was replaced by "Western history and religion" in the interests of truth in advertising. Students were told that Search was meant to be the beginning of their exploration of the humanities, not the end of it. They were encouraged to take courses on non-Western topics that were available elsewhere in the curriculum. Over the years, this answer has silenced students more than satisfied them.

A third perennial challenge for the Search course, more latent recently than in the past, is that of faculty recruitment and assimilation. Recruiting talented and energetic faculty to teach just about anything is easier when colleges enjoy a buyers' market for academics than when, as inevitably will happen, the sellers regain the upper hand. When that day comes, the lack of tangible incentives to teach in Search may hinder faculty recruitment, as will the apparent disincentives of time away from the discipline and uncertain teaching evaluations. The college was fortunate in being able to draw on the heroic recruiting abilities of Fred Neal in the sellers' market of the 1970s. But the timely arrival of heroes on the scene should not be an element of institutional planning.

In addition to these perennial challenges, three newer ones confront the Search course. One is faced by every college and university: how to make intelligent use of computer-based educational technologies. As with almost all other new technologies, the advantages computers offer are instantly apparent, the costs subtle and hard to discern. Distressingly, humanists in the academy, usually so sensitive to the complexities of technological change, have been less reflective about these trade-offs than one would expect them to be. One frequently hears, for example, about students who are silent in class but come alive in listserv discussion groups. The question that people in the humanities should be raising, however, is this: Should students be encouraged to think that transmitting messages from the solitude of their terminals is an adequate substitute for joining discussions in the company of their fellows? Similarly, the wonders of information retrieval and display often are treated as an unalloyed good in college courses. But to the extent that electronic bells and whistles distract students from the hard work of reading and thinking deeply about serious and complex works and expressing themselves in intelligent, evidence-based arguments, they disserve them.

The other two challenges are particular to Rhodes. In 1998 the president of the college, in conjunction with the board of trustees and after an extensive campus-wide discussion, added "to serve God" to the preamble of Rhodes's mission statement as a way of reaffirming the college's historic Presbyterian commitment. This gesture was especially ambitious in the light of the gradual secularization of higher education that, since the 1960s, has influenced Rhodes, along with many other church-related colleges and universities (Hatfield, 1996; Marsden, 1994). How the new mission statement will affect the curriculum (the Search staff feels that it already does its part by satisfying the Bellingrath-Morse Foundation's standard) is uncertain. The creation of new courses that include a service component, rather than the alteration of existing courses, appears to be the college's more likely response.

The second Rhodes-specific challenge to Search comes, strangely enough, in the form of tribute to the course. A summer 1998 faculty committee on the curriculum, which was appointed by the dean and charged to think boldly about curricular issues, offered as its major proposal the creation of a six-credit-hour capstone course for seniors, designed to help students "in developing a personal philosophy." The committee suggested that Search provide the setting for the capstone course. To make this possible, second-year Search would be moved to the senior year.

The ad hoc committee's proposal was strenuously resisted by the Search staff and by most of the faculty as a whole. Divorcing the second year of Search from the first would remove the rationale for both years' chronological organization—second-year

Search by design and first-year Search by omission. (What would be the basis for having the first year continue to end in the fifth century A.D.?) As one staff member said, "I don't know what this new course would be, but it wouldn't be Search." The critics succeeded in defeating the proposal at an early stage. Nonetheless, the impulse to place Search at the center of the curriculum is evidence of its strength as a program. As in the Bellingrath-Morse controversy two decades earlier, the college's tendency when it wants to solve a problem is to look to Search for the solution.

Notes

1. This summary of the origins and development of the Search course is based primarily on Nelson (1996c), Hatfield (1996), Llewellyn (1996), and Vest and Cullen, 1996.

2. Although it lurks offstage, another important centralizing institution is the Bellingrath-Morse Foundation's requirement for Bible and Bible-related study as a condition of its contribution to the college's endowment. However disturbing the idea of allowing an outside agency to constrain a college curriculum may be, one practical effect of the policy has been to remove an inherently contentious issue from the table: the amount of Jewish and Christian material that should be included in the course. To be sure, the staff spends a great deal of time discussing which biblical and Bible-related writings should be assigned and how they should be presented on the syllabus. But the requirement performs in such discussions the same function as the control rods in a nuclear power plant, limiting the explosive potential of the inherently combustible material. The requirement also keeps Search from succumbing to one of the stranger trends in modern higher education: the slow disappearance of close study of the Bible from courses that avow to present the enduring and influential texts of the Western tradition.

References

Allardyce, G. "The Rise and Fall of the Western Civilization Course." *American Historical Review,* 1982, *87,* 695–725.

Armour, E. "On Diversity and Conflict." In M. Nelson (ed.), *Celebrating the Humanities: A Half-Century of the Search Course at Rhodes College.* Nashville, Tenn.: Vanderbilt University Press, 1996.

Bennett, W. J. *To Reclaim a Legacy: A Report on the Humanities in Higher Education.* Washington, D.C.: National Endowment for the Humanities, 1984.

Bloom, A. *The Closing of the American Mind: How Higher Education Has Failed Democracy and Impoverished the Souls of Today's Students.* New York: Simon & Schuster, 1987.

Botsford, E. "Freshman Discovers College Means Study." *Sou'wester,* Oct. 20, 1946.

Cooper, W. R., and others. *Man in the Light of History and Religion: A Syllabus.* Memphis, Tenn.: Southwestern at Memphis, 1945.

Cullen, D. E. "Of Great Books and Conflicts." In M. Nelson (ed.), *Celebrating the Humanities: A Half-Century of the Search Course at Rhodes College.* Nashville, Tenn.: Vanderbilt University Press, 1996.

Davis, J. H. "Man in the Light of History and Religion: A Humanities Course at Southwestern." In Earl J. McGrath (ed.), *The Humanities in General Education.* Dubuque, Iowa: W. C. Brown, 1949.

Diehl, Charles E. Letter to Theodore M. Greene. Morgan Archives, Rhodes College, May 14, 1945.

"Dr. Neal Says Farewell to Man." *Sou'wester,* Apr. 26, 1985.

"The Great Centuries." Morgan Archive, Rhodes College, 1944.

Hatfield, D. W. "Curriculum Innovation, 1958–1975." In M. Nelson (ed.), *Celebrating the Humanities: A Half-Century of the Search Course at Rhodes College.* Nashville, Tenn.: Vanderbilt University Press, 1996.

Johnson, A. T. "Report of the Dean." Morgan Archives, Rhodes College, Aug. 1950.

Lacy, L. "On Faith and the Critical Method." In M. Nelson (ed.), *Celebrating the Humanities: A Half-Century of the Search Course at Rhodes College.* Nashville, Tenn.: Vanderbilt University Press, 1996.

Llewellyn, R. R. "'Man . . . the Measure,' 1975–1985." In M. Nelson (ed.), *Celebrating the Humanities: A Half-Century of the Search Course at Rhodes College.* Nashville, Tenn.: Vanderbilt University Press, 1996.

Marsden, G. *The Soul of the American University: From Protestant Establishment to Established Nonbelief.* New York: Oxford University Press, 1994.

Morgan, W. *The Architecture of Rhodes College.* Columbia: University of Missouri Press, 1989.

Nelson, M. "Celebrating the Humanities." *Rhodes Today,* Summer 1996a, pp. 12–18.

Nelson, M. *Celebrating the Humanities: A Half-Century of the Search Course at Rhodes College.* Nashville, Tenn.: Vanderbilt University Press, 1996b.

Nelson, M. "The Founding Era, 1945–1958." In M. Nelson (ed.), *Celebrating the Humanities: A Half-Century of the Search Course at Rhodes College.* Nashville, Tenn.: Vanderbilt University Press, 1996c.

Nelson, M. "The Amateur Hour." In M. Nelson (ed.), *Celebrating the Humanities: A Half-Century of the Search Course at Rhodes College.* Nashville, Tenn.: Vanderbilt University Press, 1996d.

"90 percent of Students Want Man Alternative." *Sou'wester,* Feb. 13, 1981.

Osman, J. "Southwestern Faculty Offers the 'Great Centuries' Lectures."
    Southwestern News, Mar. 1945, pp. 6–7.

Searle, J. *The Campus Wars: A Sympathetic Look at the University in Agony.* New
    York: World Publishing Co., 1971.

Streete, G. C. "The Feminist Search for Values." In M. Nelson (ed.),
    *Celebrating the Humanities: A Half-Century of the Search Course at Rhodes
    College.* Nashville, Tenn.: Vanderbilt University Press, 1996.

Vest, J. M. "Influences Beyond the Walls." In M. Nelson (ed.), *Celebrating
    the Humanities: A Half-Century of the Search Course at Rhodes College.*
    Nashville, Tenn.: Vanderbilt University Press, 1996.

Vest, J. M., and Cullen, D. E. "Redefining the Search, 1985–1995." In
    M. Nelson (ed.), *Celebrating the Humanities: A Half-Century of the
    Search Course at Rhodes College.* Nashville, Tenn.: Vanderbilt Univer-
    sity Press, 1996.

Veysey, L. R. *The Emergence of the American University.* Chicago: University
    of Chicago Press, 1965.

Chapter Five

The Core Curriculum at Eckerd College

Lloyd W. Chapin

Since its opening in 1960, Eckerd College has had an interdisciplinary, values-oriented core curriculum. Structure, content, and course titles have varied, but the core requirement itself has remained. Both the college's continuing educational commitments and its efforts to adapt these commitments to changing circumstances have found their clearest expression in the core. To trace its history is in many ways to trace the educational history of the college as a whole. Moreover, an analysis of how and why Eckerd's particular core has changed and evolved may also offer insight into the broader history of American liberal education since the 1960s.

The Original Commitments

Eckerd was founded as Florida Presbyterian College in 1958, at a time when there was a national sense of need to expand higher education opportunities and to improve their quality. Members of the United Presbyterian Church, U.S.A., and the Presbyterian Church, U.S., who shared this national view, first working independently and then jointly, concluded that there was a clear need for a church-related liberal arts college, innovative in character and superior in academic quality, in the rapidly growing state of Florida.

From the beginning, four basic commitments governed the planning of the new institution. First, it was to be a college that would stand in the best of the liberal arts tradition. Second, it was to be a Christian college, meaningfully related to the Presbyterian church. Third, it was to be dedicated to the highest standards of academic excellence. And fourth, it was to be a pacesetting institution that would demonstrate to other colleges more effective ways to facilitate student learning. The principal features of the academic program were a strong interdisciplinary core curriculum extending over four years that focused on value questions; an emphasis on independent study that found influential expression in the introduction of the winter term and the 4–1–4 academic calendar to American higher education; an emphasis on international education that resulted in the creation of many opportunities for students to study overseas; and strong majors designed to give students close study and prepare them for graduate school.

Florida Presbyterian College flourished in the 1960s. *Time* magazine described it in 1966 as a "college that has grown from vacant lot to excellence in six short years" ("Coming of Age at Six," p. 82). Its educational program earned a national reputation for innovation and quality, and the winter term concept was adopted by more than three hundred colleges.

In June 1971, Clearwater businessman and philanthropist Jack M. Eckerd pledged $1.5 million to pay off the college's existing operating debts and an additional $8.5 million to be paid into the endowment. In grateful recognition, the board of trustees voted unanimously to change the name of the college to Eckerd College, effective July 1, 1972. Eckerd's gift provided a major lift to the college, critical to its survival at a time when the national environment was becoming increasingly difficult for small, private colleges. The decline in the traditional college-age population, the lower standardized test scores of high school seniors, the rapid expansion of the public sector of higher education, the emergence of the drug culture, and the spread of student unrest converged to threaten the stability of many institutions. Eckerd, still relatively new, financially fragile, and with only a small body of youthful alumni, was especially vulnerable. Enrollment declined sharply from a high of 1,114 in 1971–72 to a low of 843 in 1976–77, along with a 15 percent reduction of the faculty and a series of budget deficits.

The college's fortunes began to improve noticeably by the early 1980s. New majors were added in computer science, international business, management, and marine science. The Program for Experienced Learners, a degree-completion program for adults, flourished. A unique new venture in intergenerational education, the Academy for Senior Professionals at Eckerd College (ASPEC), brought more national attention. Enrollment and Scholastic Aptitude Test scores in the residential college began a steady climb, and the number of faculty increased. The college returned to balanced annual budgets, eliminated the accumulated debt in the current operating fund, and began to build endowment.

Today, with more than twenty-two hundred students, the college has the largest enrollment in its history, has completed new construction with more still under way, and has recently conducted a successful capital campaign. Through all of these developments, the commitments that guided the college at its founding have continued to define its character: a commitment to the liberal arts and sciences; to a meaningful relationship with the church; to academic excellence; and to be an innovative, pacesetting institution. During the course of the college's history, these defining characteristics have continued to find their clearest expression in the interdisciplinary, values-centered core curriculum. In tracing the evolution of the core, especially the first-year course, one can see how the college has responded to the various forces that have challenged its original commitments.

The Earliest Version

Originally the core curriculum was envisaged as a four-year, eight-semester sequence that all students would take and in which all faculty members would participate. The first-year course, entitled "Western Civilization and Its Christian Heritage," was designed to study "religious, scientific, social, economic, and political development, and literary, artistic and musical works" from "the pre-Greek era, Greece, Rome and the Middle Ages, . . . the Renaissance to the beginning of the 19th Century." Particular emphasis was to be "placed upon the impact of the Judeo-Christian tradition and its meaning as it relates to all knowledge. The historical-redemptive message as revealed in the Holy Scriptures is seen as central in the interpretation of man's sojourn" (*Bulletin*, 1959, p. 5).

The second-year course bore the same title and covered the nineteenth and twentieth centuries. The third-year course, "Civilizations of Asia," was designed to broaden students' perspective by providing a cultural and historical analysis of the civilizations of Asia and their interaction with Western civilizations. In their senior year, students took "Christian Faith and Great Issues," a study of the relevance of the Christian faith to current community and world issues. Each course involved a combination of weekly lectures or presentations to the entire class by experts in the field and small group discussions.

The sequence of core courses was designed to address a number of objectives. One was to provide a common educational experience for students regardless of their field of specialization. As John Bevan (1964), the founding dean of faculty who played a key role in the development of the curriculum, wrote, "Underlying the design of the core program is the conviction that knowledge is unified and that at the heart of the academic experience there should be a unified, rather than departmentalized, approach to understanding" (p. 100). This commitment to the unification of knowledge found expression not only in the required participation of all students and the course's interdisciplinary content, but also in the expectation that every member of the faculty would contribute, or, as Bevan put it, "a four-year plan of study drawing its staff from the faculty in all academic areas so that in any one year 60 per cent of the total faculty is involved."

Another objective was "to equip the student for the formation and articulation of informed, independent, responsible judgments of value." This meant attention to the development of analytical, dialectical, and writing skills as necessary preparation for making value judgments in addition to acquiring specific information. Even the culminating course in the senior year, on Christian faith and great issues, was "not designed to indoctrinate but to challenge students to think through social, economic, and political issues in the light of their own personal value systems."

All of the core courses eschewed reliance on secondary sources. Students were to grapple directly with seminal works. The readings in Western civilization came from the Bible, Homer,

Plato, Aristotle, the Greek tragedians, Augustine, Aquinas, Dante, Machiavelli, Luther, Shakespeare, Voltaire, Darwin, Marx, Freud, and Camus. Asian readings included selections from the Buddha, Lao-tzu, Confucius, Mencius, the Qur'an, and Murasaki. For the "Christian Faith and Great Issues" course, prominent persons directly involved in these issues were brought to campus to give public lectures.

The earliest version of the Western civilization course inevitably reflected its cultural time and place. Its proclaimed focus on "the historical-redemptive message as revealed in the Holy Scriptures as central in the interpretation of man's sojourn" gave the course an evangelical cast not surprising in a southern Protestant environment. The course materials were indeed an expression of "man's" sojourn in the sense that only the works of male authors were included. Perhaps most striking of all from a postmodern perspective, with its acute sense of the relative and fragmented character of all human claims to truth, was the confident assertion that the interdisciplinary nature of the course was justified by "the conviction that all knowledge is unified." Nonetheless, the course was a bold departure from the typical freshman Western civilization course taught exclusively by humanities faculty relying on the lecture method and secondary sources. Its subject matter and its staffing were drawn from a wide variety of disciplines, including the social and natural sciences. The texts were primary sources and, aside from the plenary lectures, classes were small discussion groups designed to engage students in the critical analysis of primary documents. Nor were the course's goals simply an informed knowledge of the past or the sharpening of intellectual skills. Its ultimate purpose was to equip students for making "responsible judgments of value."

The initial core sequence was visionary in some respects. By employing a pedagogy that emphasized the use of class time for the critical examination of primary texts, the courses anticipated the coming decline in reliance on lecturing and increased emphasis on active learning. Basing a broadly interdisciplinary approach on a belief in "the unification of knowledge" may seem questionable in today's more skeptical epistemological climate, but the inclusion of subject matter from the humanities, the arts, and the social and natural sciences did recognize that human perspectives of reality are necessarily mediated by different methodologies and that no one perspective can be taken as absolute. The focus on equipping students to make and explain informed value judgments enabled the college to retain the traditional liberal arts goal of strengthening moral character while maintaining the important distinction between education and indoctrination. Moreover, by adding a course on Asia in the third year whose purpose was to focus the "attention of students on cultural forms, institutions, and historical movements which lie outside their own tradition and which are becoming increasingly significant for our civilization," the core sequence anticipated the rising importance of having students come to terms with non-Western cultures.

Project '73

By the early 1970s, the original core sequence with its integrated interdisciplinary and chronological approach in the first two years, focus on the Judeo-Christian perspective, confidence in the unification of knowledge, and emphasis, for a cross-cultural perspective, on Asia was dissolving. There was an increasing concern for addressing contemporary issues rather than developing historical understanding, and a growing sense of the need to address and explore cultural diversity rather than to rely on the classic texts of Western civilization. Although the "Christian Faith and Great Issues" course retained its place as the culminating course for the senior year, the earlier sections of the core sequence clearly treated Christianity more and more as simply one intellectual option among others. These changes are not surprising in a period when many cultural assumptions were undergoing challenge in American society and in higher education. Disillusionment with America's Vietnam policy, the rise of the civil rights movement, widespread drug use, the emphasis on individual autonomy, and the questioning of traditional authorities all served to challenge carefully structured core curricula that focused on Western civilization and the Judeo-Christian tradition.

The college's curricular stresses were accentuated by growing financial difficulties, declining enrollment, the departure of some of the key figures who had founded the college, and, in 1972, the change in name. It was clear that if the college was to survive and flourish, it was time for a major effort at renewal. Much of this effort centered, not surprisingly, on the curriculum.

In 1973 the faculty, by now a blend of founding faculty, who had been with the college since the early 1960s, and others who had been hired as enrollment grew, approved a comprehensive revision of the academic program. Project '73, as the revision came to be known, inaugurated major changes in the core sequence, the academic calendar, and faculty organization in an effort to cope with tensions that had already begun to undermine the coherence and vitality of the original core sequence. The changes were also intended to make the college more attractive by renewing its reputation as an innovative pacesetting institution.

Under the revised calendar, freshmen first encountered their faculty mentor as the instructor in their first college course, a seminar that was the centerpiece of a new three-week term immediately preceding the fall semester called Autumn Term. Autumn Term (perhaps a misnomer for August in central Florida) was developed as a broader and deeper period of freshman orientation designed to give students an intensive foretaste of college living and academic work. Autumn Term projects were developed by individual faculty members and were designed to provide new students with an intellectually stimulating start to their college studies by allowing them to choose an appealing topic taught by someone with special enthusiasm for it. The Autumn Term experience created a strong bond between the faculty mentor and his or her twenty student associates. Each Autumn Term group and its mentor continued as a discussion section of the two-semester freshman year core course.

The core course, while retaining an interdisciplinary approach, a reliance on primary sources, active learning, and the periodic participation of all faculty members, underwent significant changes in content and acquired a new set of titles. The intent was to respond to the sense shared by many faculty and students that the course needed to be more demonstrably relevant to contemporary issues. The first semester, "Inquiry and Human Nature," focused on "problems of defining human nature and viewpoints taken by different disciplines such as anthropology, psychology, and the humanities" (*Catalogue*, 1976–77, p. 22). There were three structural units: Inquiry and the Ascent of Humankind, Problem Solving Explorations, and Inquiry and the Future of Humankind. Assigned texts included selections from Plato, Augustine, Luther,

Madison, Thoreau, Marx, and Darwin, as well as contemporary readings from Bronowski, Skinner, and James Watson. What was described as "man's sojourn" in the 1960s had now become "humankind's ascent," and the theme of the "unification of knowledge" had now become "the problems of defining human nature and viewpoints taken by various disciplines."

The second semester of the course became "Values and the Search for Spirit." Its objectives were "(1) to explore the spiritual dimensions of mankind; (2) to probe one's own identity; (3) to encourage respect for each other's beliefs; (4) to encounter the range of spiritual reality in art and act; (5) to consider the importance of faith for life on Spaceship Earth." Five major issues (meditation, suffering, redemption, action, and vision) served as the core. Students were to experience specific "spiritual dimensions (Art, Altered States of Consciousness, Yoga, Tai Chi, Adventure, Selfless Service, etc.)." Assigned texts included selections from the Bible, the Tao, Angelou, Castaneda, Hesse, Jung, King, and Wiesel. In this revised version of the first-year course, religion was still a central concern, but rather than emphasizing the influence of the Judeo-Christian tradition in making value judgments, the focus was on cultivating religious experience. At first this may appear to have been a surprising turn, but in fact, it reflected the faculty's efforts to respond to a tendency among young people in the late 1960s and early 1970s to turn away from conventional intellectual and ethical definitions of religion and toward a greater interest in mystical and experiential approaches.

Project '73 did away altogether with the second-year Western civilization core courses. In their place, students were required to take two courses from a category called "Modes of Learning." These courses, whose announced purpose was to help students learn how to learn and to develop the skills necessary for doing more advanced work in a particular field, were, in fact, the introductory courses to various disciplines. Thus, the original four-course sequence in Western civilization was reduced by half, and the remainder was replaced by what was, in effect, a modest disciplinary distribution requirement. The original two-semester sequence of Asian studies required in the junior year now became a requirement simply to take two area studies courses in cultures "other than one's own." To complete the general education sequence, Project '73 replaced the two-semester senior course, "Christian Faith and Great Issues," with the requirement that students take four courses in the junior and senior years from among a group of courses called "Values Sequence Colloquia." These covered a wide range of topics, such as business and society; ecology, evolution, and natural resources; justice, law, and community; science, technology, and human values; and secularism and personal values. Their shared purpose was to help students understand themselves and their beliefs so that they could "learn how to evaluate critical issues of the day and eventually formulate [their] own value system, or philosophy, to live by." To underscore the emphasis on values, the entire general education sequence, including the two first-year core courses, the area studies courses, and the values colloquia, was designated "The Values Sequence."

At the same time that it was reorganizing the general education curriculum and the calendar, the faculty reorganized itself. When the college opened in 1960, the faculty was divided into three traditional academic areas: the arts and humanities, the social sciences, and the natural sciences and mathematics. As part of Project '73, the faculty reorganized itself into six collegia: Behavioral Sciences, Comparative Cultures, Creative Arts, Letters, Natural Sciences and Mathematics, and Foundations. Foundations was the designation for the group of faculty serving in any one year as freshman mentors. The other groupings were based on a shared method of inquiry and were designed to overcome traditional departmental and disciplinary boundaries by bringing together those faculty and their student majors who shared a similar approach to learning. The collegia sought intentionally to foster the interrelatedness of knowledge and the importance of interdisciplinary work.

Viewed as a whole, Project '73 reflected the college's effort to respond to the challenges posed by the cultural upheavals of the late 1960s and accentuated by declining enrollments and a series of unbalanced budgets. This curricular response, especially the changes in the general education curriculum, sought to make the program more appealing, as well as more relevant, by focusing on contemporary issues and student concerns. There was a greater awareness of the issues posed by a global society and cultural diversity. There was more emphasis on faculty attention to the needs of individual students and a desire to provide students with more flexibility in their choice of courses. There was a greater concern for learning how to learn and for the differences in various modes of inquiry.

One of the most striking aspects of Project '73 was its diminished confidence in a common core of knowledge as the necessary foundation for a liberal education. The original two-year sequence based on primary texts of Western civilization studied in chronological order with an emphasis on the centrality of the Judeo-Christian tradition had become a one-year sequence organized thematically around contemporary issues of identity and purpose. The Asian studies sequence had been fragmented into a choice of area studies. "Christian Faith and Great Issues" had been replaced by a range of values colloquia, and different modes of learning had become a curricular category of their own. Moreover, by 1973, there was no longer any required science or foreign language. In many respects, the idea of a core curriculum based on common content had been replaced by an emphasis on the diversity of human ways of knowing and choosing, as well as the freedom of students to choose among options. Even so, the Project '73 curriculum retained important elements of continuity with its predecessor, including a strong emphasis on the value of interdisciplinary study and the development of the capacity to make informed value judgments. Pedagogy relied primarily on using primary sources, substantial writing, and class discussion, that is, active learning. Every member of the faculty was still expected to participate in the delivery of general education, most notably by periodic participation in the Foundations Collegium as an Autumn Term mentor and discussion group leader in the first-year course.

Project '73 brought major changes in the Eckerd curriculum or, as the 1976–77 catalogue cover asserted, "Bold New Directions." As it pursued these new directions, the college sought to be faithful to its original commitments to liberal education, a meaningful church relationship, excellence, and innovation. Nevertheless, it cannot be denied that Project '73 diminished explicit attention in the curriculum to the Judeo-Christian tradition. Eckerd had moved a long way from the original call for a course in which "the historical-redemptive message as revealed in the Holy Scriptures is seen as essential in the interpretation of man's sojourn." This shift in emphasis, although questioned by some leaders of the college's

church-related constituency, did not evoke sharp criticism, probably because even the revision retained a strong emphasis on values
education and the importance of religion in human life.

The curricula of the 1960s and 1970s represented divergent
ways of understanding liberal education. The curriculum of the
1960s certainly included skills development, but it also stressed
the mastery of a particular content. The Project '73 curriculum,
on the other hand, was not completely indifferent to content, but
for its architects, content could vary as long as students acquired
the intellectual tools that liberate the mind. This tension in liberal
education has a long history. One can see it perhaps most clearly
in the encounter between classical Greco-Roman education with
its emphasis on the seven liberal arts—all of which are essentially
skills—and the early Christian church with its emphasis on theological and moral content. In a famous example in his *Confessions,*
Augustine of Hippo conveys a sense of this tension when he
laments that the pagan teachers of his youth cared more
about how he pronounced the word for a human being than
how he treated human beings (I, 18). In the history of Florida
Presbyterian College and Eckerd College, the tension can be seen
most clearly in the changing character of the Foundations core
sequence. In the 1960s, the sequence sharpened intellectual skills,
but these skills were linked to a specific content: major texts in
chronological order in the history of the West followed by materials from Asian civilizations. Project '73 reduced the core sequence
from three years to one and shifted the focus to the exploration of
contemporary themes.

Important elements of Project '73 proved to be popular.
Autumn Term in particular was considered a great success. Students rated the experience highly, and the parents of entering
freshmen liked the idea of a lengthy, personalized orientation
period at the beginning of the academic year. Faculty enjoyed the
opportunity to create and teach seminars on their favorite topics
to small groups of eager, conscientious new students. Students also
liked the freedom to choose from among a variety of courses to fulfill the components of the general education program once they
got beyond the year-long freshman core sequence. The reorganization of the faculty into collegia worked well. Faculty found regular contact with colleagues who shared similar methodological

orientations stimulating, and they were able to communicate with each other more readily across traditional disciplinary boundaries.

Yet despite the effort put into creating Project '73, many faculty members became increasingly critical of key features. A primary target was the first-year core course sequence—not surprising since it has always been the focus of curricular thought and debate. Many came to believe that the organization of the sequence around contemporary themes had resulted not only in the loss of a historical sense, but also in the increasing use of topical articles (on, for example, the American family, the female athlete, or being a hospice volunteer) that did not merit the required attention of all students. The general, although not universal, complaint was that the course did not lay a strong foundation for further study.

An increasing number of faculty criticized other elements of the new program. It became apparent that it was not possible to address meaningfully such abstract issues as the distinctive modes of inquiry in introductory courses. Moreover, identifying a particular list of courses as "values colloquia" seemed to suggest that other courses did not teach values. From the standpoint of keeping faith with the college's commitment to be meaningfully related to the church, there was no clearly established curricular setting in which students engaged in a serious intellectual encounter with the Judeo-Christian tradition. Finally, there was growing dissatisfaction with the absence of foreign language, science, and mathematics requirements.

These accumulating complaints about Project '73 were all, in one way or another, a criticism of its tendency to deemphasize the importance of specific content. Western civilization, Asian civilization, the Judeo-Christian tradition, foreign language, science: all of these clearly defined elements in the initial curriculum were treated as options. The focus was on self-exploration, contemporary issues, modes of inquiry, and valuing.

Synthesis

By 1979, the faculty was ready to undertake a major revision of Project '73. The revision, which was adopted in the fall of 1980, was an effort to combine the strongest features of the two earlier curricula. A measure of its success is that it remained virtually unchanged for fifteen years, a time during which the college's fortunes improved significantly. Many factors contributed to this forward movement, but a stable curriculum supported by faculty, administration, and trustees, and generally well received by students and parents, certainly played a part.

The revised curriculum retained the most popular features of Project '73: Autumn Term, freedom for students to choose from a range of courses to fulfill parts of the general education program, and the collegium form of faculty organization. But it also made changes. The clearest indication of the thrust of the revision can again be found in the first-year core sequence. The names of the courses were changed from "Inquiry and Human Nature" followed by "The Search for Spirit," to "Western Heritage I and II." Once more the course became a survey of the development of Western civilization by means of the examination of classic texts. Beginning in the fall semester with selections from the ancient Greeks and Romans and the Bible, the course moved forward chronologically to the twentieth century, where it concluded with works by T. S. Eliot, Woolf, Wiesel, and King. Because certain recurrent general themes emerged—the self, community, and the transcendent—the texts served as the occasion for reflecting on enduring issues. But the other main purpose of the course was to give students a common grounding in the West's cultural heritage.

Course pedagogy still stressed active learning and skill development. The mentor-led sections, which met twice weekly following a Monday lecture to the entire class, relied on group discussion, student presentations, and essay writing. But as in the original curriculum, the importance of skill development and personal reflection was balanced by a belief in the value of knowing a particular content: the cultural heritage of the West. Even the natural sciences were included, with readings from Aristotle, Galileo, and Darwin. Two members of the science faculty—a chemist and a physicist—coauthored a textbook on the history of science designed specifically for the course. A book of art history supplemented the focus on written texts. There was also a conscious effort to include works by women (Hildegard von Bingen, the Seneca Falls Declaration, and Woolf) and minorities (Douglass, Du Bois, and King). Every member of the faculty, regardless of discipline, continued to serve periodically as a freshman mentor and leader of a discussion section. Through this practice, the college stressed that, whereas in other courses faculty members model the role of the expert, in the first-year core sequence, they model the role of the liberally educated person who can make productive intellectual use of any significant nontechnical work.

Another significant change in the revised curriculum was to eliminate the Modes of Learning and Values Colloquia categories and replace them with specially designated courses divided among five perspectives: aesthetic, cross-cultural, environmental, social relations, and Judeo-Christian. The purpose was still to give students some opportunity for choice in fulfilling general education requirements, but also to be more specific about content. Students were expected to take at least one course in each of the first four perspective categories and a core course in the senior year called "Judeo-Christian Perspectives on Contemporary Issues." To the requirement of writing proficiency, the new revision added that students must demonstrate proficiency in foreign language and mathematics at the first-year college level.

"Judeo-Christian Perspectives," which became a requirement for all seniors in the fall semester, involved weekly lectures or plenary sessions on topics of contemporary importance, such as biomedical ethics, world hunger, environmental pollution, gender or race relations, and peace and war, followed by small group discussions led by the interdisciplinary team of faculty who were responsible for the course that year. Participation by all faculty in the course was encouraged but not required. The course itself was to serve as a capstone to the general education program by engaging students in future-oriented reflection on issues they were likely to face during their lifetimes, guided by the intellectual resources of the Judeo-Christian tradition.

A comparison of the 1980 revision and the original curriculum of the 1960s shows a revival of several key elements: the first-year focus on Western civilization, the senior-year focus on Christian faith and contemporary issues, and the requirement in foreign language. This revival was the result of the faculty's sense that the Project '73 curriculum needed more intellectual substance and a greater attention to the traditional sources of contemporary culture. The amount of time devoted to these requirements, however, was substantially reduced. Western civilization was now two semesters instead of four, "Christianity and Contemporary Issues" was one semester instead of two, and the level of required foreign language proficiency was reduced from three years to one. A major reason for this reduction was the desire to minimize the identification of specific content areas with liberal education and to increase the freedom students would have in planning their curriculum. This desire was consistent with the Project '73 architects' view of liberal education as primarily skill development. It was also motivated at least in part by the pragmatic judgment that a more diverse curriculum with more options would be more appealing to students than a highly structured set of core requirements. Here one can see at work two powerful factors that always undermine core curricula. One might be called philosophical—the view of liberal education as primarily the acquisition of intellectual skills—and the other psychological—the natural tendency of students to press for as much freedom of choice as possible.

Another powerful factor that also makes it difficult to sustain a core curriculum, and even more difficult to reinstate after it has been given up or reduced, is the power of academic disciplines as expressed programmatically in majors and reinforced by the dynamics of the academic profession. Most college and university faculty members enter the profession because they fall in love with a subject or discipline and want to spend their lives with it. The culminating degree for entry into the profession—usually the Ph.D.—is essentially certification that one is a professional researcher in a specialty. Continuing advancement as an academic professional in the world beyond one's immediate institution depends almost entirely on research that has led to publication. On the other hand, liberal arts colleges, while valuing scholarly expertise, place primary emphasis on the importance of teaching and mentoring students. The result is that faculty members often experience a degree of tension between, on the one hand, their initial sense of vocation, professional training, and the broader professional context, and, on the other hand, the needs and expectations of a college committed to providing a comprehensive liberal education. This tension is even greater when a college such as Eckerd expects its faculty to devote a significant amount of time to teaching interdisciplinary core courses.

Fortunately, some faculty come to identify primarily with an institution's core curriculum. But for the majority of faculty, the most congenial way to cope with this tension is through preserving significant involvement with their discipline. Here they can concentrate on the subject that drew them to the profession in the first place, work with students who also find the subject appealing, and even use information gathered in connection with their courses as a basis for scholarly publication. The result is that it is extremely difficult to persuade faculty who have been teaching within their field to shift time and effort to interdisciplinary core courses. This difficulty helps to account for the difference between the Eckerd curriculum of the 1960s and the curriculum that went into effect in 1980. The faculty members who taught the strong core curriculum of the 1960s were recruited for that purpose and shared the enthusiasm generated in creating a new institution. The college faculty of the 1980s had had a substantial period of time, facilitated by the revisions of Project '73, to build a strong set of majors in which they took pride and whose place in the curriculum they were reluctant to see diminished by an increase in core requirements.

As a result, the 1980 revision combined elements of the two earlier programs. The shift of the first-year core back to a focus on Western civilization, the restoration of a senior core on the Judeo-Christian tradition, and the reinstitution of a foreign language requirement were consistent with the spirit of the original curriculum. The opportunity for students to choose from among a range of perspective courses was reminiscent of the original curriculum's emphasis on content by virtue of specifying the value issues with which students must be familiar, but it was also consistent with Project '73's emphasis on opportunities for choice. The fact that the number of required core courses increased by only one ("Judeo-Christian Perspectives on Contemporary Issues") over the number required in Project '73 is indicative of the faculty's reluctance to reduce the time they and their students devoted to their disciplines.

One way to describe the 1980 revision is as a curriculum by consensus, perhaps the only possible outcome for a twenty-year-old institution with a diverse faculty and a tumultuous enrollment and curricular history. Another way to describe the revision is as a creative synthesis that balanced an emphasis on content with an emphasis on skills, combined a measure of freedom with a strong core experience at the beginning and at the end, sharpened and strengthened the focus on values education, and still left room for strong majors.

Confronting the Future

Throughout the 1990s, Eckerd College flourished. Enrollment increased modestly each year; SAT scores stayed close to 1200; the student body was truly national in character, with a strong international component; operating budgets were in balance; campus facilities expanded; new educational programs for adults brought the college national attention and generated substantial net revenues; and the college completed successfully the largest capital campaign in its history. Yet there has been an increasing sense that the college, like other independent liberal arts colleges—even the strongest—faces serious, possibly life-threatening challenges. Perhaps the most serious of these is the problem of high tuition. For two decades, cost increases at colleges like Eckerd have far surpassed the income increases of American wage earners. Enrollments at public institutions have soared as parents and students have begun to weigh the perceived value of a degree against its cost.

Closely related to the issue of cost is the challenge of changing demographics. The pool of potential applicants for colleges like Eckerd has been steadily shrinking since the 1970s. In 1995 less than 10 percent of SAT takers had combined SAT scores of 1000 or above and incomes of $70,000 or more. Nationally, this equaled only about 80,000 students. Of the students enrolled in private colleges in the 1990s (about 17 percent of total undergraduate enrollments), 40 percent are nontraditional, that is, students not likely to enroll on a full-time basis in full-service residential colleges. Moreover, the fastest rates of growth are among Asians, Hispanics, Native Americans, and African Americans—groups that, with the exception of Asians, have not typically been a significant portion of the residential private college applicant pool. Closely related to the issue of cost is a growing vocationalism. Parents and students, more than ever before, want an expensive college degree to lead to a well-paying job. This eye to the financial future affects students' choice of courses and major and creates increasing demands for career counseling, internships, and job placement. Compounding this pressure is the fact that for many the undergraduate degree is only a prelude to graduate study. In order to bear the additional cost of tuition for graduate school, parents and students now want to pay less for an undergraduate education.

Another major challenge has emerged in the 1990s: rapid and dramatic developments in educational technology that offer exciting new opportunities to improve student learning. They may also provide ways to make the personalized kind of education Eckerd offers more cost-effective. At the same time, the cost of acquiring, upgrading, and maintaining the infrastructure for such technology is substantial. Moreover, the pace of development in the future promises to be so rapid that it is difficult to determine in advance the wisest way to invest institutional resources. Other entities are already emerging—some outside traditional higher education—that are committed to offering prepackaged and distance-learning programs at prices far lower than typical residential college tuition. As a result, the rapid development of educational technology poses both great opportunities and serious challenges.

These challenges taken together underscore that the liberal arts college in the 2000s confronts a far more competitive environment than the college of the 1960s did, and is likely to do so for the foreseeable future. Eckerd competes with a large and diverse public sector ranging from community colleges, to relatively small, selective, academically strong, residential state colleges, to large state universities with honors colleges. Eckerd also competes with prestigious and comparably priced private colleges and universities with longer histories of excellence, larger and older networks of alumni and donors, and larger endowments. Like other traditional academic institutions, Eckerd will also face increased competition from for-profit enterprises that use their financial resources and the new communication technologies to develop a full range of educational services for the general public.

Increasingly aware of the need to respond to these challenges in the external environment, the college decided in 1993 to undertake a major review of the educational program. The purpose of the review was twofold: first, to determine what liberal arts college graduates in the twenty-first century need to know and be able to do, and second, in the light of this determination, to construct an educational program that will enable the college to respond effectively to challenges in the external environment.

The revised curriculum that emerged is, perhaps surprisingly, essentially a modification and strengthening of the curriculum approved in 1980. Once again, changes in the first-year core course encapsulate the nature of the revision as a whole. The title has been changed from "Western Heritage" to "Western Heritage in a Global Context." The course focuses on the cultural foundations of European-American civilization while taking into account some of the important contributions of other major cultures to the increasingly global civilization that constitutes the modern world.

Course materials continue to be representative selections from enduring classic and widely influential materials with due regard to the natural sciences as well as the social sciences, humanities, and the arts, and to the development of the Judeo-Christian tradition. Format and pedagogy remain a combination of classwide presentations and small discussion sections. The classwide presentations bring the entire first-year class, numbering between 350 and 400 students, together, typically on a Monday morning, for a plenary session in a teaching auditorium. Discussion sections are designed to follow up on these sessions and explore the assigned reading.

The course itself is organized around a series of themes: the hero, justice, truth, and the sacred in the fall semester; power, nature, freedom, and hope in the spring semester. For each theme there is an assigned reading from one or more classics in the Western tradition, accompanied by one or more classics from outside the West. The readings proceed in a roughly chronological order. For example, the course currently begins in the fall with readings from the *Odyssey,* Mencius, *Antigone, The Republic,* the Bible, and the *Tao Te Ching.* The course ends in the spring with readings from Basho, Hurston, Moltmann, Achebe, and King.

During the spring semester, the cadre of faculty who are scheduled to participate in the course the following year plans the syllabus under the direction of the associate dean of faculty for general education. A general understanding exists that there will be at least some continuity in the readings from year to year so that faculty members do not face a completely new set of texts each time. Nevertheless, there are always changes as faculty members learn what texts evoke the most thought, discover new texts, or revive old favorites. Changes also result from a continuing debate between those who prefer traditional classics and those who advocate more room for what they see as the underrepresented voices of women, minorities, and other marginalized groups. The debate is affected by the extent to which one perceives the West's cultural heritage as something to be celebrated or contested. The result, at Eckerd at least, has been what Martin Luther King, Jr., called creative tension: vigorous, productive debate among various perspectives and a constantly shifting consensus rather than stalemate or sharp division. In spite of differences over texts and topics, there seems to be general agreement that students need a deeper understanding of their cultural heritage, even if only to critique it, and that the most effective way to attain this is through serious intellectual encounters with substantial texts that are accessible to general readers.

The revised curriculum has added to the existing graduation proficiency requirements in writing, mathematics, and foreign language two more requirements: oral communication and information technology. Fulfillment of the new requirements is linked closely to the first-year core course. Faculty leaders of the "Western Heritage in a Global Context" discussion sections are to provide opportunities for students to develop oral presentation skills to meet a set of faculty-approved standards. Faculty leaders are also to provide opportunities for students to develop and document the ability to make use of electronic communication and to retrieve, use, and evaluate information gained in this way in pursuit of scholarly activity.

The contextualizing of Western, or what is now specified as European-American, civilization by the use of non-Western materials is clearly a response to the development of an increasingly global civilization, as well as the increasing ethnic and cultural diversity of college students. The integration of an information technology proficiency requirement into the course is a recognition of the growing importance of communication technology in general and its power to contribute to student learning. The active learning pedagogy that has always characterized the course relies more and more on e-mail, news groups, and use of the Internet.

From the beginning, persons appointed to the faculty have been expected to participate in teaching the general education program, including its first-year core course. Announcements of faculty positions include a reference to "willingness to participate in the college's values-oriented interdisciplinary general education program." A litmus test for finalists during the interview process is the question, "What is your reaction to teaching in the first-year core course on a regular basis?" The answer, of course, is almost always positive in one way or another, but search committees weigh carefully the thoughtfulness and enthusiasm of the response. For example, "Well, I have no objection," is not considered particularly impressive.

Faculty who teach in the first-year course participate in a week-long workshop immediately following spring commencement in order to prepare for the fall. They return for a two-day session immediately before Autumn Term. They also meet together weekly throughout each semester to discuss the assigned texts and develop teaching strategies for the week ahead. In recent years, participating faculty have received an extra stipend in recognition of these special responsibilities. Participation in the course is also given special consideration by the Academic Standards Committee, which evaluates faculty performance for promotion and tenure. Students' ratings of the course and of the quality of instruction in their particular section provide the committee with significant comparative data available nowhere else in the curriculum. Here one can see how students rate different instructors in essentially the same context. Strong or weak ratings are an important factor in personnel decisions.

It is significant that through several major revisions, the principle of universal faculty participation has remained. It is also true that some faculty are more enthusiastic than others and that universal participation requires sustained encouragement by the administration and faculty leadership. The personal and wider professional pull of disciplines remains strong. One of the great values of universal participation, a value sufficiently recognized by faculty over the years to sustain support of the principle, is as a source of academic community. The first-year core course is the intellectual meeting ground not only for students but for faculty as well. Here faculty have the opportunity to get to know one another better and to share different perspectives across boundaries that often divide the academic world. Many find this highly rewarding. The shared experience of teaching and mentoring in Foundations also serves to nourish a sense of responsibility for the curriculum as a whole and keeps the issues of learning and teaching at the forefront of community attention.

Still, the new curriculum's heightened expectations for mentoring, especially in the first-year program, have helped to make clear the need for a stronger program of faculty development. The immediate response has been the creation of a new position—associate dean for faculty development and intergenerational learning—to administer a program of expanded workshops on teaching and the inclusion in the capital campaign of funds to endow faculty development activities.

The latter part of the new dean's title recognizes the additional responsibility for facilitating interaction between faculty and members of the Academy of Senior Professionals at Eckerd College (ASPEC). This organization, founded in 1982, has more than two hundred carefully selected members who have retired from successful careers in a variety of fields and who make themselves available to the academic program as well as participate in a variety of other ASPEC programs. One of their most valuable roles is to serve as "discussant colleagues." They are carefully paired with faculty members, at the faculty member's request, to serve as class participants in discussion-based courses. Here again the first-year core course was the initial testing ground and has seen the program's most notable success. Faculty find the ASPEC members valuable catalysts in discussion, and students welcome the different points of view they often provide. ASPEC members serve as a further supplement to the mentoring program by offering students perspectives—and sometimes helpful contacts—based on a lifetime of experience.

The new curriculum has also made three important changes in the Perspectives section. The Cross-Cultural Perspective has been renamed the Global Perspective and redefined to mean courses that provide an encounter with "cultures and/or histories whose bases . . . or world views differ significantly from those of the Western European or North American tradition." To the four existing perspectives, in which courses are to be taken in the sophomore and junior years—the aesthetic, environmental, global, and social—a fifth has been added—the scientific—so that students will have at least one course that deals directly with the scientific method. The focus of the senior-year core course—"Judeo Christian Perspectives on Contemporary Issues"—has shifted from an examination of ethical responses to social issues to an exploration of meaning, purpose, and value. In the light of this shift, the course has been renamed "Quest for Meaning." The idea is to change the nature of the course from one that emphasizes applied ethics to one that explores underlying philosophies of life and systems of value. The goal is for students to attain a clearer sense of the relevance of the Judeo-Christian tradition as well as of other belief and value systems to perennial human concerns.

The most recent revision of the educational program is an attempt to strengthen the curriculum approved in 1980, which was itself an effort to synthesize the strongest and most popular features of the first two versions: the college's original curriculum and Project '73. Still, a number of people in the college community believe that the revisions do not go far enough and that the college needs to undertake more radical change. These calls for change tend to focus on the need to adapt more fully to the revolution in educational technology.

The college has already committed itself to a substantial investment in technological infrastructure. All student residence halls, faculty and administrative offices, the library, and many classrooms are now connected by fiber-optic cable and have access to the Internet. Students and faculty rely increasingly on electronic communication for teaching and learning. Sections of the core courses make more and more use of technology for communication between mentors and their student associates, for newsgroups, for research on various topics, and, of course, for word processing. The more ardent advocates of educational technology have called for even greater reliance on computers to provide information transfer in courses, especially at the introductory level, so that faculty are free to devote more time to individual guidance, especially at advanced levels. They envision a significantly different delivery system with a correspondingly significant change in the role of faculty. For the most part, current faculty are willing and, in many cases, eager to use the new technology, but many remain concerned that excessive reliance on it will depersonalize the kind of education that is one of Eckerd's strengths and that they themselves find most rewarding.

Assessing Student Response

What can be said about the effect of the core on the students for whose benefit the program is designed? One would expect student response to required courses to be less positive than their response to courses they choose, and student ratings of the core sequence have never on average been as high as the ratings for electives or courses in their major. On the other hand, core courses have generally rated well (no lower than 2 on a scale descending from 1 = excellent to 5 = poor), and students often rate their particular section of the core at the top of the scale. Students overall rate the most recent version of the freshman core, "Western Heritage in a Global Context," at 2.0. This compares with an average rating of 1.7 for all Eckerd courses.

The course that has always struggled most to elicit a positive student response has been the senior core. Here the inherent resistance to a required course is increased by the fact that it must be taken by seniors who are at the stage in their education when they want to focus on their individual interests and enjoy maximum freedom. Their resistance is compounded by a perception that it is a religion course with a moralistic direction ("I already know what my values are!"). Even so, the overall ratings for what was "Judeo-Christian Perspectives on Contemporary Issues" and is now called "Quest for Meaning" remain in the 2 range, and individual faculty and particular sections are often rated as excellent. The very fact that the college reinstituted such a senior-year course in the 1980s after the lapse of almost a decade and has decided to continue it in a revised version indicates the seriousness with which Eckerd takes its commitment to giving expression in the curriculum to its church-related mission.

Another interesting aspect of student response to the senior core is that the older students in the adult degree completion program (the Program for Experienced Learners) have always rated the course more highly than the traditional college-age students enrolled in the residential program. Those who have already had some experience of life's complexity apparently find the course a welcome opportunity to engage in reflection on fundamental ethical and social as well as personal issues.

Assessing objectively the effectiveness of an interdisciplinary core program that is unique to the institution is difficult. Questionnaires and exit interviews can provide insight, but no standardized measures are directly relevant. The closest the college has been able to come to a comparative assessment has been through its participation in the Higher Educational Data Sharing Consortium (HEDS) Senior Survey. HEDS consists of eighty-seven liberal arts schools defined as Baccalaureate One (national liberal arts colleges) under the Carnegie system of classifying institutions of higher education. In the survey administered to graduating seniors in 1997, Eckerd students consistently rated themselves "very satisfied" to "satisfied" or their capacity "moderately" to "greatly enhanced" with core curriculum–related aspects of their education (in comparison with other participants in the survey) (Table 5.1).

Although one should be cautious about interpreting these data, it seems clear that Eckerd students rate their educational experience positively in the areas most relevant to the core sequence. They are particularly appreciative of the quality of

Table 5.1. Comparison of Eckerd Student Response with Peer Group.

	Eckerd (Percentage)	Peer Group (Percentage)
Overall satisfaction with education	92	90
Academic advising	94	76
Humanities and the arts	95	95
Science and math	88	85
Social sciences	93	93
Skills and knowledge	93	91
Think analytically and logically	94	90
Relate to different peoples	69	64
Moral and ethical issues	76	74

academic advising, the enhancement of their general knowledge and basic skills, and their improved ability to think analytically and logically, cope with cultural diversity, and deal with moral and ethical issues.

Whatever the reaction of students may be, alumni of the college, especially those who have been out several years, tend to look back on the core sequences as among their most valuable educational experiences. Often they observe that they failed to appreciate them adequately at the time but now see how important they were. Contributing to this positive assessment is that these courses are the shared experiences that link them to their classmates, the faculty, and other generations of alumni. But it is also true that living longer usually brings them to the realization that the texts and themes of these courses are often the texts and themes that are central to their lives.

The Frail Vessels of Human Affection

Many gibes exist about revising a college curriculum. Perhaps the most notorious is the analogy to moving tombstones in a graveyard. Faculty are often criticized for being too slow and too self-serving to bring about necessary change. Students and alumni often declare that the most important things they learned in college were outside the classroom. Yet after many years as an academic dean, I would offer a more positive assessment. George Eliot once justified making young women the dynamic centers of her novels by noting, "In these frail vessels is borne onward through the ages the treasure of human affection." A curriculum, the particular structure for ordering the content of student learning, is also such a vessel. It may appear frail because changing conditions require constant revision. Still, it is the vessel, the primary carrier from one generation to the next of what we know and treasure, of what we believe, and for what we hope.

Throughout the history of Florida Presbyterian and Eckerd College, the general education program, particularly the core sequence, has been, to extend Eliot's metaphor, the prow of the college's vessel in a sea of changing circumstances. In its history one sees at work most clearly the direction of the college's education aspirations. One also sees how that direction has been adjusted in response to many different forces. No doubt these adjustments and revisions will go on as the college seeks to keep faith with its founding commitments to the liberal arts, to excellence, to a meaningful relationship with the church, and to be a pacesetting institution.

References
Bevan, J. "Florida Presbyterian College: New Adventure in Education." In W. H. Stickler (ed.), *Experimental Colleges.* Tallahassee: Florida State University Press, 1964.

Bulletin of Florida Presbyterian College. St. Petersburg, 1959.

"Coming of Age at Six," *Time,* Dec. 9, 1966.

Eckerd College Catalogue. St. Petersburg, Fla., 1976–77.

Chapter Six

The Humanities Program at Davidson College

Brian J. Shaw

As the Davidson Humanities Program approaches its fourth decade, it looks back on an illustrious past and ahead to a surely unsettled future. Inaugurated in 1962 as an intensive interdisciplinary program introducing first- and second-year students to the Western tradition from its beginnings in the ancient Near East to the present, Humanities (or "Humes") has established itself as a pillar of the curriculum, enjoying strong administrative support and a large and spirited student following. Nevertheless, faculty enthusiasm has recently waned. Persistent questions about Humanities' identity—Is it a great books program or an extended Western civilization course?—compounded by growing skepticism among the program's faculty about either project and increasing demands on them to engage in disciplinary research, have provoked an inescapable crisis. As a recent external examiners' report declares, "The original idealism and vision that created the program some thirty years ago no longer exists." Indeed, the report continues, "Most [faculty] participants hate the program more than they love it, and see no guiding intellectual purpose to the enterprise" (Hoag and Riesenberg, 1997, p. 1).

To rekindle enthusiasm by offering a new generation the opportunity to claim ownership of a program conceived decades ago and in important respects unaltered since, a recent

Humanities task force recommends that instructors be offered increased autonomy to shape their sections and draw on their own disciplinary training and perspectives. Davidson's administration, too, in concert with Humes staff, has undertaken to relieve the program of its traditionally heavy burden as the principal avenue for introducing the college's 1,600 students to close work with faculty in small group settings. In place of a program serving approximately one-third of first- and second-year students, a smaller Humes now forms but one component of a new and comprehensive array of first-year seminars. Nonetheless, if few faculty envision Humanities as continuing to occupy its traditionally preeminent place in Davidson's curriculum, many still believe that the need remains for a two-year, interdisciplinary program to introduce at least some students to the signal ideas and events that have shaped European and U.S. cultures. The challenge facing Davidson is to forge a new vision around which an increasingly diverse faculty grown estranged from the pedagogy and interests of their predecessors can enthusiastically unite.

Origins of the Program

Davidson's Humanities Program, like others that emerged during the 1960s at other southern liberal arts colleges associated with the Presbyterian church, both borrowed freely from the celebrated "Man" course at Southwestern at Memphis (now Rhodes College) and enjoyed the vigorous support of the church's Division of Higher Education (Vest, 1996, p. 139). As such, from the beginning Humes sought not only to provide an alternative to the increasingly technical character of much of American higher education at mid-century, but also to emphasize the centrality of biblical faith and Christian culture within a genuinely liberal education. Toward these ends, the program's founder, Daniel D. Rhodes, who came to Davidson College, in Davidson, North Carolina, from Southwestern at Memphis in 1960 as professor of religion and philosophy with the mandate to establish Humanities, recruited colleagues from a variety of departments. Once assembled, they devised an inaugural syllabus for the first year divided into five study units: "Prehistory and the Ancient Near East," "The Old Testament Period," "The Greek Period," "The Roman Period and Christian

Beginnings," and "The Medieval Period" (*Humanities 11–12*, 1962–63, p. v).

As David Kaylor (personal communication, July 1998), a professor of religion who joined Humanities in 1965, attests, faculty participants expressly conceived the program as an attempt to integrate diverse scholarly disciplines and "as a matter of course" framed this endeavor within a "Christian liberal arts context." Rhodes and his colleague in Humes from the department of Bible and religion, Max Polley, were ordained Presbyterian ministers, and the other four members of the inaugural program, drawn from the departments of philosophy, classics, history, and English, were all active members of the Presbyterian or Methodist church. Indeed, Rhodes and Polley incorporated into the first two semesters of Humanities enough of the two mandatory Bible courses they taught that students could apply their participation in Humes toward the college's graduation requirement in biblical study. Like their colleagues at other church-related colleges, Humes faculty resolved to emphasize the Hebrew and Christian contributions to "Western civilization" not simply as a remote cultural inheritance but as a vibrant contemporary presence.

If the program's founders conceived Humes as an enterprise marked indelibly by a Christian (and especially Reformed) faith, so too did they view as central the program's interdisciplinary nature. Like others who rejected the growing compartmentalization of American higher education by embracing alternatives such as Chicago's and Columbia's great books courses and the general education movement, Rhodes and his colleagues insisted on the inescapable interrelatedness of knowledge. Thus from the beginning Humes presented a syncretic view of the diverse intellectual tributaries coalescing throughout the centuries to form an identifiable "Western tradition." The introduction to the 1962–63 syllabus announces this unmistakably and declares the following as the program's guiding assumptions:

(a) that the modern educative process has been too concerned with training the specialist rather than educating the whole man; (b) that even undergraduate liberal arts education has been tempted to multiply courses beyond necessity and to overdepartmentalize; (c) that excessive use of the analytic method has

contributed to an unnecessary fragmentation of knowledge; (d)
that synthesis can and should accompany analysis, even at the freshman and sophomore levels; (e) that the past, present, and future
are inextricably intertwined; and (f) that the life and achievements
of Western man can and should be seen in meaningful patterns.
[*Humanities 11–12,* 1962–63, p. v]

Indeed, lest students miss the full pedagogical and philosophical import of this explicitly narrative account of European (and
later, in the second-year program, North American) culture and
society, the syllabus numbers among Humes's benefits a "sense of
the meaning and organic unity of the Western tradition" and a
"grasp of the meaning of human existence" (p. iv). Organizationally, in the program's daily operations these same presuppositions
provided staff members a framework within which to structure
what might otherwise have appeared as a bewildering array of
assigned readings drawn from no fewer than eighty primary and
secondary texts. From the first semester's exploration of *Gilgamesh*
through the second semester's concluding reading of *The Canter-
bury Tales,* Humes recounted an expansive tale of progressive development culminating in the medieval "attempt to synthesize the
Graeco-Roman and the Judeo-Christian traditions into a Christian
Europe" (p. v).

To aid staff members themselves to perceive the "meaningful
patterns" woven throughout the Western tradition, Humes faculty
met daily to allow participants with expert knowledge of the materials under study to share it with colleagues and provide questions
for upcoming class discussions. As George Labban, a professor of
classical studies who taught in Humes during that first year, recalls,
participating in faculty study sections, as well as meeting with students six days each week—twice as often as other courses, since
each semester of Humes counted as a double course—was an
extraordinarily enriching as well as arduous experience. Not having hitherto ventured extensively beyond his own field, teaching
in Humes was "an incredible experience" that indelibly impressed
on him the "inescapably interdisciplinary nature of all knowledge."
Indeed, Labban viewed his dual role as alternately expert and amateur not as a weakness but rather as one of Humanities' greatest
assets. Labban gratefully attributes to his years in Humes both his

acquaintance with previously unfamiliar materials and, even better, his deepened appreciation of the role that classical authors played in shaping patristic and medieval literatures (personal communication, July 1998).

Although taught by a different group of faculty members, the capstone year of Humanities, "The Western Tradition from the Renaissance to the Twentieth Century," offered initially in 1963–64, shared the guiding assumptions and organizational structure of the first year's program. Chaired by Bradley Thompson of the history department, Humanities 21–22 assembled two historians, a political scientist, an English professor, and two professors of religion. Supplementing them were guest lecturers from the departments of art history and economics. Like the staff of Humanities 11–12, Thompson and his colleagues offered an inclusive sweep of the signal events and cultural achievements of the Western tradition, alternating in roughly equal measure formal lectures for all of their approximately 90 students (out of a sophomore class of about 250 students) with small group discussions. Indeed, the second year encompassed no fewer than eight thematic sections, from "The Emergence of the Modern Political and Economic Structure" to "The Later Nineteenth Century." During the year's 180 class meetings, participants read selections of works by more than ninety authors, both primary and secondary, from Machiavelli's *Prince* to Kierkegaard's *Fear and Trembling*. Although the second year's staff limited its examination of the Western tradition to just five centuries in contrast to the three millennia explored in the first year, their perspective was no less broad and integrative.

In addition to sharing with the first-year program a thematic organization and narrative sweep, and actually giving rise to these similarities, was a common set of pedagogical, moral, and spiritual convictions. As the 1963–64 syllabus declares, overly specialized curricula, such as those increasingly prevalent in American higher education after the world wars, ran the risk of producing technicians unable to see beyond the cramped confines of their own fields. Such a situation, the second-year staff believed, threatened a lamentable educational loss, since "the well educated man must have as the heart of his learning a broad understanding of the humanities." Worse yet, it exposed both students and society at large to frightening existential and political perils. As Thompson and his colleagues cautioned, "If we do not see beyond our own horizons, we lose all identity as individuals and end like those in the *Brave New World* without History, Literature, Religion, Philosophy or Science, confined to the performance of merely technological tasks." On the contrary, they warned, "Man must know himself and his tradition in order to be free" (*Humanities 21–22, 1963–64,* p. lii).

Also prompting the two staffs, and with them Davidson's trustees and administration, to embrace such a comprehensive program deeply imbued with moral and spiritual purposes was the college's desire to facilitate the achievement of its traditional educational goals. As a church-related institution dedicated since its founding in 1835 to educating the "whole man" (Davidson did not admit women as degree candidates until the 1970s), the college had always demanded that students complete a rigorous set of core courses. In 1962–63 these included a year's study of freshman composition, a year-long survey of English literature, two courses in Bible, two in religion, a year of mathematics, two years of foreign language, a year of natural science, and a two-semester Western civilization course. Participation in the new Humanities program allowed students to satisfy all of the history requirement and no less than three-quarters of those in English, religion and Bible. Thus, introducing Humes helped students meet an extensive set of core requirements and allowed the college to reaffirm its long-standing convictions that education "for technical mastery alone is only partial education" and that to "professional skills must be added moral integrity and spiritual awareness" (*The Davidson College Reference Catalogue, 1962–63,* p. 18). Like the first curriculum adopted in 1838 mandating rigorous instruction in Latin and Greek (electives were not available until the 1870s), course offerings during the 1960s, including the new Humanities Program, faithfully heeded the admonitions of Robert Hall Morrison, Davidson's first president. Far from being divorced from each other and from moral virtues, Morrison admonished, "religion and education" must "blend their influences" to "promote order, temperance, justice, benevolence, faith, humility, and holiness" (quoted in Beaty, 1988, pp. 3–4; see also Shaw, 1923).

Subsequent Developments

During the years immediately following Humanities' inauguration, both years' staffs undertook minor syllabus revisions in response to their initial experiences. (They did so independently, since Humes functioned without a program chair until 1984.) These consisted primarily of efforts to trim the number and length of readings and writing assignments. As Daniel Rhodes recalls, during the summer of 1963 he and his colleagues "had to revise the syllabus . . . in light of some remaining unrealistic expectations" (quoted in Vest, 1996, p. 156). Even if Humes did meet six days a week and accounted for fully half of students' course work during their first two years, demands remained formidable. The 1962–63 syllabus called for students to read excerpts from no fewer than eighty books; a decade later the 1974–75 syllabus listed required readings from almost seventy—despite the fact that during the intervening years the number of available class days had fallen as a consequence of college-wide calendar changes from 180 annually to 150. Similarly, while the 1962–63 syllabus required students each semester to complete four in-class exams, seven two-page papers, and one "library" paper of eight to ten pages, the 1974–75 first-year syllabus demanded six reviews, eight longer themes, and one research paper of twelve to fourteen pages. In fact, as these very minor alterations indicate, Humes changed relatively little during its first dozen years. Assignments remained substantial, course readings were still organized chronologically, and class meetings alternated between large group lectures and smaller seminar discussions. Finally, unchanged too was Humes's interdisciplinary and narrative structure, as well as its substantial inclusion of biblical and other religious writings.

If organizational and thematic changes during Humanities' first two decades remained minor and few, however, the years since have witnessed a number of developments, testifying not only to the program's continued pride of place in Davidson's curriculum but also to growing pedagogical controversies. Humes's transition, in fact, from an enterprise uniting a fiercely loyal faculty and students to one still enjoying considerable student support but beset by chronic staffing problems, a diminished sense of common purpose, and abiding disagreements about how—and even whether—to continue it, is one that emerges in even a brief recounting of its development. No special events in themselves announce the division of this history into clearly demarcated periods, but an admittedly arbitrary division of the program's thirty-six years into three equal segments usefully lends some narrative unity of its own. This division also coincides, if only fortuitously, with at least a few signal events.

Humanities, 1962–1974

The first development of consequence during the program's first twelve years was the college's adoption of the so-called Blue Sky Curriculum for the 1968–69 academic year. The new curriculum not only abandoned Davidson's traditional semester system with its six-day class weeks for a new trimester calendar with no Saturday morning classes but also inaugurated a substantially less structured curriculum. Most notably, and considerably affecting Humes, the new curriculum reduced the twelve-hour (four-course) requirement in Bible and religion, including mandatory courses in "The Old Testament" and "The New Testament," to the completion of just two courses in the renamed department of religion. It also reduced the required semesters of English composition from two to one, and awarded credit for two courses (of a total of three) needed for graduation in the new social science curricular division to students completing Humes. In other words, the total number of class days available to the now six-term, rather than four-semester, program not only decreased from 360 to 300, but the mandate for Humes to satisfy a substantial portion of an extensive graduation requirement in biblical studies disappeared. In response to the first change, both years' staffs set about trimming the program's assignments to fit the new format. Rather than undertaking any fundamental reorganization, "the work done at that time was essentially a matter of paring" (Rhodes and Maloney, 1977, p. 1). As for the second change, the relaxed college mandate in Bible and religion led both Humes teams, and especially the first-year staff, progressively to reduce the number of class meetings allotted to them. Thus if the 1962–63 syllabus devoted thirty sessions to the "Old Testament Period," that of 1974–75 allotted just twenty-one. For its part, the second-year staff, which during

1963–64 spent sixteen sessions studying Reformation theology and history, dedicated half as many in 1975–76.

It is important to note that Humes's organizational and pedagogical continuity during these twelve years, like the relative diminution of biblical and religious studies itself, echoed broader developments throughout the college and higher education generally. Curricular reform was very much on the agenda nationally as colleges liberalized graduation requirements, welcomed an increasingly diverse student body onto their campuses, and deemphasized their traditional missions as molders of upright, and usually Christian, character (Marsden, 1994). In this spirit the *1968–69 Davidson Reference Catalogue* (p. 14) announced the new curriculum as an exciting occasion to "provide flexibility, challenge, and opportunities for increased student responsibility" within a variety of educational "tracks," including even an "independent study track" permitting students to forgo supervised participation in regular courses and determine their own course of study. The impetus for all these changes emerged from the college's new conviction that "the strength of the liberal arts college of the future lies in a demonstrated willingness to innovate and to hold the student primarily responsible for his own education." Davidson's longstanding conviction precisely to the contrary—that a fixed curriculum with no or very few electives best allows faculty to inculcate in students not just special competencies but explicitly moral virtues like "temperance, justice, benevolence [and] faith"—was now, if not absent, at least considerably in abeyance.

And indeed, the reduction in time devoted to the study of religion in Humes and in the curriculum at large mirrored sweeping changes in campus life. By 1969 compulsory daily chapel services were abolished. Just a few years later, in 1972 and 1974, the faculty recommended that non-Christians be eligible for tenure; final trustee agreement came in 1977 when the college bylaws were amended to welcome as permanent faculty "non-Christian persons who can work with respect for the Christian tradition even if they cannot conscientiously join it" (Beaty, 1988, pp. 384, 394). At the same time that students and faculty were becoming denominationally more diverse, they also became more racially and sexually heterogeneous. After years of faculty appeals, Davidson's trustees in 1970 undertook the racial integration of the college, calling on the president to "enroll students from a variety of racial, economic, social and geographical backgrounds" (Beaty, 1988, p. 395). Just two years later the trustees voted, again with overwhelming faculty support, to admit women as degree candidates. Given the extent of these changes, Humes itself could not remain unaltered, although their consequences for the program's reading lists and format remained inconclusive. As it happened, the diminished role of biblical and Christian materials in both years of Humanities was hardly matched by a proportional introduction of materials reflecting new concerns and perspectives. No text assigned in 1973–74, for instance, was authored by a woman, and the first-year syllabus still declared to an audience now containing women students the program's continued dedication to "educating the whole man." Similarly, only two of Humes's three hundred class meetings during that year were devoted to the study of "non-Western cultures" (two lectures in the first year examining "Byzantium and the Rise of Islam" and "Islam and Its Bid for the West"). The latter session recommended only as optional reading excerpts from the Qur'an. On the other hand, while leaving non-Western and women's perspectives unrepresented, the second-year staff required students to read works by Martin Luther King, Jr., and Huey Newton.

Despite these modest developments in Humes and the larger ones taking place throughout the college, however, the program remained essentially unchanged. In particular, its foundational demand for synthesizing, interdisciplinary knowledge to make explicit the "meaningful patterns" in the "life and achievements of Western man" remained unaltered, and despite the need to squeeze the program into an abbreviated calendar, both its narrative structure and comprehensive, thematic organization remained constant. So did its staff's vigorous commitment, with a steady core of seven faculty members regularly devoting fully half their teaching efforts to Humanities and another seven ordinarily committing a third (*Humanities Program Self-Study Report,* 1974, p. 1). Six of the eight faculty teaching first-year Humes in 1973–74 were, in fact, the program's founding fathers.

Constant too was students' tremendous enthusiasm for the program, as gauged by both growing enrollments and surveys of junior and senior Humes alumni. Accordingly, by 1974, increasing demand had prompted the college to expand the number of sections in each year from the original six to eight and to offer as well an advanced independent study option for a limited number of seniors. That same year the *Davidson College Self-Study Report* (p. 131) recommended that Humes prepare to expand beyond eight sections in order to guarantee the program's availability to at least 40 percent of the incoming class. A working paper written by Professor Sam Maloney just two years earlier at the request of the dean of the faculty, John Bevan, even explored the possibility of requiring Humanities as a core graduation requirement. In the face of formidable staffing challenges and the general trend begun in 1968 toward increased curricular flexibility, this proposal provoked little enthusiasm, but it and a 1974 program self-study, as well as steadily increasing enrollments, all revealed impressive student support. So, finally, did quantitative surveys of 1968 and 1973, which revealed that more than 93 percent of Humes alumni "would recommend the program to others and would take it again if they had the opportunity" (*Humanities Program Self-Study Report*, 1974, p. 3). Clearly, if Humanities did not change in essential ways during this time, there arguably was little reason to. Students and faculty alike remained fiercely loyal to its pedagogy and aspirations.

Humanities, 1974–1986

The first, more or less subterranean rumblings of faculty dissatisfaction with Humes emerged during the next twelve years, from about 1974 until 1986. Most striking, along with the continuing diminution of class sessions devoted to religion, this period witnessed the infusion into both years of new instructors increasingly less inclined to embrace the methods and concerns of the program's founders. Rhodes, the originator and sole director of the first-year program from 1962 until 1980, retired in 1984, and of the 1986–87 first-year staff, only Kaylor and Polley remained from the program's early years. Eight of the fifteen staff members that year, in fact, were assistant professors, some hired under the auspices of a grant from the Andrew W. Mellon Foundation explicitly to recruit new faculty. Others joined in order to meet departmental obligations to the program. Only three staff members were full professors with extensive experience. Indeed, during the next decade, no fewer than nine of these fifteen faculty would withdraw from the program, either permanently or for extended periods, many for reasons deriving at least in part from profound reservations about its pedagogy and organization.

Not coincidentally, some junior faculty already teaching in Humes or contemplating joining it harbored real concerns about the adverse consequences of participation for their scholarly productivity and professional security. Teaching outside their normal competence in such a time-consuming enterprise did little, after all, to enhance their status in an increasingly precarious job market. Although excellence in teaching remained the preeminent qualification for tenure at Davidson, an accomplished publishing record became progressively necessary to secure tenure at Davidson and elsewhere. As a 1983 outside consultants' report documents, Humes faculty were by now a younger and more diverse group and much more likely "to challenge rather than to accept inherited patterns of institutional organization . . . and settled patterns of intellection." They were also, the report notes, "'market-conscious' in a way that older faculty members can scarcely credit" (Levich, Martin, and Rabb, 1983, p. 3). Perhaps not surprising, this potent mixture of scholarly skepticism and professional anxiety eventually collided with the determination of some senior staff to resist substantial changes in a program in which they had invested so much, a collision that eventually prompted some untenured members to withdraw their loyalty. Regular weekly meetings to discuss and revise course readings still took place, but often more uneasily. Some junior faculty were reluctant to jeopardize their close personal as well as professional relations with senior members, and in some cases, they even feared adverse consequences for their tenure prospects should they challenge the program's fundamental structure and purposes too vigorously. All of these developments inaugurated a new period, lasting into the present, of chronic and occasionally acute staffing difficulties, especially in the first-year component.

One indication of the marked generational divide emerging during this period is the stark contrast between the conclusions of two Humanities reports presented just six years apart to the new dean of the faculty, T. C. Price Zimmermann. The first, *Summary Report on the Humanities Restudy,* authored by Rhodes and Maloney of the department of religion, summarizes the recommendations of twenty staff members who met during the summer of 1977 to evaluate the program and suggest ways to improve it. As Maloney and Rhodes report, faculty during these five weeks sought to verbalize the "unstated assumptions" guiding the program, including the mandate to educate "the whole person" and to impart "knowledge of the sources of our culture." They reaffirmed too as central program aims the "discernment of patterns in the western intellectual tradition" and "an awareness of the interrelatedness of all knowledge" (Rhodes and Maloney, 1977, p. 3). On the basis of these conclusions, staff members resolved to make minor changes in approximately 30 percent of the assigned readings, revise daily study guide questions, and adjust "the amount of time and attention given to various disciplines." Rhodes and Maloney presented these revisions as the products of "the first total faculty rethinking of the whole program since its inception." Certainly, nowhere in the report did they indicate that the staff perceived a need to change Humes's guiding principles or organization or that they harbored doubts about its fundamental good health.

The second report, authored just five years later by three outside consultants invited to campus by Davidson's administration, offers a strikingly different portrait of the program. Not content, as were the participants of the 1977 summer workshop, to equate a robust reaffirmation of Humes's traditional assumptions and goals, together with minor revisions in readings and lectures, with its "total rethinking," these authors spoke of Humes's accomplishments exclusively in the past tense. In the present they described only an imposing array of problems and shortcomings. In particular, along with the persistent skepticism of some younger faculty about the program's pedagogy and organization, the report's authors, including Ted Rabb, a Princeton University historian, and Marvin Levich, a professor of aesthetics at Reed College, inventoried a formidable list of weaknesses, including the following:

- The reluctance of some departments "to participate vigorously in the program"
- Humanities' "only adventitiously interdisciplinary" character
- The superficiality inherent in Humanities' commitment to "coverage" and its consequent reliance on reading brief and fragmentary excerpts
- Inadequate instruction in English composition

Rather dismissively characterizing Humes as "a history-of-ideas affair" offering students little beyond a "skeleton . . . of facts" and "a name-and-identity awareness of intellectual monuments of the western tradition," the consultants urged the college to undertake a "serious re-examination" of its methods and aspirations and to begin a process of "experimentation" in order to revise them fundamentally. One experiment they recommended was to halve the number of students in Humanities and complement it with a "parallel course" in which "the major work . . . would occur in the discussion sections, each of which . . . would choose its own documents and define its own interest, thereby making the most of whatever experience and talents its leaders have" (Levich, Martin, and Rabb, 1983, pp. 4,6).

Predictably, many senior faculty vigorously repudiated the report's findings. But Davidson's administration, along with many junior faculty whose allegiance was less to a program conceived two decades ago than to the specialized disciplines in which they had recently been trained, did not. As a consequence, shortly after receiving the consultants' report, Zimmermann announced that the "imminent departure from the course of some key founding members" provided an apt occasion "to recapture the spirit of innovation by means of a major revision which will have the participation and hence the loyalty of a new generation of teachers." In the same memo, he announced the creation of a new post of program director to assume administrative responsibility for the entire program, as well as his and President Spencer's choice to fill it. Later, he made known the administration's plans to submit as part of the revision process a proposal to the National Endowment for the Humanities (NEH). That proposal (which proved successful) included among its provisions a summer workshop, the appointment of two distinguished visiting scholars, and new opportunities for faculty to audit the program before joining (Zimmermann, 1983; see also Spencer, 1983).

In the end, however, despite the likely prospect of these measures to reinvigorate Humes and make teaching it more attractive, staff members responded more energetically to the dean's proposal to reorganize the program administratively than to his calls for a "major revision" of its pedagogy and methods. Heatedly denouncing the administration for initiating both the reorganization and the NEH grant process without adequate prior consultation, most senior faculty and even many junior members demanded the recision of each. Unfortunately, in the uproar over these essentially procedural and jurisdictional issues, the original summons issued by the administration and the outside consultants to recast Humanities in ways that would ignite the enthusiasm of younger members was effectively ignored. The concerns of junior faculty in particular, to which the dean's memo had originally appealed, were thrust aside by the altered terms and participants of this new debate. For their part, many senior faculty, echoing the "Rethinking" of 1977, confidently declared the program fundamentally sound and in no way in need of substantial revision. In their favor, they could point to the subsequent success of the NEH application, "Strengthening the Humanities at Davidson College," whose ultimate version they, and not the administration, eventually determined, as well as to additional quantitative surveys of Humes alumni conducted in 1976 and 1982, which, like their predecessors, revealed persistent student enthusiasm (*Humanities Program Self-Study Report,* 1976, p. 3; *Humanities Survey 1989*). Consequently, despite by now chronic staffing difficulties and the estrangement of many junior faculty, very little changed in either Humes's organization or its guiding principles. In the light of future events, it appears that a signal opportunity to address these concerns had been lost.

Humanities, 1986–

If the concluding years of Humanities' middle period saw little substantive change, subsequent ones witnessed crucial developments whose cumulative effects have made unavoidable a definitive reckoning with the program's deep-seated tensions. Among these, in particular, are three that together have prompted an open crisis: additional calendar changes mandating a significantly diminished number of class sessions available to accomplish the program's still quite ambitious goals, loudly voiced and no longer subterranean dissatisfaction with Humanities' guiding principles, and acute staffing difficulties. Indeed, indications of a crisis include yet another highly critical report by external examiners in 1997 and a contemporary survey of staff members confirming their lackluster enthusiasm (Hoag and Riesenberg, 1997; *Humanities Faculty Survey,* 1997). Signs include as well, and strikingly so, a request by seven of the eight members of the department of religion to deny Humes students credit toward the college's graduation requirement in religion. Humanities, the signers argue, offers "mere exposure . . . to a limited range of religious texts" and does "little to challenge stereotypical and prejudicial understandings of religion generally, and Jewish and Christian traditions in particular." Worse, they allege, absent genuinely "critical treatment" by scholars "trained in a particular discipline" and presented instead by "teachers with little or no expertise," religious texts "fall prey to readings that are at best banal, and at worst trivializing" (Csikszentmihalyi and others, 1997). The bare familiarity that Humes students gain, they declare, hardly substitutes for the knowledge and competencies obtained by those completing departmental offerings.

That professors of religion should feel so alienated from a program shaped by a previous generation from their own discipline speaks volumes about the program's current woes. Participation in Humes, after all, once provided students the equivalent of three courses toward Davidson's then–four-course religion requirement. But at least as revealing as this dissatisfaction is the argument offered to justify it: one alleging a fatal lack of competence by instructors from other departments to teach religious materials. An earlier generation led by members of the department of Bible and religion had championed Humes as a welcome alternative to increased academic specialization. In the view of Humanities' founding generation, Humes sought to combat the "fragmentation of knowledge" and the tendency to "over-departmentalize" that accompanies the contemporary concern "with training the specialist rather than the whole man" (*Humanities 11–12,* 1962–63, p. iii). Now, on the contrary, members of that department insistently distance themselves from Humes precisely because the knowledge it imparts is insufficiently grounded in the specialized methods and perspectives of their discipline.

The developments precipitating this remarkable reversal arguably stem not from any qualitatively new or unanticipated events after 1986, but rather from a steady exacerbation of the problems already present then. For one, Davidson's return in the 1988–89 academic year to the semester calendar abandoned two decades earlier with the adoption of the Blue Sky Curriculum, together with the reluctance of Humes staff and other faculty to continue the program as a sequence of five-day-a-week courses in a curriculum now comprising two- or three-day-a-week courses, inevitably necessitated yet another reduction in the number of available sessions. Thus, from a six-term program comprising 300 sessions, Humanities shrank in 1988 to a four-semester sequence providing the equivalent of five semesters' meetings: 225. (During the first and last semesters, the program met three times per week, and during the middle two, it met for four and a half sessions per week.) Just a few years later, in 1992, the staff abandoned this cumbersome arrangement, and Humes shrank again to a normal four-course sequence, thereby reducing the number of class meetings to just 180. In other words, by the 1992–93 academic year Humanities had available just 60 percent of the sessions it had had five years earlier and precisely half the number it had enjoyed at the program's start. Yet during this time its goal of offering students a comprehensive sweep of the Western tradition from its beginnings in the ancient Near East to the twentieth century remained essentially unaltered. Not surprisingly, the temptation to provide an even more hurried examination of the key events, texts, and "meaningful patterns" of almost four millennia became an inescapable mandate. If the 1983 outside evaluators' report already chided Humes for its historical superficiality and reliance on reading brief excerpts rather than entire works, these defects grew progressively more severe as the mismatch between the program's expansive goals and shrinking opportunities to meet them inexorably grew. With Humes's reduction from the equivalent of eight courses to just four, not only many junior faculty, but some senior members too, joined an ever-louder chorus lamenting the program's superficiality and lack of coherence.

Even without these strains imposed by college-wide calendar changes, the increasing faculty disaffection with Humanities' fundamental assumptions would likely have continued and even intensified. Most dramatically fueling disillusionment with what the outside evaluators in 1983 had termed Humes's "settled patterns of intellection" has been the progressively diminished currency of the "grand narrative" underlying the program. Articulated not simply in informal protests but also in a number of position papers written in 1997 by Humanities instructors at the administration's invitation, this disillusionment strikes at the heart of the program's pedagogy. Nor, quite significantly, is it any longer confined to the junior ranks. On the contrary, as one senior English professor argues, Humes's "very outmoded conception of a cultural narrative" neither speaks convincingly to the scholarly convictions of current faculty nor prompts students to "interrogate and challenge" the wide variety of issues raised by course readings (Gibson, 1997). Another Humanities instructor, a tenured historian, argues that the "naïve . . . definition of 'Western Civilization' which is *implicit* (although never really articulated) in the course" not only stymies critical examination of course materials but actively misleads. Participants, he laments, "march forward from the Greeks and Hebrews through the Romans to medieval Europe, and thence, of course, to the modern West, as if that were the fundamental narrative structure of the past" (Berkey, 1997).

Significantly, and just as worrisome for Humes's continuation in anything like its current form, little of this dissatisfaction can be attributed to a narrow—and as some senior members hope, fashionably fleeting—infatuation with postmodernism. On the contrary, while Lyotard, Derrida, Foucault, and others undoubtedly have left their impress on some faculty, this disaffection sinks considerably deeper and more diverse roots. In the language of the inaugural syllabus, a program dedicated since its inception almost four decades ago to tracing the allegedly "meaningful patterns" woven throughout the "life and achievements of Western man" cannot expect to speak to the scholarly concerns and disciplinary allegiances of most faculty who have come of age within the last two. Not just the postmodern "incredulity towards metanarratives" (Lyotard, 1989, p. xxiv), but the myriad influences of feminism, cultural theory, and non-Western studies on all fields, as well as developments peculiar to each discipline, have worked to estrange many faculty from the core assumptions and methods of the program's founders.

Anyone doubting this need only inventory the research interests of current Humes faculty or, better yet, contrast the kinds of courses they and their departmental colleagues offer now with those available a generation ago. A quick perusal of the 1962–63

Davidson catalogue reveals that courses in religion then focused overwhelmingly on the study of the Bible, church history, and Protestant theology. On the contrary, only a slender majority of those listed in the *1998–99 Announcements* center exclusively on Hebrew or Christian topics. Separate courses examining the Hindu, Islamic, Buddhist, and Daoist traditions, together with others exploring religious practices and beliefs from a variety of faiths, are nearly as plentiful. Indeed, many of the courses that still examine Christian and Hebrew topics bear little resemblance to their predecessors, exploring instead novel topics like "Autobiography and Religion," "Woman and Body in the Christian Tradition," and "Poets, Prophets and Priests." By the same token, although for decades faculty in the department of English organized courses principally into canonical and chronological groupings, traditional offerings like "Shakespeare" or "American Literature to 1900" now compete for student interest with "Caribbean Literature," "Film as Narrative Art," and "Studies in Literature by Women." Courses in other departments are similarly heterogeneous and, not surprisingly, just as little receptive to the grandly narrative assumptions still undergirding Humanities.

In the context of all these developments, the tumultuous events of 1997 and 1998 really ought not to surprise anyone: the dramatic request of the religion department to withdraw religion credit from the program; the scathing 1997 external examiners' report (Hoag and Riesenberg, 1997, p. 1) characterizing Humanities (in the words of its own staff) as "'a shell of a program,' 'adrift,' 'inert,'" and "'without an identifiable focus or will'"; a survey indicating little faculty confidence in the program's ability to develop students' capacities to read and think critically; and the need to reduce the first-year program beginning in 1998–99 to just six sections (a total of 88 students from a first-year class of 472) due to the diminishing number of faculty members willing to teach the program. On the contrary, in the context of both a steadily shrinking calendar within which to accomplish Humes's goals and the growing faculty estrangement from them revealed by the 1983 program self-study, these dramatic events are perhaps not so much unexpected as overdue. A small minority of faculty still respond to Humes's woes by declaring it "a stable . . . part of the Davidson curriculum" and dismissing "challenges to its fitness" as "idiosyncratic and/or politically motivated" (Manning, 1997). Such claims, however, convince few. More plausible is the recent verdict of the external examiners that Humanities "is a weary operation and some of those involved can't or won't see how weary it is" (Hoag and Riesenberg, 1997, p. 1).

Yet even this conclusion is hardly as definitive as many critics believe. For if the sometimes traumatic events of the late 1990s prompted a crisis, its resolution remains undecided. Chronic disaffection surely exists, but so does a sizable reservoir of staff loyalty and enthusiasm. Thus, when critics point to the 1997 external examiners' report and other recent documents and events to establish the severity of Humes's deficiencies, program supporters hail just as enthusiastically some genuinely impressive achievements. Preeminent among these is the establishment of the E. Craig Wall, Jr., Distinguished Teaching Professorship of Humanities, a position made possible by the award in 1993 of another major NEH program grant. Together with large private gifts to the college, this award supports a rotating chair to honor outstanding Humes instructors and facilitate the entry into the program of new faculty. In addition, Humes advocates can cite quantitative surveys in 1989 and 1997, which, like consistent enrollment figures, indicate continuing strong student support. Finally, and just as important, program defenders invoke the steadfast commitment of Davidson's administration. Like his predecessor, John Kuykendall, who retired as president in 1997 to assume teaching duties in the department of religion—and significantly, in Humanities too—Davidson's new head, Robert Vagt, remains an outspoken program advocate. A Humes alumnus himself and the father of two program alumnae, Vagt calls Humes a "seminal course" that "continues to be roundly endorsed by . . . those who have marked its effect upon their lives." Accordingly, Vagt believes, "the life expectancy of such a program is quite good" (personal communication, July 1998).

Nonetheless, despite these impressive achievements and the vigorous support of Davidson's administration, alumni, and students, Humes's committed defenders no longer constitute a clear majority of its faculty. Although program stalwarts at an earlier critical juncture successfully stymied a concerted push for major revisions, they cannot now. Consequently, the crucial question facing Humes as it enters its fourth decade is not whether, but precisely how, to change in order to secure the loyalty of a new generation of teacher-scholars. Although nothing can be predicted with complete assurance, it appears exceedingly unlikely that the Humanities program of 2002—if there is one—will substantially resemble that of 1962 or, for that matter, that of 1999.

Whither Humes?

Whether Humes exists in 2002, during the next few years it will almost certainly become smaller, organizationally looser, and less central to the college's curriculum than it traditionally has been— or at least this will happen if staff members conscientiously implement the recommendations of the 1997 Humanities task force and if Davidson's administration proceeds with plans, adopted in 1998, to offer Humes as but one of three tracks within a new array of first-year seminars. As the seven members of the task force recommend, Humes ought to retain its current organization as a four-semester, chronologically structured, team-taught program, but it also should grant instructors considerably greater autonomy within this framework. Most significant, and with the administration's blessing, the task force proposes that each semester's staff jointly decide on a small number of "intrinsically significant core texts" and allow individual instructors to supplement them if they wish. In addition, faculty would have a free hand to approach all course materials "in the manner they deem most appropriate" and devise their own tests and writing assignments. The only remaining mandates are that instructors provide "some basic historical context for . . . the texts and issues" they explore and that during the first year they assign enough written exercises to allow students to satisfy the college's requirement in English composition (Berkey and others, 1997, p. 1).

It is significant that during the 1997–98 academic year, the Humanities task force was just one of three charged to offer recommendations for revamping Davidson's first-year curriculum; a second revisited the requirement in English composition, and a third examined individual faculty proposals for first-year seminars. Accordingly, the Humes task force devised its recommendations explicitly with an eye to facilitating the program's integration into this new curriculum as simply one variety of first-year seminar, all

designed to "introduce entering students to a collegiate community of learning, provide settings for focused study and small-group
interaction, and offer opportunities to fulfill core requirements"
(Williams, 1998, p. 1). Indeed, task force members proceeded with
full awareness that some faculty, including some prominent Humes
staff, envision the new first-year seminars as not merely comple-
menting Humanities but perhaps even replacing it (Krentz, 1997).
They therefore took especially seriously the challenge not merely
to revise the program to retain the loyalty of current instructors,
but also to recruit new faculty by giving them the attractive option
of designing their own seminars.

Persistent Challenges

Challenges, task force members and others acknowledge, will confront the new program, however it is redesigned. In particular,
although the new format should remedy some complaints, it will
surely leave others unaddressed and even prompt new ones. Like
any other compromise, the autonomy model offers neither Humes
defenders nor critics all they desire. Thus, on the one hand, some
program stalwarts have resisted the task force's proposals, since
they regard them as offering an inherently unstable arrangement
likely to degenerate into a chaotic amalgam of courses integrated
in name only. Some critics have responded just as unenthusiasti-
cally, dismissing even a restructured Humes as a pale approxima-
tion of the virtues making first-year seminars attractive. In
particular, they argue, first-year seminars can provide faculty opportunities to explore a limited number of texts free of Humes's traditional mandate for broad topical and historical coverage.
Although the autonomy model should ameliorate staffing problems by attracting faculty formerly estranged by Humes's strong
narrative unity, it seems just as likely to alienate others. As the program's chair, Hansford Epes of the department of German and
Russian, cautions, although some will welcome the chance to offer
expansive readings of particular texts, others will be more appre-
hensive. Those teaching in the first semester, for example, who
possess the expertise to explore Thucydides' *History* deeply will
happily seize the opportunity, but staff who do not may feel isolated and adrift. After all, Epes points out, few professors even at a

liberal arts college possess the competence to discuss comfortably for weeks at a time texts as heterogeneous as Thucydides' *History*, Sophocles' *Oedipus the King*, Plato's *Republic*, and the Hebrew creation accounts in Genesis.

At this critical juncture there also looms the fundamental issue raised explicitly by the 1997 religion department memo and implicitly by the two outside evaluators' reports in 1983 and 1997: the conflict between advocates of generalist and specialist educational programs. Indeed, even a cursory look at the first-year fall semester syllabus for 1998–99 fuels the worst fears of disciplinary specialists that a radically autonomous program *especially* offers occasions for "banal" or "trivializing" readings of core texts. In a semester exploring "The Hebrew Scriptures," "The Homeric Age," and "The Classical Greek World," only a minority of lectures are presented by faculty who are expert in these fields. Instead, a professor of German lectures on Genesis and Sophocles, an analytic philosopher on the Hebrew Bible, and a historian on the *Iliad* and "Building the Parthenon." Remarkably, none of the semester's six instructors possesses graduate training in biblical studies, and one is not even a regular faculty member. Even some program advocates regret the extent to which staff members during this semester operate outside their fields, but they nonetheless defend the program's pedagogy. Humes instructors, they argue, are hardly ignorant of these materials, and the opportunity for first-year students to witness how even "mere generalists" productively explore these texts is itself valuable. Reading Genesis or *Oedipus the King* should not exhaust itself simply in technical mastery, but rather in appropriating these texts' lessons for living. In any case, advocates insist, these criticisms remain beside the point, since Humes avowedly introduces entering students to these materials. It in no way pretends to impart the competencies that departmental study does.

Remarkable too, and equally suspect to faculty wary of the program's own distrust of disciplinary expertise, is another problem attending even a thoroughly "autonomous" Humanities: Humes's continuing to grant credit toward some graduation requirements despite its paucity of faculty from the relevant academic departments. Under the auspices of the new model, students completing Humes continue to receive credit for one course in literature and another in religion. Yet of the twenty-six sections of Humes during the 1998–99 academic year, the departments of English and religion—two traditionally heavily contributing departments whose members have grown especially estranged from the program's foundational premises—provide only one each. At the same time, three departments toward whose requirements Humes provides no credit—political science, art history, and physics—collectively contribute seven teaching positions. In other words, Humes students receive credit toward requirements in religion and literature by virtue of instruction provided by faculty whose own training falls well outside these disciplines. Surely, critics argue, such a situation is not merely anomalous, but unacceptable for a liberal arts college priding itself on the expert quality of its instruction.

Finally, and no less unsettling to faculty disgruntled with Humes's "generalist" pedagogy, is the formidable array of tasks the revised program inherits. Many Humes staff, as well as faculty in the department of English, vigorously protest the awarding of composition credit to students completing Humanities. To expect a four-semester program to impart general competence in writing, they argue, while simultaneously providing effective instruction in no fewer than four distinct disciplines (history, philosophy, religion, and literature) is simply unreasonable. Already in 1983, in fact, among other criticisms, the outside evaluators faulted Humes for its failure to "deal adequately with problems in writing" (Levich, Martin, and Rabb, 1983, p. 3). Even now, as one otherwise enthusiastic supporter ruefully acknowledges, Humes fails "to blend the teaching of writing into a curriculum that is already overloaded with content requirements" (Thornberry, 1997).

Fundamental Questions

Ultimately, as formidable as all these challenges are, even more fundamental is the question of what tasks the program should attempt now that its original raison d'être of "educating the whole man" by providing a sweeping narrative of "the life and achievements of Western man" appears increasingly unconvincing to ever larger numbers of faculty. Quite simply, what purpose remains to a program conceived by a previous generation of instructors—

exclusively white, Protestant, and male—who still believed in the "organic unity of the Western tradition" and spoke singularly of "the meaning of human existence," as did the authors of the 1962–63 syllabus?

A full response to these queries lodges inextricably in the larger and often acrimonious debates about liberal education agitating American campuses everywhere. So-called traditionalists plead the continued relevance of great books and Western civilization programs to the worthy projects of crafting healthy souls and committed citizens, goals very much a part of Davidson's traditional educational mission. As Gertrude Himmelfarb argues, such courses "encourage students to rise above the material circumstances of their lives and to liberate them intellectually and spiritually by exposing them, as the English poet Matthew Arnold put it, to 'the best which has been thought and said in the world'" (quoted in Nehamas, 1991, p. 260). Scholars on the cultural and political left, on the contrary, recommend a less canonical and more multicultural program of study. They urge this approach particularly for its alleged ability to foster habits of Socratic questioning and empathetic understanding, habits that Martha Nussbaum (1997, p. 21) argues constitute "an indispensable part of a worthwhile life for any person and any citizen." Indeed, Nussbaum insists, conservatives' worshipful attitude toward great books and their rigid placement of them within a narrative of uniquely Western achievements actually betray their ignorance of, not devotion to, the books' profoundest lessons: "It is an irony of the contemporary culture wars that the Greeks are frequently brought onstage as heroes in the 'great books' curricula proposed by many conservatives. For there is nothing on which the Greek philosophers were more eloquent, and more unanimous, than the limitations of such curricula" (p. 33).

Yet even if one finds admonitions like Nussbaum's unconvincing, there still remains the unavoidable question of why a humanistic education need assume the form of a two-year, team-taught, interdisciplinary course at all. Why not instead, many ask, simply allow students to encounter great ideas and texts in regular departmental courses, supplemented perhaps by first-year or even capstone senior seminars? Considering the by-now virulent disaffection among many Davidson faculty with general education courses, as well as the resistance of still more to conceiving their efforts in either Humes or their own departmental offerings as attempts to fashion "good persons" or "good citizens" of any kind, such proposals, they insist, demand serious consideration. After all, although writers as different as Allan Bloom (1987) and Richard Rorty (1989) believe that reading Homer, Shakespeare, or Nabokov ought ideally to make students more virtuous, others certainly do not. Thus, while some faculty believe that humanities courses of any sort must entail essential "civilizing" or "citizenship" functions, others legitimately approach texts as occasions for strictly formal analysis. Still others invite students to explore them as articulations of persistent existential dilemmas, or perhaps even as particularly interesting ideas in their own right, independent of any moral and political concerns. This being the case, it seems unclear why—to say nothing of how— two dozen professors possessing strongly differing convictions ought regularly to agree on a common set of readings and approach them with identical methodologies and purposes. Not all humanistically trained faculty, they remind us, embrace the distinctive variety of intellectual history or *Kulturgeschichte* that has shaped Humes since its inception—nor ought they. Any mandate that they should, in fact, appears not only unreasonable, but after one removes the cohesive narrative that once provided the program's organizational unity, as the new "autonomy" model does, otiose as well.

In the face of objections like these, program advocates can offer at least two responses: one quite plausible and the other less so. The first substantially embraces the recommendations of the 1997 Humanities task force that Humes be revised to allow instructors autonomy to determine their own section's assignments and that the program be offered to students as but one of three varieties of first-year seminars designed to introduce them to close work in small group settings. The advantages of this response are several. For one, it allows faculty still enthusiastic about and considerably invested in Humes—most of whom are excellent teachers and who include recipients of state and national teaching awards—to continue teaching a program they love and recruit others to it by their example and excitement. For another, this response allows the college to satisfy persistent student demand for an interdisciplinary, chronologically organized introduction to the signal cultural achievements of the Western tradition. Finally, and not insignificant, it dovetails with the oft-stated wishes of

Davidson's administration that Humes continue in some form and that it be staffed by faculty claiming enthusiastic ownership of its aspirations and methods.

The second response, by way of contrast, insists that the program persist essentially unchanged and that it reach the same number of students as it has traditionally. This response is both quixotic and subversive of faculty morale and collegiality. It undermines collegiality because it would demand the participation of professors who have abandoned the program or declined to join it. Only if the minority of faculty still dedicated to Humes enlist the administration's aid to conscript colleagues into a program whose foundational assumptions they reject, can this response succeed. And it is quixotic because it ignores the multiple calendar changes since Humes's inception, which have dramatically reduced the number of class days available to accomplish its comprehensive goals. As even one staunch program defender acknowledges, "Humanities has suffered" on account of these reductions, and if the program plausibly is to meet the tremendous demands on it, "serious consideration" needs to be given to its reversion to a five-day-a-week schedule (Manning, 1997). But this change appears extremely unlikely for any number of reasons—no Davidson course, for example, has been offered five days a week since 1987—and its attainment, in any case, would make teaching Humes even less attractive, especially to untenured faculty. Professors at Davidson as elsewhere confront a very different job market from that faced by Humes's founding generation, one that confers greater rewards on scholars with impressive publication records than on those exceptionally dedicated to interdisciplinary teaching. Steadfastly to ignore this and to demand instead that faculty discount their specialized training and interests to refashion themselves as accomplished generalists would only exacerbate Humes's already acute staffing difficulties.

Finally, in addition to prompting these concerns, any response to the program's current woes that calls for maintaining its current form and pride of place in Davidson's curriculum ignores as well, and just as fatally, the long history and diverse roots of faculty dissatisfaction. Much of the estrangement from Humes is neither recent nor reducible to a single cause. In particular, far from arising chiefly, as persons unfamiliar with Davidson might suppose, from the sort of postmodern or left-wing assault on "Western values" that conservatives like D'Souza (1991) and Kimball (1990) decry at other American colleges, this unhappiness has for decades united faculty otherwise divided by quite heterogeneous scholarly interests and political sympathies. Although some professors' scholarship clearly—and appropriately—reveals the influences of recent developments in feminism, cultural theory, and multicultural studies, the faculty as a whole is hardly a cauldron of postmodern theorizing.

Fortunately, Humes's staff members have yet to call on the administration to conscript their colleagues into the program. Happily as well, few are tempted to cast the debates about Humanities' future in starkly political (or acerbically personal) terms, since it is only too apparent that liberals and conservatives are readily found on both sides of this fundamental issue. Nonetheless, those who desire Humanities to retain its traditional organization, size, and centrality in Davidson's curriculum need to make clear precisely how they would achieve these goals in the face of diminishing faculty commitment. At the very least, they must specify what staffing mechanisms they recommend, short of duress, to attain them.

Until these means are articulated, there remains no viable strategy for advocates to pursue save embracing the task force's recommendations to refashion Humes as a smaller and more autonomous program comprising just one variety of first-year seminar. No other response exists that both meets their needs and allows other faculty to satisfy their own. Under these terms, program loyalists can freely explore the signal texts and events of the Western tradition as they traditionally have; faculty equally in love with great books but estranged from Humes's narrative structure can likewise claim effective ownership of the program; and others can complement both these efforts by their own labors in first-year seminars to impart disciplinary perspectives and competencies. At a time especially when economic pressures drive colleges to produce ever greater numbers of technically trained professionals but dwindling numbers of humanistically educated persons, a catholic embrace of what Dryden called "those milder studies of humanity," and not a divisive insistence on any one curricular means to them, is called for (quoted in Engell and Dangerfield, 1998). By urging this embrace, the task force offers an especially promising opportunity to all faculty to join in advancing them.

References

Beaty, M. D. *A History of Davidson College*. Davidson, N.C.: Briarpatch Press, 1988.

Berkey, J. "Humanities Position Paper." In Davidson College, *The Humanities Program: Prospects for Renewal*. Davidson, N.C.: Davidson College, Sept. 1997.

Berkey, J., and others. *Humanities Task Force Recommendations*. Davidson, N.C.: Davidson College, Dec. 2, 1997.

Bloom, A. *The Closing of the American Mind: How Higher Education Has Failed Democracy and Impoverished the Souls of Today's Students*. New York: Simon & Schuster, 1987.

Csikszentmihalyi, M., and others. Memorandum to the Educational Policy Committee. Davidson College, Feb. 21, 1997.

Davidson College. *Davidson College Reference Catalogue, 1962–63*.

Davidson College. *Davidson College Reference Catalogue, 1968–69*.

Davidson College. *Davidson College Self-Study Report for the Southern Association of Colleges and Schools*. Davidson, N.C.: Davidson College, 1974.

D'Souza, D. *Illiberal Education: The Politics of Race and Sex on Campus*. New York: Free Press, 1991.

Engell, J., and Dangerfield, A. "The Market-Model University: Humanities in the Age of Money." *Harvard Magazine*, May–June 1998, pp. 48–56.

Gibson, G. "Position Paper." *The Humanities Program: Prospects for Renewal*. Davidson, N.C.: Davidson College, Sept. 1997.

Hoag, R., and Riesenberg, P. *The Davidson College Humanities Program: External Examiners' Report*. Mar. 1997.

Humanities 11–12, The Western Tradition to the Renaissance. Syllabus. Davidson College, 1962–63.

Humanities Faculty Survey, 1997. Davidson, N.C.: Davidson College, 1997.

Humanities Program Self-Study Report. Davidson, N.C.: Davidson College, Jan. 31, 1974.

Humanities Survey 1989. Davidson, N.C.: Davidson College, 1989.

Humanities 21–22, The Western Tradition from the Renaissance to the Twentieth Century. Syllabus. Davidson College, 1963–64.

Kimball, R. *Tenured Radicals: How Politics Has Corrupted Our Higher Education*. New York: HarperCollins, 1990.

Krentz, P. "Position Paper." In Davidson College, *The Humanities Program: Prospects for Renewal*. Davidson, N.C.: Davidson College, Sept. 1997.

Levich, M., Martin, T., and Rabb, T. *Report of the Consultants*. Davidson, N.C.: Davidson College, 1983.

Lyotard, J.-F. *The Postmodern Condition: A Report on Knowledge*. (G. Bennington and B. Massumi, trans.) Minneapolis: University of Minnesota Press, 1989.

Manning, R. J. "Position Paper." In Davidson College, *The Humanities Program: Prospects for Renewal.* Davidson, N.C.: Davidson College, Sept. 1997.

Marsden, G. M. *The Soul of the American University.* New York: Oxford University Press, 1994.

Nehamas, A. "Serious Watching." In D. R. Hiley, J. F. Bohman, and R. Shusterman (eds.), *The Interpretative Turn.* Ithaca, N.Y.: Cornell University Press, 1991.

Nussbaum, M. C. *Cultivating Humanity: A Classical Defense of Reform in Liberal Education.* Cambridge, Mass.: Harvard University Press, 1997.

Rhodes, D., and Maloney, S. *Summary Report on the Humanities Restudy.* Davidson, N.C.: Davidson College, Sept. 26, 1977.

Rorty, R. *Contingency, Irony, and* Solidarity. New York: Cambridge University Press, 1989.

Shaw, C. R. *Davidson College.* New York: Fleming H. Revell Press, 1923.

Spencer, S. R., Jr. Memorandum to the Faculty on Humanities Program Revision. Davidson College, Feb. 22, 1983.

Thornberry, M. T. "Position Paper." In Davidson College, *The Humanities Program: Prospects for Renewal.* Davidson, N.C.: Davidson College, Sept. 1997.

Vest, J. M. "Influences Beyond the Walls." In M. Nelson (ed.), *Celebrating the Humanities: A Half-Century of the Search Course at Rhodes College.* Nashville: Vanderbilt University Press, 1996.

Williams, R. C. *Memorandum to the Faculty on First-Year Seminars.* Davidson College, May 1, 1998.

Working Paper: A Proposal for the Expansion of the Humanities Program to Constitute a Common Educational Experience for All Students. Davidson College, 1972.

Zimmermann, T.C.P. Memorandum to the Humanities Staff on Program Revision. Davidson College, Feb. 3, 1983.

Chapter Seven

The Experimental College Program at Berkeley

Katherine Trow

The goals set for programs of general education in the humanities are frequently stated in lofty and abstract terms. Catalogues and brochures speak of students' gains in critical thinking, increased writing proficiency, and becoming better citizens. Attempts to measure the success of these courses and programs, indeed most studies of student outcomes in higher education, are usually paper-and-pencil surveys done either at the time or just after the courses are completed. Although these surveys may reveal the level of satisfaction students express with a course or program at that time, they can hardly address the long-term effects, which in many cases represent the true and lasting value of liberal arts courses.

An important consideration in researching the full impact of interdisciplinary programs of general education in the humanities is that some of their effects, and perhaps their most important effects, cannot be realized until some time has passed. These kinds of programs are best assessed through intensive interviews with alumni many years after they have participated in such a program. Because of the greater expense and difficulty of locating graduates

This chapter is based on my book, *Habits of Mind: The Experimental College Program at Berkeley* (Berkeley: Institute of Governmental Studies Press, University of California, Berkeley, 1998).

many years later, and the greater time required to conduct personal interviews and analyze the information they produce, these long-range studies are most often rejected in favor of the short-term, short-answer survey. Although many of those surveys can be useful (Pascarella and Terenzini, 1991), to discover just how deeply and in what ways these courses have affected the lives of their former students requires thorough interviewing. Former participants who have reached an age of mature judgment can more clearly identify the meaning such an experience has had for their lives. Their insights can have implications for the development of future programs and for ways to improve current ones.

Another advantage of such an approach is that it enables us to examine discontinued experimental programs that may have been successful in their educational aims and therefore have lessons for undergraduate curriculum and teaching reform today (Levine, 1978). Such a case is the Experimental College Program at the University of California at Berkeley. Founded in 1965 by philosophy professor Joseph Tussman, it was an adaptation of Alexander Meiklejohn's Experimental College at the University of Wisconsin forty years earlier.

History of the Experimental College Program

Meiklejohn, a dean and professor of logic at Brown University before becoming president of Amherst College, had been asked by President Glen Frank to found and chair an independent college at Wisconsin. His Experimental College lasted just five years; it was closed in 1932 ostensibly because of lack of funds but primarily because of lack of faculty support in the rest of the university, many of whom felt threatened by the "questioning, the controversy, the sheer exhilaration, camaraderie and freedom [the College] generated" (Brown and others, 1984). A controversial and influential educator, Meiklejohn inspired programs with similarities to his at St. John's College, Old Westbury College, San Jose State University, Kenyon College, and Evergreen State College, as well as at Berkeley.

Tussman had been a student of Meiklejohn at Wisconsin, but in the late 1930s and early 1940s, a few years after the Experimental College had closed in the early 1930s. After serving in World War II, Tussman taught at Berkeley, where he became involved in the loyalty oath fight in the early 1950s (Gardner, 1967), then left to teach at Syracuse University, and later Wesleyan University. In 1963 he returned to Berkeley and became chairman of the philosophy department. Through all this time, he had carried with him Meiklejohn's vision of undergraduate reform. Early in 1964 (before the student revolution sparked by the Free Speech Movement) Tussman began negotiations with the administration at Berkeley to start the Experimental College Program, modeled, with some changes, after Meiklejohn's Experimental College at Wisconsin.

There were more similarities than differences between the two programs: both had as their aim the education of young citizens for democracy; both were nondisciplinary two-year programs rather than a collection of separate courses; both concentrated on periods of history (Tussman adding seventeenth-century England to Meiklejohn's original use of fifth-century Greece and Federalist and contemporary America, called the "Athens-to-America" curriculum); both used weekly all-college lectures, small seminars, and weekly individual sessions with faculty; and both were to occupy virtually all of the students' first two years and fulfill their curricular requirements for that two-year period.

One difference between the two programs was that Tussman's faculty taught full time in the program, and Meiklejohn's faculty taught two-thirds time in his college and one-third in the regular university. Meiklejohn had greater freedom in hiring than did Tussman, and his faculty were paid more than regular faculty, but that was not the only cause of resentment among regular faculty at Wisconsin. Another difference was that there was no significant resentment of Tussman's program among Berkeley faculty.

These differences did not affect the operation of Tussman's program. Both programs established intellectual learning communities focused on a central theme. Tussman (1997) said of his version, "It was . . . based on what I understood, or perhaps fantasized, of the Wisconsin experiment." Because the two programs were more similar than different, and Tussman's the closest model of Meiklejohn's, the two are often referred to together as having a common conceptual basis.

The Meiklejohn-Tussman reform of undergraduate education abandoned the usual system of required courses and electives—what Tussman calls the "wasteland" of the first two undergraduate years of most colleges—especially at research universities such as Berkeley, where emphasis is put on preparation for specialized research careers. He argues that those two years (called the lower division at Berkeley) have become simply a holding period in preparation for the last two undergraduate years (the upper division), when students begin study in their major fields. Furthermore, he says, undergraduate education has lost its sense of an independent mission: that of initiation into the privileges and responsibilities of society. Tussman believes the current system of a set of loosely organized, mostly unrelated courses is a wasted educational opportunity and should be converted to programs with coherence and integration and an organizing principle different from that on which the second two years, with their emphasis on majors, is based. He favors the "program" for the first two, lower-division years over the course, or set of courses, because it can be coherently organized around a theme, although, he says, not necessarily the one he chose for the Experimental College Program, which was education for democracy. (In this scheme, the first two undergraduate years, which focus on fulfilling requirements prior to the major, is the "first program"; the second two years, which consist of courses in the major, is the "second program"; and the "third program" is graduate studies.)

The curriculum Tussman (1997) chose was centered on four periods "full of crisis and turmoil" illustrating moral problems confronting democratic society throughout history:

> The Greeks constitute for us a great exemplary episode. Its dramatic center is the Peloponnesian War seen through the eyes of Thucydides. But everything we read illuminates that tragedy. Homer is in the background, Aeschylus, Sophocles, Euripides are brooding commentators, Plato reaps its lesson. It is an unparalleled chorus for the basic human plot. We echo it in everything we do. . . . In the seventeenth century . . . we pick up the other great cultural strand of our lives. It gives us the King James Bible, Shakespeare, Hobbes, and Milton—the Judeo-Christian tradition in a strain especially constitutive of the American tradition and character. As for America, we take the covenant, the Constitution, the law, and the court, the living complex institution, as the thread that guides us in the attempt to understand what we are up to. [pp. 90–91]

How the Program Operated

One hundred and fifty students enrolled in both of the two-year cycles that the program ran. They were taught by six professors, or in the first year of the first program by five professors and five teaching assistants. Applications and letters of invitation were sent to all entering freshmen during the summers of 1965 and 1967. Applications returned numbered a little over 300 for each of the two two-year cycles, representing close to 10 percent of the entering class of 3,303 in 1967. (No figures are available for 1965, but it can be assumed they were similar.) Tussman recalls there being somewhat more female than male applicants. Students were selected at random from two hats: one for women and one for men. The only requirement for admission was that students had passed the reading and writing screening test that all University of California freshmen took to determine whether they had to take a basic writing course their first year. This requirement was to ensure that students could devote all of their time to the program—except for one "outside" course, which they were to use preferably to satisfy university language requirements. The program itself carried forty-eight units of credit; a regular course added to that each semester brought to sixty the total number of credits earned by program students, allowing them to enter the upper division as juniors with both the social science and humanities requirements of the College of Letters and Science fully satisfied.

Applicants were advised in the invitational letter that those interested in majoring in subjects with heavy requirements such as science or music might have difficulty fulfilling those substantial requirements while in the program. Nonetheless, one former student whom I interviewed for the study was able to graduate with a science major by taking required science courses in summer school. In addition, students were allowed to drop out of the program at any time they wished during the two years, taking twelve units of credits for each completed semester with them back to the regular university.

In contrast to the regular course system, the program instead consisted of lectures for the whole group based on the readings and in which all faculty participated, small seminars of ten or fifteen students led by individual professors, an additional seminar led by program students with no faculty present, and individual tutorials with each student for the purpose of going over the papers they were asked to write every two weeks or so on assigned topics. Students regularly spent an average of two to four hours weekly in lectures, four hours in seminar, and one hour in tutorials. The remainder of their time in the program was spent reading, writing, and in informal discussions. The entire program (with the exception of the large lecture) was conducted in one building, an old fraternity house built in 1893 by English architect Ernest Coxhead and recently sold to the university. The House, as it was called, is an example of the "First Bay Tradition" descending from the arts and crafts movement in England and is of some architectural significance (Trow, 1998). Having virtually the whole program take place in an inviting space encouraged informal discussion among students and faculty, and among students themselves, who did not live there but could use the House for informal discussion, reading, playing music, and cooking occasional meals.

There were no classes, no examinations, and no grades except a pass or fail for those who wanted to transfer. Students were therefore not competing with each other for grades or trying to impress faculty members for better grades; they could instead identify with the program as a common academic enterprise. Reading exclusively original rather than secondary sources (except, by necessity, the Greeks and other non–English language writers in translation) enhanced the students' sense of the responsibility they took for their own education.

Taken together, abandoning separate courses and classes for a coherent two-year program with a theme, reading the curriculum composed of original sources together with faculty, and meeting in one physical location that they could use for other purposes helped to create a unique learning community within the larger university. Meiklejohn has been called the "father to the learning community movement" (Gabelnick and others, 1990), and he and Tussman together can be considered the creators of the prototype learning community. The Tussman program, together with Meiklejohn's program, can be thought of as interdisciplinary in the sense that it was not taught from a single disciplinary standpoint. Faculty in the first two-year cycle came from the departments of political science, philosophy, mathematics, sociology, and rhetoric. Tussman preferred to call it adisciplinary or nondisciplinary, implying that it had nothing to do with disciplines.

The Role of Faculty

Tussman's reform was not only based on a radically different conception of lower-division studies; it also necessitated radically new and personally more demanding ways of teaching for the members of the Berkeley faculty who staffed the Experimental College Program, at least in the first cycle. Faculty members were expected to teach, that is, to lecture, publicly, in the company of colleagues rather than *in camera,* as in the usual classroom, although seminars and tutorials were conducted by individual faculty alone. This form of team teaching in the program theoretically has the advantage of reducing the temptation for the teacher to "perform" for an audience of students rather than to teach, and for all teachers to focus together on what students are learning. In order for this approach to be successful, however, faculty members have to work closely together.

This level of cooperation was not achieved during the first two-year cycle. Tussman had chosen his first set of program faculty from among his colleagues at Berkeley for their reputations as strong teachers, but his plan was somewhat sketchy, and there was no structure of authority. Faculty had not met as a group before the program started, leaving them to interpret much of the program's plan without guidance from Tussman. Soon after the first cycle began, it became evident that several faculty had differing views from Tussman about how to run the program, and some gave in to the temptation to become gurus to the students. Debates and arguments ensued, some of them quite bitter. Weekly faculty meetings scheduled with the intention of talking over the curriculum were disbanded after the first unsuccessful meeting.

Another obstacle to the harmonious operation of the program appeared soon afterward. Tussman had found it difficult to persuade colleagues to take time off from their research and graduate teaching, and he found only five faculty members for the first year. Their decision to add six teaching assistants to fill out the teaching roster was made against Tussman's better judgment, after he lost in a three-to-two vote. Later, when some of the teaching assistants were found to be subverting faculty authority in their relations with students by telling them not to follow faculty directives, the faculty voted unanimously to discontinue their contracts for the second year. Oddly enough, this incident cleared the way for Tussman to assume the previously lacking authority in the program; in his own words, "as if by general consent, without comment," he was left in charge.

Tussman did not repeat the same staffing mistake in the program's second two-year cycle. Instead of looking among Berkeley faculty, with the authority given him by the university administration and with the concurrence of the academic senate, Tussman instead hired five former students and friends at colleges outside the University of California system, some from as far away as British Columbia. This change produced a much better operating program and a much happier leader. Meetings of the faculty to plan for the year took place over the summer, the faculty planning seminar was revived and held weekly, and communications were vastly improved over the first cycle. Tussman (1997) said, "I remember the second run seminar as the most exciting, the most significant intellectual and moral experience of my whole life, unmatched, unapproached by anything I experienced in four decades of interesting university life" (p. 30). Arguments and debates among faculty continued, but on a much different basis: "The basic agreement on fundamentals in the second group made possible vigorous running disagreement on almost everything else. . . . I emerged after four years reassured that education could still be thought of as the initiation of the new generation into a great continuing and deeply rooted civilization" (p. 32).

The program ran smoothly during the second two-year cycle and ended in 1969, graduating into the upper division about two-thirds of its students, as the first cycle had done. Yet the program was not resumed the following year. Ironically, the very change in staffing during the second year that resulted in such harmonious relationships and a successful program produced a staffing situation impossible for Tussman to reproduce. These second-cycle teachers could not be given tenure at Berkeley because the program was not a department. Unable to take more than two years away from their own jobs, they returned to their colleges and universities, leaving Tussman to struggle with the problem of finding a new set of teachers—but from where? Although the chancellor approved of the program and asked for a proposal for its renewal, the vice chancellor would not—indeed, could not—grant it tenured faculty positions. Tussman had run through his list of potential faculty from Berkeley. In the end, he gave up, even though both the chancellor and the College of Letters and Science had approved the continuation of the program. So in 1969, after having received national attention when it began ("Intellectual Immersion," 1968; Peterson, 1969), the program disappeared. And in the political, social, and educational chaos of Berkeley in the late 1960s and early 1970s, it did not appear to be missed. It should be noted, however, that during its years on the Berkeley campus from 1965 to 1969, the program remained largely unaffected by political events on the campus. For instance, some of its students went on strike in their "outside" classes, but never in the program. (A fuller account of the effects of the campus political turmoil on the program and the program's effect on students' political attitudes is given in Trow, 1998, chap. 12.)

The Study

Many years after it ended, I heard Tussman talk about his experiment in a seminar at the Center for Studies in Higher Education on the Berkeley campus. In an effort to discover what former students now made of this noble-sounding educational venture, so unusual for Berkeley or any other large, public research university, I began a pilot study using interviews with four former students in the program (Trow, 1987). The pilot study was fruitful; these four people remembered vividly their experiences in the program and freely shared them with me. With the help of a grant from the Fund for the Improvement of Postsecondary Education at the U.S. Department of Education, I expanded the number of interviewees to forty during the fall and spring of 1989 and 1990. By that time, these former students had had eighteen to twenty years to reflect on their experiences in the program and offer judgments about its meaning to their lives. I chose twenty from each of the two cycles—ten women and ten men—in order to simulate the ratio of the numbers who had enrolled in the program. I interviewed only people who had completed the program to ensure that they all had had equal exposure to it. (Further descriptions of the interviews, the questionnaire, and comparisons with a control group of forty-five former Berkeley students who had applied to the program but had not been selected in the random acceptance process are provided in Trow, 1998.)

Some Findings

Interviews opened with the question, "What has been the major impact of the program on your life?" and the answers usually revealed the participants' predominant views of the program. In order to trace possible differences between the first and second two-year cycles and between men and women, their answers to that first question are reported separately in each of those four categories. The major impacts that first-cycle women noted were educational gains in the form of a better understanding of what education is all about, being able to use primary sources, learning to be independent thinkers, becoming intellectually awakened, and gaining more confidence in dealing with the rest of their undergraduate and graduate education. They talked about the sense of security they found in this small program as beginning students in a large university. They also testified to the more personal gains in self-esteem they felt were a result of their participation, with the exception of one, who thought she was not mature enough and confident enough at the time of the program to profit from it. Few mentioned the curriculum, and one woman said that although the content was interesting to her, it was not as important as the process of learning itself:

> I realized I enjoyed intellectual pursuits. It wasn't just to go to school and get a good grade, but there was something beyond that. I went to graduate school partly as a result of the program. [a political scientist]

Learning from primary rather than secondary sources was important to several women:

> It was a terrific advantage that we were taught from primary sources rather than secondary sources. Rather than reading what

somebody else thought about Euripides, you actually sat down and read it first and thought about it yourself. . . . I think it became more apparent to me later on, when I got my degree in political science. Being forced to be independent and be an independent thinker. . . . Learning how to make choices about how I would spend my time, and realizing that I ultimately had to take charge of my own learning. [a lawyer]

Two other women thought that being in the program helped them adjust to being in a large university. They compared their success to the problems of adjustment their sisters had who attended the University of California at Berkeley but were not in the program.

Men from the first cycle had things to say about the long-range impact that they could see only after some time had passed. One businessman spoke about its long-lasting effects:

[The program] showed me that whether I'm talking about the Minoan period, or classical Greek period . . . the same fundamental issues were important in each one of them. The same political issues, organizational issues, social issues, inequality issues. In a way the Tussman program was like a global village in terms of ideas. Now, the program to me is like a net, an intellectual net, and it has just stretched over time.

Women from the second cycle also gave the opportunity to work from primary sources as an important benefit of the program. They added other themes:

Another major impact has been that I learned to value institutions in our society. I learned to value the contribution that institutions make to the social fabric and I've chosen to work in State service. It's a vocation to me, to choose an institution to be a part of. [a civil servant]

It forced us, in a way most undergraduates are not, to think for ourselves. There's no question that directions for the future came out of the program. I think it was one of the best decisions I could have made for my education. I feel the foundation in law and the nature of government, of society, of man, is all useful. I didn't go along with it in the form that we got it, but the questions are still *the* questions. [a teacher active in community service]

The major impact was probably not real evident to me until I went into the second two years of college and started comparing what other people's experience had been with their first two years. I felt like I had the best of both worlds. [a businesswoman]

Men from the second cycle looked back on their time in the program and saw the central importance of the concept of community, as well as other values instilled and encouraged in the program, and its long-lasting and even cumulative effects:

As I look back on it, I recognize that it has to do with my belief in community and how important it is to be part of a community, whether it's a neighborhood, whether it's a city—making community a better place. [a businessman]

The impact is, that I realize, twenty years later, that I had a very unique and very privileged opportunity to look at problems of social living through some of Western history. . . . It lived up to my ideal, or fantasy—the small group seminars with professors. I thought those were really a special opportunity, really a privilege to be sitting in there with a group of maybe six or eight or ten students and a senior professor, and everyone intimately involved, engaged in the subject matter, as opposed to a professor standing up in front of 150 people, talking and watching you try to write it down and maybe you are daydreaming. The intimacy of it, that was the best. I learned to take seriously the whole problem of what is ethical behavior for individuals in society? What do we owe to society? That's what they were trying to say—"Let's look at how it's been addressed over different snapshots in human history. . . ." It was the high point of my academic career, no question about it. [an economist]

Other men spoke of the program's cumulative effects, and of the habits of mind it created. A lawyer told me,

The impacts were subtle. They become apparent more and more as you get older. It educated us, taught us how to read, how to learn for ourselves. I take that back—it didn't teach us how to do it, it got us into the habit of doing it. It took us from the bad habits of cramming for exams and feeding back to people what they wanted to hear, to actually seeing what a person has to say and deciding for yourself whether that's something useful.

Another lawyer said this:

The thing that's lasted is that as I've grown older, the impact accumulated in a weird way. The longer I've lived with these books and with the clear strains that go through these great mature thinkers, the more I see that that's true personally in my life, and also in terms of my overview of history and culture and the present. As you get older, you just know more, and you live more, and you have suffered more losses, and you have more sense of the complexity of the world. And these books have always been there [for me]. So it's managed to inform the way I think even now. That's the big impact.

Other men talked about realizing the aims of the program:

Towards the end of the program I got this sense of a tradition that you could become part of, and I have great respect for it, because it still guides me now. It was a foundation experience for me. The development of your mind. . . . The idea of a community of scholars, of being associated with the same faculty members, the same students primarily over two years with a physical location identified with this house here. The chance to grow up with a group of people experiencing the same things that you were. This . . . learning how to look at issues, seeing how things we're looking at today can be viewed as what was going on in the *Iliad* thousands of years ago. That there is some sort of continuity to human experience no matter how different the things may seem today. And the basic foundation of our Western thought is as valid now as it was thousands of years ago . . . the overall point being trying to produce people, voters who can think. And the only way you can think and make an educated choice as a voter, as a member of a democracy, is to understand how this whole system has been put together. What the roots of it are . . . the roots of American democracy. [a teacher]

Comments from two other men demonstrate the importance of the program in their lives:

It always comes up, ideas that were talked about in the program. They do constantly touch on things in my life today. It has given me a background in which to think about how to make decisions, whether these are actual day-to-day life decisions, or just philosophical ones. It's provided a basis of knowledge, a system of looking at political philosophy, and having something to refer back to. It's organized my thoughts in a way. That would be the lasting value. It certainly has had a probably profound influence I still don't fully understand or appreciate. [a businessman]

It awakened me to issues that continue to be near and dear to me. Questions of human nature, and political activity; a question of natural law and moral law, and first principles. And what is the relation of person to person, of man to man, man to his fellow citizen, of states to each other. The issues brought up in the program seem to be still critical and still crucial. . . . When you've been dipped into the canon, or into the Western tradition, you realize that the Western tradition is not a monolithic thing. It's an actual living thing, but you can't really know that until you get into it. . . .

I can't tell you if it would have helped or hindered a given career track, but for the uses to which I put my mind and soul, it was great. I can't think of anything better. It was really my education. The place where I really got down in the muck and sort of chomped around, [laughs] in the really stewy and fermented parts of . . . the human mind and soul. That's where I really . . . did my work, you know. I mean, I really found out things there. . . . It furnished me with intellectual material on which to work for the rest of my life. [a literary editor]

Differences Between Cycles and Between Men and Women

Not everyone interviewed for the study said that the program had had such profound effects on their lives, although each reported some gains and benefits. The examples provide vivid evidence of the best effects of the program. It is not accidental, nor is it intentional on my part, that these last comments from second-cycle men take up considerably more space than the others. In analyzing all the responses to the question about the major impact of the program from all four groups—women and men, first and second cycles—I found that although women from the second cycle had some things to say about the content of the program, it is these men from the second cycle who had the most to say about the lasting effects of its substance on their lives.

Comments about the major impact were divided into three groups:

- Comments dealing with the impact of the content of the curriculum: the educational and moral purpose of the program itself, education for democracy; the recurrence of great ideas over time; values and ethical considerations put forth by the program; the concepts of citizenship, of community
- Responses concerning the effects of the educational structure of the program: the coherent two-year program; the substitution of lectures, seminars, and tutorials for regular university classes; the absence of grades and exams; the training for independent thinking; the nondisciplinary nature of the curriculum; the use of primary rather than secondary sources; learning how to think, write, and speak and how to integrate these skills with each other; and other features of the learning community—the continuity of books, ideas, faculty, students, and setting over the two-year period
- Benefits of a more personal nature: the sense of belonging that the program created; the ease, comfort, and protection it offered entering students; the confidence they gained through their experiences there and how that carried over to the upper division in the regular university and beyond

From these categories of responses, the following major findings emerge:

- Responses falling into the last two categories look much the same for all groups. All four groups of male and female, first- and second-cycle participants put roughly equal emphasis on the categories of educational and personal gains from the program. There were no major differences among any of the four groups.
- All four groups differ in the emphasis they put on the first category, curricular content. Twice as many participants from the second two-year cycle (twelve participants), men and women together, as the first cycle (six participants) said the major impact of the program had come from the content. And twice as many men (twelve participants) as women

(six participants) from both cycles said the content had had a major impact.

The total number of respondents (forty) is not large, making the subgroups even smaller and not appropriate for statistical tests of significance; also the group as a whole may not be a representative sample. Collectively, however, they do represent roughly one-fifth of the students who completed the program during its two-cycle, four-year existence, and the differences are therefore suggestive of the entire group of program graduates. Thus, the differences among some of the groups that emerge here deserve attention and explanation.

The first category, curricular content, appears to be most crucial to understanding the differences in effects between the two cycles of the program. The first cycle could be thought of as the program's maiden voyage. Tussman and the faculty he recruited often disagreed about the program's goals and means of achieving them; they did not meet together regularly; and conferences with students were held on a haphazard basis. During the second cycle of the program, the faculty remained constant throughout the two years and were largely unified. They met as a group each week, and conferences with students were held on a regular, scheduled, and more frequent basis. There were no teaching assistants to intervene for faculty.

The second-cycle faculty were much more cohesive as a group and apparently conveyed the purpose of the curriculum more effectively to more students. This supposition is supported by the fact that although some of the former students from the first cycle demonstrated many of the educational and personal benefits of the program, a notably greater number of participants from the second cycle were able to express the meaning of the curriculum more fully. Several from the group of second-cycle men reported spending much time in the House, reading, playing music, and talking. Some said they brought in firewood for the fireplace, cooked spaghetti dinners on weekends, and published a poetry journal, all aspects of the learning community that the founders of the program had intended to encourage. (Although some women were part of this group, men apparently outnumbered them, and by chance, none were interviewed.) In spite of those differences in responses concerning the content of the program among first- and second-cycle participants and between men and women, the educational and personal effects of the entire program remained approximately the same for all four groups, making the differences in responses about content all the more striking.

The fact that women as a whole had fewer comments to make about the content of the program than did men is open to interpretation. It may be that this group of women placed more value on the educational and personal effects of the program than they did on the content. (Women also talked less about the program in general during the interviews. The longer interviews tended to be with participants, both men and women, who talked about the curriculum.) Perhaps the way the program gave women confidence in their academic abilities, awakened their awareness of intellectual interests, and eased their way into the upper division at Berkeley overshadowed the significance to them of the more abstract intellectual and ethical content. Although they mentioned community involvement in their current lives about as often as men did, they may not have linked that with the content of the program. Carol Gilligan (1982) concludes from her research that females come to have a more contextual and less abstract morality than males. Although this may have been a factor, there may be another explanation for the gender difference based on the way women students related to the program's all-male faculty. At the time of the program, in the mid- and late 1960s, the women's movement had barely begun to have an effect on the campus, and only a handful of women taught at Berkeley (Hunter, 1997). Tussman said he tried to recruit a woman teacher for the second cycle of the program but was unsuccessful.

Implications for Faculty-Student Relations

The differences between men and women may also be a reflection of the crucial importance of close faculty-student relations. It seems reasonable to assume that in order for the content of the program to have the most substantial overall effect on students, their relationship had to be close in the academic sense, allowing for argument, debate, and intellectual give-and-take. Half of the women in the first cycle remembered wishing for more and closer faculty contacts, as did a few in the second cycle, indicating that women may have been shyer about initiating such contact and needed to be drawn out, especially in the first cycle, in which student-faculty tutorials were not regularly scheduled. When students were too shy or hesitant to engage faculty or allow faculty to engage them in the intellectual substance of the program on a one-to-one basis, perhaps that substance was less likely to have affected them.

Second-cycle faculty were not hesitant to engage students, both men and women, in debate. One woman from the second cycle told of a close student-faculty relationship she established with a professor that was initiated by his calling her into his office to ask why she had not been at his lecture the day before. When she explained that she had attended a political demonstration instead, an "intense debate" ensued between them about responsibility and the value and place of political action. In the end, he suggested to her more viable ways of protest open to students. She came then to see the whole program as a

> forum—a place where you could actually work out the issue for yourself with some support. I appreciated the fact that I wasn't just at loose—trying to figure this all out by myself, but there was some opportunity for dialogue and for dealing with it.

This former student's case illustrates two important aspects of the program: that it was small and intimate enough for her to have been missed in a lecture and that faculty paid close attention to the moral and cognitive development of their students. Not writing exams and grading students, and not bearing the entire burden of lecturing for a quarter or semester, faculty were freer to concentrate on the intellectual development of their students than they would have been in the regular university. With students writing papers every two weeks or so (in contrast to once a semester in the regular university), attending small seminars with faculty weekly, and holding informal discussions daily in the House, faculty could track the progress of their students much more effectively than in an ordinary classroom setting.

The papers lent themselves especially well to the task. They were collected into individual student portfolios and, along with each seminar professor's comments, became records of cognitive development. Tussman (1997) called the papers "fever charts"—diagnostic tools in the "quasi-therapeutic art of teaching," in contrast to the "performing art of teaching." He used them to identify students' bad habits that needed curing: using "grandiose or fluffy language, repeating too much of what they had read, using figures of speech that were just a little bit off."

In his study of cognitive and moral development in college students, William Perry (1970) outlines the changes in students' thinking that mark the transition from a belief that knowledge is absolute and answers clearly right or wrong, to an increasingly complex understanding of the contextual relativity of both truth and choice. His developmental scheme "concerns precisely a person's 'moral' development, in the sense of his assumptions about values and responsibility. . . . Since each step in the development presents a challenge to a person's previous assumptions and requires that he redefine and extend his responsibilities in the midst of increased complexity and uncertainty, his growth does indeed involve courage" (p. 44). In discussing the instructor's encouragement of risk, Perry describes the good teacher as one "who supports in his students a more sustained groping, exploration, and synthesis" (pp. 211–212). The good teaching in the program, as defined by Perry, was made possible by the intimacy of its learning community, which allowed for close student-faculty relations.

This discussion of the effects of the program on participants has dealt only with what they perceived to be the major impact—what they picked out as the foremost effect on their lives as they viewed it some twenty years later. There were many other important effects of the program.

One of the most prominent aspects of the interviews as a whole was the way in which participants talked about educational issues. Their experiences in the program seemed to establish a great many of them as experts in their own education and as thoughtful observers of higher education generally. Sometimes the interview came to be almost a kind of educational forum—a place to discuss their beliefs about education as they described how the program inaugurated a lifetime pattern of concern about education and learning.

Another important effect of the program had to do with academic identity and academic self-esteem. A common response of participants to a question about how the program affected their academic self-esteem was to observe that in general many entering freshmen were forced to recalibrate their estimates of their own intelligence in view of a new set of peers, a great many of whom had been valedictorians and salutatorians of their high school class. Coming from being "big fish in small high school ponds," they found themselves little minnows in the university ocean, struggling to find their academic place. The absence of exams and grades in the program helped some students to focus instead on what they were learning, but a few of those students who depended on grades for assessments of their academic worth were uncomfortable without that yardstick.

Nevertheless, many of these former students found in the program something more important to take the place of grades. In identifying with the program, they could feel that they were part of an educational elite. One woman, a librarian, said that her academic self-esteem became in the program

> a whole new thing. It changed my views because I just always thought I would be at the top. I realized I wasn't going to be the "A" student in every single class in every single subject. The program helped me through that—what must be a real difficult period for most people. And I think that's probably why you get the high freshman drop-out rate. I think a lot of people hit that and just give up. . . . At the same time you discovered that you weren't going to be at the top of this group the way you were in high school—you also had a cushion there, something that made you feel it didn't matter that much. You weren't just in there learning for the grade. You weren't learning the one thing that the teacher wanted you to learn and write back on the test. So it was a better way of learning, like learning to learn instead of trying to remember.

Almost all study participants reported no problems in adjusting to the upper division after graduating from the program, except for the disappointment and let-down some expressed. "It was like going from technicolor to black and white," one said. "I felt like a spectator versus more of a participant the way I felt in the program."

Replications of the Experiment

The value of the Experimental College Program is demonstrated not only by the evidence from testimony of former students presented here, but also in the number of its replications on other campuses. The programs at San Jose State University in California and Vico College at the State University of New York at Buffalo were early copies, Vico College lasting ten years until all the original faculty had left. The curriculum of the Meiklejohn-Tussman plan was adopted as the Arts I first-year program at the University of British Columbia in Vancouver and recently celebrated its twenty-fifth anniversary. At Malaspina College in British Columbia, initiated by a former Arts I student, it has been adopted as a two-year junior-senior program in conjunction with the University of Victoria. There is even a vestige of Meiklejohn's Experimental College at the University of Wisconsin, begun in 1948 and reorganized in 1981; it is undergoing another revision as part of a group of learning communities there. In the late 1980s, Evergreen State College in Washington adopted much of the Meiklejohn-Tussman plan, which has led to the formation of the Washington Center for Improving the Quality of Undergraduate Education, a statewide consortium emphasizing both faculty and curriculum development in the form of learning communities. This in turn has given rise to its many replications or adaptations across the country (Gabelnick and others, 1990). So the model is adaptable, and modified versions of it endure, even if some of the original Meiklejohn-Tussman principles are sometimes sacrificed.

Lessons from the Program

This study has shown, as others have, that students generally learn best in small groups in which cooperation rather than competition is the rule (MacGregor, 1987). It demonstrates what teachers have long known: that students often need encouragement to make contacts with faculty in the form of regularly scheduled appointments and that there are students who welcome coherent course programs. But it also illustrates that many students in their first two years are glad to have the sequence of their instruction laid out for them in spite of all the electives available. And Tussman has shown that ordinary college students can master difficult material when the assumption is that they can and when learning takes place in a supportive learning community.

The results of the study have demonstrated the value to the effectiveness of such programs of a variety of pedagogical approaches to undergraduate education: team teaching, the accumulation of students' papers over a period of time in portfolios, individual tutorials, lectures focused on understanding the readings rather than on simply imparting information, emphasis on the students' responsibility for their own education, and, most important, the establishment of a learning community through the sharing of a common curriculum as well as through faculty sharing intellectual power with students.

The study was not intended to be a full-fledged evaluation of the program as a whole but rather a look at the long-term effects as reported by former students. But from what they have to say, it seems fair to conclude that the Experimental College Program was successful enough to have produced both short-term gains and lasting positive effects for these participants. It has been successful enough to have spawned successors. Tussman's only real failure, that of not solving the problem of staffing the program with either tenured or nontenured faculty, was an administrative failure rather than an educational one and may have served to help others following him to avoid that pitfall. For example, Malaspina has built strong ties to administration and regular faculty in order to ensure support.

Seventy years is not an insignificant span of time for a plan of reform to stay alive in a system of state institutions of higher education that is hardly more than two hundred years old. The fact that Meiklejohn's and Tussman's programs and their closest successors have mostly appeared at large, public universities is an indication of the need recurrently expressed to bring more liberal and humanistic education to these institutions, which are usually focused on research rather than teaching and on professional rather than liberal education.

Lessons have already been learned and put into practice for surmounting the difficulties of establishing programs like this that may go against the grain of the host institution. Using Tussman's

Experimental College Program as a template, the following are some of the major characteristics of the more successful parts of these programs:

- A sound, long-range solution to Tussman's staffing dilemma, involving perhaps enough tenured faculty from the beginning to ensure its continuation as at Malaspina or some combination of tenured, visiting, and junior faculty as at Evergreen State. It is necessary for faculty to be in basic agreement about the purpose and methods of the program, and they should meet regularly to discuss the curriculum and student progress. It is also important for faculty to have some preparation during the summer preceding the opening of the program, as Tussman learned the second time around.

- A coherent curriculum reflecting the faculty's confidence in its ability to tell students what to read and a curriculum that is not subject to whims and fads. This does not preclude some room for occasional additions and deletions, but when the basic curricular structure is open for constant debate, the debating is unceasing and corrosive.

- If the curriculum has a moral dimension, it will be more challenging and meaningful to students. It need not be the "Athens-to-America" moral curriculum that Meiklejohn and Tussman used, but if it does not advance ethical and cognitive development, it will not take advantage of this particular time in students' lives when, moving outside the moral authority of the family and striking out on their own, they are especially receptive to ethical concerns.

- The establishment of a learning community. As in Tussman's program, continuity of faculty and students over a two-year span allows for familiarity and trust to develop and provides the setting for that rare experience when everyone, faculty included, shares a common reading program. The absence of exams and grades allows a spirit of cooperation to take the place of competition. A stable academic environment helps students to form academic identities. A physical location for the exclusive use of the program adds significantly to the formation of that identity and encourages informal but important student-faculty interaction to take place. Malaspina has recognized this and has built a separate building in which to house its program.

• Individualized instruction permits students to receive the kind of faculty attention and support necessary to help them make the moral and cognitive steps required to progress to higher developmental stages. It also helps to make the curriculum accessible to all students, not just an elite cadre of honor students.

• Requiring undergraduate students to use original rather than secondary sources is a potent device to develop critical and independent thinking. The usual reliance of students on textbooks and secondary sources, encouraged by most faculty, discourages them from exploring for themselves the meaning of required readings. The message that faculty recognize the validity of students' ability to think for themselves encourages that ability.

• A program using a variety of pedagogical methods and a team of faculty with different teaching styles and different approaches to the same coherent curriculum but a common purpose offers students with different interests and abilities an extended range of learning possibilities. Students can find in this diversified approach something for everyone.

Adaptations of the Program

The key to the success of the Meiklejohn-Tussman replications appears to lie in their ability to adapt to their circumstances, altering somewhat the original plan in the course of adaptation. At Malaspina, science has been added to the curriculum, helping to fulfill graduation requirements but also adding to the required reading that Tussman purposely kept at a minimum. Wisconsin's Integrated Studies Program is not a separate college, as was the original Experimental College, and students have the flexibility to take as few or as many of its courses as they wish, when they wish, although perhaps at the price of less coherence than in the original college. Evergreen's curriculum has been broadened to include all courses taught there. These changes may seem heretical to supporters of the original Meiklejohn-Tussman model, but if adaptations enable new programs to survive, it may be worth some sacrifice of purity in order to keep alive this tradition of curricular reform. Universities themselves may become more receptive to such programs as research makes more apparent their positive long-term effects on students. As to the supposedly elitist character of the curriculum, the pendulum may yet swing away from the Europhobic tendencies so prevalent recently and back toward more recognition of great works in the Western tradition (Miller, 1997; Rothstein, 1997).

A program modeled after Tussman's would have distinct advantages for certain types of students for whom universities currently express concerns, such as students who feel alienated from their educational experiences. Commuting students, for instance, would clearly benefit from having a place and a program on campus to call their own and in which they could meet faculty and fellow students informally. They could thus be provided even greater opportunities to connect with faculty than regular courses and on-campus housing can usually offer. Older students and students coming from disadvantaged backgrounds often live at home to avoid the expense of on-campus living, and they would stand to benefit from a program that affords "a home away from home" not only in the physical and psychological but also in the intellectual sense. Similarly, students who come to college less well prepared academically than others can benefit from this kind of individualized teaching and emphasis on cooperation in a learning community, which reduces the advantage of prior knowledge and puts them on much the same footing as their more advantaged peers. Unlike many other academic programs, there is no particular high school preparation necessary for such programs, other than university-level competency in reading and writing.

Significance of the Long-Term Effects

The long-term effects of programs such as Tussman's Experimental College Program demand recognition. They represent the harvest of "seeds planted over time," as one former student put it. As an example, just before I wrote this chapter, a former participant in the program whom I had interviewed for the study nine years before called to tell me she had changed her mind about some of the things she had told me then. She had been at the time of the interview the least positive of all the informants about her experiences in the program. However, she has recently begun to reevaluate her time in the program in the light of a renewed interest, first kindled there, in the readings. She said she had "finally understood what Joe Tussman was up to" in tracing Western political thought from its origins in Greece through to America's traditions.

In spite of recently taking classes in the classics at major universities in the area, she found "no classes did what the program did"—that is, took the readings out of the disciplinary context of history, classics, archeology, and so forth, and introduced them directly to the students with no intervening criticism or secondary analysis, revealing the scope of "some of the greatest writing and thinking that has survived over the centuries." Even reading the *Odyssey* from cover to cover now in one class did not give her the context that she remembered from the program. She explained that when she entered the program, she was only seventeen, had just left her family for the first time, and in that socially and politically disruptive time her only "context" had been her "own personal self," which did not allow her to take advantage of what she now sees as a "brilliant" program of study.

This postscript again illustrates the importance of development during a person's lifetime in assessing a program's worth. The former student's judgment of the Experimental College Program clearly has changed over the years as her lifetime experience has changed. Now, almost thirty-five years later, she finds herself ready for "the program." What could serve as a better illustration of Henry Adams's prophecy: "A teacher affects eternity; no one can tell where his influence stops"? No one yet knows where the influence of Alexander Meiklejohn, or Joseph Tussman, or of the Experimental College Program, will end.

References

Brown, C., and others. "Alternative Education: Trends and Future Implications." In R. M. Jones and B. L. Smith (eds.), *Against the Current: Reform and Experimentation in Higher Education.* Cambridge, Mass.: Schenkman, 1984.

Gabelnick, F., and others. *Learning Communities: Creating Connections Among Students, Faculty and Disciplines.* New Directions for Teaching and Learning, No. 41. San Francisco: Jossey-Bass, 1990

Gardner, D. P. *California Oath Controversy.* Berkeley: University of California Press, 1967.

Gilligan, C. *In a Different Voice: Psychological Theory and Women's Development.* Cambridge, Mass.: Harvard University Press, 1982.

Hunter, D. "Berkeley Women at Century's End." *Berkeleyan,* Nov. 5–11, 1997.

"Intellectual Immersion at Berkeley." *Time,* Mar. 15, 1968. p. 78.

Levine, A. *Handbook on Undergraduate Curriculum.* San Francisco: Jossey-Bass, 1978.

MacGregor, J. *Intellectual Development of Students in Learning Community Programs 1986–87.* Olympia, Wash.: Washington Center for Improving the Quality of Undergraduate Education, Evergreen State College, 1987.

Meiklejohn, A. *The Experimental College.* New York: HarperCollins, 1932.

Miller, J. "The Academy Writes Back: Why We Can't Close the Book on Alan Bloom." *Lingua franca,* 1997, 7(3).

Pascarella, E. T., and Terenzini, P. T. *How College Affects Students.* San Francisco: Jossey-Bass, 1991.

Perry, W. G. *Forms of Intellectual and Ethical Development.* Austin, Tex.: Holt, Rinehart and Winston, 1970.

Peterson, E. "The Program Has Helped Me Know That I Don't Know." *Mademoiselle,* Aug. 1969, p. 261.

Rothstein, E. "Culture Wars Go On, But the Battle Lines Blur." *New York Times,* May 27, 1997.

Trow, K. "The Experimental College Program in Retrospect: An Exploratory Study." Unpublished manuscript. July, 1987.

Trow, K. *Habits of Mind: The Experimental College at Berkeley.* Berkeley: Institute for Governmental Studies Press, University of California, Berkeley, 1998.

Tussman, J. *The Beleaguered College.* Berkeley: Institute for Governmental Studies Press, University of California, Berkeley, 1997.

Chapter Eight

The Heritage Program at Millsaps College

W. Charles Sallis

Proudly publicized by Millsaps College and widely recognized beyond the campus, the Heritage Program celebrated its thirtieth anniversary in September 1998. In 1968 the Millsaps faculty had departed from years of tradition to create a humanities program that integrated history, literature, religion, philosophy, and the fine arts into a single elective course of study. Over the history of the program, 36.5 percent of all Millsaps freshmen have chosen to satisfy their core humanities requirements by this means. Other students, including those who are unable to take Heritage because its enrollment reaches capacity early in the preregistration process, satisfy their humanities requirements through interdisciplinary topics courses.

Millsaps College, founded in 1890 in Jackson, Mississippi, by the Methodist church, is a predominantly liberal arts college with an undergraduate enrollment of approximately twelve hundred students. Its coeducational student body is evenly divided between men and women; 45 percent come from outside the state. The average American College Test score of entering freshmen is 27, and about 40 percent of graduates continue their education in graduate or professional programs. In 1912 Millsaps became Mississippi's first institution of higher learning to be accredited by the Southern Association of Colleges and Schools (SACS), and in

1988 it received the first and only Phi Beta Kappa charter in the state. Oral and written departmental senior comprehensive examinations have been required since 1933.

Millsaps faculty and administrators who have been involved with Heritage are virtually unanimous in crediting the careful attention to detail at its beginning in 1968, continuous evaluation and renewal by its core faculty, and periodic review by outside consultants for the program's vitality. It is now "the jewel in Millsaps' academic crown." The college's report for admission into Phi Beta Kappa described Heritage as a "model program" and one of the significant strengths of the college. When the Millsaps faculty approved a new interdisciplinary core curriculum in 1991, with changes affecting virtually every academic department, it insisted that the basic structure of Heritage remain a central part of the core curriculum. A successful 1991 grant proposal by the college to the John S. and James L. Knight Foundation to help underwrite the new curriculum touted the "highly successful" Heritage Program as "one of the distinctive features of the curriculum." A faculty review of the core curriculum in April 1998 (Millsaps College, 1998, p. 11) reaffirmed that assertion by stating that Heritage "has long been the College's most widely and favorably recognized distinctive program."

In the thirty years since the first Heritage class met in September 1968, 3,070 Millsaps freshmen have studied the humanities in this program under eight directors, thirty-four professors, and numerous guest lecturers and artists from both on and off campus. Of those freshmen, 1,626 (53 percent) were women and 1,444 (47 percent) were men. In sixteen classes, women were in the majority; in ten classes, men were in the majority, and four classes were essentially evenly divided.

Program Origins

In fall 1963, at the annual Millsaps College faculty retreat, Dean Frank M. Laney, Jr., asked the faculty to undertake an extensive curriculum review. Throughout the 1963–64 academic year, Laney held regular meetings with faculty groups. In 1964–65 he appointed a Curriculum Study Committee to compile data and recommendations for a curriculum revision proposal to be presented to the faculty. In summer 1965 its findings were refined by the Summer Curriculum Study Committee.

The Summer Committee (1965) noted that one of the deficiencies in the Millsaps curriculum was that "no provision is made for allowing the student to come to an understanding of the interdependence and interrelationship of the several academic disciplines" (p. 8). It also noted the absence from the curriculum of non-Western studies and twentieth-century issues courses.

To rectify these omissions the Summer Committee recommended the creation of four interdisciplinary courses: "Man in Western Civilization and Culture" (later called "The Cultural Heritage of the West," or Heritage Program, with fourteen semester hours credit in the freshman year); an interdisciplinary science course for nonscience majors in the sophomore year (twelve hours); "Non-Western Comparative and Area Studies" (six hours); and a three-hour senior capstone course, "Twentieth Century Issues and Values." Heritage was the only proposal enacted at that time. The interdisciplinary science course was not established until 1984, and the non-Western and twentieth-century issues courses were never implemented due to a lack of funding and commitment on the part of the faculty members most directly involved in the projects.

Heritage was to be staffed by faculty members from history, English, and philosophy and religion, with art and music faculty conducting weekly fine arts laboratory sessions. Because of departmental staffing problems, philosophy faculty lectured but were not members of the Heritage staff. Collaborative interdisciplinary teaching would expose students to a variety of teaching styles and was perceived as a "significant way" to "provide the foundation stone" for students' academic careers at Millsaps. As they examined "seminal ideas, the pivotal events, the discoveries and movements which form the basis of Western Culture," students would "develop . . . [the] capacity to think, to assimilate the related ideas, to articulate . . . thoughts, and to write with lucidity."

The humanities would be studied as a coherent whole so that students would perceive "the inter-relationship and the interdependence of the several academic disciplines and realize that no discipline 'is an island'" (Summer Curriculum Study Committee, 1965, p. 10). Because the program would involve Millsaps faculty members from other academic departments as guest lecturers and bring to campus speakers and performers, the entire college would benefit from a truly integrated humanities educational experience. "This course is recommended [as an option for freshmen]," the committee concluded, "with the belief that it would not only provide a more stimulating and challenging program of study to the student, but that it would also enrich the dialogue between the disciplines and enhance the academic climate in general" (p. 12).

The committee noted that similar programs existed at other colleges and universities. The proposed course was quite similar to the Man in the Light of History and Religion course at Southwestern at Memphis (now Rhodes College), for example. Nevertheless, there was a difference: "The Southwestern course . . . is handled primarily by professors from the Departments of History, Philosophy, and Religion. . . . Our course would be much richer with greater emphasis upon literature and the arts" (Summer Curriculum Study Committee, 1965, p. 11). Later Robert Padgett of the English department, the chief architect and first director of the Heritage Program, pointed out two "unusual if not unique" features of Heritage:

> First, it attempts to blend the insights and perspectives of a greater variety of disciplines into one master course than do most such Humanities courses. Second, our course recognizes and emphasizes the fact that many aspects of our cultural heritage do not yield themselves up fully to discursive analysis alone; they must be experienced, not just talked about. Therefore we make an unusual effort to expose the student directly to generous selections of literary works and to primary documents of history, philosophy and religion. The laboratories are especially important in this regard in allowing the student to experience directly masterworks of art, music, and drama through the media of films, slides, recordings, and live performances. [Padgett, 1993, p. 1]

Thus was the Heritage Program at Millsaps conceived. Nearly thirty years later, Padgett recalled:

> Probably everyone associated with the founding of the Heritage Program has his or her own sense of where it all started. My own conviction is that it grew out of a feeling shared by many of us in the College—especially in the Humanities area—that to do our jobs best—that is, to provide a truly rich liberal arts education—we

needed to know more than our specialized training in our fields provided us with. I remember in particular how often in the early sixties, when I was first struggling to teach a course in World Literature, I would go to Tom Jolly in Ancient Languages for help with Greek and Latin literature or to Madeleine McMullan or Frank Laney in History for help with the "backgrounds," and Madeleine, who was bravely asking her western civilization students to read "Oedipus the King" and other literary works along with political and social history, would come to me for advice on how to handle certain literary issues. We often said in those days how nice it would be if we could team-teach a course someday. Little did we know what lay just ahead. [Padgett, 1993, p. 1]

Another recommendation of the Summer Committee was for a closely related and parallel English grammar and composition course. This four-hour course was to be taught in conjunction with Heritage with the general purpose of introducing basic literary genres and enabling students to improve writing skills through writing on ideas and issues associated with their Heritage reading assignments. Thus, both courses would be mutually enriched.

The faculty approved these proposals over opposition from some traditionalists who harbored reservations about the validity of interdisciplinary courses, and the task of implementation and finding resources began. Dean Laney secured a grant for three faculty members to accompany him in 1966 to a conference on interdisciplinary studies. Padgett (1993) remembered this as an invaluable experience:

We as a team created the basis for the first syllabus of the Heritage 101–102 course; we had the opportunity to have our work critiqued by people who had had extensive experience formulating and working in interdisciplinary and team-taught courses and to question them about problems and pitfalls. (I remember particularly one invaluable piece of advice we received from a scientist-participant: "Don't start a team-taught interdisciplinary course in any area without a staff of fully committed teachers who believe in what they're doing.") [p. 3]

In 1966 Millsaps was awarded a Strengthening Developing Institutions grant under Title III of the Higher Education Act of 1965.

Padgett was appointed director of Heritage in 1967, and the first classes began a year later. The year was spent, Padgett wrote in 1993, on "the immensity of details that had to be worked out—the determination of the proper format, the day-to-day syllabus, the acquisition of appropriate textbooks (interdisciplinary materials were rare then), formulating grading procedures, planning staffing and scheduling that crossed departmental lines, establishing support materials for the library, recordings, slides, maps, films, etc." (p. 4).

In September 1968 the first Heritage class met with 77 students— 26.7 percent of the 288 freshmen who enrolled in the college that fall. It was the beginning of what Padgett called "a unique and demanding adventure." A multidisciplinary team of "fully committed teachers who believed in what they were doing" assisted the director (Padgett, 1993, pp. 3–4).

The students were given a detailed syllabus for the entire semester, which specified daily readings from several textbooks, major literary works, and selected readings distributed for particular lectures. A week's schedule consisted of four lectures, one music or art laboratory session for the entire group, and two meetings of discussion groups of fifteen students each—seven hours in all. The discussions were designed, Padgett (1969) explained, to "explore in more detail those questions and issues they have found most relevant in their reading and in the lectures." Also there were a number of required cocurricular events, "which are intended to extend the learning experience beyond the threshold of the classroom and the library to the theater, the concert hall, the art gallery, and the world at large" (p. 3).

The core faculty was highly enthusiastic about Heritage, but many, perhaps most, students felt differently. Vern Pack (1969), a Heritage student during the course's first semester, summarized the Heritage experience in the campus newspaper, *The Purple and White*:

> A student of Heritage feels overworked and overwritten. Many feel that the course "stinks" or is a trap. This may be true now, but in June the sentiment will probably change. If one can live through Heritage, one may be a better person for it. An overload of reading matter, a first semester problem, has been solved second semester by indicating what must absolutely be read, what may be read, and

what may be discarded by those who have need for social life. Tests cannot be crammed for. An overall synthesis is necessary. In other words, it behooves a Heritage student to study early and sleep well. Unfortunately this is difficult because there are assignments up to the night before a test. When asked to comment on the Heritage program at the end of a long, painful week, . . . [Professor] McMullan said, "The students are the saving grace," but Dr. Reiff only sighed, "Thank God, it's Friday."

There were other problems, too. Padgett later recalled that one of his most difficult tasks was coordinating the companion English composition course with the Heritage classes, a problem that continued until a revised curriculum went into effect in 1992:

The aims were to provide practice in written and oral expression of ideas and to provide a more aesthetic approach to literature (by a focus on structure and form and diction and by comparing modern examples of a theme or genre with works studied in Heritage) while Heritage provided insight into the historical forces that helped shape a literary work, but students seemed to prefer that the classes turn into additional discussion sessions for the literature read in Heritage. [Padgett, 1993, p. 5]

But as he later remembered, "with the frustrations came compensations." Heritage provided learning experiences for faculty as well as students:

We all agreed at the beginning that at least for the first two years we would all attend all the lectures and laboratories and we soon discovered how important and valuable that experience was: in addition to letting each of us experience the same shifting of perspectives that the students were experiencing, it gave us all new insights into different teaching styles and exposure to approaches to interpreting texts and symbols we might not otherwise have encountered. . . .

   One of the most exciting parts (but occasionally one of the most exhausting parts) of directing the program in those first two years was the fact that our grant included sufficient income to allow us to bring to the campus and to the Jackson community free of charge a number of cultural programs of extraordinary international repute and quality. . . . [pp. 3–7]

Padgett (1969) ended his first semester in Heritage on an optimistic note. "It is too early yet to gauge the success of this experiment. We know the operation of the program is not perfect, and we are already involved in revisions and improvements. In general, however, the signs have been encouraging, and not the least important, I believe, is the fact that the Heritage Program has earned the accolade of Horatian satire in the *Purple and White;* and Horatian satire, I've been taught, expresses not only worthwhile criticism of the subject, but commitment to its real values and some affection for it" (p. 4).

Growing Pains

Tense times lay ahead for the program. Heritage developed a reputation for being extraordinarily difficult, and the staff was both worried and shocked when only 60 of 286 freshmen (20.9 percent) registered for the course the next fall. A year later, in the fall of 1970, the enrollment dipped to an alarming low of 43 of 252 entering freshmen (17 percent). In an effort to discern the problem questionnaires were distributed among former Heritage students, non-Heritage faculty members, and freshmen who declined to take Heritage. *The Purple and White* of October 13 reported that the major criticism "seems to be one concerning the degree of successful integration of areas covered. Some areas such as English and history are covered more thoroughly than areas of religion and philosophy." It correctly pointed out that "it is also evident that present history and history of the past 100 years have been neglected." Another problem cited was "the extreme demand placed on students in the course to complete requirements of the program." Surprisingly, 18 percent of the incoming freshmen who did not choose Heritage said they were unaware of "the availability of the program" and had therefore given little consideration to it when choosing classes. When asked who advised against taking Heritage, the paper reported that the most frequent response was "Millsaps upperclassmen or former students."

But Padgett (1993) remembered that "the students who enrolled continued to be some of the best and they evaluated the course as worthwhile, so we felt our experiments were working; by the fall of 1971 our first class—now seniors—had begun to appreciate the integration of their studies and the skills in reasoning they had developed and they encouraged their entering friends to risk the course, and our enrollments surged to eighty-eight that fall . . . and by the next fall the enrollment rose to ninety-seven" (p. 7).

From the beginning, the faculty noticed the camaraderie that developed among the Heritage students despite their grumbling. This was important in two ways, Padgett (1993) later reflected: "First, that esprit carried them through a demanding course of study (especially the first year when we had to admit that we had asked too much reading of freshmen and set about trimming the syllabus to more reasonable proportions as we went along) and, second, it left most of them with a sense of accomplishment that made them eventually some of our best recruiters in later years." By that time, Padgett recalled, "We . . . were providing study and discussion guides to focus the assignments more effectively" (p. 7).

Padgett (1993) believes it was probably during the third year that the Heritage Program came of age: "It was during that year's fall semester final exam that I entered AC-215 [the Heritage lecture hall] and descended its [nine] tiers (its circles?) to find inscribed in Gothic script on the blackboard: 'Abandon hope all ye who enter here' (the motto over Hell's gate in Dante's Inferno). I knew then that the Heritage Program had arrived. We had passed through despair and self-pity to wit and irony."

When Padgett took a well-deserved sabbatical in 1973–74, Frank Laney, who had left the deanship to return to the history department as chair, became the interim director. A 1974 grant proposal, written primarily by religion professor T. W. Lewis in consultation with Padgett, was made to the Phil Hardin Foundation in Meridian, Mississippi, to endow the Heritage Program and to provide for a full-time director. (Padgett had not only directed Heritage but lectured and led a discussion section as well as teaching two English classes.) The Hardin Foundation approved the grant, and subsequent grants for the next seven years provided annual funding for the program. The grants were crucial for the future of Heritage, because the college faced annual deficits in the mid-1970s. In 1983 a matched challenge grant from the National Endowment for the Humanities provided $600,000 to endow Heritage. Its financial status was secure.

Padgett returned to direct the program in 1974–75. A search undertaken to secure a full-time director tapped Richard Freis, who came to Millsaps from the University of California at Berkeley, where he was finishing his Ph.D. and teaching in the Division of Interdisciplinary and General Studies. In his midyear report on the Heritage Program, Freis wrote, "I was a member of the policy committee of that Division, and was engaged in a study of interdisciplinary programs throughout the United States. I was therefore in a position to recognize the superb judgment that had gone into the conception of the Heritage program, in its general structure and the details of its syllabus; I was not and am not acquainted with a more skillfully conceived freshman interdisciplinary program anywhere in the country."

The Hardin grant allowed Freis and Heritage staff members to spend the summer of 1975 reviewing policies and procedures of the program. Freis (1975) wrote, "It was because I had the opportunity for such an 'internship' period during the summer months of 1975, and thus was given the time to study the needs of the program, that the transition from Professor Padgett's directorship to my own occurred so smoothly" (p. 2). Attention was given to the syllabus, the coordination of staff meetings of the core faculty, and the improvement of student morale.

Padgett (1993) recalled that Freis's

> most important contribution, as I see it now, was providing a philosophic and thematic core for the program, a vision and coherence gradually developed over the years; this vision doubtless grew out of his own classical heritage and his early experience of interdisciplinary work in his undergraduate years at St. John's of Annapolis, but it was a product of his own poetic and spiritual imagination (which were both broad and deep) brooding on the works and events and issues. He is a poet and a charismatic teacher and he deployed those powers upon the students and the vigorous young faculty who joined him in those early years. [pp. 9–10]

Padgett's evaluation was correct. More than anyone else connected with Heritage, other than Padgett himself, Freis gave direction that guaranteed the future success of the program. In annual reports, foundation proposals, and interviews in the college and local Jackson newspapers, Freis successfully articulated the philosophical and pedagogical underpinnings of the Heritage Program. In *The Heritage Program* (1980), Freis observed that "interdisciplinary programs are notoriously unstable." He felt that successful interdisciplinary programs had common principles: clarity of precise goals and rationale; detailed planning of each semester's syllabus; coordination of and consultation with the core faculty on a regular basis; constant monitoring, periodic review, and revision when needed; support of students; careful faculty selection; and faculty development.

Freis addressed the question of student morale:

> An interdisciplinary course such as Heritage requires a great deal from freshmen students and potentially places considerable pressures on them. . . . We have tried to make sure that the students know from the start and at every point what is expected of them; we have tried to present a predictable framework within which the students can take responsibility for arranging their efforts and managing their time; we have tried to make the examinations central and consistent and the grading standards consistent between the various staff members; we have tried to make the presentations of material as clear as possible, both intellectually and in terms of the technical aspects of presentation; we have tried to display the interrelationships between the various subjects which the program treats. . . . [pp. 3–4]

Freis further articulated Heritage's task of imparting intellectual skills to its students:

> Heritage seeks to train the students in the skill of *synthesis,* the bringing together of diverse aspects of a subject into a coherent whole, a large, integrated picture, in which both the similarities and differences of the related elements are given their due; the skill of *analysis,* the breaking down of a subject or work into its constituent parts and governing principles; and the skill of *intellectual imagination* or *empathy,* the ability to go out of oneself into a culture, work, or situation which is initially foreign, to see and experience it in its own terms, from the inside. There are also many subordinate skills, such as self-responsibility, efficient assimilation of diverse types of material and practice of diverse modes of learning, which the Program addresses and tries to inculcate. [p. 4]

A crucial and vital part of the Heritage Program is its special projects and extracurricular events that are open to the larger Jackson community as well. For example, Heritage was part of a funding network that "cooperated to provide a residency for the Erick Hawkins Dance Company, which provided not only a performance but lectures and workshops dealing with issues in dance history and art criticism and aesthetics" (Freis, 1980, p. 4).

Other extracurricular activities were presented for the benefit of Heritage students and indeed the entire Millsaps community over the years. Each semester's syllabus lists and recommends such extracurricular activities as listening to classical music, watching selected educational television programs, visiting the local art galleries and museums, and attending plays, lectures, concerts, operas, and other live performances. For certain special events, attendance was required. Heritage students also were encouraged to attend on-campus theater, music, film, and literary presentations. The fall 1996 syllabus required students to attend and write reviews of two extracurricular events (from a long list).

In 1980, after directing the Heritage Program for five years, Freis was granted a year's leave of absence to write poetry and work on an opera based on the hero of the *Iliad*, Achilles. When he returned to direct the program in 1981–82, he requested a rotating directorship in order to provide released time from the duties of directing Heritage. Rick Mallette of the English department, who had joined the Heritage staff that year, was prepared to move into the directorship. He did so when Freis became scholar-in-residence for three years (funded by a private benefactor) to complete his own work. Padgett (1993) believed that Mallette and Freis complemented each other in valuable ways. He wrote, "I tend to think of Freis as the broadener, the enricher, Mallette as the concentrator, the focuser." When Mallette completed his three-year term in 1985, Freis was ready to return to the program.

Reform and Change

After sixteen years and three directors, the time seemed appropriate for a review of the program by the Heritage staff, assisted by an outside consultant. Paul Lacey, a professor of English with extensive experience in interdisciplinary teaching at Earlham College in Richmond, Indiana, came to Millsaps in January 1985.

Lacey interviewed all Heritage directors and acting directors, all ten current and past faculty participants, and students (those currently enrolled in Heritage and upperclass students who had taken Heritage), and he had extended conversations with Dean Robert H. King. He found that the goals and outcomes of the program were "well understood and agreed upon by students and staff." The students with whom he had conversations "looking back on their experience stress that it was demanding, rigorous, a great deal of work. . . . They learned how to write, how to make connections between works and concepts, how to synthesize large amounts of material" (Lacey, 1985, pp. 1–2).

Lacey observed this about the faculty:

> The faculty speak of the intense pressure they feel to achieve both broad coverage and depth of reading in the course. They are concerned that the parent departments of the Program should receive appropriate emphasis. Meeting these goals requires that faculty be skillful lecturers—able to condense great amounts of background, to "popularize" ideas without trivializing them, to present ideas cogently and lucidly. The lectures, preeminently, need to demonstrate the arts of analysis and synthesis. Teaching the course, by general agreement, is intellectually exciting. "The most exciting intellectual enterprise" of his life, according to one faculty member. The source of "fantastic intellectual development" for another. The course has allowed its staff to "continue with the unfinished business of being educated." [Lacey, 1985, p. 2]

To be a successful lecturer in Heritage, all agreed, one needed to be both a specialist and a generalist and to have the collegial support of the other faculty members. Lacey continued:

> The work of the course is both draining and anxiety-producing for faculty. In describing this experience, faculty tend to emphasize the stress of lecturing: one is required to communicate ideas to students of widely varying abilities and to do so before colleagues with the highest teaching and intellectual standards. One has only a single lecture to deal with a topic; each lecture must be a model of lucidity and an exciting performance. Both faculty and students said that the high energy and enthusiasm of the lecturers were essential for overcoming the passivity of listeners which occurs in

any large lecture course. Students cite as an important value of the course that faculty are lecturing on their favorite subjects. Faculty report a stimulation for them in being allowed to develop new interests by preparing lectures in those areas. Given all that rides on each lecture, it is no wonder that, even after a particular lecture has been well-honed over several years, it is common for the lecturer to have trouble sleeping the night before it is to be delivered. Nor is it surprising that staff, while remaining enthusiastic about the Program and their own development through it, report needing to be rotated out after three years, to overcome the exhaustion which it produces. [Lacey, 1985, p. 2]

Lacey's assessment, which confirmed the experiences of Heritage participants, included general recommendations for improving syllabi, lectures, discussions, examinations, and the use of guest lecturers.

When Mallette resumed the directorship in 1988, he fostered the development of the fine arts presentations so that they were more fully integrated into the weekly schedule. Women writers and gender issues were added to the syllabus. Mallette introduced the first Heritage reading anthology when, as Padgett (1993) said, the "Age of Xerox" arrived" (p. 11).

Padgett (1993) further commented on this decade: "Throughout the eighties Freis and Mallette were also concerned with expanding the scope of the course to focus more on recent history and even to consider the future; after all, the original Heritage course had been designed to be followed later by a Twentieth Century Issues course, so we had given relatively little attention to Modernism and contemporary history. By the eighties that neglect was growing more and more obvious. By the nineties the calls for multicultural studies and greater diversity in curricula were being heard as well" (pp. 10–11).

During the 1980s several events converged to create an atmosphere of reform and change. A key feature of the adult degree program, established in 1982, was the required entry seminar, designed by Padgett, to introduce adult students to liberal arts, critical thinking, and writing. These students could major in traditional fields or design interdisciplinary majors. An interdisciplinary science course, first proposed in 1965, was implemented for nonscience majors in 1984 as "Science and the Human Prospect." Faculty members in biology, chemistry, and physics developed the course after participating in a 1982 Workshop in the Liberal Arts, sponsored by the Lilly Endowment. Heritage faculty met in week-long presemester workshops in which they learned about learning styles, collaborative learning, and team-building skills. As a result, Heritage was immeasurably strengthened.

The Millsaps Writing Program, which encouraged "writing across the curriculum," was established with the hiring of a director in 1985 and an assistant to the director in 1988. Intensive week-long writing workshops for faculty were held the week following graduation in 1987, 1988, and 1989. In 1989 the faculty adopted a "writing across the curriculum" graduation requirement that stipulated that students must take a writing-intensive course (in any department) in their junior or senior year. Beginning in the fall of 1989, freshmen and sophomore students were required to assemble a writing portfolio for assessment by faculty members for writing proficiency. This initiative was supported by the Writing Center (established in 1986) and by a Fund for the Improvement of Post-Secondary Education (FIPSE) grant in 1990. "The intent of the requirement," reported Dean King, was "not simply to make students better writers but to promote their intellectual development through writing" (King, n.d., pp. 4–5).

An informal faculty study group met periodically during the 1980s to discuss women's issues. The faculty approved the establishment of a women's studies concentration, and many faculty members incorporated more scholarship about women into their courses. The Heritage staff, in a major revision of the syllabus, led in this regard. In his 1989–90 Report on the Heritage Program (p. 2), Mallette reported thirteen new or revised lectures, with three of them concentrating on women's issues: "Images of Women in the Late Seventeenth Century," "Nineteenth Century Feminism," and "Freud and Feminism."

Comprehensive Curriculum Review

As a result of the intellectual climate created during this period and in keeping with recommendations of Millsaps's Long Range Planning Commission in 1985, a faculty task force began a comprehensive review of the curriculum in 1988 and reported to the faculty in the fall of 1989. In the spring of 1990 the faculty elected six of its members to a curriculum review committee to consider several possible curriculum models. The status of Heritage was never an issue in these discussions. In February 1991, the faculty voted by a two-to-one majority to institute a new core curriculum to be implemented in the fall of 1992. There was general agreement that the major impetus for changing the curriculum was the intellectual climate created at Millsaps during the 1980s that emphasized active and collaborative learning.

A central feature of the new curriculum was its interdisciplinary approach to learning, something that Heritage had accomplished for more than twenty years. A memorandum from the newly created Core Council in August 1995 reminded the faculty that the Heritage Program "has been a premier program of the Millsaps curriculum. Its long and successful history of interdisciplinary teaching was the model for the new curriculum's revision of the Arts and Letters Core." When the Curriculum Revision Committee proposed ten core topics courses to replace the traditional general education curriculum, Heritage and the humanities courses (Core 2–5) "were seen as two ways to the same goal, with both programs providing different emphases—Heritage offering students a comprehensive and global overview of the human narrative and Core 2–5 offering students in-depth treatments of selected moments of this story."

Each Core 2–5 interdisciplinary topics course has a focus in at least one area: history, literature, religion, philosophy, or fine arts. Students must choose four courses from at least three of these areas and from all the historical periods (ancient, premodern, modern, contemporary). Team teaching is encouraged. Each course has a particular theme; the primary goal is not to transmit broad areas of knowledge (as in a traditional course) but rather to enable students to develop intellectual skills and abilities for critical thinking and proficient writing.

What are the skills and abilities that the Millsaps faculty believes are essential to be liberally educated? The following core abilities are listed in the college catalogue and have appeared in each Heritage syllabus since fall 1992:

> *Reasoning*—the ability to think logically and reflectively, to analyze critically and constructively
>
> *Communication*—the ability to express one's thoughts and feelings coherently and persuasively through written

and oral communication and to work effectively in
collaboration with others

Historical Consciousness—the ability to understand the
achievements, problems and challenges of the present with
perspectives gained from a study of the past

Aesthetic Judgment—the ability to understand and appreciate
creative responses to the world and to develop one's own
modes of creative expression

Global and Multi-Cultural Awareness—the ability to understand
and appreciate a variety of social and cultural perspectives

Valuing and Decision-Making—the ability to understand and
appreciate differing moral viewpoints; to make carefully
considered, well-reasoned decisions; and to make a mature
assessment of one's own abilities, beliefs and values

Implementing the new curriculum made great demands on
faculty members who were teaching core courses. They now had
to design new courses, work with colleagues, and learn about fields
other than the ones in which they were trained. But as was
reported in the college's proposal to the Knight Foundation in
1991 (pp. 8–9), "Some of the faculty have already had extensive
experience with collaborative teaching through their participation
in Heritage. They have worked with colleagues from other disciplines in the selection of readings, the preparation of discussion
guides, and the setting of examinations."

When the faculty adopted the new curriculum, it included the
charge that the Heritage Program become global in its scope.
David Davis, a historian who taught world civilization and African
and Near Eastern history, was named director of Heritage in 1992
with the task of making that transformation. Davis worked with a
faculty committee to implement changes.

Important changes were made in the early 1990s. A structural
change added a discussion session and eliminated one lecture per
week, so there were now three discussion sessions and four lectures. This change added to the faculty workload: ten hours in six
discussion sessions and four lectures plus one hour for the weekly
staff meeting. An ideological change occurred with the addition
of a global and multicultural perspective along with a name change
to "Heritage of the West in a World Perspective." Short writing

assignments of one to three pages per week, a longer paper of eight to twelve pages, and four unit examinations per semester were required. Heritage students and professors would engage in e-mail conferences outside class, and the Heritage web page (http://www.millsaps.edu/www/heritage/) provided on-line readings for each semester plus links to other sites.

To encourage active learning and responsibility for one's own learning, several new exercises were added: an autobiographical paper, "What is my heritage?" questions for discussion sessions, short response papers after presentations, historical simulation games, weekly writings, major semester papers, peer reviews of drafts, and projects in which student teams create Heritage presentations and plan discussion sessions.

In spring 1995 the Core Council conducted an assessment of the Core Curriculum and then invited Barbara Lawrence, the director of Institutional Research at Idaho State University, to visit the campus as a consultant. The Heritage Program, an integral component of the Core Curriculum, was included in this assessment. After an intensive and productive assessment, the conclusion was that the core curriculum "was on track," true to the vision the faculty adopted in 1991. There were, however, a number of ways in which the curriculum could be strengthened. Noting that Core 2–5 offered "a very challenging course of study," the council observed that "when students in focus meetings were asked to comment on the Millsaps core curriculum as a whole, they often were quite positive, particularly when they compared their educational experience in the core with the education of their friends in other institutions. There were elements they wanted us to do better—but they generally did not feel oppressed or burdened by the demands of the core curriculum" (Millsaps Core Council, 1995, p. 7).

All agreed that the Core 2–5 option allowed students more time to work on writing and thinking skills begun in Core 1, "Introduction to Liberal Studies," required of all freshmen. Core 2–5 students have two years to engage in the intensive writing assignments of their classes. Heritage "cannot in a single year, allow students the time to mature as writers." The council noted that the Heritage staff was aware of this difference and that "current [Heritage] students have commented how much more carefully they are writing and thinking" (Millsaps Core Council, 1995, p. 4).

Referring to faculty discussions and workshops at Millsaps in the 1980s on critical thinking and learning stages and styles, the council sounded a somber note: "A large number of the faculty who were part of this movement are now in their fifties or nearing retirement, and several leaders have left the College for other reasons. But the College has not fully initiated the younger faculty into this culture of pedagogy or made pedagogical innovation important to them" (Millsaps Core Council, 1995, p. 6). It then recommended that faculty be sent to off-campus workshops on critical thinking, learning stages and styles, writing, and pedagogy. Pedagogical development should be supported through faculty development grants, and efforts by younger faculty to bring creative methods into their teaching should be rewarded in faculty evaluation. This, of course, would include Heritage faculty.

In April 1998 the second stage of the review of the Core Curriculum was completed at the request of Dean Richard Smith and the Core Council. Heritage director Steven Smith and the Heritage staff submitted an exhaustive review of the Heritage Program to the faculty. They discussed the advantages and disadvantages of Heritage and the questions that had been raised in the course of the curriculum review process.

Advantages included some obvious benefits. Heritage provides a "big picture" of the humanities that allows freshmen to "make major discoveries about non-Western cultures." The constant rotation of new and returning faculty into Heritage offers invaluable interaction with colleagues in other disciplines. "Since the presenters usually cannot even pretend to 'cover' their subjects, they instead make focused *arguments* that the audience is invited to assess critically as regards both the conclusions drawn and the procedures followed." There is time during two semesters to give personal attention to students and to include "desirable extras" such as the cocurricular cultural events (Millsaps Core Council, 1998, p. 13). These advantages account in large measure for the continuing popularity of Heritage.

Disadvantages of Heritage were equally apparent. Because Heritage cannot deal with any field as well as Core 2–5 topics courses do, it "pushes students to excel in generalizing more than in looking closely or thinking strictly." Since few faculty are trained to teach non-Western cultures, this part of Heritage suffers.

Because of the intensity of preparing Heritage lectures, especially those involving non-Western issues, and of the burden of keeping up with the heavy reading assignments, it has been challenging to recruit new faculty to take on these responsibilities. Heritage is also extremely demanding for students, and many are overwhelmed by the course expectations. As a result, some students lose the momentum necessary to sustain the work. Many resort to doing the "minimum necessary for a respectable grade," and "as for the number of activities involved, there are so many that Heritage often comes to be experienced more as a grind than as an adventure." Smith added, "Over the years, Heritage faculty have wrestled with the issues addressed above. Some of the disadvantages may yet be further ameliorated; certain disadvantages may have to be accepted as trade-offs, if Millsaps is to retain a program of this sort" (Millsaps Core Council, 1998, pp. 13–14).

The findings by the Heritage faculty were echoed in various ways in the anonymous student evaluations gathered at the end of semesters. Since the beginning, students have been given opportunities to evaluate the Heritage Program. In addition, they can offer criticisms, comments, and suggestions anonymously throughout the semester. These assessments are kept only for the previous two years. In the 1997 and 1998 evaluations, the comments ranged from extreme satisfaction to extreme disappointment. In general, the discussion sections had the highest praise from students, who applauded the closeness, the focus on the interchange of ideas and active learning, the purpose of Heritage, and their own intellectual growth. The following comments are from students who rated Heritage "excellent" or "good":

> This course has challenged my traditional views in a manner that made me see different perspectives and challenged my ability to present my perspectives clearly with logical arguments to back them up.

> It has taught me to think in new ways. This course has truly been a benefit to me. I see how all the disciplines are connected and can't really be separated.

> I have never learned so much in a course. I have learned more about subjects I didn't like and have come to enjoy. I feel as if

I have truly gotten the complete liberal arts education through Heritage. It has really made me think.

It has challenged me to think at a different level.

My greatest reward was all the new knowledge acquired and how I was able to apply it to my life.

Nevertheless, many students complained about such matters as the overwhelming workload, the inconsistency of grading they perceived among Heritage section leaders (a persistent issue that appeared early in Heritage's history), and the early-morning Thursday class, among others. The following are comments from students who rated Heritage "average" or "poor":

This course tries to cover *way* too much material *way* too fast so that we only touch on various events in history. [The most rewarding aspect of the course for this student was "the fact that I don't have to take any more history when this class is over."]

Heritage dictates your schedule. Some days we had discussions, lecture, and a required extracurricular event at night—while having to read more for the next day. *Too* much required of us!

I have not been pleased with Heritage. I feel like I am being questioned for my religious beliefs and often times I feel the faculty mocks us for our faith. Being at a Methodist school, I don't think my Christian beliefs should be constantly criticized. My faith was questioned/ridiculed and I found it to be a boring class. I would *not* tell anyone to take Heritage in the future.

One student who rated Heritage as average was clearly conflicted by the experience: "Perhaps because I was so worried about my grade the whole time, I couldn't get too much out of it. There was entirely too much work given that one couldn't possibly do it all." Yet, the student wrote, "Heritage is a very fulfilling course and I have learned more about my history and myself than ever before. It is an exceptional program."

A persistent concern is that students who choose the core topics alternative rather than Heritage may not "develop comparable knowledge and skills." Associate Dean Judy Page addressed this issue in the core review of April 1998: "Heritage teachers remind us all that even though Heritage is structured as an historical narrative, there are necessarily many gaps and omissions in coverage. Heritage also includes the kinds of in-depth exercises and textual analyses that core topics courses require." Actually, offering two ways to meet core requirements is an advantage: "Some students benefit from the fast-paced year-long course and others from the slower assimilation of core topics. Heritage cannot accomplish everything in one year that is structured into core topics in two years. Students do not develop in the same way; nor is it possible to do the same amount of writing" (Millsaps Core Council, 1998, p. 10).

Other college programs are at least tangentially connected to the Heritage Program if not indeed its offspring. In September and October 1980 Richard Freis and Charles Sallis adapted a portion of the Heritage syllabus for a seminar for a group of executives from Unifirst Bank for Savings, then the largest savings and loan association in Mississippi. The seminar, called "The Humanities and the Rise of a Global Technological Civilization," met once a week on campus for eight weeks and discussed readings by Machiavelli, Bacon, Hobbes, Mill, and Marx and Engels, among others. This seminar was very well received by these men and women from the business community and provided a model for the Leadership Seminars in the Humanities, which were established in 1988.

In 1987 Millsaps submitted a proposal to the National Endowment for the Humanities requesting a three-year grant to provide start-up costs for Leadership Seminars in the Humanities. The seminars are now in their second decade, and ten Millsaps faculty members who served in Heritage have successfully directed seminars.

Conclusion

The fall 1998 Heritage syllabus introduces the purpose of the Heritage Program to the members of the Millsaps Class of 2002 who will graduate in the twenty-first century: "As you better comprehend the interwoven dynamics shaping the world we have inherited, you should begin to view yourself as an active and essential participant in shaping our future world. Heritage will provide a variety of learning situations in which you can develop the skills that will empower you as a discerning consumer of information, sensitive leader, and responsible citizen in the global community. As an essential part of your liberal arts education, and as an integral part of your core experience, Heritage will help you develop skills essential for life-long learning."

No doubt the same sort of challenge was issued to the 1968 Millsaps freshmen who were members of the first Heritage class. In the words of the Millsaps Statement of Purpose that was current when the Heritage Program began, Millsaps College sought to give students "breadth and depth of understanding of civilization and culture," to broaden their perspectives, to enrich their personalities, and to enable them "to think and act intelligently amid the complexities of the modern world" (Millsaps College Catalog, 1968–69, p. 4). A generation later these words still ring true, and the Heritage Program has played a major role in keeping this pledge.

References
Freis, R. *Report on the Heritage Program.* Jackson, Miss.: Millsaps College, Dec. 31, 1975.

Freis, R. *The Heritage Program.* Jackson, Miss.: Millsaps College, Nov. 1980.

Freis, R. "Heritage Program Proposal to the Phil Hardin Foundation." Jackson, Miss.: Millsaps College, Nov. 7, 1980.

King, R. H. *Assessment and Institutional Change: The Millsaps Story.* Jackson, Miss.: Millsaps College, n.d.

Lacey, P. A. *A Report on Millsaps' Heritage Program.* Jackson, Miss.: Millsaps College, Jan. 1985.

Lawrence, B. *Assessment of the Millsaps Core Curriculum.* Jackson, Miss.: Millsaps College, Apr. 1995.

Mallette, R. *Report on the Heritage Program, 1989–1990.* Jackson, Miss.: Millsaps College, 1990.

Millsaps College. "Grant Proposal to the John S. and James L. Knight Foundation." Apr. 3, 1991.

Millsaps College Catalog, 1968–69, 1997–1999.

Millsaps Core Council to Millsaps Faculty, Aug. 18, 1995.

Pack, V. "Heritage Buttermilks." *Purple and White,* Feb. 28, 1969, p. 4.

Padgett, R. H. "An Introduction to the Millsaps Heritage Program." *Major Notes,* 1969, *10*(3), 3–4.

Padgett, R. H. *A Brief History of the Heritage Program: Some Highly Personal Musings and Remembrances of Things Past.* Jackson, Miss.: Millsaps College, 1993.

Report of the Curriculum Revision Committee, August 1990.

Summer Curriculum Study Committee. "Proposal for a Revised Curriculum." Jackson, Miss.: Millsaps College, Sept. 1965.

Chapter Nine

The Humanities Program at the University of North Carolina at Asheville

Margaret J. Downes

Since 1969, the University of North Carolina at Asheville's (UNCA) four-year, four-course Humanities Program has provided the heart of each student's education at this designated liberal arts campus of the University of North Carolina system. Humanities, as the program is commonly known, actually began in 1964 at Asheville-Biltmore College, which in 1969 became incorporated into the state system as UNCA. Since 1964, this interdisciplinary program has been planned and taught by an interdepartmental staff—at first by nearly all the faculty in the traditional humanities disciplines and, for the last twenty-five years, by faculty drawn from departments across the university, including the natural and social sciences. UNCA emphasizes excellent undergraduate teaching by a faculty strong in scholarship and is able to attract to the Humanities Program experienced instructors, including several department chairs and award-winning professors, along with junior faculty. As any healthy program must and should, Humanities has altered its contours over the years as faculty, administrators, and students have responded to changing conditions and opportunities. For all of its changes, however, the program remains probably the most notable and most widely recognized entity at the university.

Program Origins

In 1963, Asheville-Biltmore College's student body numbered approximately seven hundred. Its small faculty and its cooperative administration, both dedicated to the college's liberal arts mission, conducted enthusiastic and intense formal and informal discussions concerning reformation of the disciplined-based general education requirements. Later that year, a faculty-elected committee decided on a new general education program. "The key decision they made was in reference to the humanities," writes the university's first chancellor, William E. Highsmith. "The committee members wanted to make a genuine break with some of the traditional methods that had divided the humanities into more specific academic disciplines, such as history, literature, philosophy, religion, art, music, history of architecture, and so on. They wanted the institution to have a strong, humanistically oriented base that would tie together many of the ideas within the broad area of humanities and show how they were fundamentally related.

The result was that the largest block of work in the general education curriculum required of all students would be six four-hour courses called the Humanities" (Highsmith, 1991, pp. 61–62). Four four-semester-hour courses would be taken by students during their freshman year (taught in "half-term mode," or seven-week half-semesters), and two during their sophomore year, providing an intensive humanities base for each student's liberal arts education. The courses were these: "The Ancient World (Beginnings to 180 A.D.)," "The Medieval World (180 to 1350)," "An Age of Transition (1350 to 1700)," "The West and the World (1700 to 1850)," "The World and the West (1850 to 1920)," and "The World in Our Time (1920 to the Present)." Nearly all, if not all (the record is not clear), of the faculty from the traditional humanities disciplines taught in this new program. By incorporating all general education requirements in the humanities disciplines into one set of interdisciplinary courses, the faculty intended to inform students better about the history of Western culture, thus encouraging them to ponder, question, and discuss ongoing human concerns with their peers and their teachers across the boundaries of the humanities disciplines.

Since the work of that first group of faculty, all decisions about the program's content and course arrangement have been made by the Humanities director and faculty. At least every few years, a Humanities faculty committee reviews and adjusts the program's goals and objectives. Traditionally, the instructors in each humanities course meet weekly to discuss course content and pedagogy, and at the end of each semester they meet to reform the syllabus. More substantive changes (in number of courses, or in restatement of the program's mission, for example) need approval by UNCA's elected faculty senate.

From those first years, the Humanities courses have begun with interdisciplinary study of the ancient Greeks, concluded with today's world, and used "Changes in Western Civilization" as the guiding time line. Humanities covers an ambitious amount of territory. UNCA has had no other general education requirements in history, literature, philosophy, or world religions, and although there always have been general education courses required in the social and natural sciences, materials from these areas have been included in the Humanities courses since the early 1970s. Basically, the early program was a set of great books courses.

The umbrella of the first Humanities Program was ambitiously large and became more stable and useful when trimmed. In 1967 the program was reduced to twenty semester hours, with content reconfigured into five courses: "The Ancient World (Beginnings to 600 A.D.)," "The Medieval World and the Renaissance (600 to 1600 A.D.)," "The Dominance of the West (1600 to 1850 A.D.)," "The Emergence of the Modern World (1850 to the Present)," and "The Modern World (Some Possible Shapes of Things to Come)." In 1970, the faculty approved dropping the fifth, futuristic, course, believing that more careful structuring would allow UNCA to keep Humanities strong and viable.

In Humanities' early years, students' sole formal instruction in writing occurred in the program, but this requirement gradually changed during the 1970s into two separate freshman courses in English composition. Another spin-off occurred in 1986 when a four-credit-hour, interdisciplinary, junior-level "Arts and Ideas" course was formed. Like Humanities, "Arts and Ideas" is a required, core general education course, taught by an interdepartmental faculty drawn mostly from the creative writing, drama, music, and art departments. The course encompasses presentations by artists of what they do and why, and requires students to engage in some form of artistic creation. Humanities courses also use the creative arts to exemplify particular points of cultural distinctiveness and change.

When the program began, Humanities courses were team-planned and sometimes team-taught by faculty from the departments of English, philosophy, classics, history, art, and music. In the early 1970s, as UNCA (and other colleges) faced some resistance to required, core general education, Humanities director Robert Trullinger successfully moved to widen the reach of the program to include both faculty and materials from the natural and social sciences. This stabilized the base of support for Humanities on campus and gave UNCA the model that continues to flourish.

For each course, students and faculty attended (and still attend) a large group lecture once each week. The custom was established (and generally is maintained) that the faculty member assigned a particular lecture should not be an expert on the assigned topic, but rather should model for the students the teacher as learner. This weekly lecture is followed by two discussion classes, in which students in groups of eighteen to twenty-five meet with an instructor. Since the program's beginnings, discussions have focused on assigned primary source materials concerned with "the story of the human race, what we have done, how we have lived, what we have desired, what we have believed" (Highsmith, 1991, p. 253). In general, complete books were assigned rather than a combination of complete works and excerpts, as is the current practice.

Program Adjustments

During the 1970s and early 1980s, Humanities continued to adjust to the turbulent post-1960s world. In 1971 the program expanded, adding "Problems in the Modern World" as a senior-level elective. In 1978, this course was dropped from the catalogue due to low enrollments. In 1973, the courses were rearranged so that "The Contemporary World" preceded "The Ancient World," "The Rise of the West," and "The Emergence of the Modern World." "The Contemporary World" was made into a catch-all course, used to give entering freshmen an introduction to the use of the library and to college life in general (study skills, the "social scene," finding one's way around campus), as well as to provide a forum for discussing various readings on the contemporary world. (UNCA's First-Year Experience Program now focuses on these freshman needs.) Which readings these were was entirely the individual instructor's choice. It soon was apparent, however, that faculty had been overly optimistic in assuming that entering freshmen would be more conversant with their present-day world than with the past. Thus, in 1978, UNCA returned to a chronological presentation of the Humanities courses, having discovered that students better understood their own world once they had studied its earlier ages. The faculty also reaffirmed their commitment to a shared syllabus for every Humanities course, having become convinced of the value of these as bases for campus conversation and knowledge.

The 1979–80 UNCA catalogue shows several major changes in Humanities. Although the four courses still covered materials from the ancient to the contemporary world, individual thematic emphases were added, at each instructor's choice, to the chronological coverage, and the courses were rearranged to be taken one in the freshman, two in the sophomore, and one in the senior year: "The Universe and the Individual," "The Quest for Knowledge and the Individual," "Mass Society and the Individual," and "The Future and the Individual." (In 1981, the courses again were renamed: "The Ancient World," "The Rise of European Civilization," "The Modern World," "The Future and the Individual.") With that rearrangement, students would experience Humanities first as an introduction to their UNCA years and finally as a senior capstone course, in which their knowledge of their majors, as well as of the materials in the first three Humanities courses, could be brought to bear in discussions. Some academic departments had expressed a preference to the director that the entire junior year be left open for courses in the majors, which explains why two Humanities courses became required in the sophomore year.

In 1996, the Humanities faculty agreed on skills objectives for each course, as follows:

"The Ancient World"

Listening, note-taking and study: Instructors should feel free to teach any effective note-taking strategy they think would be useful.

Reading: The students will develop their skill in active reading by working on a writing assignment emphasizing analysis or "close reading" and the annotation of texts.

Writing: Students will write an analysis or "close-reading paper" requiring a clear statement of thesis, the use of quotations from the text, and a demonstration that the student understands how the quotations provide an explication of the text and support the thesis.

Discussion: The students will take an assigned problem or issue and discuss it in a small group session. A member of the group will write up the results of the discussion.

"The Medieval and Renaissance World"

Listening, note-taking and study: The students will receive instruction on how to study for essay examinations and how to write more advanced essay responses than those they composed for "The Ancient World."

Reading: The students will practice reading from appropriate secondary material, as a way of enhancing their primary reading and of incorporating research into their own prose (see *Writing* below). In discussions, they may be asked to quote directly from research sources and evaluate the statements to which they refer.

Writing: Students will review the work on the statement of a thesis, introduced in "The Ancient World," and extend it to serve within a brief research essay. Instructors may suggest that the students use the thesis to show how the topic of their research reflects the Medieval or Renaissance culture. For this objective, instructors may find it useful to limit the resources students employ (see *Reading* above).

Discussion: In small groups, students will be responsible for leading a discussion of the texts to explore major themes. The small group work may then form the basis for full class discussion.

"The Modern World"

Reading: The students will practice the skill of reading critical or interpretive essays on course material.

Writing: The students each will write a critical research essay and will design their own topic in consultation with the instructor. Their research will be aimed toward exploring/critiquing a cultural, political, aesthetic, or scientific perspective and making an evaluation based on their research and thought.

Presentation: Students, either individually or in small groups, will prepare a presentation on an assigned topic designed to focus on subject matter ancillary to a given session's theme. They will deliver their presentation to the class.

"The Individual in the Contemporary World"

Reading: Students will practice the reading of a broad range of texts, possibly controversial in nature, with a view to placing an author's ideas in an immediate cultural, historical, and political context. The emphasis for reading skills will be the use of texts to construct a more deeply informed worldview, one which both examines the present to take into account contemporary intellectual debate and looks back over the past to discover the underlying connections emphasized throughout the Humanities sequence.

Writing: The students will analyze the arguments of texts in a paper exploring an issue related to the course themes. Research will be aimed at exploring multiple perspectives as they inform a set of cultural, political, aesthetic or scientific issues and then drawing from this exploration an informed conclusion or a resolution of apparent contradiction. Instructors, of course, should determine the specific parameters of this assignment.

Presentation: Each student will be asked to prepare a brief, individual presentation to be delivered to the class.

Since its early days, changes in the program have been guided by and often initiated by its director, a faculty member appointed by the vice chancellor for academic affairs after consultation with the advisory council of chairs, a body comprising one appointed and four elected members. Until 1985, the director was given one course of reassigned time per semester; he or she had no budget and no secretary. In 1985, in response to demands created by growing enrollment, the reassigned time was increased to two courses per semester; the director was given control of a modest budget (now at the thirtieth percentile of UNCA's department and program budgets); and the program was given a three-quarter-time secretary (full time as of 1997–98).

As the university has grown (the full-time-equivalent [FTE] students more than quadrupling, since 1970, to thirty-one hundred FTEs), the director has come to depend more and more on faculty coordinators to organize each of the four courses. Each coordinator, appointed by the director, makes sure that a revised syllabus is in place each semester, runs the weekly faculty planning meeting, meets biweekly with the other coordinators and the director, and helps out in a number of other ways. In the 1990s, the coordinators were permitted one course of reassigned time from the vice chancellor for academic affairs' budget so that they could be replaced by adjunct faculty in one course in their home department. In practice, however, these duties have been performed gratis nearly half the time, without request for this reduced teaching load.

In 1984, Chancellor Highsmith retired and was succeeded by David G. Brown, a strong proponent of the Humanities Program. Brown had been attracted to UNCA by its reputation for providing a solid liberal arts education for all students and "agreed with the long-held premise that the humanities program was the core of each student's interdisciplinary study." In support of this stance, "one of his first major decisions regarding curriculum enhancement was to channel $50,000.00 above and beyond regular funding to three areas, of which the humanities program was one" (Highsmith, 1991, p. 244).

Brown's "thrust funding" allowed Humanities to conduct seminars directed by on- and-off campus scholars, as well as other faculty development activities. The longest-lasting and internally beneficial project begun with this money was the creation in 1984 of a Humanities Faculty Internship Program, which the vice chancellor for academic affairs has continued to support. Michael Ruiz, chair of the department of physics (and an outstanding classical pianist), suggested the idea, having himself taught a Humanities course for the first time without graduate education in much of that course's philosophy, poetry, and other traditional humanities content. Thus, since 1984, in order to prepare and encourage faculty who are new to a Humanities course, internships permit the reassignment of three hours of class time to new instructors during the semester before they first teach that course. (UNCA's annual teaching load is twenty-four semester credit hours, with the possibility of a reduction of three hours for an approved special project.) Although each intern works primarily with a mentor well experienced in Humanities teaching, he or she is strongly encouraged to visit the sections of all who are teaching the course, both to learn the materials better and to observe pedagogy. The intern also attends the weekly faculty planning meetings for his or her Humanities course.

Without the internships, it would be far more difficult to recruit and retain excellent teachers. Although some faculty occasionally intern without benefit of reassigned time (due to short-handedness and an insufficient pool of part-time faculty in their department), the offer of reassigned time is encouraging to all. In the experience of the program, giving a stipend for interning is no substitute for reassigned time. Occasionally, experienced Humanities instructors intern in a Humanities course different from the one in which they have been teaching; to date, seven faculty have taught all four courses, and seventeen have taught more than one, an experience that both enriches their teaching and simplifies the director's job of assigning instructors to the four courses each semester.

Current Contours, Conventions, and Controversies

Thanks to the internships, a generous faculty, and the generally positive profile of the Humanities Program on campus, 71 of UNCA's 155 full-time faculty teach at least one Humanities course. They want to do so not only because the experience is intellectually stimulating, but also because tenure, promotion, and merit raise decisions take into serious consideration their contributions to interdisciplinary programs in general education. Most of UNCA's faculty realize the benefits of teaching at an institution that is credited both inside and outside its walls with a strong interdisciplinary core general education program. Most also are aware of the internal benefits of the greater collegiality encouraged by interdepartmental participation in such a program.

Although nearly half the faculty can teach Humanities courses, other campus duties prevent their regular and predictable annual participation. Since the early 1970s, outside consultants to the program have remarked on its need to have some permanent claim on the use of faculty. This goal has not yet been attained due to complications such as the creation, since 1986, of more interdisciplinary programs (Arts and Ideas, Women's Studies, International Studies, Africana Studies, and Multi-Media), the growth in the majors, and the assignment (permanent as well as ad hoc) of increasing numbers of faculty to administrative positions. In 1998–99 (including summer 1998), 124 sections of Humanities were taught, 73 percent by full-time faculty. But there was no guarantee that these same faculty, or *any* 73 percent of UNCA's faculty, would teach Humanities in subsequent years. This leads the director to depend on a cadre of highly qualified and enthusiastic part-time faculty (all have master's degrees; a few have the Ph.D.), most of whom stay with the program for several years. Although the pay for adjunct instructors is slowly increasing, it remains low—under six hundred dollars per semester credit hour.

The director must work constantly to obtain and retain faculty, but this work is fruitful in part because Humanities always has had support from the university's chancellor and the vice chancellor for academic affairs. These administrators have regarded the Humanities courses as central to UNCA's mission and have entrusted the faculty with control of the program through its director, its course coordinators, and a strong faculty senate.

As a sixteen-hour, core general education requirement involving a wide range of faculty, Humanities is UNCA's most prominent campus program and thus seems to many to be the obvious place to experiment: with inclusion of greater gender, racial, and cultural diversity; with service learning (using community service by students as a pedagogical technique, particularly in teaching the contemporary materials in "The Future and the Individual"); and with peer mentoring (faculty helping each other with their teaching)—all current examples of pursuits within the program. With nearly everyone on UNCA's rather small campus interested in and in some way affected by what is going on in Humanities, suggestions, questions, and debates about its workings are inevitable. For UNCA, Humanities is a large program, drawing in nearly half of the full-time faculty and all of the students. Approximately 120 to 125 sections are scheduled each year, including the summer term. Thus, every UNCA professor has at least one departmental colleague who has taught, or plans to teach, in the program. For this and other reasons, Humanities is a popular topic of conversation.

This general interest has resulted in healthy alterations in the program throughout its fairly long life, adjustments that have contributed to the longevity of Humanities. It is, by and large, a faculty-forged, faculty-run program, which by its interdisciplinarity (and its internships) helps to keep the walls between departments from becoming thick or opaque. Humanities helps to keep UNCA's faculty conversing—not infrequently about the effectiveness of the program and how it could be improved. The program's centrality to the mission of the university has kept it interesting to UNCA's administration, some of whom have participated in the program as interns or as lecturers at the weekly large group sessions.

The university community not only watches what happens in the Humanities Program, but also reviews and reassesses it in a number of ways. UNCA's first formal review of its general education programs and courses, by a senate-elected committee in the period 1982–1985, included debate about the Humanities Program's goals and objectives ("Is it really interdisciplinary?") and its four-course sequence ("Is sixteen credit hours excessive? enough?" and, "Why this particular sequence?"). But these debates were short-lived. The Humanities Program was approved unchanged, probably because it traditionally does change—all the time. (The fact that it was discussed toward the end of the three-year general education review also played some role in its easy and quick approval.) UNCA's second formal general education review began in fall 1999 and most certainly will address issues of diversity and coverage in Humanities, as well as the difficulties in achieving ongoing and predictable departmental commitment of faculty to the program. There undoubtedly will be speculation about the feasibility of other arrangements of the sixteen credit hours currently allotted to Humanities and about the current, basically chronological arrangement of the program's courses and materials. Certainly the issue of just what interdisciplinary means will be revisited, as will the issue of teaching "out of field."

Because the faculty who teach any of the four Humanities courses are never exactly the same from one semester to the next, the program is regularly under review as new perspectives flow into group discussions and decision making. The inclusion of new instructors and interns also presents an annual need to review and revise the program's goals, course requirements and policies, syllabi, and choice of textbooks. Newcomers often end up changing a Humanities course, changing the contours of the program in the process. For example, in 1997, a professor of Chinese history and culture began teaching Humanities; the first two courses now reflect his influence. In "The Individual in the Contemporary World," a number of new faculty (including two from the Sudan) called for a focus on international human rights, a topic now dealt with more explicitly in that course.

There are other regular avenues for program review and improvement. The weekly one-hour planning meetings for each course give faculty a chance to review (and refresh) the upcoming week's large group lecture and to share ideas about how best to teach the following week's assigned readings. Newer instructors ask questions and make suggestions that lead their more experienced colleagues to rethink the ways the course has been conducted. Regular weekly meetings began in 1983 and continue to the present. (Before that year, Humanities faculty met frequently but less predictably.) When faculty began these formal weekly meetings, they often were reluctant to admit that they could not teach everything on an interdisciplinary syllabus well. This reserve thawed eventually, but catalysts still have to be added regularly to keep humility respectable. An esteemed colleague's admission of ignorance does much to encourage his or her peers to make similar admissions, and thus to move the group toward greater knowledge.

At the end of each semester, each course's faculty (that semester's and the next semester's) meets to review the strengths and weaknesses of the course and to revise its syllabus. Biweekly, the Humanities director meets with the four course coordinators, an invaluable advisory board. These meetings also help to keep the four courses coordinated with each other. Occasional full-year or semester-long faculty seminars involve perhaps one-third of the Humanities faculty. (The most recent, on ancient through contemporary human rights, was conducted in 1999–2000.)

Two or three times each semester the entire Humanities faculty meets in plenary sessions. About half to two-thirds of the faculty attend. (Attendance is voluntary, but the director issues many personal invitations.) In 1998, for example, members of the Humanities faculty gathered three times to share teaching tips: once to hear several teachers' five-minute reflections on the sufficiency of multiculturalism in the Humanities curriculum and twice simply to socialize. Thus, Humanities changes according to the general will of the faculty who teach it, with final decisions being made by the director, sometimes in consultation with the vice chancellor for academic affairs.

Probably the program's richest self-review took place at the first Humanities retreat, following the conclusion of the spring 1998 semester. This three-day event took place at a pastoral spot just outside Asheville. Thirty-two faculty (including two part-time faculty) attended, representing all participating departments and faculty ranks, a range of scholarly interests, and a wide spectrum of political leanings. Seventeen participants chose to stay overnight. The format alternated small group and plenary discussions of the syllabi, textbooks, and program goals and objectives; about half the waking hours were spent in relaxation and informal conversation. Because of the location (green, fresh, calm, and generally inviting), the timing (postgraduation, pre–summer school), and the intensity (the location was isolated), the retreat was highly successful. Two major goals were met: first, those in attendance became aware of what is included in all four syllabi (most knew about just one syllabus); second, program goals and objectives were openly debated, leading to plans to make a final (for the next few years, at least) decision about them during the academic year. These questions, for example, arose: What is the overarching objective of the program—if we have one? What is the future of globalism in the program?

In modeling these processes of review and renewal and in several other ways as well, the Humanities Program is central to the university's curriculum and campus culture. First and foremost, it exemplifies UNCA's mission to provide excellent, interdisciplinary teaching. UNCA exercises selective admissions criteria: in fall 1998 the entering students' mean high school grade point average was 3.66 on a 4.0 scale, and their mean Scholastic Aptitude Test score was 1142 (the national mean was 1017). Many of UNCA's students have never traveled beyond western North Carolina, and many are the first in their families to attend college. Thus, the Humanities

Program provides an important opportunity for them to venture further intellectually into the world, as well as into their own (and their fellow students' and teachers') academic and personal capabilities. The requirement that each Humanities student attend three or four cultural events on or off campus during the semester expands their realization of themselves as budding cosmopolitans (and certainly adds to the size of the audiences for these events).

UNCA's primary aim, like that of each Humanities course, is to help students realize themselves as unique, well-informed, active members of a global community of learners and doers. The instructors, each venturing beyond his or her discipline, show the students just what it means to be a learner, even when one already knows a lot. As part of their learning, students in Humanities courses are required to participate in classroom discussion of the weekly large group lectures and the assigned primary source readings. To the faculty's gratification, these discussions often continue outside class, with faculty, with fellow students (even in the gym locker rooms), and in non-Humanities courses. Apparently students are connecting their Humanities general education with their other learning.

Humanities often is the place where initiatives begin on campus. For example, the university's first (of three, to date) interdisciplinary endowed chair, a National Endowment for the Humanities (NEH) Distinguished Teaching Professorship, was appointed in 1997. This professorship is combined with the directorship of the Humanities Program for a three-year term. As NEH Professor, the Humanities director receives two additional hours of reassigned time per semester to improve teaching in the Humanities program—for example, by organizing workshops, setting up peer mentoring relationships among faculty, and encouraging and helping to fund professional travel. Because the majority of the Humanities faculty are regular departmental faculty, the teaching improvements encouraged by these NEH-funded mentoring activities ultimately benefit the whole campus. For example, a substantial part of the NEH funding in 1997–98 was used to award small stipends of two hundred dollars each to faculty who chose to undertake individual projects to improve student learning in Humanities. Thirty-nine faculty completed such projects.

The NEH endowment also funds the replacement of the NEH professor in his or her department. With NEH's approval and that of the university's vice chancellor for academic affairs, the Humanities director/NEH professor decided to use these funds to establish the first national NEH postdoctoral fellowship in teaching in the humanities. The holder of this new fellowship, a two-year appointment, learns much about life at an undergraduate institution that emphasizes teaching and, in turn, teaches his UNCA colleagues new things about his academic specialty. He (or she, perhaps, in future appointments) also will be responsible for visiting his graduate campus to share his experiences with doctoral students planning careers in college teaching. The Humanities director serves as main mentor to the NEH postdoctoral fellow.

The director provides general mentoring and encouragement by annually reviewing the written student evaluations of each instructor. Each Humanities instructor is required to have students evaluate at least one of his or her sections per semester. Comments on these, as well as on an instructor's other contributions to the Humanities program, are included in an annual report by the director to that instructor's department chair. When the university was smaller, the director used to observe each instructor's teaching annually. Since this is no longer feasible, the director visits the classes of new faculty, the classes of faculty notably praised or panned by students, and the classes of faculty who invite her to do so.

Since 1988, two innovations at UNCA have proved especially helpful in invigorating Humanities teaching: service learning (the incorporation of five to fifteen hours, depending on the instructor, of community service related to class readings and discussion) and teaching circles (informal, small, and regular workshops in which faculty cooperate in presenting informed points of view on a particular topic). Service learning, which received substantial national recognition during the 1990s, is currently employed as a highly successful pedagogical technique by about half of the instructors of "The Individual and the Contemporary World," and the practice is spreading in that course and elsewhere in the university's curriculum. The other technique—the teaching circle—is a favorite among Humanities faculty. During summer 1998, for example, five Humanities teachers gathered weekly to investigate ways in which new kinds of hands-on learning might improve Humanities education. Other Humanities teaching circles were designed to focus on the diverse roots of momentous nineteenth-century European political movements and "Options for the Future: Construction Instead of Destruction."

All faculty development activities sponsored by the program are open to the whole campus community. Potential new Humanities faculty are especially welcomed, as leaders, participants, or observers. This not only helps to keep campus-wide conversation going, but also helps in attracting new faculty to the program. Recruiting new faculty, probably the most time-consuming responsibility of the director, is cause for both joy and distress. The campus-wide networking that takes place as a result of this recruiting, but also and especially from the interdepartmental teamwork in the courses, fosters smoother progress at university meetings in general. The faculty has learned to talk with each other more easily, with little of the defensiveness and suspicion that so often can result from departmental isolation. The chance to teach the interdisciplinary, team-planned Humanities courses attracts the campus's more active faculty—those drawn also to UNCA's Arts & Ideas, Masters in Liberal Arts, Women's Studies, International Studies, Africana Studies, and Multi-Media programs, and to new courses in their own departments, administrative assignments, fellowships, and off-campus scholarly assignments. As a result, it is not always predictable who will be part of the next year's Humanities faculty. There is therefore an obvious need for departmental commitments of agreed-on numbers of regular faculty to Humanities, but there also are variable conditions within those departments that prevent finding a pat formula to answer Humanities' need.

The director visits department chairs often, explaining the program's staffing needs and the ways in which its contents might complement that department's courses. Excellent teachers are pursued, sometimes for years, to recruit them into the program. As new tenure-track faculty are hired, it is increasingly common to require the benefiting department to agree to commit one of its faculty to one or two additional Humanities sections per year. Since many department chairs regularly teach Humanities, their cooperation and support are readily forthcoming—that is, when their own department's courses are covered. A cooperative effort by the director and the vice chancellor for academic affairs holds promise that an acceptable plan soon may be constructed for departmental commitments to Humanities.

Currently, however, the department chairs' general goodwill toward Humanities, and that of the successive vice chancellors for academic affairs, assures the program (if the director keeps asking) of a respectable portion of full-time faculty participation. Since the beginning, the vice chancellors for academic affairs have supported this goal and have made it known that participation in interdisciplinary programs (and Humanities is the largest) is seriously taken into account when faculty are considered for tenure, promotion, or merit raises. They also have consistently supported the Humanities Internship Program for new instructors. Both the department chairs and the vice chancellor for academic affairs usually (moving toward always) include the Humanities director among those scheduled to interview candidates for new or replacement tenure-track faculty positions. This practice not only helps to acclimate new colleagues, but also clarifies to them the university's interest in having them teach in the program.

Once faculty are convinced that they may well enjoy teaching Humanities (thanks in part to the Internship Program) and that their careers at UNCA will be enhanced by their participation, their willingness still can be blocked by the out-of-class time commitment involved. Humanities students are required to write formal papers in each course, increasing from five pages without research in the first course, to fifteen to eighteen in the last, based on research such as one might expect from seniors. Essay exams are the rule in all Humanities courses, and frequent out-of-class discussions with students are the norm. Some of the reluctance of regular faculty to sign on has been overcome by the official reduction (as of spring 1997) of the maximum Humanities class size to twenty-two students. (It had climbed, through overenrollment, into the thirties in some cases.) Faculty also are encouraged that each instructor can exercise some individual choice concerning what his or her syllabus includes—10 to 25 percent of the course content, depending on the course faculty's decision—and by the principle that each syllabus is to be essentially a core syllabus. Another encouraging plan is being considered: a way to allow faculty to bank Humanities credit hours that are over and above the twelve hours of teaching required each semester. Since each Humanities course is four semester credit hours, faculty often teach thirteen hours per semester, without additional compensation. The banking plan would grant an instructor, after three such semesters, a semester-load lightened by one three-hour course.

Since teaching well is of highest importance to the Humanities faculty, and to UNCA faculty generally, substantial attention is given to what, and how well, students are learning. When a notable number of students call for a change, through formal, end-of-course evaluations or through other means, they are paid serious attention. For example, in 1989, the African American Student Association requested a meeting with the Humanities director and the course coordinators to discuss the lack of African materials in the program. This was a gap, the Humanities administrators concluded; as a result, a year-long faculty seminar on the topic was conducted. Twenty-five faculty participated, compensated by a stipend of two hundred dollars each (though half refused this stipend, preferring to use the money to bring in outside experts). Following group readings, discussions, and meetings with visiting lecturers, the faculty ended up including African materials in each of the four course syllabi.

In general, faculty response to student perceptions often leads to change in the four syllabi. Yet student satisfaction with the Humanities courses varies. Freshmen often find the courses intimidating: reading primary source materials and being expected to participate in discussions can be unnerving, and sitting through even the best hour-long lecture can be "boring" to someone just out of high school. These lectures have improved over the years, in part because the greater Asheville community is invited to attend (addressing a noncaptive adult audience tends to encourage a lecturer) and in part because the faculty has, by and large, heeded its own caveat: "Aim at students rather than at colleagues in your own discipline."

Over the years, UNCA's reputation has grown. The 1998 *Princeton Review*'s "The Best 311 Colleges" called UNCA "one of those relatively unknown gems in higher education." The university also has been named a "best buy" among American colleges in the 1996, 1997, 1998, and 1999 *Fiske Guide to College,* and was included in the *Fiske Guide*'s 1993 special, one-time listing of the nation's ten best public liberal arts institutions. The Humanities Program frequently has been mentioned in these publications as exemplary. It has become increasingly clear to the university's entering students that the Humanities Program is an important part of what they can expect from their education. By senior year, most students find their Humanities experience valuable. A recent *Program Assessment Survey* of graduating seniors, produced in September 1997 by UNCA's Office of Institutional Research, indicates that the Humanities Program rated above the university mean in all applicable (since it is not a department) categories: "environment for learning," "scholarly excellence," "quality of teaching," "faculty concern for students," "student view of the curriculum," and "student satisfaction with the program."

Certainly one of the most notable alterations in the Humanities Program since 1985 has been its provision of a fuller global context for the study of traditional Western patterns of thought and development. The choice of core texts reflects this change. Decades ago, all courses used Harcourt Brace's *The Classics of Western Thought* as a core text and one or another "Western civilization" text. In the mid-1980s, the program continued to assign chapters from a Western civilization textbook, and the faculty for each of the four courses developed its own core primary source reader (*The Asheville Reader,* volumes 1–4, published by Copley), which included more evidence of cultural and gender diversity. In 1998, volume 1 of *World Literature and Thought* (Harcourt Brace) was adopted for the first course, "The Ancient World." New editions of *The Asheville Reader* are being prepared by faculty teams for "The Medieval-Renaissance World," "The Modern World," and "The Individual in the Contemporary World."

The vitality of the current and ongoing efforts to find sufficient balance between the traditional and the global in the Humanities Program is exemplified by the 1998–99 inclusion in "The Ancient World" core syllabus of religious texts. Besides reading traditional biblical materials (chapters from Genesis, Exodus, Jeremiah, and Job; the Sermon on the Mount; and selections from Paul's letters), the students study religious texts from Mesopotamia, Egypt, Ethiopia, India, China, Greece, and Rome.

In 1996–97, an elected Humanities faculty committee debated whether to use a Western or a world civilization textbook as core to the program—and which text that might be. After substantial investigation and conversation, the recommendation, accepted by a clear majority of the Humanities faculty, was to adopt Gloria Fiero's *The Humanistic Tradition* (third edition, in six volumes, McGraw-Hill), which was phased in course by course over four semesters. Fiero's presentation, which is both historic and thematic, smoothly and sensitively incorporates other world cultures in her chronological presentation of Western cultures.

The Future

The Humanities Program doubtless will alter in many ways as it searches for a well-balanced incorporation of Western and non-Western materials. The program's goal is to assist the university in producing as graduates strong and knowledgeable citizens who can comprehend ways in which threads of diverse cultures are interwoven in the fabric of our culture. A primary goal of Humanities is to help students understand the sources of our predominant American paradigms, lest they, as young citizens, be unable to recognize these sources, and thus be less able to decide whether, and how, to alter the culture that these have produced. Perhaps continued use of historically based courses will accomplish this goal; perhaps a large change will be necessary—for example, to thematically rather than chronologically arranged courses. Whatever is decided will have to take into account that nearly half of UNCA's regular faculty must be both willing and able to deal with the new materials. Thus, time and budget for ongoing Humanities faculty development activities are regular needs.

As new technology—and the budget to purchase it—has become available, it has been incorporated into the Humanities Program. This has necessitated a specific kind of faculty development. (Humanities often shares technology, along with its purchase price and faculty training, with other programs and departments on campus.) Before 1990, the program's technological reach rarely extended beyond use of slides, filmstrips, videotapes, records, and audiotapes to supplement reading materials and enliven the weekly lectures. Since then, purchase of slide collections and videotapes has continued, mostly to increase holdings of non-Western materials. As faculty and students have become more techno-adept,

Humanities has extended its reach into newer and more expensive technologies. The program now has two scanners (one for text, one for slides), two portable TV-VCR-laserdisk players, a lecture-hall laserdisk player with large-screen projector, and several computers with Internet access in the main and in some adjunct offices. All full-time faculty have Internet access in their offices. Three multimedia classrooms now exist on campus, and since faculty demand for these is increasing, a fourth is under construction. In 1998, thanks in large part to a few enthusiastic faculty members and an excellent Humanities secretary, use of the web increased to include publication of syllabi, large group lecture notes and outlines (a huge savings in printing costs), class schedules, and a web page that includes a faculty list with a "click-on" to each faculty member's e-mail address (http://www.unca.edu/humanities).

The incorporation of new technology in Humanities will increase. The president of the University of North Carolina system, Molly Broad, has marked this initiative as one of her main goals, and UNCA's new director of the Teaching and Learning Center, Charles Bennett of the department of physics, is strongly inclined to support pedagogical improvement projects that employ current technology. A respectable component of the Humanities faculty, however, somewhat leery of "tech-toys," resists moving too quickly away from traditional teaching methods. While not completely unhealthy, this reaction does make it apparent that further tech-training needs to be made available.

Besides continuing to improve diversity in the four syllabi and make better use of technology in teaching, other Humanities program goals are the gradual widening of its interdisciplinarity to represent more adequately, for example, the history of science, the permeation of our culture by technology, the aesthetics of mathematics, and the investigation of the human psyche. As new faculty enter the program, such widening is being debated.

Further needed improvements include better faculty recruitment. Academic departments must be convinced to commit a reasonable number of faculty slots to Humanities on an annual and ongoing basis; what "reasonable" means will vary from department to department and from time to time. (This commitment may well occur by administrative mandate, following sufficient conversation.) There is a need as well to continue to seek sources of funding other than the state budget for program improvement. And, of course, the new assessment of learning plan for Humanities needs to be tested and refined. In general, goals will be sculpted as the scope of problems and opportunities alters—locally, statewide, and beyond.

More than one-third of a century ago, when it was founded, UNCA's young Humanities Program was grand in scope, comprehensive in design, and pivotal in expressing the goals of and setting the course for the institution. The program remains so, through the responsiveness of a campus community dedicated to fulfilling its public liberal arts mission.

Reference
Highsmith, W. E. *The University of North Carolina at Asheville: The First Sixty Years.* Asheville: University of North Carolina at Asheville, 1991.

Chapter Ten

The Foundation Year Programme at King's College

Margaret Heller

In 1972 the University of King's College in Halifax, Nova Scotia, introduced the Foundation Year Programme (FYP) as an alternative approach to university education for first-year students. FYP treats the historical development of Western culture through the consideration of major works of literature, philosophy, theology, political and economic theory, the visual arts, and music. With a current enrollment of around 230, the program is a single course taken in the place of four full-year classes, usually by students enrolled in an arts degree. As well, there are thirty-five students in the first year of the King's bachelor of journalism honors degree, for whom it is required, and twenty in science, who can choose to take a shorter version of the program. Called in a guidebook to Canadian universities "the most exciting, most demanding, and

I thank the many individuals who gave me their time to talk about the Foundation Year Programme and the University of King's College. My gratitude especially goes to Patrick Atherton, Elizabeth Edwards, Angus Johnston, Henry Roper, and Colin Starnes for their assistance. Many thanks also to the staff of the King's Library, Patricia Chalmers, Janet Hathaway, Drake Petersen, and Elaine MacInnis, and to Pat Dixon, administrative assistant to the Foundation Year Programme.

most valuable first-year program in Canada" (Frum, 1987, p. 59), King's Foundation Year has a national reputation and draws roughly half of its students from outside the maritime provinces, particularly from Ontario.

Foundation Year and King's

The name of the course states its educational goal: Foundation Year seeks to provide a foundation for further education through the study of many of the foundational works of the Western tradition. The name also points to the program's importance for King's. FYP came into being during a period of crisis, when the existence of the university itself was in doubt, and it proved to be the means by which King's "refound" itself, becoming the basis for its immediate survival and eventual prosperity.

Although it is Canada's oldest English-speaking university, King's was, and still is, one of the smallest, with an enrollment of around 850. Founded in 1754 in New York as an Anglican college, King's closed during the American Revolution and in 1789 was reestablished in the small town of Windsor, Nova Scotia, by Loyalists who had fled the new republic. During the nineteenth century, while the former King's in New York flourished as Columbia, King's in Nova Scotia remained small and unpopular. Although it had the backing of the established authorities, the college managed to alienate the province's mainly non-Anglican population, and they built their own denominational schools. As well, in 1820 the nondenominational Dalhousie University was established in the provincial capital of Halifax, and it soon became Nova Scotia's major institution of higher learning.

After its main building was destroyed by fire in 1920, King's moved from Windsor to Halifax with the aid of the Carnegie Foundation and entered into association with Dalhousie. Under the terms of this association, King's put into abeyance its power to grant the B.A. and B.S. degrees and provided the new Dalhousie-King's joint faculty of arts and science with eight professors paid for by the Carnegie endowment. Yet King's retained its university status, keeping its own campus, board of governors, administration, and endowment, as well as its divinity school, which trained men for Anglican ministry.

From 1920 until the establishment of the Foundation Year Programme in 1972, King's did little more than provide a distinctive residential life for Anglican students attending Dalhousie. Its one form of academic endeavor on its own campus, the divinity school, was tiny, and by the late 1960s it was on the way to forming a separate ecumenical college, the Atlantic School of Theology, with two other denominations. Deeply in debt and challenged by the government of Nova Scotia to justify its receiving public funding, King's almost allowed itself to be collapsed completely into the much larger university. But in the end, it refused this option and chose instead to try an educational experiment. King's turned its crisis into an opportunity to create a new way of educating undergraduates to counter the numerous failings that in the 1960s had come to be associated with the contemporary multiversity.

This second foundation of King's, almost two hundred years after the first, has been a success. On the basis of the Foundation Year Programme, which gave King's levels of enrollment and financial stability unprecedented in its history, King's was able to establish a school of journalism in 1978 and an upper-year interdisciplinary program, called Contemporary Studies, in 1993. The university is now experiencing more expansion with the introduction of two new interdisciplinary programs, Early Modern Studies in the fall of 1999 and History of Science in 2000. In 1971 King's had thirteen professors (eight in arts and science departments at Dalhousie and five in the newly established Atlantic School of Theology); in 1998 it had thirty-eight full-time faculty members, some in Dalhousie departments but most in King's programs. Although the Foundation Year Programme is only a first-year course, it is "the cornerstone upon which the new King's has been built" (Godfrey, 1979, p. 1).

King's and Dalhousie

The new King's does not stand completely on its own. With the exception of the one-year bachelor of journalism degree, all degrees offered through King's include classes taken at Dalhousie to a greater or lesser extent. Foundation Year students, for example, complete their first-year requirements by taking electives in Dalhousie departments. The following year they can, as King's students, enter the second year of a regular degree program at Dalhousie (a significant number of its departments, including classics, English, history, philosophy, and sociology, consider FYP to be equivalent to their own first-year offerings), or they can enter a program of King's that still includes courses taken on the other campus. Ever since the two institutions formed an association, King's has attracted students who want a small college experience along with access to the resources of a major university.

The relationship between King's and Dalhousie is extremely complicated, with elements of both autonomy and dependence. Despite the close connection, King's has managed to preserve its independence in governance and to foster a distinctive collegiate ethos. Dalhousie, with an enrollment of about fourteen thousand students and an orientation toward the sciences, graduate studies, and professional training, provides a kind of foil to King's, which prides itself on the quality of its undergraduate teaching in the humanities. King's students hold fiercely to their identity even when in upper-year courses in Dalhousie departments.

But the relation between the two is not one of simple opposition, for the Foundation Year Programme was to a large extent the result of an internal critique at Dalhousie that could find no effective expression within that institution's culture and structures. Foundation Year continues to think of itself as providing an alternative to the kind of education students receive at Dalhousie or any other large university.

The Organization of Foundation Year

FYP operates as a single integrated unit rather than as a series of unrelated courses in separate departments. It takes a nondisciplinary approach to what it teaches, stressing the interconnectedness of various aspects of culture. Foundation Year's nondepartmental and nondisciplinary nature has required the development of a distinctive structure, which can be seen in the organization of its curriculum, instruction, appointments, and governance.

Curriculum

The course is organized according to chronology, moving through six "sections": the Ancient World, the Middle Ages, the Renaissance and Reformation, the Age of Reason, the Era of Revolutions, and the Contemporary World. Each section, about four weeks long, is the responsibility of a coordinator—a faculty member who organizes its reading list and lectures, provides an overall interpretation of the section, and relates it to the rest of the course.

Foundation Year teaches each year an almost unchanging core of texts, including *The Epic of Gilgamesh*, Genesis, Exodus, the Book of Job, *The Republic*, the Epistle to the Romans, *Confessions, The Song of Roland, The Proslogium, The Summa Theologica, The Divine Comedy, The Oration on the Dignity of Man, The Prince, Meditations on First Philosophy, Leviathan, The Social Contract, The Communist Manifesto*, and *The Waste Land*. There is also a core of authors whose works vary, including Homer, Sophocles, Aristotle, Luther, Shakespeare, Hume, Mill, Nietzsche, Mann, Wittgenstein, Heidegger, and Sartre. And there are a number of writers whose works are not part of the core but have been studied on and off over the years, such as Sappho, Erasmus, Voltaire, Burke, Mary Shelley, Baudelaire, Schöpenhauer, Dostoyevsky, de Beauvoir, and Lyotard. The ideal of the course is to consider complete books rather than selections, but this is often tempered by practicality.

The FYP curriculum is not unlike that of other liberal arts programs, yet it has some distinctive features. While some great books courses make a leap from Augustine to the Renaissance, for example, Foundation Year's Middle Ages section receives considerable weight as the period of the formation of fundamental European ideas and institutions. The institutional emphasis in this interpretation of the medieval world explains certain choices of texts, such as a letter of St. Paul in the New Testament rather than a Gospel. One component that distinguishes Foundation Year from similar American programs is its focus on European developments: it is the French and not the American Revolution that is of central importance in the Era of Revolutions section, for example.

Instruction and Evaluation

Foundation Year students are expected to read a large number of texts in a short period of time. Plato's *Republic* is read over three days, for example, and Mary Shelley's *Frankenstein* in one. FYP asks its students to consider the books they read in three ways: through listening to lectures, participating in tutorials, and writing essays.

The class meets for two-hour lectures on the designated material—four mornings a week for most students and three mornings for those taking the shorter version, which means they do not attend on Thursdays. Thursday lectures tend to be on the visual arts or music, or on books that can be treated separately from the other readings of the week. In each section of the course, some lectures are given by its coordinator and others by lecturers from the FYP teaching staff or Dalhousie faculty. Although lecturers focus on the reading of the day, they also endeavor to provide a certain amount of historical background and bring out connections with previous works. What they are not meant to do is outline current academic debates concerning particular texts or speak from the vantage point of specialized scholarship.

Following the lectures are one-hour tutorials, which are discussion groups of about fourteen students led by a tutor. Tutorials are central to the teaching of the program, being the place where students are challenged by their tutors and their peers to engage with the material. For the sake of both continuity and variety of instruction, a tutorial group meets with what is called its main tutor for three of the six sections of the course, and for the other three sections it meets with three different tutors. Because students remain in their groups the whole year, each tutorial develops a distinct sense of identity.

Every two weeks an essay is assigned. The essay questions, set in a regular meeting of the tutors, often arise out of what was said in lectures or tutorials, and they focus on problems that can be discussed with reference to the primary texts alone. Twice a year longer papers are assigned, requiring the use of secondary sources; these are meant to encourage students to become familiar with the library. Foundation Year prides itself on its success in teaching first-year students to write well. Essay grades are the major component in their evaluation, but there are also exams: two midterms, which are short-answer tests of factual knowledge, and two sets of oral exams, which assess the students' overall grasp of the material.

The Foundation Year Programme is an intense, all-consuming experience for students and instructors alike. Its continual demands and rapid pace can be a source of great frustration. As one student wrote in the college newspaper, "I have yet to meet the dynamo for whom this programme was intended"

(Bowden, 1995, p. 21). And yet most who enter FYP complete it: each year fewer than ten students drop out. Even when frustrated, students show remarkable dedication to Foundation Year while taking it and extraordinary gratitude for it later, if a lament such as this one by a graduating student is any evidence: "When I wrote a paper, it was an event in the late, great, Western tradition. . . . Weep, weep, weep for me, it is no more" (McLean, 1996, p. 18).

Faculty Appointments

Much of the success of the program is due to the quality of those who teach in it. Foundation Year is lucky to be able to take advantage of the resources of Dalhousie, which it draws on for many of its lecturers. But the program has also worked to foster its own style of instruction. King's' institutional independence from Dalhousie has given FYP the freedom to develop appointments that best suit its needs. Because Foundation Year's curriculum is not divided by discipline and because a great deal of cooperative teaching is required, regular departmental models for the most part have not been followed.

Although all of the types of academic positions in the program have undergone considerable modification over the years, Foundation Year has had to wrestle especially with that of the tutor. The distinction between the positions of coordinator and tutor may appear to be the same as between professor and teaching assistant, but this does not capture the true nature of either. The duties of a coordinator in organizing a section and giving some lectures in it are less than those involved in designing and teaching a course. A section is formed through extensive consultation and cooperation with colleagues, and there is a spirit of continuity at work that serves to discourage much tinkering from year to year. On the other hand, the duties of a tutor go beyond what is expected of a teaching assistant. Tutors are responsible for teaching the curriculum of all the sections of the course and for assessing the academic progress of their students. The importance of the tutors has always been recognized by King's, which has given them appointments with higher status and remuneration than are usually accorded teaching assistants.

The first tutors were appointed as junior fellows, one-year positions considered appropriate for those in transition to further studies or permanent jobs elsewhere. But in the 1980s FYP began to renew the appointments of some individuals for a number of years to ensure the continuity and quality of its teaching. Foundation Year needed to find a way to make longer-term appointments in the tutorial staff for the good of the program and to limit the number of renewals of those holding junior positions for the sake of equity. Accordingly, a continuing renewable position of senior fellow was established in 1998 to give accomplished tutors a more stable appointment, and the junior fellowship, called the teaching fellowship since 1994, now can be renewed only twice. Tutors who want to continue to teach in Foundation Year after three years must apply for and receive a senior fellowship. The current tutorial staff (1999–2000) has five teaching fellows and two senior fellows.

The teaching fellows come from a wide variety of backgrounds, the most common being philosophy, classics, political theory, and English literature. Almost every year there is an opening for a teaching fellow; the position is advertised annually within Canada and receives a large number of applications. It is a continuing debate within the program whether individuals with extensive publication records and years of teaching experience are overqualified for this junior appointment. Even with the impressive qualifications of many of the applicants, finding good teaching fellows is not an easy task, for successful tutors have attributes often not discernable from their curricula vitae or from interviews, such as an ability to teach outside their own area of expertise and a willingness to contribute to a common enterprise. Inculcating new tutors into the ways of FYP is one of the major concerns of the program's director.

Gradually King's has also created a number of long-term or tenurable professorial appointments in Foundation Year. As the program and the university expanded, both needed to develop a King's-based professorial faculty to draw on for a variety of administrative roles rather than relying on those who already have full commitments in Dalhousie departments. Beginning in the mid-1980s, King's gave professorial appointments to some tutors, primarily to those who were asked to take up administrative positions. Foundation Year now has a complement of eight professorial appointments, some tenured and others on the tenure track. FYP professors are part of the administration of the college as vice president, the director and associate director of Foundation Year, and the director of the new Early Modern Studies Programme; many serve as section coordinators, and many are cross-appointed to teach in other King's programs. In any given year, most of these continue to tutor in Foundation Year.

Governance and Review

The governance of the program follows the collegiate model: administrative positions are cycled through the faculty, and administrators are expected to continue to teach. The FYP director, appointed for a three-year term, is responsible for the academic and administrative functioning of the program. He or she is assisted by an associate director. A thirteen-member council—the section coordinators, the FYP professorial appointees, and some other members of the King's faculty—advises the director on academic policy and recommends appointments. A council of tutors was created in spring 1999 to give the tutorial staff more influence as a body.

Foundation Year undergoes an extensive review process. At the end of each year there are individual student evaluations of tutors and lecturers in the form of questionnaires and comment sheets. As well, each tutorial group chooses a representative to meet with the director and associate director and discuss the curriculum and other concerns students might have. This meeting can last as long as eight hours. After the final term ends, there are the Tutors' Review, the Coordinators' Review, and the General Council, which includes two representatives of Dalhousie's Faculty of Arts and Social Sciences. Dalhousie also reviews Foundation Year every seven years on the model of its unit reviews.

Origins of Foundation Year

Although Foundation Year's organization has undergone continual evolution in response to the results of its various modes of self-assessment, the basic framework of the program has been remarkably stable. From today's vantage point, when FYP seems solid and well entrenched, it is easily forgotten that it began as an experimental course whose early years were full of struggle and conflict and whose future was by no means assured.

As with other courses that study the great books of the Western tradition, Foundation Year's curriculum has attracted its share of critique and controversy concerning its neglect of women authors, privileging of works of high culture, and Eurocentrism. Foundation Year can be seen as of a piece with the long history of traditionalism and elitism at King's, which went hand in hand with its origins as a Loyalist Anglican college. There is much about King's that might support the view that it merely represents a kind of conservatism, including the survival of traditions of wearing gowns and formal meals, the continued presence of Anglican clergy, the resistance of the chapel to new liturgies and women priests, the numerous faculty with degrees from Oxford and Cambridge, and the largely white student body.

Yet this is not the whole picture of contemporary King's. Along with its conservatism has been a dynamic that has fostered experimentation and risk. Much of the evident traditionalism of the college has been invented identity, not substance. FYP was formed out of various kinds of radical critiques of education in the 1960s, not in reaction against them, and the program has never stressed the preservation of a heritage, only its comprehension. The history of the Foundation Year shows a complex interplay between traditionalism and radicalism, which at times have been opposed and at other times in alliance.

Foundation Year began as a last-ditch effort to save King's from a complete merger with Dalhousie, which it was contemplating as a solution to its financial problems. King's needed to discover a unique academic role for itself in order to persuade the provincial government that it was worth supporting as an independent university. In 1970 the college was fortunate to find as its new president Graham Morgan, a graduate of Oxford and a King's professor in Dalhousie's sociology department, who embarked on a determined program of institutional renewal.

For Morgan, a new academic mission at King's involved fostering a renewed sense of collegiality. His interest in nineteenth-century social theory perhaps contributed to his belief that the fragmentation of the contemporary university curriculum and the apathy of contemporary university students could be overcome by creating a college community. Morgan intended to give substance to the collegiate ideal of communal life in which intellectual, social, and spiritual concerns were integrated. Such an ideal spoke to the institution's traditional identity as a small residential college on the Oxford model, aimed at educating the whole person rather than the specialist scholar. This ideal would find its concrete expression in the creation of the Foundation Year Programme.

In 1971, the president and two other members of the faculty, as members of the board's special committee on a new academic role for King's, drew up a proposal for the creation of a first-year program that would offer an alternative to the now typical "cafeteria-style" array of electives by providing an integrated treatment of the historical development of Western culture. The program would have a core curriculum of significant works taught in a nondisciplinary manner to show the interrelation of theology, literature, philosophy, politics, arts, science, economics, and social structures. The committee hoped that such an approach would counter the widely lamented problem of student apathy. It wrote in its proposal: "It is apparent that the onus of responsibility lies with the faculty to give meaning and purpose to the undergraduate curriculum in such a way that the student is fired with enthusiasm at the prospect before him. That prospect should be one in which there continually unfolds a series of insights and connections which propel the student to deepen his understanding of his heritage and hence of himself and his own time and place" (Atherton and others, 1971–1972, p. 3).

In proposing such a program, the committee drew on not only the collegiate ideal that King's had inherited but also the dissatisfaction that many at Dalhousie felt with the direction their university had taken. The 1960s was a time of tremendous growth at Dalhousie, due largely to government financing. The relatively small provincial university was becoming a multiversity, with professional schools, graduate programs, and research institutes. As Dalhousie's core arts curriculum was being replaced by a proliferation of elective courses and the education of undergraduate students was being subordinated to the requirements of specialist scholarship, many worried that the quality of its teaching was suffering.

The Hegelian Critique

A few resisted Dalhousie's new direction. The classics department became the center of one countervailing trend, led by its head, James Doull. Doull was a Hegelian philosopher who encouraged his students to go to the roots of contemporary assumptions by examining their origins and development. He taught in classics because he believed that the comprehension of the present needed to begin with a close study of ancient Greek philosophy. But his concern was with recuperating the thought of the West as a whole, from classical antiquity to the medieval Christian world as it arose out of Augustinian theology, to the older modern period of European culture.

Doull's endeavor to comprehend contemporary presuppositions through the history of thought inspired colleagues and students alike, and he attracted to classics in the mid-1960s a small circle of bright students who stood out at Dalhousie for their intellectual passion. Several of these would later become involved in the Foundation Year Programme, and over the years numerous members of FYP's teaching staff have been influenced by Doull in some way. The role he has played in the development of the program has been indirect but profound, giving it what has been described as "a decidedly Hegelian flavor" (Benjamin, 1989, p. 21).

The emergence of a distinctively King's kind of Anglicanism during the 1970s and 1980s was also largely the work of members of the Dalhousie classics department. Ordained clergy on the faculty, associated with classics, Foundation Year, and the chapel, laid special emphasis on regaining a knowledge of the roots and development of Christian doctrine during the patristic period and through the Middle Ages. The particular weight and interpretation given to the medieval section of the program was greatly influenced by their work.

A King's student in the 1970s playfully characterized the whole school of thought clustered around Doull and classics as "Canadian-nationalist-aristotelian-thomist-hegelianism" (Kirby, 1975, p. 6), decidedly opposed to the mainstream Anglo-American approach taken in other Dalhousie departments, not to mention conventional Anglicanism.

Left-Wing Radicals

The other major attempt to make university education meaning-ful in the late 1960s originated in Dalhousie's expanding social science departments. Sociology in particular was full of young radical professors who attracted students interested in social analysis for the sake of social transformation. Activist faculty worked to revolutionize the conventional curriculum and style of teaching, and some of them became involved in the early years of FYP, seeing in it the possibility of an alternative education that would bring into question the status quo.

It is common to think that the 1960s radicals introduced a kind of flakiness into a previously rigorous university education. But a closer look, at least at Dalhousie, gives another impression. University teaching in the 1960s was dry, exam driven, conventional in its methods, and unconnected to the deeper strivings of its students. Even prominent scholars lectured from textbooks, and the basic mood of students was one of anti-intellectualism. The radicals' demands for "relevance" were also demands for engagement, significance, and rigor.

The involvement of faculty radicals in setting up a course with a core curriculum shows the close connection between traditionalist and radical critiques of the modern university during this period. President Morgan, as an example, was a left-wing sociologist who sought to recover some of the older values of collegiate life.

Approval

Although the proposed first-year program had support from these various sources, gaining acceptance from Dalhousie was a difficult matter. For one thing, the program's integrated historical approach made it academically unconventional and, for most at Dalhousie, academically suspect. For another, the program seemed to fall outside the terms of the articles of association of the two universities, which limited King's ability to teach arts and science courses.

But by the spring of 1972, Dalhousie's board of governors had agreed to approve Foundation Year as an experimental course, and Dalhousie's English, classics, German, political science, and sociology departments agreed to deem it equivalent to certain of their first-year classes. King's in turn agreed to compensate Dalhousie for the work of those professors in the joint faculty of arts and science who became FYP coordinators, and on its own appointed a director to administer the program and three junior fellows to run tutorials.

As the Foundation Year Programme was being launched, Morgan wrote presciently, "I myself consider it to be the beginning of a very serious direction for King's: that is, that we should increasingly see our University as an institution devoted primarily to a particular kind of undergraduate education" (Morgan, 1972, p. 2).

The 1970s: Conflicts

Foundation Year began as an alliance of members of the Dalhousie-King's joint faculty who shared a critique of liberalism and the multiversity serving it. They were all in their different ways historicists in that they all had overarching narratives of the development of the West as it moved through distinct historical periods. Yet the sources of their metanarratives were different, and these competed for dominance. The program was soon riven by ideological clashes, and its early conflicts were resolved only when one side, which included President Morgan, left in 1977.

The first director of Foundation Year was Wayne Hankey, an Anglican priest and an alumnus of King's who had been a student of Doull and active in radical student politics during the mid-1960s. Hankey worked to formulate a unifying argument that would give an overall meaning to the history of the West. He wrote in the first introduction to the program: "We are endeavouring to understand the roots of our culture, to see how it produced what it did and to judge—given that what it has produced is dying—whether we wish to return to those roots to build again or if we must renounce all and give ourselves over to the whirlwind" (Hankey, 1972).

Hankey was responsible for articulating much of the program's distinctive character and ethos, which it retains today; there is still a sense, although less explicit, that the development of the West can be grasped as a whole through its intellectual and institutional traditions. But he was not the only one in the program with a definite interpretation of history. The coordinator of the Contemporary World section, for example, was a Maoist sociologist who taught that the history of the West was culminating in Third World struggles against capitalist imperialism, concerning which "the relevance of Lenin's diagnosis should be self-evident and all the more compelling" (Gamberg, 1973, p. 74). The program found itself divided into two camps, with the classicist/Hegelians on one side and the sociologist/Marxists on the other. Many students found the conflicts exciting as Foundation Year became the battleground for their conversion.

The divisions finally came to a head in 1976–77 over the question of appointing new tutors. The nature of the authority of the president and the director over this aspect of the program was unclear, and each wanted someone sympathetic to his side. Both Morgan and Hankey had a sense of ownership of Foundation Year, and their conflict became bitter and personal. When Morgan attempted to relieve Hankey of his post as director, the issue became one of faculty rights, and the president did not receive the support he had been looking for from the board. Just at this time his term as president was coming up for renewal, and Morgan decided not to re-offer, eventually resigning his King's professorship as well and transferring to Dalhousie. All the left-wing social scientists also decided to leave. "Canadian-nationalist-aristotelian-thomist-hegelianism" now prevailed.

The break between the classicists and the sociologists left in its wake hard feelings at Dalhousie for a long time, adding to that university's general suspicions about the interdisciplinary Foundation Year Programme. These suspicions were fueled in part by the ongoing rivalry at Dalhousie between the classics and philosophy departments concerning the true nature of philosophy, for the Hegelian approach to the history of thought in the former was an anathema to the strongly analytic bent of the latter. The hostility felt toward classics and, by extension, toward Foundation Year came to the surface in two reviews of the program with two different results.

The First Review

In December 1977, the chair of Dalhousie's philosophy department formally asked the faculty of arts and science to inquire into Foundation Year because he was worried that neither "the general conception of the Programme [nor] its conduct day-to-day is intellectually respectable" and that "there is strong prima facie evidence that it has proved a disaster": "Students there, it seems, are rather systematically indoctrinated in a peculiar ideology, one that rejects out of hand much of the students' own culture: their philosophical traditions, the traditions of Western democracy, their heritage in science, especially in the formal sciences and in the empirical social sciences" (Martin, 1977, pp. 1–2).

In response, the faculty of arts and science set up a committee to review Foundation Year in spring 1978, and it completed its work in fall 1980. The results were extremely positive. The committee found that FYP was academically solid and that it did at least as good a job as any other first-year course in laying the groundwork for upper-year studies. Numerous interviews showed that the program was highly regarded by its students and that there was no indoctrination into a single point of view.

As the review committee had discovered, the early battles for metahistorical domination were not the whole story of the program. It was important to those who began Foundation Year that it be rigorous. FYP students were asked to read a large number of difficult books, listen to challenging lectures, engage in tutorial discussions, and write essays on a regular basis that required close reading of the texts. Even during its troubled early years, the academic promise of Foundation Year was being fulfilled to a surprising extent. Not only did it prepare students for further university work as well as did Dalhousie, but a trend would emerge by the early 1980s in which those who had taken FYP actually tended to do better in their upper-year courses, winning a disproportionate number of Dalhousie's departmental medals and earning a disproportionate number of Dalhousie's honors degrees.

The Second Review

The fallout at Dalhousie from the ideological conflicts of the mid-1970s continued to plague the program into the early 1980s. In 1982 a new review committee of the faculty of arts and science ignored the findings of the previous review and revisited concerns about FYP's ideology. The 1983 report of this committee was hostile: it accused Foundation Year of endeavoring to indoctrinate its students against modernity and recommended that Dalhousie no longer accept it as equivalent to four full-year courses. If this recommendation had been accepted, Foundation Year would have been unsustainable financially. But the findings of the second review were based largely on hearsay and memories of earlier battles. In the end, the Dalhousie faculty became convinced that the committee had failed to document its case, and the report was thrown out in 1984. Following this experience, Dalhousie agreed to regularize its reviews of the King's program.

The second Dalhousie review did not reflect the changes that had taken place in Foundation Year beginning in the late 1970s. A consequence of the earlier conflicts had been that FYP had not reached its hoped-for enrollment of one hundred students, and so it had failed to alleviate the college's financial problems. In 1977–78, following the upheavals of the previous year, enrollment had dropped substantially, from sixty-one to forty-one students. A different style of leadership needed to be found if both Foundation Year and King's as a whole were to flourish. With a new president and a new director, the college and its flagship program took a new turn.

The 1980s: Collegiality

John Godfrey, president from 1977 to 1987, was a King's professor in Dalhousie's history department. Like Morgan a graduate of Oxford, Godfrey also promoted the ideal of King's as a small, residential college in which academic, social, and spiritual life were interconnected. During his presidency the various structures that Morgan had put in place came into their own. While the former president had possessed the drive to establish new institutional forms, Godfrey had the flair to bring them to public notice. Godfrey worked hard to give King's a certain image in the public eye and to create an Oxbridge style of college life. Traditions were restored or, more often than not, invented. Godfrey's flamboyance helped to smooth things over internally and make King's and its distinctive academic work better known. Enrollment began to increase steadily, allowing King's to post a small budget surplus in 1979–80. By 1984–85 the college had an enrollment of more than five hundred students, almost double that when Foundation Year began. The program itself had over four times its original enroll-ment of thirty students.

During the 1980s, the goal of completely integrating all aspects of campus life, with Foundation Year as its basis, was to a large extent realized. The student body in the early 1980s was large enough to support numerous college activities and small enough to form a close community. Most students were from Nova Scotia, although the majority were no longer Anglican. Founda-tion Year's teaching staff was united by a common background of the classics department, the Anglican Trinity College of the Uni-versity of Toronto, or Oxford and Cambridge. Many tutors lived in residence as dons, and a lively collegiate life developed around the senior common room.

Under the directorships of Colin Starnes (1978–1984) and Angus Johnston (1984–1988), the teaching in Foundation Year gradually took on a new character. The course moved away from the rather dismissive stance toward the contemporary era that had followed the departure of the left-wing social scientists, and instead began to give a more evenhanded account of the history of thought. The former hostility toward Foundation Year on the part of many at Dalhousie lessened, and after the defeat of the hostile review of 1982–1984, FYP found that it had a surprising level of support in Dalhousie departments. As its reputation grew in the mid-1980s, enrollment in Foundation Year began to climb to unan-ticipated heights with an influx of students from central Canada. By 1989 the program had more than two hundred students.

The 1990s: New Challenges

In the 1990s, King's entered yet another phase of its existence. Per-haps the early 1970s can be considered as fitful infancy, the 1980s as sunny childhood, and the 1990s the troubled adolescence of a maturing institution. During that decade the college faced new questions about its future, caused particularly by declining gov-ernment funding for higher education and new challenges to its kind of teaching. It also had to grapple with stresses caused by its very success. The expansion of enrollment in Foundation Year brought in its wake unanticipated problems of growth, the sepa-ration from past habits, and self-questioning.

Controversies over the Curriculum

The most recent period can be marked by another review by Dalhousie, this one completed in 1994. Both its internal and external reports praised FYP's many accomplishments, the excellence of its teaching staff, and the originality of its approach. No longer was the future of the program put into question; the review was instead a thoughtful appraisal of some of the methodological and intellectual problems that needed to be faced. Its principal criticism was that FYP was too monolithic in its sense of what should and should not be included in the curriculum, and the review recommended that the program find ways to incorporate writings by women, recognize the contributions made by non-Europeans to European culture, and broaden the range of its approaches to the past. In the 1990s, therefore, FYP had to wrestle with the same issues concerning the Western canon that have confronted other such courses.

Women

The issue of the place of women writers in the program appeared in its earliest student evaluation and resurfaced on and off through the 1970s and 1980s. The curriculum was made up exclusively of works by male authors, and even what was said concerning women by these authors was ignored in the lectures, although at least half of Foundation Year's students were female. As well, the program had an exclusively male faculty for a long time: between the academic years 1973–74 and 1981–82, no women were hired as junior fellows, and there were no women coordinators or joint professors. Only occasionally was a female professor from Dalhousie invited to lecture.

This began to change in the mid-1980s. Women began to be appointed as tutors, and, in response to pressures from students and the alumni, the program introduced a lecture on feminism in 1987. Foundation Year appointed its first woman director in 1990–91. But such changes were not enough to satisfy the more pointed criticism that the curriculum received during the 1990s.

In 1993 a letter to the editor of the *Bulletin of the Canadian Federation for the Humanities* chastised Foundation Year for evidently thinking that women writers were not important enough in the development of Western culture to be included in its curriculum (Bohm, 1993, pp. 7–8). FYP's director responded by pointing to the prominence of female characters in many of the program's key texts as evidence that it did not neglect women's importance (Roper, 1993, pp. 8–9). This reply led to an internal debate over what FYP's stance really was. Five tutors—three women and two men—wrote a letter to the director that, while generally supporting the program's approach, concluded by saying: "We are sometimes disappointed with the acceptance by our colleagues of the [Western] tradition's silence on the oppression of women" (Edwards and others, 1993, p. 2).

In response to pressure from some students and members of the teaching staff, there are now several lectures that consider writings by women (8 out of 107 in 1998–99), and the lecturers have been somewhat more willing to address what male authors had to say about women instead of passing over this material in silence. But students themselves do not agree about the importance and treatment of the issue. While some campaign to get more women writers onto the reading list, for example, others complain that their inclusion is mere tokenism, or that the assigned works by women are not really "great," or that any lecturers who draw special attention to what authors say about women are importing contemporary values into the past.

Race

With the exception of the exchange in the *Humanities Bulletin,* the debate about gender issues in Foundation Year has been internal to the program. Much more public have been the controversies over the treatment of race in FYP's curriculum and the accessibility of King's to minority students. Nova Scotia has an aboriginal population and a fairly large black community. Both groups are underrepresented at King's, and this is often laid at the door of Foundation Year.

Accessibility to the school of journalism is most at issue. Foundation Year is the required first year of the four-year journalism honors degree, the only such degree in the region. Black and aboriginal students have argued that a course on the Western heritage should not be the only gateway for those who want to be journalists. In 1991 a group of visiting black high school students walked out in protest after a Foundation Year presentation. Hostility to Foundation Year hit the local news media in 1995 when two black journalism students accused the program of being racist in a public forum during Black History Month.

Although FYP's faculty and students defended the program against the charge, there was general acknowledgment that serious questions had been raised about some of the premises underlying the course. The university also realized that it would need an active commitment to the goal of racial equity if it were to attract more minority students, and it has put in place increased scholarship support. So far there have been only a few additions to the curriculum of Foundation Year, such as Jean Rhys's *Wide Sargasso Sea,* that touch on issues of race. To a large extent, this reflects the European focus of the course. It may also be that lecturers often think it better to say nothing, rather than the wrong thing, about racial concerns.

Dilemmas

The controversies about the place of women in FYP's curriculum and the accessibility of King's to minority students have brought to the fore some of the dilemmas that can face a distinctive academic program in a small college. King's had needed to find a unique academic role for itself in order to survive at all. It chose to base its future on Foundation Year, a program with a defined curriculum focused on the development of the Western intellectual tradition. If, to satisfy the demands for a greater diversity of choices, Foundation Year's curriculum became broader, it might fall into the diffuseness that often characterizes interdisciplinary endeavors. The program, and the college as a whole, are still working to find the correct balance between the two goods of coherence and accessibility.

Contemporary Studies Programme

Since the introduction of Contemporary Studies in 1993, some of the previous discontent about Foundation Year's limitations has been defused, for the new program has made possible the serious consideration of topics difficult to include in FYP. Contemporary Studies continues Foundation Year's emphasis on important primary texts but extends its range of concerns. In many courses, feminist, postcolonial, and African American writings are central. The establishment of this program has proved to be one way in which those who teach and study at King's can engage with some of the assumptions that lie behind Foundation Year.

A Changing Campus

The creation of an upper-year interdisciplinary program at King's is but one aspect of the changing character of the campus during the 1990s. The kind of collegiality that Foundation Year's founders hoped for and largely achieved in the early 1980s has become less possible, and even less desired, in the face of new goals and new constraints. King's has moved away from the older corporate model of a community integrated in all its aspects. To be sure, collegiality has not disappeared. Visitors from other universities are often struck by the extent to which it persists. But for a variety of reasons, both external and internal, the identity of the college has altered substantially.

Problems with Growth

Although King's traditionally has drawn on the maritime provinces for its students, Foundation Year's reputation began in the late 1980s to attract a substantial number from Ontario, often from private schools. This seemed to threaten the distinct character of the King's student body, and in the early 1990s limits were placed on enrollment in the college and a quota was imposed on non—maritime provinces students admitted to FYP. Both measures were short-lived. But since then the social division already existing between maritimers and the more privileged students from central Canada has widened and often been a source of friction. On the other hand, King's and Dalhousie have benefited enormously from the contributions made by students who would not have come to Halifax if it were not for Foundation Year. Part of the motivation for the creation of Contemporary Studies and other upper-year programs has been to retain out-of-province students.

The expansion of FYP also meant the expansion of its tutorial staff. Because the teaching fellows now come from a greater variety of backgrounds than in the 1980s, new ways of fostering collegiality have had to be sought. And now that the Foundation Year

Programme accepts as many as 250 students, its structures have become more formal. The very scale of the program has militated against some of the more casual and personal relations between faculty and students of earlier times.

But there have been cultural changes as well. A collegiate life centered on the residences is no longer possible because few students now want to live on the campus beyond their first year, and few Foundation Year tutors wish to be residence dons. Students are also increasingly demanding of their tutors' time in their quest to improve essays and grades, and this, as well as the greater pressures on tutors to publish, has added to the stresses felt by those teaching in the program, to the detriment of community life.

Technology

New technologies and a kind of technological thinking have also posed challenges to traditions of teaching the humanities that Foundation Year has carried forward. Technological change has sometimes been resisted successfully, sometimes not. In Foundation Year, the book, the human voice, and face-to-face teaching are still central, and there is a strong aversion to any suggestion of accessing texts through the Internet, submitting and responding to papers via computer, or teaching through taped lectures. Various compromises have been accepted: an unexpected increase of class size in 1995 necessitated the move into the dining hall for lectures and the use of microphones for lecturers, and some students with special needs tape the lectures and tutorials. Other innovations have initially been resisted and then endured as inevitable, such as numerical teaching evaluations. In general there continues to be a rearguard battle against the constraints imposed by technological systems.

The kinds of modern technology that have been enthusiastically embraced in Foundation Year have involved the reproduction of art. Within its budgetary limitations, FYP has repeatedly attempted to improve the quality of the sound system and the presentation of slides, and the program's inability to show films to the class as a whole is considered to be a serious lack. A new building to house the Foundation Year lectures is planned to open in 2001. In part, the design of this building represents a recovery of the acoustics and aesthetics of the old-fashioned lecture hall, but it also is meant to give Foundation Year access to high-quality audiovisual equipment.

The Chapel

Another sign of the times is the altered and diminished role of the King's Chapel. After the divinity school left King's in 1971, the chapel became for a while, paradoxically, more vitally connected to the life of the college than perhaps ever before. Some key members of Foundation Year's teaching staff were ordained, and their work in the chapel was closely linked to their teaching. In the latter part of the 1980s, however, the King's Chapel became the center of traditionalist resistance to the new Anglican prayer book and the ordination of women, and its stance of opposition put it on the margins of the church. Given the chapel's identification with a rather narrow and increasingly ineffectual tendency, and given the growing number of Foundation Year students and faculty with different or no religious backgrounds, the question is what kind of role Anglicanism, for the sake of which the original King's was founded, will play in the future life of the college.

Affirmations

The various challenges faced by FYP and King's in the 1990s have led to unanticipated opportunities and accomplishments, as well as to stresses. The expansion of the college has made possible the flourishing of an exceptionally vibrant student intellectual and artistic culture on campus. Although the King's identity now has a different character, and although it is hard to say precisely what that character is except that it is no longer Anglican and Anglophilic, campus spirit is as strong as it ever was and King's students are fervently loyal to their college. They are also impressively talented, running numerous publications, a theatrical society that has been the launching pad to professional careers, a filmmakers society, and a dance collective.

The presence of so many interesting and intelligent students has also enriched Dalhousie, a university whose exemplary arts departments seem to count for ever less as it strives to "meet the highest performance standards" and to "strengthen its market position" (Traves, 1998, pp. 4–5).

Conclusion: On Spirit

This has been a story of the genesis and development of a successful and distinctive kind of undergraduate education in a university that faced an uncertain future. The reasons for that success are various, but a few elements stand out. Although closely associated with another institution, King's has not belonged to it; this small university has managed to retain the autonomy required to be able to create and then modify new programs in its own way. King's was also fortunate in the early 1970s to have had no established departmental structures or interests on its own campus to contend with. The Foundation Year Programme could never have survived at Dalhousie, given that university's strong research ethos. The creation of Foundation Year was contingent, then, on King's having just enough institutional presence and just enough absence.

King's also has been fortunate in its traditions. Much of the early history of the college was characterized by a conservatism that resisted the spirit of progress. Its opposition to modernizing trends was at times merely reactionary. Yet King's kept alive an educational inheritance, that of Oxford, which in the late twentieth century served as a humane alternative to the research-oriented multiversity. The traditionalism of King's paradoxically made it more receptive to the radicalism of the 1960s; both were opposed to the utilitarianism and overspecialization that had come to characterize modern higher education.

The *Geist* of Foundation Year

The Foundation Year Programme's curriculum is very similar to that of other great books courses. Yet the assumptions that underlie much of its teaching, as well as its strengths and particular limitations, are to a large extent uniquely its own. Hegelian philosophy played an important role in forming the particular character of Foundation Year. But if the program can still be considered Hegelian, it is only in relation to remnants of certain traditions and assumptions, not through an explicit teaching. Hegel may continue to be the *geist* of Foundation Year, but he is a very hidden *geist* indeed.

Nevertheless, the program differs from other courses with a similar curriculum in its strong sense of historical periodization and development. Although works taught in Foundation Year are believed to be great, they are also chosen for how they illuminate their age. Each section or historical period of the course has an argument concerning what uniquely identifies it, how it came out of what went before, and why it was superseded. Foundation Year has, or at least aims to have, a definite narrative line in which the unresolved conflicts or contradictions of one age lead to the next.

Strengths

The Hegelian inheritance has given FYP many advantages. The program possesses a drive for coherence, both within the six sections and in their interrelation. It also possesses a strong impulse to make connections. Although the program has a tendency to favor philosophy and theology, it is committed to relating these to other aspects of culture, especially to literature and the history of institutions.

Another strength of FYP is its insistence on the importance of arguments. Although its students are in their first year and are reading many difficult texts, usually for the first time, the program teaches them to be confident that they can say something of value; they are encouraged to feel that they do not need to subject their understanding to the authority of experts. Students learn how to engage with the arguments of complex readings through listening to lectures and in tutorial discussions, and then they learn to develop their own arguments in their essays. The early suspicions of many at Dalhousie that Foundation Year's approach is amateurish or illegitimate have been silenced by the evident academic accomplishments of those who have come out of the program and into their courses.

Limitations

Foundation Year's *geist* has also been the source of many of its particular limitations. For one thing, the program's drive for coherence has an exclusionary effect. The logic that underlies FYP's argument exercises a powerful pull over the selection and reception of texts. It is evident when certain readings are not important to the overall narrative of the course, for they are not taken up in the web of connections that the coordinators and other lecturers weave throughout.

That the students are aware of the inner spirit of FYP is demonstrated over and over again in their year-end reviews, in which they simultaneously complain that there is too much philosophy and that certain important philosophers are left out, that there is too little history and that the history readings and lectures are not necessary to the program, that there need to be more women authors and that the works by women already studied are not really significant.

These contradictory complaints point to the inherent conflict between demands for comprehensiveness and for coherence in the program. Attempting to satisfy the first will always offend against the second. No matter how many works are added by women authors, for example, they always seem externally imposed, since none of them have a place within the narratives that currently inform the curriculum. Received conceptions of the Western philosophical tradition are not amenable to the inclusion of historically marginalized voices.

Another limitation of FYP is that philosophy typically attempts to grasp all other forms. By endeavoring to make past thought comprehensible in philosophical terms, Foundation Year can neglect what is distinctive about particular works or specific forms of expression. Literature has often been considered primarily as a source of images that can aid theoretical understanding. Similarly, the Hebrew Testament has been interpreted within a framework repeatedly criticized for its Christian assumptions and philosophical categories.

Finally, although the program claims that its subject is the historical development of Western culture only, and that other cultures are equally worth studying, the development of the West is at times unconsciously identified with the development of humanity as a whole. The ghost of Hegel hovers over the arguments presented in some lectures, which seem to suggest that what is not Western has not yet discovered the essential divide between the natural and rational realms. Especially in the past, "the East" was treated as having a kind of primal unity against which "the West" came to self-consciousness.

Recently more attention has been given to non-Western thought, including the Egyptian background to Greek philosophy and the Islamic contribution to medieval theology. Overall, however, the origins and implications of some of Foundation Year's assumptions concerning historical development have yet to be thought through.

Possibilities

Foundation Year's particular approach has been the source of both its distinctive accomplishments and its limitations. FYP has made difficult choices, favoring definiteness and coherence over neutrality and inclusiveness. Perhaps in the future a different conception of historical development will give the program new meaning. Although FYP's inherited set of assumptions may have impeded a more complex consideration of what is Western, the program has also shown a remarkable ability to evolve. Those who teach in FYP always have to remind themselves and their students that despite its apparent ambitions, Foundation Year does not propose to give a complete account of what it studies. It cannot include everything of value, and indeed it already includes too much. We always need to say to ourselves: "It's only a first-year course!"

References

Atherton, P., and others. "University of King's College First Year Integrated Programme." Proposal submitted to the King's and Dalhousie Boards of Governors, 1971–1972.

Benjamin, C. "Lost in Thought." *Cities*, Sept. 1989.

Bohm, A. "Letter from Professor Arndt Bohm, Carleton University." *Bulletin of the Canadian Federation of the Humanities*, 1993, *16*(1 and 2).

Bowden, L. "Flip Your Wig." *Watch*, Mar. 1995.

Edwards, E., and others to Henry Roper, Director of the Foundation Year Programme, Dec. 1, 1993.

Frum, L. *Linda Frum's Guide to Canadian Universities*. Toronto: Key-Porter Books, 1987.

Gamberg, H. "Section VI: The Contemporary World." In *The Foundation Year Programme Handbook, 1973–1974*. Halifax: University of King's College, 1973.

Godfrey, J. "The President's Report." In *Report of the President, University of King's College, 1978–1979*. Halifax: University of King's College, 1979.

Hankey, W. "Faculty of Arts and Science Foundation Year Programme (K100)." Insert into *The University of King's College Calendar, 1972–1973*. Halifax: University of King's College, 1972.

Kirby, T. "Quintillian Debate Activities." *Tidings*, Winter 1975.

Martin, R., Chairman of the Philosophy Department, to Dean Gray and Faculty Council, Dec. 6, 1977.

McLean, A. "Pondering a Life Without Jouissance." *Watch*, Mar. 1996.

Morgan, G. "Report of the President." In *Report of the President, University of King's College, 1971–1972*. Halifax: University of King's College, 1972.

Roper, H. "Professor Henry Roper, Director, Foundation Year Programme, King's College, Halifax, Replies." *Bulletin of the Canadian Federation of the Humanities*, 1993, *16*(1 and 2).

Traves, T. "Letter to Alumni: A New Vision for Change." Dalhousie, Spring 1998.

Chapter Eleven

The Intellectual Heritage Program at Temple University

Stephen Zelnick

Temple University was incorporated in 1888 with a precise mission to the Philadelphia community. Its founder, Russell Conwell, a minister and leader of the Baptist Temple (hence Temple University), recognized the buried talents among the laboring mill workers of the city and the need to provide a true university education for talented men and women. Many responded to this opportunity, and Conwell spent the remainder of his life raising funds to realize his dream. Temple College quickly added professional schools (dental, medical, law, pharmacy, education) and a divinity school. Temple University, including its professional schools, was among the first institutions to enroll women and African Americans.

Although Temple University had been a private institution for most of its existence, in 1965 it was integrated into the commonwealth system as a state-related institution. Since that time, state support, as a percentage of overall budget, has fallen steadily; no more than a third of the university budget is now supplied by the Commonwealth of Pennsylvania. Since Temple University has only a meager endowment, its budget depends substantially on enrollment, which has made planning difficult and educational policies unstable. In the 1990s, faculty learned to live with permanent crisis.

Temple University is located in a part of the city that has badly deteriorated, and in the mid-1980s the president's executive cabinet considered relocating to the suburbs. However, because the university is so deeply identified as urban, the president rejected that proposal. Since then, the immediate neighborhood has improved and seems poised for a revival. Major building projects are transforming the university, including several new residence halls, signaling an initiative to attract out-of-state students to enroll and live on campus. This strategy is the result of demographic studies that argue that Temple cannot survive without appealing to a new constituency.

In fall 1999, these dramatic investments in infrastructure began to show results after many years of decreases in undergraduate enrollment. Temple is most proud of the diversity of its 14,000-member undergraduate student body (22 percent African American students, 14 percent Asian American students, and 3 percent Latino American students) and of its harmonious ethnic and racial relations on campus. Academically, Temple students tend to require basic courses to prepare them for college-level work. They come from nonprivileged backgrounds and from high schools with relaxed standards (SAT scores average near 950). Temple's Honors Program, however, is beginning to attract students with SAT scores in the 1300 to 1400 range.

A recent reorganization of Temple's schools and colleges intends to make the university's offerings more easily understood by prospective students. For example, the College of Arts and Sciences has been split into the College of Liberal Arts and the College of Science and Technology. These changes have disrupted old patterns for the faculty and were carried out without faculty participation. The university administration also is looking to technology and a workforce with more full-time adjunct and part-time faculty to adjust its budget to enrollment uncertainties. Several graduate programs have been curtailed, and some face elimination. Although Temple is a Research I University, justification for that ranking comes largely from its medical school. There is a new initiative to adjust Temple's undergraduate programs to serve the postindustrial city, signaled by the recently approved School for Recreation and Leisure Studies, which will offer programs such as Hotel Management and Tourism.

Origins of the Intellectual Heritage Program

The Intellectual Heritage (IH) Program at Temple University was created in 1979 in the College of Arts and Sciences. IH was a central fixture of the college core, which was primarily a set of distribution requirements. The concern at that time was to ensure that at least one course in the college core would focus on traditional study and be free from the specialist focus of the majors. There was, however, a secondary agenda. The two-course IH Program was also a way to employ faculty in the humanities and theoretical social sciences at a time of falling enrollments in those disciplines.

The original design of the Intellectual Heritage Program contained the following parameters: (1) the courses would present only excellent, time-tested works; (2) students would read primary texts and not anthologized snippets or summaries; (3) the works would follow a chronological sequence and stress the history of ideas; (4) the works would be predominantly Western (that is, European and American); and (5) the works would represent many disciplines, including the sciences. The program was designed by a faculty committee, with support from the dean. Faculty who participated in the design recall with pleasure the excitement and cross-disciplinary learning they experienced. Although the two courses that make up the IH Program were never designed to be taught by a faculty team, from the beginning participating faculty visited one another's classes and traded "guest appearances." That collegiality continues into the third decade of the program.

In its first version, IH served only students enrolled in the College of Arts and Sciences. The two courses—IH051 (the ancient Greeks to the Renaissance) and IH052 (the Enlightenment to the modern era)—were taught in many sections, with section size capped at twenty-five students; however, the total number of sections rarely exceeded thirty in any semester. All the sections were taught by tenured (or tenure-track faculty) from humanities and social science departments. Although the general plan was to have a common syllabus, approximately one-third of the texts were chosen by each individual instructor. This freedom resulted in some program incoherence, but there was sufficient continuity among the faculty to maintain the integrity of the program.

Building collegiality has been particularly important in courses that include so many disciplines and so many difficult works. The Intellectual Heritage Program faced this challenge by instituting a seminar series that continues to this day. Every two weeks, faculty meet to discuss one of the texts, a discussion usually initiated by a presentation from one of the IH faculty. The topics may focus on the interpretation of the text or on pedagogical matters. Discussions are usually invigorating and informative and build the sense of faculty community, a great strength of the program.

Major Changes

By far the greatest change over the years has been the extension of Intellectual Heritage from a course required only of arts and sciences students to a requirement for all university students. In 1986, the Temple faculty adopted a university-wide core curriculum. The Intellectual Heritage Program was installed as the "core of the core" and was enthusiastically supported by the faculty. Because the provost at that time, Barbara Brownstein, worked to create a university-wide outlook, she was able to dispel much of the turf politics that have caused problems since. However, one should note also that in the mid-1980s Temple enjoyed expanding enrollments and generous resources. The adoption of the IH051 and IH052 requirements by all schools and colleges took five years to complete. By 1991, the Intellectual Heritage Program served all undergraduates and had grown far beyond its original dimensions. Currently, each IH section enrolls thirty-two students (honors classes continue at twenty-five), and the program offers approximately 120 sections each semester.

Another critical change in IH has involved staffing. Originally all IH faculty held tenure and tenure-track status, and most faculty were from disciplines congenial to a great books curriculum: English, religion, philosophy, classics, history, and the theoretical areas of sociology, anthropology, and political science. Now, because of economic pressures (years of declining enrollments and dwindling commonwealth support) and the rationalization of the university workforce (for example, an aggressive retirement incentives program and no replacement hiring), there are fewer tenured faculty available for assignment to general education teaching, and the great bulk of teaching (over 80 percent) is done by full-time adjuncts and part-time faculty.

This shift produced both positive and negative results. On the positive side, full-time adjuncts concentrate on core instruction and become expert generalists and experienced teachers of novice students. Most full-time adjuncts are hired directly to teach Intellectual Heritage by the program director (the others are hired by departments and fulfill only part of their teaching load in IH). Given the weak job opportunities in precisely those disciplines most closely related to Intellectual Heritage, the applicants hired on adjunct, year-to-year contracts are extremely well-educated and talented teachers. Many see teaching in general core courses as an attractive alternative to the standard, research-based professorial career. But because Temple adheres to the American Association of University Professors (AAUP) time definition for tenure decisions, which mandates a seven-year limit for full-time adjunct faculty, IH faces inevitable turnover and loses its best and most experienced teachers. Still, the supply of excellent replacements continues to provide the IH program with talented instructors. On the negative side, heavy use of adjuncts has caused IH to lose support and status among the tenured faculty who control the committees that administer core curriculum.

Intellectual Heritage 051: Content, Goals, and Methods

Over the years, the content of IH051 and IH052 has changed little. The changes somewhat reflect the "canon wars," adding a few non-Western texts. However, Intellectual Heritage maintains its original outlook. Gandhi has been added, but so has Adam Smith. Some original titles (Einstein on relativity) proved too difficult. In other cases, discussions in faculty seminars have recommended new emphases. In past years an advisory committee made text decisions. Recently, however, with the reduced involvement of tenured faculty, the director has made text decisions. Even so, the two IH courses look much like the courses offered twenty years ago.

The first of the two courses (IH051) is organized around three units: the Greeks, the Scriptures, and the Renaissance.

The Greeks

This unit begins with short works, which allows instructors to start the course even while students are still completing their registration and book purchases. Another purpose is to introduce close reading, which is best done with shorter texts. Most instructors begin with a selection of Sappho poems. Teacher and students read together, see structure, hear the voice, reconstruct the rhetorical situation, and observe the play of discrete information of many sorts and also the work of the class in coming to agreement on principal themes. Sappho's eroticism surprises students, both because they do not imagine that old texts can be sexy and also because her presentation is unembarrassed and close to their own experience. That these poems are homoerotic adds to the surprise. The additional challenge for students is to discover Sappho's religious thought. We accord polytheism a rational defense, discussing the advantages of having many gods and trying to imagine this in our own day (some classes conclude that we are polytheists without admitting it). Beginning the course with material that in one sense is familiar and in another is utterly strange introduces recognitions that continue to be part of Intellectual Heritage.

Next comes Pericles' Funeral Oration from Thucydides' *History of the Peloponnesian Wars*. Although serious students of Thucydides recognize his complex purposes in reconstructing this speech, the IH approach is to read it face on as praise for the democratic city. Typically students explore the form of this democracy, the cultural values that flow from that form, and the benefits claimed for both. Of course, students are also invited to compare Periclean Athens (including the issues of slavery and the narrow scope of citizenship) with their own democratic society. Most decide they prefer Athens and its direct democracy even though they are repelled by the exclusiveness of Athenian citizenship. Also, they find topics such as the citizens' pride in the city's physical magnificence and abundance of goods thought provoking.

Greek drama offers instructors two options: Aeschylus's *Oresteia* or Sophocles' *The Theban Plays*. The *Oresteia* introduces topics of law, a continuing issue in both courses, and explores the savage background of Greek legend and mythology. *Antigone* also treats of law, and *Oedipus the King* is savage enough, too. With Sophocles, there is the added opportunity to witness a debate in Athens between Periclean secularism and religious tradition. One question asked of students is, "What do the Greeks believe?" The answer, of course, is "many conflicting things." This understanding helps students resist the tendency to totalize and simplify the past.

Students seem comfortable reading plays, although few have ever seen a play performed live on stage. The human drama, and specifically the conflicts between strong-willed people, often in familial turmoil, has an immediate power for students. The theme of the mighty falling because of their arrogance appeals to democratic readers across the centuries. On the other hand, some deeper issues in the plays are difficult for students. They too easily simplify the confrontation between Antigone and Creon (Creon is bad because he is a politician; Antigone is good because she opposes authority) and are truly baffled (as they should be) by the concept of fate in *Oedipus the King*. Still, Greek drama engages students emotionally.

Plato's dialogues introduce students to complex thinking. The rationalism of Socrates and Plato's deep hostility to democracy give them more to puzzle over. Selections are read from *The Republic* and one or more dialogues, usually *Euthyphro* and *The Apology*. With Plato the emphasis is on several key issues: the dialectic process, theories of knowledge, the utopian construction of the state, the conception of the psyche, the critique of democracy, and the role of the philosopher. In many ways, the Allegory of the Cave is a signature moment in Intellectual Heritage. Students think about what it means to be a cave dweller, to receive all their thoughts from the human noise and onrush of images and rumor about them, and to do so unthinkingly. The teachers then press hard to help students understand what it would require to break loose and take the upward journey (an isolating and disorienting ordeal) and to seek certain knowledge in place of wayward notions. Some faculty have devised elaborate routines to dramatize this transformation because it defines the purposes of the course and the sort of changes students who take this journey can expect.

Instructors press students to think in agreement with Plato's argument, and especially with the notion of essential truths, a challenging journey for these post-everything students. The rule of the program is that no one can criticize a way of thinking until he or she understands it. This pedagogy of advocacy was promoted at conferences many years ago by Peter Elbow, the writing specialist. He proposed that to study anything, we first need to agree with it and find confirming instances and arguments to fill out the case for that position. He then recommended turning against the text to understand counterarguments. Only then, he proposed, is a meaningful discussion possible. IH teachers advocate and then look to succeeding texts to dismantle the argument of the one that the class is then reading. So, just as classes spent time confirming Pericles' praise for democracy, they push hard to justify Plato's contempt for democracy. The issue of who is correct is premature; the first issue has to be, "What can one think about this question?"

The Scriptures

Plato raises questions about polytheism and thus assists in the course's transition to monotheism. Among the many choices from the Hebrew Bible, Intellectual Heritage assigns the first third of Genesis, the middle third of Exodus, a selection of Psalms, and either the Book of Job or the first twelve chapters of Isaiah. Most students know some of these materials, but in a juvenile way. The aim in IH is to present the biblical materials as worthy of mature study, with emphasis on the complexity of the text, but more so the human complexity in these ancient writings.

Genesis offers both the Creation story (or stories) and the Eden events. Because the Garden story is so familiar that it has lost its significance for students, instructors revive this old story by posing challenging questions: for example, why isn't God responsible for the Fall (he is the tempter, isn't he?), and how can he justly punish our parents so severely? Classes wrestle to make sense of the story against challenging objections. Students are intrigued by this radical re-viewing of an old tale. They learn how to regard a text with care.

The technique of posing problems and encouraging students to use the text to solve them (for example, what do we learn from Genesis 2–3 about the meaning of "in the image of God"? How are the punishments imposed on Adam and Eve appropriate to their transgressions?) sharpens student reading. This pedagogy of posing problems for the students to solve provides a valuable alternative to the lecture-or-small-group-work debate. Here, the instructor is directive in proposing the questions. However, the students must commit themselves to the task of solving the problem. There is lecturing since the instructor cannot form the problem without explaining a good deal; students commit themselves to working toward a solution, and the result belongs to them.

Exodus returns the class to themes of law and nation building encountered with the Greeks. Aren't the "stiff-necked" Israelites the desert cousins of Plato's cave dwellers? Is it the democratic Aaron or the authoritative Moses who exemplifies leadership? Why do the Jews begin with the law and respect for law? The course explores the Ten Commandments to understand their particular importance and the order of their presentation (an excellent exercise is to ask students to order them as people might today). The students then scrutinize the logic of the narrative—the arrangement of events, for example, and the purpose of repetition. They focus on the training of Moses, the hero as liberator, from timid man to God's adviser and bold lawmaker. Exodus is, among many things, an excellent opportunity to teach narrative and its implications.

Students also read a selection of Psalms. Psalm 23 is required, not only because it is well known but also because it organizes several critical themes of Judaism into a highly charged and efficient text. Reading Psalm 23 allows the exploration of a familiar text for fresh meaning. It is a shock to students, for example, to recognize the triumphalism of "in the presence of my enemies." This exercise reveals how much the Jewish text has been supplied a Christian reading. A linguistic example is the King James mistranslation of the last line, which implies eternal salvation of the soul, a concept alien to the original Hebrew text. Psalm 22 is also remarkable for its appropriation by the Christian Gospels. Students learn something about how the Bible was constructed and the relation between the Hebrew and Christian traditions.

The Book of Job, required reading in the original version of Intellectual Heritage, has become optional and recently has been taught less often. Faculty report that although the dramatic situation is intriguing and links well with *Oedipus the King* on the issues of human suffering and God's purposes, the full work is difficult reading since students bog down in the close debates. The teachers have sculpted a lean version of Job to make it more accessible.

The opening twelve chapters of Isaiah form something like an epic. The extraordinary sweep of history presented here provides a new dimension to the course; the preference for social ethics over ritual is powerfully expressed, and the portrayal of a messianic redemption, with phrases well known to Christian students, provides an unexpected introduction to the New Testament. It is important to study a major prophet since the prophetic voice is so strong in the Hebrew Bible. The condemnation, within a religion, of its own people for failing their religious calling is extraordinary. That prophetic voice is also well known in American culture; the rhetorical force of Martin Luther King, Jr., for example, belongs to this tradition.

The New Testament reminds us even more forcefully how familiar students seem to be with and how little they actually know of religious texts. Among the readings are the Gospel of Matthew, the opening to the Gospel of John, and I Corinthians 13. Classes ask: What has changed in the transition from Judaism to Christianity? What does Jesus mean by "fulfilling" mosaic law? What consequences flow from universalizing God's message to all peoples? What does the coming of the Kingdom entail? Another emphasis is the familiar language and sayings that have been so influential to Western thinking, even into the present day. I Corinthians 13 focuses on the radical departure of Christianity from classical Greek conceptions of active perfection. So along with acquainting students with the materials themselves, we continue to stress the continuity and disjuncture in the ongoing discussion of values, faith, and truth.

The Qur'an is unknown to most students and provides a third instance of monotheism. Surprisingly, the Qur'an is closer to Judaism than to Christianity, and students find attractive its refusal to separate this world from the next. Generally they approach the Qur'an with grim prejudices. To study it tests whether students have learned to read texts fairly. Instructors ask them to understand why Islam is amassing converts and try to appreciate the particular attractiveness of the Qur'an. Classes also read comparatively, exploring the similarities to and differences from the Hebrew Bible and the New Testament.

Teaching religious texts has some dangers. Students do not always separate the study of texts from assertions of faith commitments. In spite of a disclaimer to students that they are studying texts and all religions are presented with respect, a few students are affronted or attempt to proselytize their classmates (Temple has a large percentage of Catholic students, many Protestants, substantial numbers of Jews and Muslims, and a small but increasing number of Buddhists and Hindus.) A few students have refused to read the texts of other religions. Instructors do their best to remind students that the objective is to understand what it might mean to be a Jew, a Christian, a Muslim, an animist, or a polytheist. There should be no threat in looking at life as a Muslim for three class hours. Still, a few students cannot put aside their suspicions.

The Scripture unit concludes with the West African epic, the Sundiata. Although this is not a scripture, it does present religious themes. The version of this oral tale that is used is heavily influenced by Islam, and its animist background shines through clearly. (The version is D. T. Niane's French-language account in English translation, since it is an oral text transmitted by each griot in his own tradition, and exists in many competing forms.) Here man is in nature and holds no dominion (as in Genesis 1). Humans share souls with animals, and totemism is not metaphoric but physically real: the hero's mother, although normally a human being, is, at times, a buffalo. Spirits, friendly and terribly evil, fill the forest, and propitiation is no mere formality. In this concept, man and nature belong together, as any modern Darwinian would agree. Again, students are challenged to assume a perspective different from their own. By comparison, Islam seems familiar.

The Sundiata also recalls some ongoing topics and anticipates others. It is IH's only true epic and as such treats nation formation, the installation of law, and the arts of statecraft. In this last matter, the Sundiata anticipates Machiavelli. Sundiata is the course's non-Western text and helps students think about what defines "Western." A list might include the objectification of nature, demystification (even in a prescientific time), literacy (Sundiata is defiantly antiliteracy), and the authority of justice rather than mere power. Sometimes one discovers more looking in from outside the windows than from the view inside a familiar room.

The IH faculty is considering adding readings from the Bhagavad Gita, which represents a nonmonotheistic scripture. In addition, its treatment of the disease of restlessness and its complex explorations of consciousness seem particularly appropriate for our times. The emphasis on nonviolence illuminates the Sermon on the Mount in a powerful way. Adopting the Bhagavad Gita would require some choices, perhaps inviting instructors to select one or two from the list of the Qur'an, the Sundiata, and the Bhagavad Gita.

The Renaissance

The Renaissance unit consists of Galileo's "The Starry Messenger," Machiavelli's *The Prince,* and Shakespeare's *Othello.* The course defies chronology by beginning with Galileo's work since it presents the break with the past most clearly.

"The Starry Messenger" (1609) is the science moment in IH051, and the goal is to concentrate on science and not on Galileo's troubles with the church. "The Starry Messenger" was written for a general audience. It reports with great bravado Galileo's first observations of the heavens with his improved "spyglass." Along the way, he breaks down the traditional view of the heavens based on Platonic conceptions and on biblical and church authority. Tracing how astronomy previously was done, without proper instruments and without the rigorous method displayed by Galileo, helps to define the nature of this revolution in thinking. Instructors also focus on qualities that scientists exhibit. Galileo is an excellent example of boldness and independent thinking, careful measurement and notation, caution in adopting conclusions, imaginative power, and individual ambition. Few freshmen students know anything about astronomy—most, for example, believe the phases of the moon result from partial eclipses—and few have thought about the qualities of scientific endeavor.

The Prince represents a similar revolution in political science. Students grasp quickly the Florentine's remark that he is abandoning "imaginary republics." Like Galileo, Machiavelli gathers his data, in this case from the annals of history, sifts through the evidence with open eyes, and reaches his remarkable conclusions. Students tend not to be shocked by Machiavelli, but they do not understand him. The distinction between nobles and the people, for example, is a blind spot for student readers; the personal integrity and discipline required of the prince is another; and, of course, Machiavelli's analytical detail eludes them. Instructors have had good success working through scenarios that begin,

"You are the newly installed prince and a small delegation of nobles comes to explain to you how you are to rule; now, according to Machiavelli, what do you do?" Finally, *The Prince* allows students to reflect on Pericles, Sophocles, Plato, Moses and Aaron, Jesus, Muhammad, and Sundiata by dividing the list into those whom Machiavelli would admire and those he would reject.

What Galileo and Machiavelli accomplished in their spheres of activity, Shakespeare accomplishes in *Othello*. In this case, the artist renders the human soul in fine detail, with impressive data and close observation. Iago, of course, is also a commentary on Machiavelli. In the amoral world Machiavelli initiates, what impedes the nonprince from using the same trickery? And how can the same man be brutal of means but noble of ends? Can a man who learns to act like a beast recall that he is a man? In Shakespeare there is also a strong Christian emphasis: Desdemona asks us to contemplate the excellence of innocence and forgiveness, and the last act of *Othello* is rich with allusion to the Gospel of Matthew, other biblical themes, and the drama of fall and redemption.

It is worthwhile at the conclusion of IH051 to demonstrate to students that they no longer read and interpret as they once did, and that this program of reading and discussion has armed them in new ways to understand books, the world around them, and themselves.

Student Progress

Many students do not pass the first IH course. Nearly a quarter either drop it or fail to achieve the required C grade. The primary reason for this failure is the poor schooling many students bring to the university; and the IH course, like difficult basic science courses, tests this readiness at a high standard. Typically students lack the discipline to keep up with the reading, take useful class notes, prepare for exams, and compose their essays—normally three or four formal essays of about fifteen hundred words each and based specifically on their reading—through several drafts. The course also requires regular attendance and class participation; instructors rate participation at from 10 percent to 20 percent of the grade. Many students are shocked at the work required. It is clear to instructors that these students are accustomed to receiving respectable grades, in high school and beyond, for little or no work.

Another source of conflict arises from the program's commitment to developing student skills and understanding. Most students, including the talented honors students, will not do well early in the course. It is not unusual for first essays to receive failing grades, even from students who are basically well equipped. The transition for many students from expressing their personal feelings to exploring textual issues with care and precision is difficult. Standards for careful draft preparation also seem to be a surprise for students. Much of the work with writing focuses, as a result, on revision. For students, this stern assessment of their work is a test of their stamina, patience, and character; many fail.

Intellectual Heritage faces pressure from the administration to relax these standards. However, although students often resent the burden of required work and the stern standards, most admit in student evaluations that they receive more attention from their IH instructors than from other faculty. The program also offers support activities, including free tutoring, a writing center, listservs for each course, and a web page. Happily, many students who are forced to repeat the course do well. As we discover in student evaluations, some credit their success at the university to their hard days in IH051.

The Intellectual Heritage Program mandates student course evaluations and gathers close to six thousand evaluations each semester. The evaluation instrument asks students for short written responses to a series of questions. A typical student evaluation notes that the student resented being required to take this course, which appears to have nothing to do with his or her major or career aspirations. In addition, respondents often note that the books were not in themselves at all interesting. However, the individual instructor was so good that she or he made the course and the readings interesting anyway; and especially toward the end of the term, the readings became more compelling. There then follows each student's list of the readings that were most important—a list that often includes half the course titles.

Faculty understand these comments to mean that as the course unfolded, the student became attracted as he or she became better able to manage the study of classic works. The instructor had indeed wielded a kind of magic—not the magic to make "bad books interesting" but to make unschooled students into readers, writers, and thinkers. It simply isn't clear to students whether the train or the station platform is moving.

Students entering IH052 are significantly different in their readiness to manage difficult readings and to fulfill the requirements of functioning university students. This assertion is supported both anecdotally and by the much higher student grades in the second IH course.

Intellectual Heritage 052: Content, Goals, and Methods

IH052 represents a new challenge. The readings in IH051 are primarily narratives (even Galileo tells a story), but the second IH course texts are more abstract. In part, this reflects the interests of those who designed the two courses: the first course was designed by faculty in the humanities, the second by social science faculty. However, the difference also reflects the shift in authority, from ancient to modern times, from narrative to scientific disciplines. Students comment that IH052 readings seem dry and difficult. The pedagogy for the second course has to recognize this shift and devise appropriate strategies.

The second course is arranged into five units: The Natural Rights Tradition, Romanticism, Revolutionary Thinkers, Nonviolent Struggle, and Imagining the World. These units proceed chronologically. However, faculty are careful that one perspective not replace another and that, for example, natural rights thinking remain a force in the course, as in our culture.

Natural Rights Tradition

Like IH051, the course begins with a short text: the opening two paragraphs of the Declaration of Independence. Instructors have long since ceased to be surprised that even in Philadelphia, students do not know the Declaration. Faculty concentrate on raising questions: Who is "nature's God?" What "laws of nature" have anything to do with governments? Why the necessity of letting "facts be submitted to a candid world"? How can we support the claim that we are born equal when we so clearly are not? Students quickly dismiss the Declaration as mere rhetoric. It does help to reconstruct the high risk taken by the signers: when "John Carroll of Carrolltown" bothers to give his home address, he is daring the British to come and find him. How many of us would do the same? John Locke's *Second Treatise of Government* supplies the answers. The goal with Locke is twofold: to explore the natural rights argument as a political force and to establish the values of the Enlightenment as a revolutionary intellectual movement.

Students suffer reading Locke. The sentences are painfully long for modern readers and his discourse relentlessly abstract. Locke's Euclidean precision pauses only rarely to offer an example. We are far from narration here, and instructors must slow down to parse critical sentences. Locke's tireless rationality (or at least reasonableness) is the best emblem of the Enlightenment, along with his faith in the basic goodness of humankind, his emphasis on individualism, and his effort to find a basis of society not rooted in force and violence. Even at this late cultural date, most students, after their initial agonizing, embrace Locke's argument and his progressive and liberal values.

These notions are then put to work by tracing their historical uses. Not only Jefferson's Declaration but the Bill of Rights, Frederick Douglass's "What to the Slave Is the Fourth of July," the Seneca Falls Resolution advancing women's rights, the *Dred Scott* decision by Chief Justice Roger Taney, Lincoln's response to Stephen Douglas on Taney's decision, and Milton Friedman's preface to *Capitalism and Freedom*: all show Locke's significance today. The study of several constitutional amendments (the Bill of Rights, plus the Thirteenth, Fourteenth, Fifteenth, and Nineteenth amendments) has deepened as instructors have learned that students know nothing about them. The discussion of slavery and the various political compromises designed to avoid the Civil War seem also to be unknown territory for these students. Although they have intense moral objections against their nation, they know little of the nation's history. The course reviews the constitutional provisions regarding slavery, with special attention to the "three-fifths of a man" compromise. Students are always stunned to discover that the slave-holding South wished, albeit only for congressional apportionment, to accord slaves full humanity, while the North, for the same political reasons, offered them none. The discussion to make sense of the three-fifths provision takes students to political issues long since buried by confused moral indignation.

As numerous students have said, the principal lesson in Intellectual Heritage is that things are never as they seem. By IH052, the issue is no longer to discover this but to learn in how many different ways it can be true.

Romanticism

Romanticism rejects the Enlightenment values in several ways and confirms them in others. By this stage, students can understand this dialectic of difference and continuity. On the one hand, romantics embrace feeling as a more reliable pathway to truth than reasoning, and they question progress, at least in the commercial and material realm. Still, romanticism shares with the Enlightenment a belief in the individual as the master of his or her fate, even if that individual is now a solitary genius rather than the public man of the Enlightenment.

Several phases of romanticism are examined in IH052: Blake exemplifies visionary protest, Wordsworth the inward journey, and Whitman exhilarating visions of progress. Emily Dickinson represents another pathway to original, solitary vision, with her own extraordinarily compressed and artful language.

Students are afraid of poetry. Somewhere in their education, they were told that poems are like Rorschachs and were invited to see in poems whatever they pleased. Soon after, students wrote little papers trusting in their freedom to superimpose their dreams onto the poems, and their teachers told them that their interpretations were wrong. Caught in this double bind, most students quite sensibly decided that reading and writing about poetry was not a game they could play and win. Somewhere there was a code to what these poems were about—a code that only teachers (and that girl in the front row whom nobody liked) knew. The IH approach, consequently, is to have students read poems in the same careful way as they have been reading other texts, with special attention to the rhetorical situation and the created voice.

Blake's shorter poems work well—"London," in particular, and also "The Chimney-Sweeper." Short poems have the advantage of showing their structure on a single page. One problem is the student's expectation that poems voice the poet's emotions directly, speaking in his or her own voice, and addressing the vaulting heavens. Finally, poems are thought so ethereal that they are about nothing in particular in this world. Reading Blake dispels these dismal expectations. The attempt to demystify poetry takes the form of a simple protocol of questions: Who is speaking? To whom? About what? In what situation? What is the problem? Is it resolved? If so, how? Although this list does not capture the poem, it does provide students a good place to start.

Wordsworth presents greater problems. The assigned texts are several sonnets, where again there is the advantage of a revealed structure. Students also study excerpts from "Preface to Lyrical Ballads" in which Wordsworth, in his own reliable prose, explains his objectives. Still, there is no escaping the difficulty of reading "Tintern Abbey." One goal is to teach students to hear Wordsworth's voice, and this is a good occasion to emphasize voice in any text. Perhaps the least developed skill among Temple students is to read aloud. Some instructors feel so strongly about this gap in language that they require student reading in class of all the texts, even Locke. The point is to help students rediscover the link between voice and writing, a critical resource in writing well. With Wordsworth, students struggle through their own initially toneless, disjointed readings toward reading with sense and passion. Instructors require students to memorize, from a few lines to much longer passages. Many students groan at this assignment; some enjoy it.

Wordsworth introduces as well the topic of alienation in the commercial city, a topic soon to be elaborated by Marx. As with all other assigned works, instructors invite students to find themselves in the text. If "the world is too much with us," where do they go for sustenance? Wordsworth's return to the simple force of nature is a theme these students know well. Although seeking the immortal soul through memory and meditation is not a step many students have taken, they are intrigued with the uses Wordsworth makes of their shared dilemma.

Whitman objects to Wordsworth's quiet repose and his unease in the city. It is delightful to discover with the students this conflict at the heart of romanticism. Whitman is our democratic poet: raucous, unlicensed, bawdy, comical, outrageous. Today most students just do not get it; in the 1960s, they got little else. They are more at home with the tight and ironic structures of Dickinson. Perhaps, too, Dickinson's pessimism and retreat to fantasy rings truer to today's students. Flamboyant affirmations embarrass; stinging uncertainties fit.

Revolutionary Thinkers

Marx, Darwin, and Freud challenge students more than any other writers. They are difficult, and their insistence on structural, causal imperatives is unsettling. These thinkers challenge the assumption, shared by Enlightenment and romantic thinking, that we shape our destiny individually. Instead, these thinkers discover forces that shape our lives but lie beyond our normal awareness. Such determinism threatens our self-esteem, and students find all three writers scandalous and relevant.

Marx takes up Locke just where individualism gives way to class, where labor is no longer the happy route to property but instead to the misery of wages. Locke and Marx share a labor theory of value. However, where Locke is confident that there is still enough free property to make the competition for ownership and appropriation meaningful, Marx looks out on a world in which nine-tenths of humanity has little or no prospect of owning anything of consequence.

Reading the *Communist Manifesto* in the post–cold war era is odd. Rather than sinking into the abyss along with the Soviet Union, Marx and Engels have acquired a new relevance as the result of the globalization of capitalism. In an irony that would have delighted Marx, he now teaches the children of capitalism what that system is, how it works, and even its destiny in commanding the world. Students are impressed with Marx's praise of capitalism and his powerful predictions of both capitalist world domination and the socialist adjustments imposed on raw capitalism. Moreover, Marx's comments on alienation and the destructive role of capitalism in reducing traditional morals to a cash nexus ring true to many students.

Most challenging is Marx's claim that the mode of production determines all spheres of activity. His model of social analysis has been highly influential, even among anti-Marxists. Students admire this act of producing a key to understanding everything. They enter also into spirited discussions of the distribution of wealth, of dramatic changes in the contemporary labor market, consumer compulsion, the emptiness of work, and other Marxian topics.

Recently selections from Smith's *Wealth of Nations* have been added to the course, providing students with a rich set of materials (along with Locke and Marx) to help them read the ideological map of our times. Coming into the university, most of these students are not equipped to read the newspaper. Exiting from Intellectual Heritage, they should be able to find their way around most policy discussions and editorials. Several instructors offer extra credit to students who publish letters in local newspapers based on IH readings.

Darwin is the IH052 scientist, with selections assigned from *Voyage of the Beagle, Origin of Species,* and *Descent of Man.* The course objective is to use Darwin to illustrate the qualities of the scientist and the insistent materialism of modern science. *Voyage of the Beagle* shows Darwin before he has fashioned his theory. Instructors want students to marvel at the precision and tenacity of his explorations of nature and the intellectual boldness of his inquiries. The young Darwin of the *Voyage* is not much older than the students, but he already shows the imaginativeness that will make him great. *Origin* introduces Darwin's theory, and here students wrestle with his unflinching materialism. Students today know so little about nature that studying Darwin provides another strong opportunity to extend their thinking. *Descent of Man* relates these perspectives on nature to ourselves.

Freud follows Darwin in the syllabus quite effortlessly, with readings from *Civilization and Its Discontents* or selected *Introductory Lectures* (on dreams and on symbolism). Freud continues the structural determinist and materialist themes in this unit. His direct assault on religious belief pains students, and his point-blank discussion of sex startles them, even in our age of immodesty. Freud also provides another collection point. His comments on the compromises between freedom and civility recall Locke, and in a different way the romantics; he also comments directly on Marxist assumptions about property and continues the Darwin-spawned discussion of biological determinism. Freud's discussion of aggression in *Civilization and Its Discontents* introduces the next unit.

Nonviolence and the Liberation Struggle

This unit presents selections by Gandhi, Martin Luther King, Jr.'s "Letter from the Birmingham Jail," and portions of a 1960 speech by Nelson Mandela. Along with nonviolence, the unit also introduces colonialism and how it has shaped the world today.

Reading Gandhi is a great relief for the students. Because the writings of the previous unit tend to be abstract and lack narrative drama, students are exhausted and sometimes discouraged. The selections for Gandhi include long pieces from his autobiography, and students seem quite relieved to be reading a story. Gandhi's idealism thrusts them suddenly in a new direction. Students resist the blank materialism of the previous unit, but then just as ardently reject the idealism of this new one. These startling juxtapositions force students to investigate their values.

Students, of course, are alert to discussions of racial oppression, and Gandhi's work provides an example not based on the African American or Latino experience but on events from another time and place. Interestingly, this displacement has many advantages in opening a discussion that would otherwise be a bit stale and bound by local experience. As the non-Western writer in the second IH course, Gandhi is particularly challenging because his criticism of Western culture is direct and uncompromising (asked what he thought of Western civilization, Gandhi answered that it would be a good idea). Students find themselves sympathetic to Gandhi's protests against Western oppression but offended at his attack on their own materialism. His religious discipline also makes students uneasy. The previous week they were troubled by Freud's forceful atheism; now they struggle with Gandhi's religious convictions and exacting personal disciplines.

Temple students revere Martin Luther King, Jr.—and know almost nothing about him. One of the delights of the second course of the IH sequence is to teach King's "Letter" and show students how King himself made excellent use of his own "IH" education. "Letter from the Birmingham Jail" illustrates how well King has integrated his readings of the Greeks, the Scriptures, the natural rights tradition, and Gandhi into his discourse and demonstrates the power that comes from apt use of them in his argument. In addition, although many students have read the "Letter" in

some previous course, they routinely comment that without knowing these source materials, they did not really understand what
they were reading. Reading King's essay becomes another opportunity for students to assess what they have been studying in both
courses and, more important, how IH has changed them. Having
the students plot their own growth and achievement is critical
to the success of these studies.

Imagining the World

As we approach our own time, it becomes difficult to designate
classics; so instructors choose one or two titles from a list of
options. The list offers Kafka's short stories, Camus's *The Stranger,*
Miller's *Death of a Salesman,* Achebe's *Things Fall Apart* or his *No
Longer at Ease,* Morrison's *The Bluest Eye* or *Sula,* Maxine Hong
Kingston's *Woman Warrior,* Gabriel Garcia Marquez's *Chronicle of a
Death Foretold,* and Wiesel's *Night.* Instructors use this occasion not
only to introduce a new perspective but also to gather in several
topics that belong to the course. For example, they ask students to
provide interpretations of Miller's *Death of a Salesman* that reflect
what Wordsworth would say, or Freud, or Marx, or Gandhi. Students are impressed with their new ability to understand works by
looking through the interpretive lenses supplied by the books they
have studied.

Prospects

The Intellectual Heritage Program is long established and quite
successful. It has received national notice—an Exemplary Program
award in 1993 from the American Association of University Admin-
istrators and recognition from the American Academy for Liberal
Education—and was singled out recently for praise by the
Commonwealth Foundation in a report on Core Curriculum in
Pennsylvania. In addition, IH serves as the center for a national
network of core text programs, the Association for Core Texts and
Courses. Nevertheless, the program faces antagonism from the
Temple faculty and administration and may not survive.

The reasons for this gloomy prospect are several. Intellectual
Heritage is radically different from anything else in Temple's

humanities or social sciences core in that it presents a fixed curriculum, uniform across 120 sections. This standardization is much resented; with so few tenured faculty available to teach regularly in the program (in fall 1998, only one out of six sections were taught by regular faculty, and several of those were new faculty), the original one-third text choice provision cannot be maintained. As the core of experienced instructors dwindles, it becomes increasingly difficult to accommodate instructor option. A few tenured faculty have resisted assignment to IH and claimed that IH, with its standardized readings, violates their academic freedom. Indeed, considering that "common text," introductory, and survey courses have normally been assigned to teaching assistants, many senior faculty interpret assignment to IH as a severe demotion in status. On the other hand, allowing inexperienced senior faculty to choose texts has caused problems. These faculty often teach within their discipline, narrowing this multidisciplinary course to fit parochial interests.

Given what an IH instructor needs to know, this problem is not surprising. Most instructors know about one-third of the material well, another third is within range, and the last third requires significant faculty education. Social science professors rarely feel comfortable teaching Wordsworth, and most humanities and social science faculty fear teaching Galileo. This means that faculty must become students themselves, and until they have taught the course several times, they will feel out of their depth.

From the beginning, the IH Program has offered seminars to support new faculty. More recently, the program established a faculty listserv that allows experienced and new faculty to discuss problems in understanding the books and in teaching them. In addition, the IH web page contains sample essays, exams, essay topics, mini-lectures, and short pieces on context and interpretation. IH has a well-appointed lounge where faculty gather for morning coffee, lunch, and end-of-the-day conversation. Every effort is made to achieve collegiality and to help integrate new faculty. In general, however, the status concerns of senior faculty prevent them from seeking assistance and from entering easily into a community that includes adjuncts and lower-rank faculty who command greater expertise. Young research faculty see IH as a distraction from their career goals, since rewards at the university are based on publication and research grants. There are no incentives offered to tenured or tenure-track faculty for teaching in the Intellectual Heritage Program and no load relief for newly assigned tenured faculty.

This problem has been sharpened by the reductions of Temple's full-time faculty. Over several years, faculty who have retired normally or been induced to retire by attractive buy-out plans have not been replaced. This means that few tenured and tenure-track faculty are available to teach in the program, which adds to its political isolation. Instead, IH depends increasingly on full-time adjuncts and part-time faculty. Although there are advantages to these arrangements (these faculty tend to be devoted to teaching and amenable to self-education), there are also political deficits. Increasingly the course is seen as belonging to a transient faculty. Nor does it help that IH accrues high enrollments while humanities and social science departments are whittled down for lack of students. Some faculty leaders have suggested abandoning the Intellectual Heritage Program and redistributing its enrollments to departments by requiring introductory disciplinary courses as core courses. These would be taught by teaching assistants, thus enlarging graduate programs and ensuring enrollment in research-related seminars. Undergraduates would, however, lose out in this arrangement.

Throughout its history, the administration has supported the Intellectual Heritage Program, but there are signs of a change. In a state-related university that offers opportunities to the children of working-class families, there is increasing pressure to serve the most narrowly conceived needs of the job market. Traditional areas of study must justify their continued existence in utilitarian terms. In this new world order, successful people will be corporate lawyers, accountants, financiers, or managers of the prison and leisure recreational industries. It seems to be more difficult to find a place for studies of classic works devoted to free thought and democratic values. The new administrators, many of them with a management agenda and seeking maximum curricular flexibility and customer comfort, see IH as an outdated and conservative villainy imposed on impressionable students.

Another dynamic is worth noting. New administrators—and there has been a parade of new provosts and vice provosts—wish to leave their mark. The best way to do this is to change what is in place, and the most "in place" program at Temple is the Intellectual Heritage Program. Bright and ambitious administrators, passing through for their two- to five-year stint, take aim at IH, almost the last vestige of traditional education.

IH's best protection has been the program's high quality, and particularly the emphasis on student development. Although administrative change agents trumpet student development, they find little attention being paid to it outside the IH Program. More important, students provide continuing testimony that although IH is difficult, they learn and develop in it. Mandatory student evaluations offer sustained testimony that students believe they benefit from their labors.

IH is also threatened by the new view of students as customers. Because Temple University has a meager endowment, enrollment shifts that are a normal result of demographics, the fortunes of sports teams, and any accident of advertising, magazine polls, or a lurid crime near campus can throw administrators into a bottom-line panic. The most recent result has been a drastic reorganization of colleges in the university based on an untested premise of expanding student choice. Intellectual Heritage is a notoriously "no choice" program since it is required of all students and the texts and standards are uniform. The course is also very difficult for many of its "customers," and so from a sales and marketing perspective, IH threatens customer satisfaction. A recent adjustment imposed by the provost's office allows students transferring into the university an automatic equivalency for many courses in our core curriculum, most notably Intellectual Heritage. This should induce happier transfers; it will not ensure that graduates know anything or can hold their own with reading and writing.

Two other forces threaten not only the Intellectual Heritage Program but all other developmental programs in the university. Because of the narrowing of faculty opportunities during the past two decades, there are no young faculty willing or able to assume directorial leadership of general education programs. Faculty at research institutions have been encouraged to focus exclusively on research and to avoid at all costs administrative work or teaching assignments that might associate them with adjuncts and teaching assistants. Indeed, promotion and tenure committees routinely reject faculty who have labored in the educational vineyard or shown enthusiasm for developmental programs. The consequences are not surprising: there are no candidates to replace the aging leaders of writing programs, American studies, Intellectual Heritage, basic mathematics, introductory foreign language, and other developmental programs. One adjustment to this remarkably bad planning may be to give these important tasks over to educational managers who have little experience with teaching and no credentials in the subject.

Finally, the refusal to recognize the professionalism of people who provide the most difficult undergraduate instruction continues. Intellectual Heritage is taught by a faculty that is more than 80 percent full-time adjunct and part-time faculty. Although the original stipulation was that the courses could be taught by no more than 20 percent nonpermanent faculty, this mandate has eroded badly over the years. With the general reduction of tenured faculty, full-time adjuncts become "regular faculty"; more recently the administration has pushed part-time instruction in IH to 33 percent. In addition, a recent effort to professionalize the full-time adjuncts, who form the core of the IH faculty (50 percent of sections taught), was to allow them to continue beyond the AAUP limit of seven years of employment if they could present a record of excellence. The proposal required periodic review every three years and a cap on the percentage of the adjunct faculty permitted to exceed the seven-year limit. Even with these concessions, a committee of senior faculty was unwilling to consider professionalizing these positions, an adjustment that has been made at many similar universities. A quick survey in fall 1996 of institutions similar to Temple University discovered that of seventeen schools contacted, fourteen permitted renewals without limit. This judgment has damaged the morale of adjunct faculty and raised serious questions about the commitment of the university's senior faculty to undergraduate education.

Conclusion

The Intellectual Heritage Program is designed to bring the very best to students who have not been well schooled and whose expectations in seeking education are narrowly vocational. Temple faculty have spent many hours recounting alarming tales of what their students do not know—words like *tempest, pious, deceitful,* and *likelihood*; the century in which the Civil War was fought; the difference between the Constitution and the Declaration of Independence—but they take this ignorance as a challenge and an opportunity. The program meets this challenge every day, with a text list and a set of standards designed to succeed. And despite obstacles, it does.

The prospects for the near future are poor. The wretched state of the tenured faculty and the hostility and new aggressiveness of the administration threaten either to remove traditional programs like Intellectual Heritage or so restructure them that they will not achieve the educational goals they were designed to serve.

It may be that we are entering a time when traditional education and real standards for learning will be reserved for an elite enrolled at elite schools and when other institutions with truly democratic missions, schools like Temple, will be retooled to service the narrowly conceived needs of the working and consuming masses. If this is true, then we will be training compliant citizens who believe and do as they are told; we will ensure that life for them is little more than working, consuming, and sensational escape—and that a heavy boulder blocks the exit from the cave.

Chapter Twelve

Tradition and Criticism in Western Culture at the University of the South

W. Brown Patterson

At the University of the South in Sewanee, Tennessee, a four-course sequence in the humanities was introduced in fall 1992 after several years of planning. It is team-taught and interdisciplinary, with participation from faculty members in art history, classical languages, English, history, music, philosophy, political science, and religion. Approximately 80 students out of an entering class of 350 elect to enroll in the sequence, which extends through their freshman and sophomore years. The distinguishing characteristic of the program is indicated by its title: Tradition and Criticism in Western Culture. The four semester-long courses, which deal, respectively, with the ancient world, the medieval world, the early modern world, and the modern world, seek to show that Western culture is the result of almost continuous dialogue and controversy. By means of lectures delivered to the whole group, small group discussions of no more than twenty students, the reading of texts, and the experiencing of works of art, students in the program come to recognize not only that the culture inherited from the past is the product of a complex and dynamic process, but that these texts and works of art raise questions that are still being discussed. Feminism, multiculturalism, and moral relativism, along with problems associated with crime, sex, and warfare, have been part of a vigorous dialogue from antiquity onward. The program examines texts and works of art within their historical context, an investigation that is illuminating in itself, and shows that the works of earlier writers and artists remain immensely relevant to today's concerns.

The Current Program

A narrative written for students in the first-semester course by its faculty team explicitly describes the process of dialogue and conflict that shaped the culture of the ancient world:

> In the course of our inquiry, we seek to acquaint students with both the diversity and the unity within ancient civilization. We examine the radical disagreements which differentiate the worlds of Homer, Sophocles, Pericles, Plato, Epicurus, Augustus, and Virgil—not only from one another, but from those of the ancient Hebrews and early Christians. At the same time, we consider how, despite their dissimilarities, the individuals and traditions of the ancient world confront many of the same basic problems and conflicts—such as the conflict between the pursuit of power and standards of justice, order and chaos, and the good of the individual and the welfare of the community. In so doing, one of our primary goals is to educate students into some of the controversies and debates which not only shaped Western culture but continue up to the present day to challenge and perplex human beings. [Humanities Staff, 1997, p. 1]

During the semester, Greece and Israel are seen as the sources of cultural traditions that helped to shape the ancient world. Socrates and David are discussed as exemplars of distinct traditions, and students are asked to consider their respective merits as archetypes of human excellence. Then, as the narrative states, "Having set up the contrast between Athens and Jerusalem, we turn to the Sermon on the Mount and the Christian ethic of *agape* love" (Humanities Staff, 1997, p. 3). The Roman historian Tacitus, as the narrative notes, called the religion of Christianity "notoriously depraved," a description that is examined from his point of view as well as from that of adherents of the new sect. The semester concludes with a general discussion by students and faculty members of the respective claims of Christianity and classical culture:

> The Christian and Greco-Roman traditions encountered one another intellectually from the first century A.D., and they continued to influence and affect one another for centuries. Is our culture today better or worse for this confluence of two traditions? [Humanities Staff, 1997, p. 3]

The second course, which freshmen take during the spring semester, begins with Augustine's *Confessions* and his interior struggle as he was confronted by the rich cultural heritage of Greece and Rome, while experiencing the powerful attraction of the Christian faith. His conversion from one way of life to another is seen as emblematic of one of the characteristic Western responses to spiritual and intellectual dilemmas. Conflicts of styles, values, and ideologies are seen in the emergence of specifically Christian art forms in Rome, Ravenna, and Constantinople. Conflicts of a theological and intellectual kind are represented by the career of Peter Abelard, the early scholastic thinker who clashed with his teachers and with such revered religious authorities as Bernard of Clairvaux. Abelard's writings raise the question in acute form of how far human beings should follow the demands of authority on the one hand or of reason on the other. The course examines Abelard's intense relationship with Héloïse and her struggle, as revealed in her letters, to come to terms with her roles as student, lover, mother, and prioress.

The course then gives attention to St. Francis's critique of the emerging commercial society of the high Middle Ages, the persecution of Jews by medieval Christians, and the warfare and mutual recriminations between Christians and Muslims, especially during the Crusades. Dante's *Divine Comedy* is seen as summing up the cultural achievements of the Middle Ages, while criticizing the shortcomings of religious and political figures of the early fourteenth century.

The last part of the course takes account of economic, social, and political decline in the West in the era of the Black Death, the Hundred Years' War, and the Great Schism in the Catholic church.

Another story also emerges here: "the resilience of institutions in the face of catastrophe, the strength of Christianity to survive crisis, and the emergence of a new kind of religious devotion as lay people sought ways to express their religious faith" (Humanities Staff, 1997, p. 2).

The third semester in the sequence, which examines the early modern world, is described in its course narrative as dealing with a period of rapid transformation, when statesmen and artists sought "to imitate ancient politics and ancient arts," the economies of Western Europe underwent unprecedented expansion, and the advent of printed texts facilitated religious reforms and revivals. The results in the early modern period were paradoxical. Renaissance optimism about human nature encountered darker views:

> At the same time, prolonged civil and religious wars tempted some
> Europeans to embrace views of human nature and human
> potential which, even today, can seem shockingly pessimistic.
> These included more cynical theories of government and some
> more skeptical attitudes towards religious traditions than anything
> on record from the preceding millennium of European culture.
> [Humanities Staff, 1998, p. 1]

The third-semester course, taken by sophomores in the fall semester, examines writers and artists whose work exemplifies these paradoxes and conflicts. They include Thomas More, a loyal friend and counselor to King Henry VIII, who sharply criticized the politics and social policies of the contemporary English government and envisioned a newly discovered land with a society based on representative government and a collectivist economy; and Martin Luther, a monk who defied the pope and challenged the assumptions of Catholic theology in the name of a biblical approach to salvation and a reformed universal church. Among artists, special attention is given to Michelangelo, whose *David* and Sistine Chapel ceiling depict the almost unlimited potential of human nature, but whose *Last Judgment* in the same chapel depicts the divine punishments that human sins have incurred.

In the third course, the history of music is introduced, beginning with the medieval plainsong tradition and proceeding into the Renaissance and baroque eras with a consideration of the place of music, both sacred and secular, in Western culture. One composition that is given detailed attention is Claudio Monteverdi's *Vespers of the Blessed Virgin* (1610), in which the composer transforms a traditional monastic evening service by introducing instrumental parts, inserting sacred songs between the psalms, and emphasizing passages in the texts with musical devices adapted from the newly emerging opera. Music is shown to reflect as well as to influence other artistic elements in the culture, to be closely related to historical events, and to have its own rational structure and emotional power.

One of the most striking contrasts examined in the course is that between two sixteenth-century Spaniards who wrote historical accounts of the conquest of Mexico. Bernal Díaz saw Cortés and his soldiers as extending the rightful claims of their king to the New World and introducing Christianity to a society that practiced human sacrifice on a substantial scale. Bartolomé de Las Casas, on the other hand, saw Cortés as treacherously and brutally killing thousands of native people, largely destroying their culture and society. Who was right? What attitudes toward a culture different from one's own are expressed by the two writers? What would a multicultural solution have looked like?

Issues of human freedom and oppression, the respective rights of individuals and governments, and the claims of reason and conscience are the focus of discussions of Shakespeare's *The Tempest*, Milton's *Paradise Lost*, Hobbes's *Leviathan*, and texts by Descartes, Locke, Hume, and Voltaire. These issues are further seen as having been at the forefront of the American Revolution, in which British colonists, including many slaveholders, achieved political independence in the name of the inalienable natural rights of "life, liberty, and the pursuit of happiness."

The final session of the third course is a general discussion addressing the question, "What lasted?" It is predictably lively and marked by disagreements among faculty members as well as students, as they seek to identify the ideas, texts, works of art, institutions, and nations that have endured—and to explain why.

The approach taken in the first three courses—representing the past as characterized by constant challenges to existing practices, ideas, and beliefs—helps to prepare students for an examination of the modern and postmodern world, in which no aspect of traditional culture has been impervious to attack and old questions are continually being reformulated, even as new questions emerge. The fourth course, which students take during the second semester of their sophomore year, begins with the French Revolution, the product, at least in part, of Enlightenment ideas of natural rights and of governments' responsibility to preserve them. These ideas, as expressed, for example, by Thomas Paine, tended to discredit all existing European governments. But the traditional order found an eloquent defender in Edmund Burke, who declined to give credence to metaphysical abstractions apart from historical conditions. Discussing the debate between Paine and Burke provides a way to understand not just revolution and reaction but also subsequent expressions of political liberalism and conservatism.

Burke was not alone in challenging the eighteenth-century thinkers' reliance on reason. In their different ways, Wordsworth, Beethoven, Blake, and Dickens can all be seen as emphasizing, as the course narrative states, "the role of powerful feelings as revelatory." The theme of conflict, treated by some romantic writers and artists—Verdi in *La Traviata,* for example—as the prelude to a conflict-free spiritual state, arose naturally in an era characterized by wars for political unification, competition in a capitalistic economy, and a scramble by many states for larger colonial empires. Conflict between social classes was the basis of Karl Marx's interpretation of history and his political ideology, just as struggle and conflict were central to Charles Darwin's theory of natural selection in the evolution of forms of life. Neither thinker left room for traditional theism. Nor did Sigmund Freud, who called religion an "illusion," based on an elemental feeling of dependency. The nineteenth century is seen as ending in disillusionment with religious ideas by many thinkers, despite the flourishing state of much organized religion. The course sees Friedrich Nietzsche's "announcement of God's death and insistence of the right of powerful individuals to create their own individual world views . . . [as] the culmination of nineteenth century thought" (Humanities Staff, 1997, p. 2).

"After Nietzsche, and with the rise of the horrors of World Wars One and Two," the narrative for the fourth semester course continues, "it became harder to maintain any kind of spiritual optimism." Conventions in the arts were violated or discarded in works such as Igor Stravinsky's *Rite of Spring* and Picasso's *Les Desmoiselles d'Avignon*. T. S. Eliot's *The Waste Land* testified to the apparently disconnected state of human experience. The loss of traditional landmarks is examined in the course with reference to several alternatives, including that offered by C. S. Lewis in *The Case for Christianity*, which argued that right and wrong are more than subjective categories and really exist apart from ourselves. In the postmodern world, this discussion of whether there is any higher truth or reality to guide human beings has become ever more prominent. In Stanley Fish's (1989) formulation, perceived objects always bear the marks of some interpretive community, and since interpretations change, the shape of perceived objects changes too (pp. 141–160). On the other hand, John Searle (1993) has argued that the existence of a real world to which true statements correspond is a necessary condition of public discourse (pp. 693–709). The course narrative notes that this issue—whether there is a higher truth or reality—is frequently raised in the *New York Review of Books*, the *New York Times* op-ed page, and other newspapers and journals. The ongoing nature of this discussion, the narrative states, "is a defining characteristic of late twentieth century thought" (Humanities Staff, 1997, p. 2). The humanities sequence ends as it begins, with the sort of questioning in which Socrates engaged (Nussbaum, 1997, pp. 15–49, 257–292). The aim of the four courses is not to resolve the fundamental problems of individual and community life, but to lead students to think about them clearly and to be able to understand and appreciate the resources of Western culture for the insights and the stimulus that they provide.

History of the Program

The University of the South consists of the college of arts and sciences—a liberal arts college—and a school of theology, a seminary for the education of men and women for the ordained ministry in the Episcopal church. In 1998–99, the former had an enrollment of thirteen hundred full-time undergraduates and the latter eighty full-time students. The university was founded in 1857 by bishops of the Episcopal church in the southern states who were ambitious to establish a center of learning in their region with the breadth of curriculum and the close attention to individual students characteristic of Oxford and Cambridge. It is frequently known as Sewanee, from the place on a plateau in south-central Tennessee where it is located (Chitty, 1993). The Interdisciplinary Humanities program was proposed as part of a thorough reform of the undergraduate curriculum that was presented to the faculty of the college of arts and sciences in spring 1990.

In its 1990 report to the college faculty, the Curriculum and Academic Policy Committee proposed revisions of the core curriculum required for graduation, the faculty teaching load, and the student course load. It called for a graduation requirement of thirty-two semester courses (in place of 123 semester hours), a faculty teaching load of three courses a semester (in place of four), and a normal student course load of four courses a semester (in place of five). Undergraduates had long been expected to satisfy a rigorous set of requirements, including a foreign language, mathematics and the natural sciences, history and the social sciences, philosophy and religion, and the arts. These requirements were redefined in the report to make clear what the various components of the core curriculum were intended to accomplish. There were some changes—an increase in the requirements in mathematics and natural science and a decrease in the requirements in English and history, for example—but the result was a deliberate reaffirmation of the importance of a comprehensive general education for all students (Curriculum and Academic Policy Committee, 1990, pp. 1–15). In addition, a renewed commitment to the teaching of writing in all courses in the college was stressed. Finally, the report noted that the Working Group on the Curriculum, faculty members who had been meeting for two years examining the curriculum under the supervision of the Curriculum and Academic Policy Committee, looked favorably on the possibility of an interdisciplinary program in the humanities for freshman and sophomore students. In May 1990, the college faculty approved the new curriculum. A Humanities Planning Group was soon appointed to draw up a detailed proposal for an interdisciplinary program to enable students who elected it to study literature, history, philosophy, religion, and the arts in an integrated way and to satisfy thereby several requirements in the core curriculum.

Where did the idea for a sequence of interdisciplinary courses in the humanities come from? In a general way the discussion in educational circles and in the serious press in the 1980s about the need for coherence, rigor, and a new emphasis on the humanities in the undergraduate curriculum played a significant part. William Bennett's *To Reclaim a Legacy: A Report on the Humanities in Higher Education* (1984) found that "most of our college graduates remained shortchanged in the humanities—history, literature, philosophy, and the ideals and practices of the past that have shaped the society they enter" (p. 1). It called on the academic community of each institution to ask: "Does your curriculum reflect the best judgment of the president, deans, and faculty about what an educated person ought to know, or is it a mere smorgasbord?" (p. 31). The Association of American Colleges, the professional organization perennially concerned with liberal education, issued its report, *Integrity in the College Curriculum* (1985), in which it found that the undergraduate degree had been devalued by a process of relaxing requirements and standards that had begun two decades before. The booklet asserted that nothing less than "the quality of American life is at stake, the wisdom and humanity of our leaders, our ability as citizens to make informed choices, and the dedication with which we exhibit humane and democratic values as we go about our daily lives" (p. 7). It called for a required curriculum that gave specific attention to the processes of inquiry, literacy, numerical reasoning, historical consciousness, science, humane values, art, international and multicultural experiences, and the study of one subject in depth (pp. 15–26).

The late 1970s and early 1980s was also the era in which Harvard College's core curriculum was introduced. Harvard's was the most widely publicized attempt to define what it meant to be an educated man or woman in the late twentieth century and to devise a set of courses to ensure that each graduate had been introduced to the major ways of thinking and learning in the arts and sciences (Keller, 1982, pp. 75–132; Patterson, 1983, pp. 192–217). Harvard's stress on modes of thought rather than on content had limitations as a way of restoring coherence to the curriculum, since very specialized courses were allowed to qualify for the core (Keller, 1982, pp. 167–188). But it helped to propel colleges and universities across the country, including the University of the South, to reexamine their undergraduate academic programs.

There were also personal and institutional factors that gave support to the idea of an interdisciplinary humanities program at the University of the South, which enjoys close relations with several of the colleges that have such a program. Faculty members and administrators at Sewanee were well aware of the programs at Rhodes College and Davidson College. I was a member until 1980 of the faculty team responsible for teaching the second year of the two-year program at Davidson. After I came to Sewanee as dean of the college of arts and sciences and professor of history in 1980, I encouraged faculty members to consider instituting a program aimed at integrating the humanities disciplines for freshmen and sophomores at the University of the South. I had found teaching at Davidson with colleagues in such a program highly stimulating and had seen how much the program benefited the students who took it. At Sewanee I strongly encouraged the efforts of the Curriculum and Academic Policy Committee and the working group when they undertook a thorough revision of the undergraduate curriculum. It was in the course of this revision that an interdisciplinary humanities program found a significant number of supporters. I was a member of the Interdisciplinary Humanities Planning Group and, after I returned to full-time teaching in 1991, became a member of the faculty team responsible for teaching the third-semester course.

The Interdisciplinary Humanities Planning Group, under the leadership of James F. Peterman, a member of the philosophy department, included members of six departments: classical languages, English, history, music, and religion, as well as philosophy. Formed in 1990, following the faculty's adoption of the report on the curriculum, this group examined the syllabi of interdisciplinary humanities programs at Rhodes College, Columbia University, Davidson College, Earlham College, Millsaps College, Occidental College, and the University of North Carolina at Asheville. It then set about drawing up plans for a program that would best serve Sewanee's faculty and students and would be consistent with the university's history and mission. The university, an Episcopal institution, aims to provide an education "in personal initiative, in social consciousness, in aesthetic perception, in intellectual curiosity and integrity, and in methods of scientific inquiry," as its statement of purpose reads (*The University of the*

South . . . Catalog, 1997–98, p. 5). By December 1990, some basic issues had been resolved: to make the program an option for students and to aim at enrolling approximately eighty students, who would receive academic credit for four courses, one each in English, history, religion or philosophy, and the arts, all areas of the core curriculum in which students are required to take courses. Each of the four semester-long courses was to treat a distinct phase of Western culture: the ancient, medieval, early modern, and modern worlds. Each semester would have a staff of four faculty members, drawn from the disciplines of literature, history, philosophy or religion, and the arts. Lectures each semester would be given to the whole group, but each faculty member would have his or her own discussion group for the semester. Discussion groups would have no more than twenty students each. The teaching of writing would receive major emphasis. The humanities departments would be surveyed to see whether there was interest among their faculty members in teaching in the program. The response was impressive: twenty-four faculty members, considerably more than the number needed, expressed an interest in teaching in such an interdisciplinary program.

In its final report of February 22, 1991, the Interdisciplinary Humanities Planning Group presented its conclusions to the college faculty and asked that body to "endorse the general framework" for the program, in order that the dean could appoint the first faculty members to teach in it (Interdisciplinary Humanities Program Planning Group, 1991, p. 6). The college faculty endorsed the program unanimously, and the dean appointed Pamela Royston Macfie of the English department as director and William S. Bonds of the classical languages department as associate director, along with ten other faculty members as members of the staff.

This faculty group met for three weeks during the early summer of 1991 to draw up specific proposals for the four courses in the sequence, to be presented for the approval of the college faculty. That approval was given in spring 1992, and Humanities 101 and 102 were offered for the first time in the academic year 1992–93. Humanities 201 and 202 were offered for the first time in the academic year 1993–94. The provision of paid faculty time in the summer of 1992 was judged to be essential in order to allow faculty members to read and discuss works outside their areas of expertise, as well as to draw up course descriptions and reading lists. The initial three-week workshop in 1992 was followed by another of the same length in 1993. Since then, a week-long summer workshop has been held each year to enable the faculty members on the staff to review the courses and revise them. In May 1996, Elizabeth Mills of the English department and the humanities program at Davidson College served as a consultant to the program and was a member of the workshop. Faculty members joining the staff are included in the workshop and participate in decisions made about the content and organization of the program.

The initial teaching staff consisted of a four-person team for each course. Although there have been several staffing changes, there has been a large measure of continuity. Nine of the original staff of twelve have continued to teach in the program.

The progress of the program has been anything but smooth. The first student course evaluations, collected each semester, were discouraging and in some cases disturbing. Some students found the lectures beyond their grasp and unrelated to the readings; some found each faculty member to be intent on pursuing his or her own interests without reference to those of other faculty members on the team; some found the reading assignments too long and complex; some were frustrated that their writing had not improved in a conspicuous way; some complained about team-written examinations as arbitrary and unpredictable. Many students seemed to feel that they were guinea pigs in an ill-designed experiment.

Unhappiness with the program also developed in several of the departments that supplied faculty members to teach in it. There was a feeling that faculty members were being siphoned off from teaching important departmental courses. There was also dissatisfaction on the part of faculty members teaching the courses, who felt that the administration was lukewarm in its endorsement of the program. This was paradoxical, since President and Vice Chancellor Samuel R. Williamson had provided funds from the Mellon-Carlton Discretionary Fund to make it possible for faculty to devote time in two successive summers to prepare to teach in the program. But when faculty criticism mounted, public endorsement of the program by the administration was barely audible.

Faculty members teaching humanities were also upset about the facilities and equipment allotted to the program. They particularly deplored the state of the audiovisual equipment and the level of technical help provided for the lectures. Classroom space proved to be short for the hours during which the sequence was taught, with the result that discussion sections sometimes had to be scheduled at other times and in classrooms not suitable for discussions. In the summer of 1994, at the humanities workshop, the faculty members then teaching in the program were asked if they were willing to teach in it for another three years. Five said yes, four said yes with various qualifications, and one said probably no. In two key departments, English and history, there was significant opposition to the program; other departments expressed reservations about supporting it unless their staffing needs were met. In the end, members of the English and history departments continued to teach in the program, largely because they were personally committed to it, and the most pressing staffing problems in other departments were successfully resolved by the administration through several part-time faculty appointments.

Initially approved by the college faculty for a three-year period, Tradition and Criticism was rigorously evaluated in 1994–95 by its own staff in consultation with the departments that provided faculty members for the program and had the largest stake in it. Suggestions and opinions were also invited from faculty members in other departments. Among the suggestions were that the departments participating in the program conduct future searches for faculty positions with the needs of the program in mind, that each of these departments rotate faculty members in and out of the program in such a way that there would be a reserve supply of faculty members trained to teach in it, and that efforts be made by the deans, the directors of the program, members of the faculty who taught in it, and faculty advisers to inform students more adequately about the program and its distinctive approach. At the end of this process, after letters and reports were circulated to members of the college faculty, Macfie recommended that the program be approved for another three-year period. The college faculty voted its approval.

By this time, significant changes in the program were already taking place, and this process continues. To some extent, each faculty team has developed its course in the way that seems to work best. This was not by design but was the result of each team's experience in teaching. At the summer humanities workshop, each team formulates its plans for the coming year, and all four teams discuss common problems together and the changes envisioned for their parts of the program. The sessions of all four semester courses originally consisted of a much larger number of lectures than small group discussions, but this has changed. The sessions of Humanities 101 are still about two-thirds lectures and one-third discussions. The rationale is that most students need to be provided a good deal of context for their study of the ancient world and that, in any case, some of the lectures are themselves Socratic in nature, involving questions and dialogue with students and faculty members. The sessions of Humanities 102 and 201, however, are about evenly divided between lectures and discussions. The idea here is that discussions enable faculty members and students to get to know each other better and that the individual faculty members should be expected to provide some of the context for the literary and artistic works discussed. The sessions of Humanities 202 are about one-third lectures and two-thirds discussions (or seminars, as they are called in this course). Faculty members in this team find that students are ready for a more extensive and searching examination of ideas in small groups.

Under its new director, William E. Clarkson, a member of the English department, the humanities program has dealt reasonably well with a range of problems. Two large classrooms are equipped for humanities lectures, and more small rooms have been designated for discussions. Some improvements have been made in audiovisual equipment and maintenance. More adequate stipends are provided to faculty members for the annual summer workshops. Assignments and lectures have been regularly revised; a good many deletions as well as additions have been made. The initial commitment to reading works as much as possible in their entirety was compromised almost at once in the case of longer works, such as the *Aeneid*, *The Divine Comedy*, and *Paradise Lost*. Recent additions have included selections from Hobbes's *Leviathan*, Hume's *Enquiry Concerning Human Understanding*, and the *Federalist Papers*. But the most important change has been in the attitude of the students in the program, perhaps as a result of information given them in mailings from the deans before they arrive on campus. Judging by their written evaluations, students seem to like the program's interdisciplinary thrust, its focus on primary sources, its combination of lectures and discussions, its stress on developing writing skills, and even the fact that the faculty members in the program do not always agree with each other about the subjects under consideration. The students attracted to the program seem to be those most likely to be able to meet the program's expectations and to benefit from what it offers. In November 1997, after another third-year review, Clarkson (1997) reported to Dean Robert L. Keele and the Curriculum and Academic Policy Committee that "our own morale as faculty members is high, and . . . the program, while it can be improved, is making a very positive contribution to the academic life of the college" (p. 1). He proposed that the college faculty be asked to approve the program on a regular basis—in other words, for an indefinite period, as programs and courses usually are. The college faculty subsequently approved it on this basis by an overwhelming vote.

The issue of the program's Western orientation and the appropriateness or inappropriateness of that orientation was faced squarely at the time a detailed description and reading list was submitted to the college faculty in early 1992. The program's Western orientation was partly a reflection of the overall curriculum in the humanities at the University of the South. But the program was never conceived as narrowly Western. The authors of the detailed description of the program—the original faculty staff—pointed out that one of its themes would be the definition of Western civilization "as it comes into contact with civilizations that do not share its language, social structure, religion or values," and that throughout the four-course sequence, faculty and students would look critically at Western culture and the West's self-perception (Humanities Staff, 1992, p. 7). This approach has been generally followed. In the case of Humanities 101, the lecture on archaic epic poetry discusses Near Eastern antecedents to Greek literature, as well as the introduction of the alphabet and the appropriation of gods from other cultures. Tacitus's view of the Germans on the border of the Roman Empire is given critical attention in lecture and discussion, and students and faculty members use the occasion to discuss the cultural theme of self and other. The presentations on the ancient Hebrews stress their view of and indebtedness to other cultures in the Near East.

Humanities 102 includes an examination of the culture of Islam and the medieval church's response to it. In Humanities 201, the great European voyages of discovery are discussed, along with the encounter between Europeans and the indigenous peoples of the lands they reached. In Humanities 202, recent radical critiques of Western culture are discussed, including the view that the humanities have traditionally been taught in ways that are ethnocentric and self-enclosed. The same semester deals with social scientific critiques of the humanities, issues of race and gender, and the challenges represented by deconstruction. In other words, the question of what Western culture was at key junctures and of how distinctive or valuable it was in specific contexts is an important part of the program. Most faculty members teaching in the program would probably agree that students taking Tradition and Criticism in Western Culture would benefit from courses in non-Western cultures. They would also agree that Western culture has an unparalleled richness and that it is eminently worth studying, both for the questions its thinkers and artists raise and for the answers they provide.

Emphasis on the teaching of clear, correct, and effective writing has been a constant feature of the interdisciplinary humanities program at Sewanee, but the approach to that endeavor has evolved considerably. At the beginning, the staff believed that it was necessary to teach students to write papers in accordance with the standards and conventions of four distinct disciplinary areas: literature, history, philosophy and religion, and the arts. Workshops were held in the first semester to help students to master the necessary techniques. In each semester, students would be asked to write four short essays, typically three or four double-spaced typewritten pages, one appropriate to each of the four areas. Within a few years, however, it became apparent that attempting to write four different kinds of essays complicated the tasks of teaching and learning, and that, in any case, a good essay should be one that would pass muster in any of the four areas. There was then a move to favor a broad view and stress interrelationships among texts and ideas: each essay should be deliberately interdisciplinary, written on a topic described in the syllabus. Since an emphasis on writing across the curriculum was a feature of the new curriculum adopted in 1991, the papers, it was felt, should be clear and accessible to the general reader, whatever her or his disciplinary orientation.

In recent years, each humanities team has developed an approach to writing that seems likely to produce the best results in that particular course. In Humanities 101 there are two papers, each intended to be interdisciplinary and each rewritten after a conference with the discussion leader. There are also eight short "response essays" that express the student's personal view of the assigned reading. Humanities 102 requires three essays, one of which is to be rewritten. Response essays are required as each discussion leader specifies. In Humanities 201, three essays are required, the first of which is to be rewritten. The first two essays are on assigned topics, and the third is on a subject of the student's own choosing. There are also eight "salient features" essays, each a one-page treatment of an important feature of or argument in the assigned work of art or text. Finally, in Humanities 202, in a version of the original plan, four essays are required, one in each of the different disciplinary areas. Twelve response essays are also required in that course. In all four courses, the stress is on developing an argument and defending it. Papers are expected to have a provocative opening, show careful and systematic treatment of evidence, and come to a persuasive conclusion. The syllabus for each course includes an essay by Clarkson, entitled "Preparing Essays for Humanities Classes," that not only describes the characteristics of a good essay but also makes helpful suggestions about using a word processor, recommending settings, format, and techniques for making revisions. The syllabi also direct students to the college's Writing Tutors' Center, where they can receive valuable criticism and suggestions from fellow students chosen for their writing ability, many of whom have taken the humanities sequence. Appropriately, the completion of the humanities sequence carries credit for two writing-intensive courses.

The importance of Jewish and Christian traditions in Western culture has been a theme of the interdisciplinary humanities program from the beginning. This is, in part, a reflection of the fact that the university was founded by bishops of the Episcopal church and is responsible to twenty-eight "owning dioceses," located in the South and Southwest. Religion, in the view of most Episcopalians, is thoroughly bound up with human culture and closely related to subjects ostensibly of secular character. The Episcopal church's emphasis on sacramental worship reinforces in many of its members a feeling that a divine mystery lies at the heart of all life and the universe itself. But the inclusion of religion in Tradition and Criticism in Western Culture is basically in recognition that the scriptures of ancient Israel, the books of the New Testament, and the history of Jewish and Christian ideas and institutions have had an incalculable effect on the shaping of Western culture.

Members of the humanities staff would probably agree with Robert E. Proctor about the universal character and value of the Greek and Roman classics, but not with his view that the texts of the Jewish and Christian religious tradition should be excluded from the humanities (Proctor, 1988, pp. 156–169, 189). Sewanee's interdisciplinary humanities course therefore includes selected books of the Bible, Augustine's *Confessions,* Bede's *Ecclesiastical History of the English People, The Rule of St. Benedict,* Dante's *Divine Comedy,* Luther's *Treatise on Christian Liberty,* Ignatius of Loyola's *Autobiography,* Monteverdi's *Vespers of the Blessed Virgin,* John Milton's *Paradise Lost,* and C. S. Lewis's *The Case for Christianity.* It also includes discussions and lectures dealing with ancient Israel, Christ and the early church, the place of the papacy in Western Christendom, the Protestant and Catholic Reformations, the idea of God in the thought of seventeenth-century philosophers, rational religion and the evangelical revival in the eighteenth century, and the place of religion in the modern world. In treating all of these subjects, Tradition and Criticism seeks to be historical and critical rather than dogmatic and to be as free from bias as its faculty teams can make it. Religious thinkers and artists, the program suggests, are as likely to raise important issues for reflection about human life and destiny as other significant contributors to Western culture.

Into the Future

The future prospects for Tradition and Criticism look favorable. The morale of faculty participating in the program is high, the program is attracting able students in increasing numbers, and administrative support has become more vocal, focused, and purposeful. There are nevertheless some potential problems. One is that faculty recruitment for the program is likely to become more difficult. Faculty members at all selective institutions, including the University of the South, are under pressure to pursue research and to publish in their disciplines. Teaching humanities can seem distracting to faculty members, particularly younger ones struggling to establish themselves in their disciplinary fields. The answer seems to be for the university to seek out those scholars for new or replacement positions in the humanities whose interests naturally lead them across disciplinary borders. Historical study, literary theory, political theory, and art history, to take a few examples, are becoming increasingly interdisciplinary. Careful, intentional recruiting of faculty members by the administration and the humanities departments to find those who have a natural interest in a program like Tradition and Criticism is needed to lay a secure foundation for the future.

Another potential problem is the tendency for many students, including some of the most serious and talented, to seek an education in subjects seen as most likely to return financial rewards. At many liberal arts colleges, business administration, accounting, and computer science have a compelling attraction for such students. At Sewanee, where the curriculum has remained focused on the traditional liberal arts, most students seem to place a higher premium on becoming well-rounded individuals than on achieving immediate practical benefits as a result of their undergraduate education. This could change, however, if the general population comes to view the liberal arts—and the humanities in particular—as an antiquated body of knowledge largely unrelated to a student's career concerns. In the final analysis, faculty members in the humanities undertake to teach their students to think clearly, write and speak effectively, and reflect on values important to a democratic society, and this effort should give the humanities at institutions like the University of the South a strong appeal if the case is adequately put forward.

A potential problem that could be more serious is the growth of a way of thinking that is skeptical to the point of being nihilist about ideas, values, and institutions. There is a kind of fin-de-siècle mood among some students and faculty in the academy generally and among thinkers elsewhere. The past is frequently seen as having little or no relevance to the present, and texts can have whatever meaning a reader or set of readers says they have. One such approach is to say that there is an infinite range of meanings for any object, no one of which is inherently more probable than another. The world is seen as fragmented, without coherence or stable structure, in physical or social terms (Taylor, 1997). Such a point of view, whether at Sewanee or at other educational institutions, ultimately undermines the serious study of Western ideas and values. Tradition and Criticism, however, can be and should be as critical of the various expressions of contemporary academic culture as it is of every other expression of Western culture. In fact, it may provide the most appropriate kind of forum in which the human condition can be considered by college students and their mentors, and in which past and present, the sacred and the secular, and urgent theoretical and practical concerns can be brought together.

References

Association of American Colleges. *Integrity in the College Curriculum: A Report to the Academic Community.* Washington, D.C.: Association of American Colleges, 1985.

Bennett, W. J. *To Reclaim a Legacy: A Report on the Humanities in Higher Education.* Washington, D.C.: National Endowment for the Humanities, 1984.

Chitty, A. B., Jr. *Reconstruction at Sewanee: The Founding of the University of the South and Its First Administration, 1857–1872.* Sewanee: Proctor's Hall Press, 1993. (Originally published 1954.)

Clarkson, W. E. Letter to Dean Robert L. Keele and Members of the Curriculum and Academic Policy Committee. University of the South, Nov. 4, 1997.

Curriculum and Academic Policy Committee. *Report to the College Faculty.* Sewanee, Tenn.: University of the South, Apr. 23, 1990.

Fish, S. *Doing What Comes Naturally: Change, Rhetoric, and the Practice of Theory in Literary and Legal Studies.* Durham, N.C.: Duke University Press, 1989.

Humanities Staff. "Interdisciplinary Humanities Program: Detailed Description and Reading List." University of the South, February 7, 1992.

Humanities Staff. "Course Narratives for Tradition and Criticism in Western Culture: Humanities 101, 102, 201, 202." University of the South, 1997.

Humanities Staff. "Revised Course Narrative for Humanities 201." University of the South, 1998.

Interdisciplinary Humanities Program Planning Group. *Final Report.* Sewanee, Tenn.: University of the South, Feb. 22, 1991.

Keller, P. *Getting at the Core: Curriculum Reform at Harvard.* Cambridge, Mass.: Harvard University Press, 1982.

Nussbaum, M. C. *Cultivating Humanity: A Classical Defense of Reform in Liberal Education.* Cambridge, Mass.: Harvard University Press, 1997.

Patterson, W. B. "Defining the Educated Person: From Harvard to Harvard." *Soundings: An Interdisciplinary Journal,* 1983, *66*(2), 192–217.

Proctor, R. E. *Education's Great Amnesia: Reconsidering the Humanities from Petrarch to Freud, with a Curriculum for Today's Students.* Bloomington: Indiana University Press, 1988.

Searle, J. "Is There a Crisis in American Higher Education?" *Partisan Review,* 1993, *60*(4), 693–709.

Taylor, M. C. *Hiding.* Chicago: University of Chicago Press, 1997.

The University of the South, College of Arts and Sciences, Catalog, 1997–98. Sewanee, Tenn.: University of the South, 1998.

Chapter Thirteen

Western Intellectual Traditions at Hendrix College

John Churchill

The Western Intellectual Traditions courses at Hendrix College in Conway, Arkansas, include lectures sprinkled among the seminars. Each of the faculty members teaching in the course delivers one or two lectures a term; mine is on Alexander the Great. By the time my lecture rolls around, we have traveled with Odysseus and felt Sappho's loves. We have met Aristophanes' unheroic Dikaiopolis and the Socrates of Plato's *Apology*. We have pondered the just soul of *The Republic* and the person of Aristotelian practical wisdom. My lecture closes our consideration of things Greek by attending to the man who, though a pupil of Aristotle, put an end to the world in which Aristotelian notions of human flourishing seemed at home. That is the historical point of the lecture: how Alexander's career ended the world of the polis.

But there are also two philosophical points. One is culturally important and contemporaneously relevant: the problem of difference. Alexander was an early multiculturalist. He faced—at least for a brief moment—problems of ethnic, cultural, religious, and linguistic difference. The other point is personally penetrating: Alexander was a nearly perfect instantiation of the ancient Greek heroic ideal. For better or worse, he lived out a barbaric warrior ethic with ruthless consistency and vigor, setting the paradigm for innumerable successors, as he himself had drawn it—directly and explicitly—from Homer's Achilles. For himself as for hundreds of thousands who fell across his path, Alexander's career was disastrous. And yet my fascination endures.

A course at Hendrix dedicated to the examination of human excellence stands in the shadow of the college's motto—*eis andra teleion* (toward human fulfillment)—with its implication that we are interested in deliberating on images of human fulfillment. Here is one such image: Alexander, the man who will conquer the world, who will outperform everyone at everything that pertains to self-assertion and the exercise of dominance over others, who expects to earn admiration and submission by the continual demonstration of his superiority in wit, skill, and strength. I sometimes think that this ethic, revived by Nietzsche and evident in action movies and other elements of American popular culture, is one of only two basic ethical positions. The other is the ethic of civic virtue, compromise, cooperation, self-restraint, and deliberation. Our look at the Greeks in the Western Intellectual Traditions course builds to the Platonic and Aristotelian versions of this calmer ethic. But because we begin with Odysseus, it seems right to close with something Odysseus would more likely have endorsed, one of the most enduring models of human fulfillment: Alexander's version of the heroic ideal.

One of my aims in the lecture is to elicit from students an admission of their own fascination with this ideal. Alexander is a beautiful man. He is quick and dashing. He wins. He even smells good. Yes, he is violent, but violence is exciting. Yes, he wastes countless human lives, but his scope is grand. Yes, he dies young, but he thereby cheats the reckoner who would have brought age and regret. He dies like a god at thirty-three, not yet a bloated, mumbling Elvis. Something there is in many of us that finds this deeply troubling pattern alluring, even though we know that it is the analogue, in political culture, of Thrasymachus's theory of ethics: as justice is the will of the strongest, so political legitimacy belongs to the most successful warrior. To elicit the allure of Alexander in a lecture—Is that to purge us of it, to expose it for examination and critique, or to reinforce and perpetuate our tendency to indulge it, to make us more inclined to fall for it again?

I do not know whether my lecture serves the warrior ethic or the civic one. But I know that Alexander is fascinating, and that this fascination is deeply troubling and needs examination.

So, too, the other lectures in the course—on women in medieval society, on the wars of religion, on seventeenth-century notions of reason and knowledge—offer for contemplation and critique selected paradigms of human flourishing, or they offer depictions, when we come, for instance, to the Atlantic slave trade, of the possibilities of profound inhumanity. Why examine these things? Why even read, for the Western Intellectual Traditions seminars, the Greek literature mentioned above, and the writings of medieval Europeans who were animated by concerns about the temporal and spiritual ends of humanity, about the bases for the legitimacy of civil government and its relation to the church, about the place of nonhuman animals in a divinely ordained order of things? Why trouble oneself and one's students with the thought of the seventeenth century: with Hobbes and Locke, Descartes and Molière? Why bother with the nineteenth century: with Nietzsche and Darwin?

To answer these questions we can hardly improve on the Socratic dictum: Know yourself. The unexamined life is not worth living. At least, the life without the self-knowledge that comes of critical examination is hardly human. It is instructive to consider that the Hendrix motto sets a course toward human fulfillment but leaves open what that fulfillment might be. The motto implies a search for the best conceptions of human flourishing and a search for their accomplishment. The Western Intellectual Traditions course is a step in that search.

History of the Humanities at Hendrix

The general mission of Hendrix College from the beginning has been to cultivate students as intellects and as whole persons through the liberal arts. The 1890 catalogue, placing itself in square opposition to the "intensely practical, utilitarian" values of the "money-god" of the Gilded Age, declared, "We do not pander to that depraved, money-born cry, 'Nothing but the practical!'" Decrying education that leaves the student "stuffed and gorged" with tables and facts, Hendrix in 1890 proposed a more truly practical education, one that by "giving development to mind and heart, building strong by building deep and broad," promised to produce "the student who has learned to think, not merely to memorize, who has secured permanent culture and wisdom," and who has become "cultured in mind and heart" (Hendrix College, 1980, pp. 10–11).

This declaration was almost certainly written by Alexander C. Millar, president of the college. Though expressed in different language at different stages during the next century, this mission has remained constant and is reflected in the college's current statement of purpose. The statement includes the affirmation that "Hendrix is dedicated to the cultivation of whole persons" and asserts that one of the ways in which this aim is pursued is to lead students "to examine critically and understand the intellectual traditions woven into the history of Western thought."

The statement of purpose envisages a set of activities—to investigate and appreciate, to examine, to develop, to explore and connect, to participate—directed toward subject matter that is in large part the traditional domain of the humanities. It also envisages a set of outcomes that are abilities, capacities, powers, and dispositions—the stuff of which humanity is made. The term Martha Nussbaum chose from Seneca, in the title of her book on liberal education, *Cultivating Humanity*, is the presiding verb in this statement: we aim to cultivate. The conviction reflected here is in the Socratic tradition. A deeply reflective education, oriented toward self-discovery and the cultivation of skills of deliberative thought, is not only more humane but also more profoundly practical than technical training.

This commitment has been honored at different times in different ways. In 1934 the college, after three years of study financed by the General Education Board of New York, undertook a "New Program," described as having been "designed to return the College to its tradition of general education" (Lester, 1984, pp. 156–157). Thomas S. Staples, dean of the college, took the lead in the study and in the program. The fundamental idea was to divide the curriculum into two parts: a general college of two years and a senior college of two years. The latter was to be disciplinarily based. The former was to provide general education through a scheme that involved four elements: humanities, natural sciences, social sciences, and "philosophic studies." The humanities element focused on the ancient world, the Middle Ages, the Victorian world, and the "modern world." The philosophic element included Bible, philosophy, education, and religion. This curriculum endured for the better part of two decades and was bolstered by the work of Hendrix faculty study groups at the University of Chicago in 1939, 1940, and 1941 (Lester, 1984, p. 158).

Robert Campbell was perhaps the principal advocate of the humanities at Hendrix in the mid-twentieth century. Campbell had earned his Ph.D. in English literature at the University of Chicago and was appointed to the faculty in 1920. He served for thirty-eight years and from 1942 to 1958 was a vice president of the college. In 1953 Campbell delivered a series of lectures on the humanities in general education. His central thought was that "the most important idea we can have in common in a free democracy is that we must be free to explore different ideas, test them out, and accept or reject them on the basis of our own judgment" (Campbell, 1953). The elements of this commitment are instantly recognizable: (1) there are profound differences among ideas, and it is important to be acquainted with these differences; (2) we need freedom to follow the imperative of exploration among those ideas; (3) processes of testing these ideas are available; (4) the judgment of the individual in assessing those ideas is essential; and (5) the critical evaluation of differences among ideas is deployed in the service of democratic society. Here we see Hendrix in the service of what Denby (1996) calls the "old ideals": nonspecialization, selfhood, and citizenship (1996, p. 14).

Campbell wrote at the height of the cold war, when the defeat of one totalitarian foe was a fresh memory, war with another loomed, and the domestic scene was heavily shaped by the paranoid, totalitarian style of McCarthyism. He portrayed education in the humanities as the most important bulwark against totalitarianism and indoctrination. His argument was Mill's *On Liberty* packaged for the 1950s in America. Denby (1996) notes the centrality of Mill in the canon's rationale: "What the books taught was not a stable body of knowledge or even consistent 'values' but critical habits of mind" (p. 355). Whatever the contemporary cultural climate—whether we seem stretched between the menaces of the "threat of international communism" and those of McCarthyism, or between the didactic virtues of the contemporary right and the poststructuralist nihilism of the left—the way to recover humane balance seems to be the same: the cultivation of rich capacities of deliberative reflection and the cultivation of humanity through the study of the humanities. In the middle of the twentieth century, this was the faith at Hendrix.

Hendrix, however, had no settled format for imparting this education of self-discovery in the humanities. By the early 1960s the college offered general education in a distributional pattern, with courses required in English, foreign languages, religion, and the three areas of humanities, social sciences, and natural sciences. In the humanities two of the options were courses designed to provide a historical grasp of Western thought. One was called "Man's Search for Values," and the other "Conceptions of Man and the World in Western Thought." Students were required to take one or the other. A social sciences course, "Individual and Society," attempted a similar task from the perspective of social, political, and economic thought.

Several influential faculty members, including two successive deans of the college, had earned Ph.D.s at Columbia. Staples, a southern historian who had written a dissertation on Reconstruction in Arkansas, served as dean from 1928 to 1949. He was succeeded by William C. Buthman, who was dean from 1949 to 1965. The third in this lineage, George Thompson, also a historian of the South who had written another Columbia dissertation on Reconstruction in Arkansas, never reached the deanship, but his was the dominant conservative voice on campus for most of four decades, ending in the early 1990s. Thompson led a Hendrix faculty general education seminar at Columbia in the summer of 1974 and was the college's principal advocate of liberal arts conceived as the perpetuation of tradition.

In the 1950s Hendrix mirrored the somnolent mood of the nation and by 1959 was sorely in need of new vigor. The infusion arrived in the shape of a new president. Marshal T. Steel was an alumnus, originally from south Arkansas, who had built an illustrious career in the Methodist clergy, culminating in the prestigious post of senior minister at Highland Park Methodist Church in Dallas. Steel's presidency reinvigorated the college with new buildings, infusions of money, increasing numbers of students, and mass plantings of half-grown oak trees. In 1965 he brought in Francis Christie as academic dean. Christie too was an alumnus, a Methodist minister who had held deanships at Mt. Union College and Simpson College, a graduate of Perkins School of Theology at Southern Methodist University, and the holder of a Ph.D. from Vanderbilt, where he wrote a dissertation on the Hebrew Bible. Christie, before returning to Arkansas, had been active in integration efforts in Nashville and Birmingham.

Christie's appointment shaped Hendrix for the next two decades. His challenge was to teach a vastly expanded student body with an only moderately expanded faculty. His strategy was threefold: (1) he introduced a labor-intensive calendar that extracted maximum teaching from the faculty; (2) he promoted a dramatically relaxed pattern of curricular requirements that prevented the high student-to-faculty ratio from creating curricular pressure points; and (3) he advocated and embodied in his own teaching and administration a deeply romantic philosophy of education that emphasized student freedom. This philosophy explicitly portrayed curricular requirements as stultifying and, not incidentally, provided conceptual support for the other two parts of his strategy. Faculty hiring during the Christie years reflected his strategy, and Christie's powerful legacy, detectable in the new century more than thirty years after the beginning of his deanship, was a faculty deeply imbued with the value of student freedom amid wide curricular options.

Christie's chief antagonist in all these matters was the last Hendrix faculty member who represented the old Columbia connection, George Thompson, former dean Buthman's self-identified heir apparent. A historian with deeply conservative educational principles, Thompson was a defender of the Old South, and the theme of restoration dominated his educational thought. He conceived the role of the humanities as the perpetuation of truths already fully disclosed in classic texts and conceived the core of education as the induction of an educated elite into leadership that would extirpate the corruptions of modernism. To Christie, by contrast, the very word *elite* was anathema, and modernism was deliverance from prejudices.

The conflict between Christie and Thompson reflected their variants of southern heritage. Christie's origins were in a piney woods blacksmith shop on the Arkansas-Louisiana border. His instincts were populist, liberal, and inclusive. His philosophy of education was a blend of Dewey and Rousseau: from Rousseau the idea that the paramount value in every student's intellectual development was freedom and from Dewey the notion that education was an activity undertaken by the learner, not an inculcative process conducted by the teacher. Thompson, on the other hand, came from the culture of the plantation. He viewed education as the cultivation and transmission of heritage and the preservation—or restoration—of a social order based more on Plato's *Republic* than on the democratic thinkers of the Enlightenment.

Christie's suspicion of tradition, scorn for requirements, and love for the freedom of the 1960s won out over the notion of preserving and transmitting heritage. In 1968 the faculty, with Christie's leadership, buried the old required courses in Western thought among a plethora of options, in the name of values such as freedom, individual design, choice, and variety. The tightly structured humanities requirement devolved into a broad selection. After these changes, education in the humanities at Hendrix centered on distribution requirements that reflected the departmentally based disciplines, and the departmental major survived as the centerpiece of the student's experience. Shards of the old curriculum survived here and there as disconnected honors offerings or bits of departmental offerings. The message of the curriculum in defining liberal education was this: students need a smattering of things in different departments, a major, and then whatever they like. A profoundly romantic structure, this system allowed the best students to follow their interests into unfettered intellectual adventure, building a unique educational identity. The best students were very well served. But this structure also allowed other students to pick their way, willy-nilly, through a sequence of courses whose only structural principle might well be a track of the major.

By 1980 Francis Christie was no longer dean, and those who had lost the curricular battles of the 1960s had regrouped and were contesting the field again. But an attempt to reinstate the old curriculum failed, because a faculty largely hired by Christie was still in the ascendant. Nevertheless, the faculty felt sufficient sympathy for the idea of placing some acquaintance with the West at the core of the curriculum to set up a requirement, in 1983, that students must take some two-term sequence in some more or less comprehensive, historically based topic: for example, the history of philosophy, the history of Christianity, an art history sequence, or the Western Heritage course. This last course sequence was the vestige of the old social science requirement, sleeping like Arthur under the hill, as the introduction to the history major. This arrangement, from the point of view of those who wished for more curricular coherence and a requirement relating to the West, had the virtue of providing every student with at least an acquaintance with historically based material. From the point of view of those who still placed primary value on student freedom, the requirement's restrictiveness was not completely vicious: students could choose how they satisfied it.

One of the options in this structure was a piece of the old humanities core, "Conceptions of Man and the World in Western Thought," which had passed from former president Matt Locke Ellis to Christie and then ultimately to me. Rebaptized as "Western Views of Humanity," this two-term course was offered to a selected, invited clientele—one freshman in twelve—who were led on a tour from Homer to Freud. The *Iliad* and the *Odyssey* began the course, followed by the *Oresteia,* Aristophanes, Plato, Aristotle, Epictetus, and Augustine. It was in the teaching of this course that I developed my own relationship with the great North African bishop and came to regard his passions, his sensibilities, and his humanity as touchstones for my own conception of humanity. It was also in the process of teaching this course that I began to reflect on what it means to read and reread the same texts annually over a period of years, sharing them with a body of students who are always the same age—the freshmen are frozen at age eighteen—while the teacher leaves youth and passes into middle age and beyond. I came to think of this cumulative experience as an important part of my own self-discovery. The faculty member's uptake on a text changes as he or she moves from the end of youth through middle age and onward, and the sense of the taught texts changes accordingly. (See Churchill, 1991.) So our experience with a text, taught over and over again, becomes a rich palimpsest, a changing map, in fact, of our own intellectual and personal development. A part of teaching in the humanities has to be self-consciousness about the changing nature of one's own continuing encounter with the texts. Too little attention, I believe, is directed toward this important feature of faculty life.

Western Intellectual Traditions Emerges at Hendrix

By 1987, a few years after I became the college's chief academic officer, new energy flowed in: a challenge grant from the National Endowment for the Humanities (NEH). The purpose of the grant was to provide faculty and curricular development monies in support of the curricular commons established in 1983. With funding for summer workshops, a cadre of faculty began to move toward a new, integrative approach to the question of common experience in a Western humanities course. This cadre was drawn largely from the faculty members who taught courses in the commons adopted in 1983. It included all the historians and philosophers, as well as representatives from English, music, theater, and other departments. The old guard—the last of the Columbia Ph.D.s—was no longer a factor; the reactionary aura of restoration had vanished, and it became possible to consider a common experience for all first-year students without the baggage of the old right. The old left, however, was still strong, and debates turned on such questions as whether it was acceptable to require any course of all students. Some members of the faculty who were not involved in the project thought such a notion was morally suspect on the face of it.

The NEH funding—with substantial support from the Pyeatt family of Searcy, Arkansas, and Memphis—provided for summer seminars in which the core cadre of a dozen faculty designed and then prepared to teach a multidisciplinary, historically based two-course sequence, which became known as Western Intellectual Traditions (WIT). From the beginning of this project, the intent was to design a required course for all first-year students. Faculty curricular design, like politics, is the art of the possible. The pedagogical aims of the designers were broad and multiple, and by no means grounded in unanimity of theory. The courses are, as much as anything, an illustration of the idea that very good things can be done jointly by people who disagree. Another dimension of the art of the possible is illustrated in the constellation of expertise that happened to be present among the faculty. We were rich in interest in the Greeks, rich in medieval expertise, rich in the Enlightenment, and interested in fin-de-siècle Vienna. It so happened that the champions of the history of Christianity and of the Renaissance, for example, did not participate in the seminars. These absences were reflected in the course design.

There was, then, no fundamental ideology driving the course design. And the specifics of the syllabus turned out to reflect an essentially accidental concatenation of faculty interests and expertise. These events reflect a deep truth about human affairs, one that runs throughout Ludwig Wittgenstein's later work. Theory follows practice. We have no consensus theory of universal reason or of universal human nature in which to ground our hope that the conventions that make social order possible rest on more than the sheer fact that much of the time we agree about how to proceed. This agreement—when it occurs—is not grounded; it is not guaranteed with metaphysical or epistemological assurances. What we have is the fact of agreement—when we do agree. When we do not agree, what we have is the viability of hope that we might, finally, and the possibility that we will be willing to continue talking in search of agreement. The WIT course was built on no greater assurance than that and is, thus, a characteristically postmodern undertaking.

So in the design of the Western Intellectual Traditions course we did not make a common theory the cornerstone of the enterprise. We did not suppose that one could contribute to the design—or teach in the course—only if one believed that the future of civilization depended on the inculcation of the traditional values of the West embodied in certain texts, or only if one believed that everyone should confront the malevolent phallo- and Eurocentric discourse of dead white males in order to overthrow its hegemony intelligently. Some of the designers believed something like the first of these; some had sympathy with the second. Some were motivated primarily by the desirability of having a unifying intellectual experience at the core of the Hendrix curriculum, believing that the fact of its commonality among students was far more important than its content.

Beginning in 1988, five years before the course was first offered, the WIT faculty met for a couple of weeks every summer.

This project had the great good luck of having a driving force who was also a skillful builder of consensus, Garrett McAinsh. McAinsh is an Emory-trained historian of Europe who had been hired by Francis Christie and had shared the Western Heritage course for years with George Thompson. He knew both sides of the old frays intimately, and so was ideally fitted for leadership. Faculties, of course, are not susceptible to leadership in any simple sense, and so the process of building the Western Intellectual Traditions course was slow, careful, and full of talk. The philosophers were insistent on certain touchstone texts. But how much of Aristotle's *Ethics* is essential? Which parts are even accessible to first-year students? Which parts of Plato's *Republic* are indispensable? Must we read all six of Descartes's Meditations? The historians were delighted to focus on four periods of history and thereby to gain the possibility of a little depth. But what about the intervening centuries? Didn't we need bridge lectures to remind students that something happened between the Peloponnesian War and the medieval papacy? What readings will best convey the situation of women in the Middle Ages? The faculty advocates of the arts battled both for a fair share of the syllabus and for an integration of art, architecture, and music with philosophy and history. The course took shape in an interplay of considerations drawn from different disciplines, ideologies, personal perspectives, and educational histories.

Among the faculty involved were those who had their own undergraduate experience of similar courses at Gettysburg, Baylor, Spelman, Reed, and Rhodes, among others. McAinsh kept the process moving, and in 1992 the faculty were presented a proposal to require a two-term sequence of Western Intellectual Traditions courses of all first-year students, displacing the options of history of philosophy, history of Christianity, Western Heritage, and so on. Readings in the courses were to be entirely primary texts. In addition to readings in history and philosophy, students would read plays, listen to music, and view art and architecture. Students were to write several essays each term. There would be lectures, but the characteristic experience of the courses would be discussion in seminars. The faculty who had designed the course and prepared to teach it stepped forward and said, in effect, "I, from philosophy, am willing to lead students in discussions of Greek statuary and seventeenth-century opera," or "I, from the music department, am willing to teach Plato and Descartes."

The specifics of the syllabus embodied the art of the possible. The first term was to deal with the Greeks and with the Middle Ages. The second would deal with the seventeenth century and the close of the nineteenth century. In each segment, not only the old acknowledged giants but also the historically marginalized would be read and discussed. Women were included at every step, but not under the aegis of a theory. In the courses' title the word *traditions* was in the plural. This pluralism was intentional, but it was not founded on ideology. It was simply a gesture in recognition of differences. In each segment, the courses would attend to the West's relations with the non-West: the Persians, Islam, and Africa, for example. This attention did not reflect a multiculturalist theory. It simply reflected the reality of these connections.

When this proposal came to a vote of the faculty, there was only mild opposition. It came from the remnant of Christie's old left, subdued in the national trend that saw the waning of the enthusiasms of the 1960s. This remnant opposed in principle the requirement of any course at all. The proposal passed because a cadre of faculty—about one in six of the entire faculty and drawn from a broad array of departments—avowed not only their support for the idea but their willingness to teach the courses. They had invested a half-decade of effort. Finally, no one who favored some approach to such a requirement thought this version was utterly wrong. The advocates of Western Intellectual Traditions had steered past the shoals of cultural and pedagogical theory.

Conduct of the Course

The courses that constitute Western Intellectual Traditions call for students to read primary texts. On this principle there has been no compromise, despite the groans of students after a few days wrestling with Aristotle. "Think of yourself," I say to the students in my own section, "as the sort of person who will come to read Aristotle with pleasure." Most of them seem to see this as a wry professorial joke at their expense; some come to see it as an Aristotelian exhortation toward their own eudaemonia. This aspect of the course has also been the hardest part for faculty: Aristotle—to stick with this clear example—is not easy for trained philosophers, let alone those whose professional expertise is in another field. But the tables are turned when the primary text is a piece of medieval music or the Parthenon. This feature of the WIT courses is also connected with the conception of what it is to teach such a course, a conception that sheds interesting light on the contemporary debate sparked by Jane Tompkins's work.

In her widely read professional autobiography, *A Life in School,* Tompkins seems to assume that the only kind of authority a teacher can have is an absolute and unchallengeable authority premised on command of the facts and theories: knowing the stuff cold. She assumes therefore—since no one could live up to that level of expectation—that the teacher must work in a state of constant peril—the peril of being shown up as a fraud. She portrays teaching as a performance of a particular sort: the exhibition of consummate expertise. This conception defines the teacher-student relationship by placing the teacher in a starkly authoritative role toward students. It is not just that teachers have to know more than the students: they have to know everything. It is not just that teachers have to be cleverer than the students: they have to be ultimately clever. The teacher is therefore in a constant competition with students to preserve the pretense of omnicompetence. All of this constructs teaching as a tension-filled, competitive performance whose focus is the teacher and whose requirement is brilliance. The judges are the students.

Tompkins proposes an alternative conception of teaching that vests in students a new authority: that of consumers, to whose preferences the teaching function must conform. The relevance of the learning experience to the state of their souls becomes the criterion of integrity in teaching, not the subject matter and the teacher's command of it. The teacher is still subject to student judgment, only not as to how well she knows the stuff but how relevant she is to the student's situation. In this redefinition of the integrity of teaching, students are still the judges, but now they assess experiential relevance rather than professorial expertise.

One solution to the problem of the locus and nature of authority in teaching lies in recognizing that teaching is not a simple dyadic relationship between teacher and student in which the content functions as a ground for transactions of status and authority.

Rather, the material—the text, the thought under discussion, the artifact under scrutiny—has primacy. Teacher and student roles can take shape in many ways in relation to it, and there are plenty of paradigms for teacher-student interaction over the material beyond the simplistic notions of didactic teaching, in which the teacher pronounces truth for the student, or vending machine teaching, in which the teacher gives the student whatever he or she wants. A teacher can be a guide on a journey, like Dante's Virgil and Beatrice, or a coach, like Socrates, or a provocative interlocutor, like Montaigne or Wittgenstein. There is a wide range of possibilities, and Tompkins's reliance on the expert performance as her model is a sorely limited conception of teaching. At Hendrix, in the Western Intellectual Traditions course, the model of the teacher as expert performer applies only to the lecture sessions. In the seminars, it is simply not an option. Necessarily, our constructions of the teaching function are different, and various.

The course depends on discussion. There is a lecture once a week, sometimes twice, in which one of the faculty members provides fodder for the seminars to follow. But the heart of the course is the seminar, a group of twenty to twenty-five students led by a faculty member who might be from music or history, economics or psychology, biology or chemistry. Originally each instructor kept the same students for two terms. Later we experimented with remixing the groups for the second term. Each method has advantages and disadvantages. Continuity provides for a quick reestablishment of conversational rapport in the second term. Extended conversations, the knitting back and forth from topic to topic, showing interesting patterns of relationship among concepts, can stretch over a wider range of material. But perhaps a section has fallen into some problematic dynamic: factions develop, or set-piece disputes are played out again and again, or things just do not work out. A change of characters can be welcome. The point, either way, is to promote discussion.

Well, what is discussion? In the early 1980s Hendrix was visited by the poet Richard Brautigan. Like the typical visiting poet, Brautigan interspersed his poems among comments to the audience. His segues from poem to poem were light patterings of disconnected talk. At one moment he finished a poem that had nothing to do with bears, cabins, or Montana, and said to the audience, "I have a cabin in Montana where the bears walk across my yard." Nice to know, but what is the point? The next poem, too, was void of connections with bears, cabins, or Montana. He regularly and intentionally violated the principles of relevance that distinguish discussion from aimless maundering. This, of course, was part of the performance and had, as such, a Zen-like purpose. He wanted to present his topics with a fresh immediacy. But he was not discussing anything.

Discussion is knitted together—not in any neat or even predictable way, but knitted nonetheless—by principles of relevance. Discussion succeeds when patterns emerge, connections are established, and relationships are created or developed. What do things have to do with each other? That is the question students really want to have answered when they ask, "What are we talking *about?*" In the best discussions it is often hard to know.

For that reason the WIT faculty developed, after a couple of years, a list called "The Big Questions." The idea behind the list was to provide a way to start answering the student who asks, "What are we talking *about?*" The confidence behind the list—and the implicit warning to faculty—is that the student's question can be answered by locating the discussion topic among the questions on the list. Among the big questions are the following: What is the relation between the human and the divine? What is a good person? What constitutes the good life? What can we know, and how can we know it? What is the proper relationship between individual and society? What is beauty, and why is it important? Is there purpose to human existence?

In the book of readings for the WIT courses, these questions are followed by a statement attributed to Francis Christie: "It's not so much what ideas are held that counts, but the way in which they are held." Of course, developing the big questions was a delightful exercise for the WIT faculty. And the WIT faculty do not suppose that the list is final, uncontentious, or free of biases of time and culture that further reflection will make embarrassing. They are simply attempts to open discussions of issues that have come up again and again, in classic texts as well as in dormitory bull sessions.

Although the WIT courses concentrate on four periods in Western history and are clearly, in this sense, Eurocentric, each segment of the course attends to the voices of historically marginalized constituencies within the European tradition, and each segment shows Europe in contact with a non-European part of the world. The virtue of concentrating attention in this way is that students have the time to read considerable stretches of primary texts. We want them to have read Nietzsche, not to have read about Nietzsche. We want them to have gathered some sense of the presiding genius of an age, not just a chronological sequence of what happened when because of what. But much is left out—actually, most is left out—of any course. Coverage of everything—or even of all the important things—is impossible. We do not pretend to cover everything, or everything important. We omit the Renaissance, for example. Some regard this as an abomination. Our aim is not coverage, any more than it is the display of expertise.

It is important to note that the formulation of the big questions followed the selection of the texts. In fact, the list of questions emerged only after faculty reflected on student anxiety about the books. "What are we discussing?" they asked. So the texts were not selected because they address these questions. Rather, the questions are a guide to the texts, generated by a reading of the texts. They inform discussion of a syllabus that begins with the *Odyssey* and moves next to Sappho. The early lectures deal with life in Athens and with Greek music and lyric poetry. We pay attention to the mechanics of the production of musical sounds in ancient Athens in order to ground class discussions in the material realities of ancient life. Then we take up the *Oresteia.* A look at Athenian polity follows on the theme of civic order that is introduced at the close of the *Eumenides,* and we treat the Peloponnesian War in two ways: straight on in Thucydides, where through the Periclean funeral oration we look at an Athenian self-conception in contrast to their treatment of the Melians, and from a slant, through the lenses of Aristophanes' *Acharnians.* In this play, the theme of civic order and its relation to the individual looms large. Some of the philosophy faculty in the course have plumped for the *Clouds* instead, but the historians, the politics faculty, and the theater faculty seem to think we have enough Socrates. For that is indeed our next stop: the *Apology* and the *Phaedo.*

Steeled by an introductory lecture on Greek philosophy, we dive into *The Republic,* reading sections on epistemology and politics. Students become acquainted with the Allegory of the Cave, the Divided Line, the tripartite theory of the soul, and the Platonic vision of social order and the education necessary to support it. Inevitably, next comes Aristotle: the physics, the metaphysics, the ethics, the politics. Sometimes, despite themselves, students come to recognize the teleological turn of mind, the empirical habit, the commonsensical, if ponderous, approach. They also gain acquaintance with virtue, the mean, and practical wisdom. They are relieved beyond expression to arrive at an examination of Greek art and architecture. At last comes Alexander, and a summing up of the Greeks.

We hope, perhaps above all else, to escape too easy an assimilation of this ancient culture into contemporary modes of understanding. Whatever truth there may be in the idea that Greek ideas have driven the development of the democratic, inquiring, scientific West, we want to preserve the otherness of the Greeks. Their civilization is at once both a distant mirror—Barbara Tuchman's (1978) phrase for the fourteenth century—and an inscrutable prism, whose examination brings into question our understanding of the Greeks and of ourselves.

This tension—the aspects of the alien and the familiar, the ancestral and the foreign—is even more intense when the course turns to thirteenth-century Europe. It is here that—having passed over the origins of Christianity—we encounter the Bible, reading selections from the Hebrew Bible and the New Testament. There are two sequences of readings: one traces the Christian appropriation of the Hebraic tradition from Creation and the Fall through the prophetic tradition to the Gospels and the Pauline writings. The other follows the same track but concentrates on images of and teachings about women. In these readings the Bible appears on the syllabus alongside other books. But as everyone who has tried it knows, it is difficult to approach the Bible as one among the books. A few students view the Bible with religious awe; their capacity to read the text and ask what it means in a scholarly setting is occluded by a reverential trance. An equal number are disabled by scorn. They are certain that everything in the Bible is either rank superstition or manipulative lie. Most, though, are simply uncomfortable. Part of the discomfort stems from the attitudes of the students at the extremes. These more moderate students are anxious not to offend, and anything they say will offend either the reverent or the radical—and perhaps both. But these moderates are also confused. Are they supposed to approach these texts with a critical eye? It is from this moderate core that useful discussion emerges, but it emerges slowly and haltingly.

The medieval segment includes a self-description of the papacy in the voice of Innocent III and a representative of Christianity's perennial minority report—anti-institutional, antihierarchical, radically egalitarian, and pacifistic—in the voice of Francis of Assisi. Some students have their eyes opened by his preaching to the birds; others deepen their scornful incredulity.

After a look at Gothic style in art and architecture, the course turns to the chivalric ideal, reading one or another of the narratives of Chrétien de Troyes. Then come Thomas Aquinas's politics, ethics, and natural law, which the students rightly detect as another dose of Aristotle, this time in Christian guise. Medieval music provides the segue to Dante, and the course ends in hell, whose variety and movement most students find a great relief, even though it is another expression of the oppressive totalizing of medieval civilization. We find in this process that the horrors of the *Inferno* have an oddly aesthetic allure.

At this point each student has written five essays: two out-of-class assignments on topics chosen at the instructor's discretion and three in-class examination papers. For the final examination, each student writes a sixth essay on an integrative topic chosen from a list developed by the WIT faculty. Examination topics might ask the students to compare the visions of human excellence in classical Greece and the Christian Middle Ages. They might ask for reflection on the roles of men and of women in these cultural periods. They might require students to compare Greek and medieval conceptions of humanity's relation to the gods or to God. They might ask for reflection on the roles of art, architecture, and music in shaping and expressing the two periods. Whatever the topic, the examination questions require students to bring ideas into comparative relations, mount arguments, defend assertions with reasons, and develop interpretations of the texts and objects they have examined.

The second term begins with the scientific and philosophical revolutions of the seventeenth century. From Newton, Bacon, and Descartes, attention moves to Molière, the Counter-Reformation, and the baroque. Music is represented through Purcell's *Dido and Aeneas,* and the perennial question of legitimating political power returns in Hobbes and Locke. No student can escape asking whether power is the sole source of political legitimacy. Are there rights antecedent to their recognition by a state? Here students recognize issues in a near-contemporary form. For example, when the trade policy of the United States toward China is debated in terms of the applicability of Western ideas of human rights to Chinese circumstances, the differing perspectives of Locke and Hobbes are of immediate analytic value. The century closes with a look at Dutch introspection, commerce, and domesticity in Rembrandt and Vermeer, and at the Atlantic slave trade. Equiano's slave narrative brings the economic boom of Europe into relation with the exploitation of African humanity and the development of the New World.

The New World has become a world of colonial empires by the next moment of the course. The theme of this section is "Modernity in Crisis," as we examine the stresses and strains to which modern civilization was subjected at the brink of the twentieth century. Darwin, on the *Beagle,* enjoys British dominion of the seas as his context. Although the theory of political liberty flourishes—Mill's *On Liberty* is our text—so does a system of economic exploitation, which we examine through Dickens's *Hard Times.* Marx remains a powerful commentator on capitalism despite the recent collapse of political Marxism, and so we get a thorough dose of the theory of alienation of labor. We look at Nietzsche on ethics. The emergence of the women's movement occupies us next: the Grimké sisters, Sojourner Truth, and the evolutionary theories of sex differentiation of Charlotte Perkins Gilman. Finally, a glimpse of William James and *The Will to Believe* is intended to offer some prospect of hope amid the turmoil.

The positioning of William James at the close of the course points to an interesting aspect of the development of the syllabus. The first thought of the faculty was to focus the last segment on late Hapsburg Vienna. The art, music, politics, literature, and philosophy of Vienna from 1890 to 1918 all seemed to presage the crisis of the West in the twentieth century. Freud would serve as a major focus. But the idea was unsustainable from the perspective of syllabus construction, and we broadened into late nineteenth-century

Europe. We have stretched the century to include a late work of Freud—*Civilization and Its Discontents*—and we have stretched Europe to include William James. What this shows is the tendency of a group of faculty, working and reworking a syllabus, to pull at the boundaries of its original intent. In the case of James, clearly the aim was to provide a hopeful counterpoint to a syllabus that otherwise would have ended in Nietzsche, Freud, and Ibsen. This faculty concern for the effect of the course on students is natural and appropriate, but in the history of syllabus development, it lies in tension with the principle of letting texts take us where they may. Both ideas are important, as the following considerations illustrate in a different way.

The WIT faculty has insisted from the beginning on giving attention to the convergence of the West with other cultures. Each of the four segments of the sequence includes an explicit look at the West's interaction with another culture. In the Greek segment, students consider the category "barbarian," as an expression of the self-understanding of the Greeks in contradistinction to the Persians, both at the dawn of the classical period and in connection with the marginal position of the Macedonian Alexander and his confrontation with the Persian empire. In the medieval period the ascendancy of Islamic civilization is the counterpoint to half-barbarian Europe, as a source of manifold advances in Western culture. In the seventeenth century, attention shifts to Africa and the New World, now linked with Europe in an invidious triangular trade in raw materials, manufactured goods, and humans. The late nineteenth-century segment includes the relations between Europe and its colonial empires.

Responsible discussion of this wide-ranging spread of topics demands a careful selection of texts. Early in the design of the courses, it became obvious that we would want to publish our own book of readings. By 1998 the book had gone into its third edition under the energetic and painstaking editorship of Lawrence Schmidt, a member of the Hendrix philosophy department. Schmidt is the Reed graduate in the group, and it is he who supplied the perspective of that college's two-year humanities course. Originally a repository of hard-to-find texts, the book, *Western Intellectual Traditions: Selected Readings,* has grown into a comprehensive compendium, encompassing most of the readings of the two courses, together with introductory notes by Hendrix faculty, a guide to critical reading, a list of the big questions, illustrative time lines, glossaries and notes to the lectures, and other aids to the students. The book of readings does not, of course, contain the works that students read in full (for example, Homer, Dante, Dickens, and Ibsen), which they must buy separately. A faculty guide, informally known as *The Great Book of Help*, contains notes and guides for discussion leaders and is made available to faculty. In it the Hendrix historians offer suggestions on the history bits, the philosophers help others with Aristotle and his ilk, the musicians tell the philosophers how to listen, and so on.

Classics and Culture

David Denby (1996) notes that Columbia's Contemporary Civilization course grew out of a course offered during World War I and was considered from the beginning "a defense of Western civilization." Literature Humanities, installed in 1937 after years of development, had as a chief purpose the purveyance of European literature to the recent immigrants who had begun to appear at Columbia. In the genesis of these courses, we can see the impetus championed decades later by E. D. Hirsch (1987) in his appeal for "cultural literacy." In a nutshell the argument is that success in a liberal society depends not on ethnicity or race, but on familiarity with the texts and topics admitted as canonical by the dominant culture. Denby thinks it ironic that such courses, with these intentions, have been castigated as marginalizing those very constituencies, along with others. The courses' intent was explicitly antimarginalizing, insofar as individuals are concerned. What neither Denby nor Hirsch recognizes as clearly, however, is that in proposing to draw individuals into the mainstream, such courses still marginalize the disparate traditions to which the assimilated individuals may have belonged by designating them to be left behind. It is well to bring students into acquaintance with the literature that will equip them with points of reference that are essential for success in the larger world; it is less well to imply that their own traditions must be jettisoned, that they have nothing to offer to that larger world, as an alternative, or as a corrective.

Still, a major virtue of the approach that Denby and Hirsch share is the insistence that acquaintance with some body of writing, commonly known, enhances one's humanity by affording access to a wealth of exemplars and paradigms without which common discourse—in some body politic—would be almost impossible. Both emphasize that such acquaintance admits to a meritocracy, not to a society in which preferment is based on ancestry. Denby argues that the left has been wrong about the role of the Western canon in providing an exclusionary hegemonic discourse. Instead of received values, he finds diversity, disparity, and a history of argument—even a history of incommensurable values and perspectives. The "West" teaches no one thing, unless that thing is a history of contention and self-criticism. At Columbia, he found that the "Western classics were at war with one other, and there was only the experience of reading" (Denby, 1996, p. 453). This realization is ironic commentary on those who suppose that the Western classics embody a transmissible univocity of value. That irony is connected with a deep philosophical point.

In the twentieth century, Wittgenstein rediscovered a philosophical perspective that reaches back as far as the ancient philosopher Sextus Empiricus. Sextus discovered that the formal, explicit rules governing any procedure will always be logically incomplete. Take any recipe in a cookbook or the directions on the back of any shampoo bottle. Read the instructions and ask yourself: "What do these directions presuppose? What do I already have to be able to do in order to follow them? What steps do they leave out? How might anyone—perversely or naively—misconstrue them?" What you will discover is that there is no end to the process of supplying supplemental rules. That means, if our aim is the reduction of a process to fully explicit rules, that our aim can never be accomplished. Knowing how to follow any rules depends on our first being trained in what counts as following the rules in similar cases. That is why Aristotle, in the *Nicomachean Ethics,* admonishes us that we will not understand deliberation about ethics unless we have been well brought up. The necessity of exemplars, in ethics and in anything else that is meant to count as a rational, rule-governed proceeding, stems from this fact. The indeterminacy to which I allude is the same as that displayed in Thomas Kuhn's exposition of the role of paradigms in scientific thought in his 1962 classic,

The Structure of Scientific Revolutions. All activities undertaken in accord with explicit and formal rules rest on a substratum of behaviors, some of which are culturally learned, some of which are simply made up on the spot, and some of which are hardwired in us for evolutionary reasons.

What this means is that cases presented to us—in learning the canons of scientific research, in ethics, in literary criticism, in whatever other field—are not illustrations but the concrete realities from which alone abstractions can be derived. Cases, then, have primacy over theoretical abstractions. They are not illustrative examples that show in concrete terms what abstractions show more clearly. Cases are the primary realities that make possible the formulation of abstract rules. A culture cannot be built on abstractions alone, on formal rules alone.

Hence—and this is the important truth embedded in what conservative commentators have been saying for two decades about the canon—there is vital importance in common experience. A culture's take on its formal rules will be coherent only to the degree that common exemplars provide the underpinning for their meaning. What common exemplars do we have? According to Denby (1996) there is a source of such common experience—real hegemonic discourse: that of commercial culture employing sophisticated tools of communication. Ours is a media society, full of representations and simulacra, most of them contrived to elicit from us predictable responses that will serve the economic interests of those who purvey them.

This cultural context—the constant manipulation of our responses for commercial purposes—bears directly on the meaning of the Hendrix College motto: "Toward Human Fulfillment" or "Toward the Whole Person." The daily experience of many people in contemporary American culture is dominated by commercial messages. Accordingly, the real hegemonic discourse in contemporary American culture lies in the mass media, and particularly in commercialism and consumerism. To buy, to consume, to identify oneself according to the sorts of products one consumes—these are the activities toward which people are urged. People know and hold in common brand names in their hierarchies, advertising images, jingles, theme songs from television shows, popular music, movies, styles of clothing. As Denby (1996) notes, the collapse of political Marxism does not mean that Marx's fundamental critique of the effects of this life on the human soul is wrong. There is something yet to learn from the Marxian critique of industrial production and consumption—something about the alienation of people from important possibilities of meaning.

A small element of that critique is immediately relevant. Life in the hegemony of commercial society is life bombarded by messages whose aim is to identify, evoke, and, by evoking, reinforce those capacities of response whose activation in the individual will work to the advantage of the sender of the message. What will make people buy this beer? These blue jeans? How do we touch that sensibility, and how do we make people act on the response we elicit when we touch it? My point, in response to the charge that the teaching of the classics reinforces uncriticized patterns of traditional value, is that it is not the reading of Homer and Shakespeare that does this; it is everyday life in our society that reinforces existing sensibilities and produces a smooth complacency. It is the experience of a consumer society that teaches that life is about the gratification of existing desires.

In an annual talk before the entering students of Hendrix College, I have for some years emphasized the paradoxical nature of our institutional aims toward them. We do not aim to gratify their existing desires, but to bring them to have new and better desires of whose nature they are currently ignorant or only vaguely aware. Their entry into this process implies that they wish to have capacities whose nature they do not now comprehend. A part of the point of liberal education—and therefore of confrontation with classical texts—is to change the sensibilities of the student: to change his or her patterns of response and capacities of feeling and understanding so that the way in which he or she fits into the world changes. For this reason it is important that these texts not be smooth reinforcers of received values and ways of responding. It is important that they be odd, challenging, even perverse. It is important that they be confrontations with the "other." This principle should hold true regardless of whether the text strikes us as truly "other"—like the barbaric moral splendor of Homer's warriors—or whether it presents to us apparent truisms of liberal culture—like Mill's *On Liberty*—but presents those truisms so consistently and trenchantly as to make them appear in their native oddity, as principles little recognized in the history of human societies.

If the aim of liberal education is to free individuals from the sway of an otherwise hegemonic commercial discourse, immersion in texts like those commonly collected in lists of Western classics is a promising way to attempt it. If the shared cultural context of our students is, as Denby suggests, saturation in the sophisticated media of a commercial society, then part of our intent at Hendrix is to provide another common experience, one that gives students resources with which to reflect, not merely images to react to. Why would a college want to do this? There are very good, even commonsense, answers to this question:

- A college with an intellectual commons offers students something to share beyond popular culture, dorm life, dining hall food, and weekend parties.
- A college with an intellectual commons offers students and faculty a shared body of acquaintance that can be presumed and relied on in later courses.
- A college with an intellectual commons offers students a better-designed opportunity to fulfill the institution's aims of cultivating their humanity, by introducing the notion at the outset and by getting an intentionally structured start on the process.

There is much that no one understands about this process. Denby posits that education is a "mystery." How is it that the books we read and discuss—though largely forgotten—still shape our sensibilities? George Eliot can explain this. In *The Mill on the Floss* Eliot's narrator, in an elegiacal by-passage, explains how our adult sensibilities are shaped by childhood experiences, which "are the mother tongue of our imagination, the language that is laden with all the subtle inextricable associations of the fleeting hours of our childhood" (Eliot, 1985, p. 94). Substituting *education* for *childhood*, who would not, on an instant's reflection, agree that the unremembered books have supplied a texture of anticipatable experience, a body of response and uptake, a sensibility not reducible to the influence of any single experience and hence not lodged with any single memory, but the compound effect of them all? This is,

ALIVE AT THE CORE

of course, not an explanation that removes Denby's mystery but a confirmation that, mystery or not, this is—as we very well know— how life works.

References

Campbell, R. "The Place of the Humanities in the Total Scheme of General Education." (Unpublished typescript.) 1953.

Churchill, J. "Odysseus's Bed; Agamemnon's Bath." *College Literature,* 1991, 18, pp. 1–13.

Denby, D. *Great Books.* New York: Simon & Schuster, 1996.

Eliot, G. *The Mill on the Floss.* London: Penguin Books, 1985.

Hendrix College. *Catalogue.* Conway, Ark.: Hendrix College, 1980.

Hirsch, E. D. *Cultural Literacy: What Every American Needs to Know.* Boston: Houghton Mifflin, 1987.

Kuhn, T. *The Structure of Scientific Revolutions.* Chicago: University of Chicago Press, 1962.

Lester, J. E., Jr. *Hendrix College: A Centennial History.* Conway, Ark.: Hendrix College, 1984.

Nussbaum, M. *Cultivating Humanity: A Classical Defense of Reform in Liberal Education.* Cambridge, Mass.: Harvard University Press, 1997.

Tompkins, J. *A Life in School.* New York: Perseus Press, 1997.

Tuchman, B. *A Distant Mirror.* New York: Knopf, 1978.

Chapter Fourteen

The Area One Program at Stanford University

Harry J. Elam, Jr., Cheri Ross

In May 1997, the faculty senate at Stanford University voted unanimously to approve new legislation for the freshman humanities requirement, Area One of four areas included in the university's general education requirements. The vote signaled the end of a two-year debate about the value and viability of this proposal for a new required year-long course sequence. The decision affirmed the university's commitment to study in the humanities for all incoming freshmen regardless of their majors. Moreover, the establishment of the new legislation set Stanford and the Area One Program on a trajectory that both builds on and breaks with the past. The new incarnation of Area One was intended to respond to recent, rapid changes within the boundaries, theories, and definitions of the humanities as well as to the equally dramatic, albeit more gradual, transformations in the interests, abilities, and educational objectives of the students now entering Stanford and other institutions of higher learning.

Discernible in the hall on that Thursday afternoon in May 1997 were faint echoes from rancorous spring faculty senate meetings nine years earlier. The debate at that time focused on content. In 1988, Stanford, in a contentious and controversial ruling, changed the first of its general education requirements, a year-long, multidisciplinary curriculum called Western Culture, from a

program solely devoted to the study of the Western canon to a
more inclusive structure that incorporated previously neglected
but important works by women and people of color. The new program was not, as many claimed, a total break with the more traditional curriculum that preceded it. Cultures, Ideas and Values—or
CIV as it soon came to be called in the Stanford system of
acronyms—preserved many aspects of the Western Culture program: chiefly its lecture-plus-discussion-section format and its
choice of eight to ten departmentally based, year-long course
sequences. Where CIV differed was in its underlying politics, based
on multiculturalism and diversity. The 1988 legislation required
that CIV courses increase students' "understanding of cultural
diversity and the process of cultural interaction, . . . confront issues
relating to class, ethnicity, race, religion, gender, and sexual orientation, and include the study of works by women, minorities, and
persons of color" (Stanford University Committee on Undergraduate Studies, 1988, p. 1).

The impact of the 1988 decision reverberated around
the country. The *Chronicle of Higher Education* called CIV "the
course that set off the culture wars" (Schneider, 1997, p. 1). For
some, including William Bennett, Dinesh D'Souza, and the editors
of the *Wall Street Journal,* the establishment of the Cultures, Ideas
and Values program dealt a death blow to the great canon of Western thought and literature. For others, it represented a long-over-
due, more comprehensive approach to the study of humanities.

Stanford's 1997 decision implicitly reaffirmed the 1988 CIV
reform of Area One's content. What it added was a focus on pedagogy. Just as CIV sought to alter the way students and faculty
thought about the humanities, the new program intends to make
a marked change in the ways humanities are taught, studied, and
practiced. The change from CIV to its newest incarnation, the
Introduction to the Humanities, and its newest acronym, IHUM,
reflects a broadening of the conception of study in the humanities,
centering on the field's disciplinary methods and tools rather than
on a specific set of contents.

This shift responded in part to a 1996 survey of graduating
seniors at Stanford who had completed their Area One requirement through the CIV program. The survey revealed that only
40 percent of the respondents felt that their CIV course had

relevance to their lives or their education. As the final report of the Area One Review Committee pointed out, "For good or ill, many students at the end of the twentieth century ask, 'why should I study the humanities or culture, ideas and values?' 'how should I study them?' 'why study the history of the past, the history of thought, the origins of culture?' For them, these questions no longer have self-evident value or answers, do not seem worthwhile, and can even seem meaningless" (Stanford University Committee on Undergraduate Studies, 1997, p. 2).

Faced with growing concerns on the part of faculty and students about the viability of CIV, the dean of humanities and sciences established the Area One Review Committee in 1995 to examine the Area One requirement over a two-year period and make recommendations to the faculty senate regarding its maintenance and improvement.

From the outset, the review committee—consisting of faculty members from within and outside the humanities—reaffirmed the importance of retaining a freshman humanities requirement. This decision was not a difficult one, even though at Stanford, as elsewhere, liberal arts curricula have recently been under attack. Critics both inside and outside the academy have come to question the relevance of a liberal arts education. The very word *liberal*—not to mention *arts*—now has pejorative connotations. Nonetheless, the review committee determined that now more than ever before— as social pressures direct students to become more singularly focused and career obsessed—there is a need for a course that compels them to think broadly about human issues; confronts significant works of literature, philosophy, history and art; and examines cultures, questions, and lessons from the past. Through engagement with such a course, students, whatever their major or career path, should become more knowledgeable about the present and better prepared to face their academic and professional futures.

The review committee then set about the task of revising the Area One Requirement's legislation to increase its relevance to the times and address the concerns raised by students' responses to the CIV program. Critical to this revision was the committee's desire to structure a course that introduced students directly to "the problems and the power of the developing humanistic enterprise in modern culture" (Stanford University Committee on Undergraduate Studies, 1997, p. 3).

Building on the strengths of CIV—the program's emphasis on learning through small group discussion as well as lecture, and its focus on primary readings—IHUM is geared toward strengthening students' ability to read carefully and critically, learn to analyze texts, and interrogate their own positions and identities in relation to these texts. It expects to foster in students the empathy and appreciation of difference that can issue from a well-developed "narrative imagination," as Martha Nussbaum puts it (1997, p. 90). It aims to make students aware of cultural differences in ancient and contemporary times and to inculcate in students an appreciation of the past's influence on the present.

These goals are broad and demanding. In order to accomplish them, the Area One Review Committee decided that a new course format was necessary. Whereas CIV had featured a choice of year-long course sequences made up of three five-unit courses taken successively in fall, winter, and spring, IHUM features a "stand-alone" first-quarter course followed by a two-quarter thematic sequence. The fall quarter course is interdisciplinary, dedicated to providing students with a general introduction to humanistic inquiry. The subsequent winter-spring course sequence studies chronologically major subjects and concerns within the humanities. Thus, the flow during the three quarters is from the general to the specific. The reasons for this change were both practical and ideological.

In the previous system, students chose their year-long CIV sequence (or "track") the summer before entering Stanford. Consequently, they were locked into this track with little opportunity for change and often found their interest flagging by spring. The new structure provides students with more opportunity for choice and change during the year. Now students choose a fall course during the summer before entering Stanford, on the basis of course descriptions and reading lists. In the seventh week of their first ten-week quarter at Stanford, after becoming acclimated to the campus and its academic rigors and benefiting from the counsel of freshman advisers about the IHUM program and the various course options, students choose a winter-spring sequence. Although Area One remains a full-year requirement, students now have more freedom within the requirement to take courses in line with their own desires and interests.

The new structure also encourages more humanities departments and programs at Stanford to take part in Area One. Previously, because of the demands of staffing a year-long course, only larger departments such as English or history, with more than forty tenured or tenure-line faculty members, could easily offer year-long CIV tracks. Under the new IHUM system, smaller departments such as drama, Asian languages, and French and Italian, with only nine or ten professors each, are eager to offer two-quarter winter-spring course sequences. The incentives for faculty members to take part in IHUM are substantial: they include personal salary incentives and funding for research assistants as compensation for the additional work associated with developing a team-taught course. Departmental incentives come in the form of increased student enrollments and potential increases in majors.

The director and the associate director of the Area One Program (the former a faculty member named to the position for a three-year term by the dean of humanities and sciences and the vice provost for undergraduate education; the latter a full-time staff member hired on a permanent basis) are responsible for recruiting courses for IHUM. They bring different faculty members together to form teaching teams. They help faculty to shape their ideas for courses according to the legislation's requirements. Sometimes the director and associate director take their own ideas for courses to likely faculty members for adoption and development. Once courses are conceived and partially developed, preliminary course proposals are presented to both the Area One Governance Board (the oversight committee for the Area One Program, composed of selected faculty, students, and administrators) and the university's standing committee on undergraduate studies. If the proposals are approved, the courses are certified for three years and become part of the next year's curriculum.

Recruitment efforts in 1997–98 resulted in a diverse array of course offerings for 1998–99. The IHUM fall quarter curriculum included choices such as "Freedom and Eros in Philosophy and Art," a course introducing students to the work of Plato and Nietzsche through the theme of artistic creation and including discussion of works in the visual arts, and "Themes and Variations," an interdisciplinary investigation of familiar stories—the tales of Oedipus, Othello, and Don Juan—cast in different media such as opera, drama, film, short story, even sociological essay. In both courses, faculty members from different departments taught together: "Freedom and Eros" teamed two philosophers with an art historian, and "Themes and Variations" brought together a musicologist with a classicist and a specialist in Slavic literature. Together with three other courses—"The Good Life," taught by professors from classics, drama, and French and Italian, who guided students through works by Plato, Shakespeare, Dostoevsky, Nietzsche, and Suzan-Lori Parks; "Desire and Its Discontents," pairing faculty from English and comparative literature and featuring works by Plato and Shakespeare in juxtaposition with novels by Austen and Joyce and poetry by Cesaire; and "Word and the World," described later in this chapter—these courses were the IHUM fall offerings for the second year of the transition from CIV to IHUM.

Winter-spring course sequences in 1998–99 were equally diverse. The classics, drama, English, German studies, history, and philosophy departments offered IHUM sequences with titles such as "Ancient Mediterranean World," "Performing the Past," "Living Through the Changes: The Literature of Transition," "Myth and Modernity," "Ten Days That Shook the World," and "Reason, Passion, and Reality." Two-thirds of the incoming freshmen—roughly 1,170 students—were enrolled in these courses, which ranged in size from 90 to 250 students. By 1999–2000, the phasing in of the new program was complete, with all 1,600 freshmen enrolled in IHUM courses.

One of the most distinctive features of the new program is its emphasis on team teaching. All courses offered in the first quarter are team-taught by two or three professors from different departments or disciplines within the humanities, aided by postdoctoral fellows in the humanities, hired through a national search mounted by the Area One Program. In both fall interdisciplinary courses and winter-spring course sequences, teaching in the new IHUM program is accomplished through large lectures and smaller discussion sections. All team members attend each lecture. The lecture format enables professors to convey to a collective body of students a coherent and concise approach to the materials. The Area One Program firmly maintains that lectures are a viable and significant educational method for developing a critical argument in relation to a work or body of works.

Large lectures, however, too often promote passive learning and alienation on the part of the students. A number of recent studies have shown that large lecture courses are less successful in producing or provoking "the retention of information, the development of thinking skills or changes in motivation or attitudes" (Erickson and Strommer, 1991, p. 165). To combat such effects, the Area One Program recruits professors at Stanford with demonstrated skill at teaching large lecture classes: professors who have outstanding ability to communicate and connect with students within the lecture format. The Area One leadership then works with these professors to make lectures more interactive and effective learning experiences. The luxury of having two or three professors and a group of teaching fellows devoted to a single course allows for innovative and exciting collaborations among the teaching team. Two faculty members might present a joint lecture, or three might join with a teaching fellow to form a panel fielding students' questions about a text. Such collaborative events open up the text to interpretation and encourage students to appreciate different approaches to analyzing a text within the humanities. To involve students further in the lecture process, some professors have organized lectures around points that students have made in web-based discussions, duly quoting and citing them in the course of the lecture. These techniques help to galvanize students' interest in the course and make them truly active agents in the educational process—in fact, co-participants in the creation of their knowledge.

Still, because of the size of these courses, students can slip into anonymity and hide in the corners of the lecture hall. For this reason the new IHUM design calls for three hours of small group discussion sections each week (divided into two ninety-minute sessions) to work in conjunction with the two hours of lecture (delivered in two fifty-minute class meetings). The size of the discussion seminars is limited to fifteen students to ensure that full student participation is both possible and probable and that the sections do not become too unwieldy for the teaching fellows who lead them.

Area One's fellows in the humanities are selected through a highly competitive search on the basis of strong evidence of teaching ability in the humanities in combination with solid scholarly potential. In addition to studying each curriculum vitae for publication and conference presentation records, search committee members carefully review each candidate's teaching evaluations and letters of recommendation; they also conduct telephone interviews with the finalists. Once hired, each fellow is assigned to one course per quarter, attending all course lectures and staff meetings in addition to teaching three discussion sections in the course. The fellowships in the humanities at Stanford are renewable for a maximum of three years to ensure the influx of new energized and energizing fellows into the program each year. The fixed term also compels the fellows to use their position in a timely manner as a stepping-stone to a tenure-track position elsewhere. The Area One leadership works with the fellows on developing their teaching skills through extensive initial training when they are hired and ongoing discussions throughout the academic year. In addition, the program supports the fellows in professional placement by maintaining job lists, providing opportunities for mock interviews and job talks, and sponsoring workshops on job-related activities, such as assembling teaching portfolios.

One of the objectives for the fellows in IHUM is to integrate discussion with lectures given by the faculty. The lectures serve as a site for disseminating information as well as a foundation for debate within the discussion sections. These presentations are analyzed for both content and argument. In discussion sections, students not only examine the texts on the syllabus but also engage the lectures themselves as texts. Accordingly, discussion leaders and students critically examine the lectures just as they do the texts on the syllabus. Effective discussion sections provide the students with insight into the works under consideration and experience in critical thinking and argumentation.

Central to the first quarter is the requirement that the courses introduce students to various methods of humanistic inquiry. The idea that there are "humanistic methodologies" just as there are "scientific methodologies" has been a subject of contention, speculation, and repeated consideration at Stanford, both prior to the institution of the new legislation and after its implementation.

Some faculty members maintain that content should govern IHUM courses, while others hold that appropriate methods of reading are dictated by texts and inseparable from their particular content. An opposed camp argues that ways of reading and thinking in the humanities—from simple but powerful forms of close reading to more sophisticated methods of analysis, contextualization, and theorizing—can be taught separately from their application to any particular set of texts.

Despite these debates, the major point that the Area One legislation asks the first-quarter courses to articulate is that humanistic disciplines undertake diverse strategies for approaching and interpreting texts. From philosophical inquiry, for instance, students can learn to use rigorous argumentation and Socratic interrogation. They can acquire the ability to assess evidence, values, and beliefs. Through historical examination, students can appreciate the text as a cultural product or even as a historical event. They can come to understand that historical research reveals unexpected interconnections among texts and contexts, as well as gain new insights into the ways that the present is constituted in the past. Literary criticism and analysis can heighten aesthetic appreciation and teach students the value of close, critical readings. It can also teach them to apply various theories about literature, language, and symbolic and cultural representation more generally, helping them gain a greater recognition of how literature shapes and is shaped by the world around it.

As methodologies migrate across fields in the humanities, these techniques and approaches are not the sole domain of any one discipline. However, the new Area One Program does hold that students can begin to develop discernible skills of textual analysis and critical approach in their first-quarter IHUM courses, which they can then apply to later course work and investigation both within and outside the humanities.

The new organization of the first quarter reinforces the idea that how students read is critical. But this emphasis on method does not mean that content is insignificant; nor does it imply that important works of literature no longer have a place in the Introduction to the Humanities curriculum at Stanford. In fact, a brief glance at the authors selected for any year's courses provides assurances to the contrary. The richness and import of the works discussed remain crucial. Supplying the students with tools for approaching complex, primary texts is at the core of the first quarter's mission. Students analyze how and why the works comment on the human condition and how and why the texts have had a lasting influence on human lives. The goal is for students to understand that complex texts are not closed systems, but open works available to multiple and variant readings. Within the humanities, ideas are always subject to debate, discussion, and disagreement.

While learning the value of different interpretations, students also come to appreciate the need for careful argumentation in support of diverse readings. The new legislation calls for IHUM courses to foster the critical thinking and argumentative skills of students through both discussion and written work. In the terms Erickson and Strommer (1991) used to describe the cognitive development of college freshmen, students should be brought from positions of "multiplicity"—in which they regard knowledge in the humanities as simply a matter of opinion—to positions of "relativism," in which they learn to value the consideration of complexity, the use of systematic analysis, and the evaluation of evidence.

In its fall quarter courses, the IHUM program specifically trains students in the close reading of texts. A repeated criticism of earlier CIV courses was that they covered too much material in too brief a time. Although their brisk pace enabled CIV courses to fulfill the mandate of diversity, it necessitated superficial readings and prevented works from being covered in depth. By the middle of the winter quarter, many students discovered the impossibility of completing all the assigned readings and resorted to reading plot summaries as a substitute for the texts themselves. When asked for ways to improve CIV, former students repeatedly responded, "Read fewer texts in more depth." Accordingly, the legislation governing the first quarter of IHUM restricts the number of texts to between three and five. This limitation enables the teaching team to cover each text carefully and intensely during the course of the ten-week quarter. Students are not only expected to read each text once, but also to reread it. Program faculty have discovered that short, weekly writing assignments, which take the place of the standard two-essays-plus-exam formula of CIV, are the key to rereading. The weekly assignments, reviewed and graded by discussion leaders, direct students to return repeatedly to the texts, approaching them in new and different ways. These assignments, in coordination with discussion sections and lectures, compel students to dig deeply into the texts and reach new understandings of the materials. Such frequent assignments have the added benefit of keeping freshmen on task. Students new to college often need to learn time management skills in order to tame a potentially overwhelming environment filled with unfamiliar distractions and unprecedented levels of freedom. In addition, frequent short writing assignments provide valuable feedback from the discussion leaders to students whose unfamiliarity with college-level evaluation standards often produces anxiety.

At least one of the three to five texts studied in each course must be from "outside the traditional Western canon." This requirement ensures both that readings in IHUM courses continue to "affirm the spirit of inclusiveness" represented in the earlier CIV legislation and that IHUM courses recognize and encourage students to understand the diversity of human experience. The phrase "traditional Western canon" is purposely ambiguous and subject to interpretation. It opens up readings in IHUM courses to works from African, Asian, and Latin American cultures, as well as from American peoples of color, women, even popular culture, that historically have not been included in enumerations of canonical texts. Consequently, the new legislation does not herald a conservative retrenchment from the concept of multiculturalism championed by the CIV legislation in 1988.

Rather, the new legislation implies a more contemporary, more nuanced, and less prescriptive reading of diversity. At times in CIV courses, works by minorities and women were added to syllabi in ways that marginalized them. For example, students might question the juxtaposition of Marie de France's *lais* with the weighty philosophical syntheses of Aquinas and Dante's magnum opus. Such inclusions of alternative, unfamiliar materials, grafted onto an apparently traditional Western thought and literature survey, threatened to derail the flow and logic of the course rather than to expand the students' sense of representative literature of a particular period. The new IHUM, in contrast, with its emphasis on methods of analysis, eschews the problematic survey model of a Western culture or world cultures course and instead encourages social categories such as race, ethnicity, gender, and class to be studied for the constitutive roles they play within the development of humanity. Thus, the critical analysis of any and every text may draw on interpretive resources such as feminist criticism, queer theory, or postcolonial studies, as well as on more traditional methods of analysis. Many new IHUM courses, for example, work with the principle that gender has been and continues to be "a fundamental condition of experience and category of analysis" (Bell, 1990, p. 300).

Rigorously maintained within IHUM, in terms of its practical implementation and ideological orientation, is a commitment to what Nussbaum (1997) refers to as "the complex transformation of [the] curriculum to incorporate a variety of approaches to human diversity" (p. 14). Developments in new disciplines of humanistic inquiry from poststructuralism to ethnic studies have changed the ways we view the processes and products of human life and, consequently, the way the study of the humanities now operates. The first quarter and IHUM as a whole are designed to make students more aware of contemporary directions in the humanities.

The 1997 legislation for IHUM also encourages that the term *text* be broadly construed to include works of visual art, drama, music, film, and architecture. The number of works studied in a course that focuses on visual arts may be greater than three to five, but the idea behind the limitation still governs the assignments: to allow students to focus more deeply on the materials. The 1998–99 fall offerings in IHUM included "Themes and Variations," a course examining works in different genres, including opera and drama; "Word and the World," which included analysis of the now classic science-fiction film *Blade Runner*; and "Freedom and Eros," involving the study of paintings, drawings, and sculptures in the discussion of the relationship between philosophy and art. By expanding the concept of what constitutes a text, these courses develop not only a deeper appreciation of different art forms but also an awareness of how these texts function within a broader system of social, cultural, historical, and ideological interrelationships.

The 1997 Area One legislation specified that the new program be phased in gradually over three years. The Area One Program enrolled one-third of the freshman class in new-style courses in the 1997–98 academic year. Two newly created fall courses—"Why Read It?" and "The Word and the World"—and two new winter-spring IHUM courses—"The Ancient Mediterranean World" and "Myth and Modernity"—accommodated these students. The guiding idea behind "Why Read It?" was that both classic texts and the humanities disciplines that study them have their own purposes and their own justifications: their own answers to the question, "Why read it?" The course responded to the new emphasis on interdisciplinary approaches through its combination of teaching personnel. Three faculty members—a drama professor, a professor of Italian whose scholarly orientation is philosophical, and a professor of history and director of the Stanford Humanities Center—lectured in the course. Discussions were led by fellows in the humanities from French and Italian, modern thought and literature, and religious studies. The faculty members designing "Why Read It?" assigned a group of primary readings from a wide chronological range and a diverse set of contexts and circumstances of production. Students read Plato's *Symposium* and Shakespeare's *King Lear* alongside Montesquieu's *Persian Letters* and Zora Neale Hurston's *Their Eyes Were Watching God*.

In "Why Read It?" the division of lecturing labor helped encourage the students to reexamine and reinterpret the texts. Each faculty member lectured at least once on each work. They approached the texts from their particular disciplinary vantage points. These diverse lectures presented the students with the possibility of different, but equally valid, readings of the texts. As a result the students learned that a scholar of dramatic performance approaches a text differently than a historian or a literary theorist does. To help emphasize this point, a roundtable discussion with all three faculty members followed the completion of each unit on a particular text. During these roundtables, all three professors engaged with each other, the teaching fellows, and the students as they answered questions posed by the students.

The teaching team for the other fall 1997–98 IHUM course took a decidedly different approach to fulfilling the requirements of the Area One legislation. "Word and the World" presented works that are world making in the broadest sense: texts that help to found cultures, political systems, notions of selfhood and humanity: the biblical Book of Genesis, the Chinese classic *Shang shu* [The Book of Documents], Descartes's *Meditations*, Shakespeare's

Hamlet, and the film *Blade Runner* (the director's cut). "Word and the World" was designed and taught by a team that consisted of a history of science professor, a professor of Asian languages, and a professor of English who codirects the Stanford Learning Lab, a new research unit in Stanford's School of Engineering that studies innovative uses of technology in education and particularly focuses on solving problems encountered in traditional pedagogical settings—for instance, the dissatisfaction students often feel with large lecture courses. Two fellows in the humanities, both literary scholars, completed the teaching team. Beyond a partnership among diverse academic departments, "Word and the World" represented a unique collaboration among the humanities, engineering, and education research: the course served as a test bed for the Learning Lab's emphasis on technology in the classroom.

"Word and the World" incorporated innovative pedagogy and computer technology at every level, from course design and lecture presentations to oral and written assignments. Students explored specially created web sites, which offered backgrounds on the assigned texts. They participated in ongoing on-line discussions of the works with other students and with faculty. Avoiding the more traditional model of a lecture course, in which a faculty member lectures while the students take notes, this course also offered groups of students the chance to prepare and present panel responses to lectures.

In order to motivate rereading of the texts and to facilitate the presentation of different approaches in the humanities, the teaching team structured "Word and the World" into two parts, each dealing with all five texts. The first five-week pass through the material presented close readings of texts, supplemented with only the most basic historical and contextual background. The faculty lecturers demonstrated literary and philosophical approaches, focusing on themes of identity and subjectivity as constituted in the texts.

The second five-week pass was organized around two types of approach, generally categorized in terms of "strands" and "contexts." "Strands" lectures explored intertextual readings among the five primary texts: for example, the notion of legitimacy and its illegitimate double in *Hamlet* and Descartes's *Meditations,* or defining "the human" in Genesis, *Hamlet,* and *Blade Runner.* In lectures labeled "contexts," faculty members provided exemplary readings that emphasized the historical location, production, and subsequent reception of the text. In focusing on how the texts were received in different places and at different times, the teaching team introduced students to the concept of the "engaged reader": the reader with a stake in a particular interpretation who develops a method or style of reading in order to displace other established readings.

During four of the first five weeks, students wrote short papers in which they exercised a specific skill, such as close reading of a literary passage or critical analysis of a philosophical argument. The second five-week segment featured two longer writing assignments, in which students analyzed an intertextual strand in the reading or researched and presented a context relevant to a particular text. These reading practices required skills that built on the ones developed in the first five weeks. Then the students employed all of these accumulated skills in the final project for the course. By forgoing the conventional final exam, "Word and the World" enabled students to display their methodological mastery, critical analysis, and deep learning in a more extended context.

For the final project, students worked in teams of three to write a tripartite textual analysis, including a close reading, a strand, and context of some element among the five primary texts in the course. Each student in a group was responsible for producing one of the written parts of the project. They were graded individually on these separate parts. As a team, they added a statement of purpose for the project as a whole and created a public presentation for the project. The students presented these projects—which ranged in form from oral presentations to web sites to puppet shows—at a multimedia fair held at the end of the quarter during the registrar-scheduled time in which the course would have administered its final exam.

The rationale for the group-based projects was to replace the standard way of organizing labor in humanities research. The final projects substituted a model of collaboration for the traditional image of the totally independent scholar, alone in a study with his or her books. In addition to offering this important experience, the teaching team intended for the group projects to improve students' oral communication skills as they articulated ideas within their groups and presented their final projects to the class as a whole.

Seven weeks into their fall quarter courses in 1997–98, freshmen in IHUM were invited to express their preferences among a number of winter-spring courses to complete their Area One requirement. Among their choices were two new IHUM course sequences: the classics department's "Ancient Mediterranean World: Civilization and Slavery" and the German studies offering, "Myth and Modernity: Culture in Germany." According to the Area One legislation, winter-spring sequences should be structured around a specific subject and informed by a definite set of themes. The classics department's two-quarter sequence examined the history of the ancient Mediterranean world, from the origins of complex societies around 3000 B.C. to the Arab conquests of the area in the seventh century A.D. The course viewed the ancient Mediterranean as the site of some of the most important social experiments in human history, which profoundly shaped the subsequent development of the whole world. The course focused on how issues of class, gender, and race influenced the social history of this period. The teaching team asked students to wrestle with uncomfortable paradoxes: Why were sophisticated literate and artistic cultures most often created for small, elite groups? Why and how did the foundation of these cultures depend on the exploitation of masses of people? How was religion used to justify social inequality? Why did the earliest forms of social egalitarianism, such as those of the Israelite kingdom and the Greek city-states, emerge alongside new inequalities resting on ethnic, gender, and class distinctions? Above all, how should the societies of the ancient Mediterranean world be defined: as complex civilizations, or as sites of systematic state violence and social oppression?

"Myth and Modernity," the other new winter-spring IHUM sequence for 1997–98, tracked the initially auspicious and yet ultimately unsettling career of the Enlightenment: the emancipation of the individual from domination by, or dependence on, external authorities—whether political, cultural, or natural. In contrast to the historical focus taken in "Ancient Mediterranean World," "Myth and Modernity" offered students a predominantly philosophical approach. Similar to the classics department's course, however, German studies organized its winter-spring offering around provocative themes and questions. In examining the promise and problems of Enlightenment modernity, the course identified mythic forms of thought and expression. It interrogated myths of art, life, and, more disturbingly, especially in the German context, race. The course prompted students to provide their own answers to its central question: Do cultures require myth, or should mythic thinking be overcome?

As these two examples demonstrate, the legislation governing winter-spring course sequences may be realized in a variety of ways. All such sequences must treat a broad historical span of at least two centuries, and the course materials, which must include selections from outside the traditional Western canon, must be presented chronologically. Like the fall quarter courses, the winter-spring sequences stress primary readings and are organized into two lecture hours and three discussion hours per week. Stanford faculty members from the department offer the course lecture, while the same group of fellows in the humanities employed in the fall quarter courses leads the discussion sections. Within these requirements, the room to maneuver is considerable. The task of developing winter-spring course sequences is appealing to a large audience of humanists at Stanford. Many of the faculty interested in offering winter-spring sequences are veterans of the old CIV program who plan to prune and reshape their three-quarter CIV course syllabi to meet the new program's requirements. Far from alienating faculty who taught in CIV and Western Culture before it, IHUM aims to include them along with newly recruited participants.

Initial reactions to the IHUM experience from students and faculty have been both encouraging and illuminating. The following are representative student reactions from written evaluations of the fall quarter courses offered in 1997–98, as well as from small student focus groups and unsolicited letters. Students testify to the ways that their IHUM courses have honed their critical abilities. Eighty-seven percent of IHUM students reported that their fall quarter courses strengthened their skills in analysis, reasoning, and argumentation, and 72 percent believed that the courses improved their ability to read in a focused way. Seventy-three percent felt that their written expression had improved, and 79 percent anticipated that the methods and skills they had developed in IHUM would be of use in other courses.

Students have responded enthusiastically to the team-taught aspect of the fall quarter courses. Ninety-two percent of those surveyed agreed that their IHUM courses provided opportunities for them to consider diverse viewpoints. Students in one focus group noted as one of the most positive aspects of their course the chance to learn from three faculty members rather than just one. They observed that the most engaging sessions for them were the team lectures in which faculty members disagreed with each other's interpretations and arguments. Rather than finding such clashes among authorities confusing or disorienting, these students felt licensed and encouraged by them to argue for their own inter-pretations of the texts.

Faculty members have discovered that designing and develop-ing a new course with a team of five or more persons, including both faculty and fellows, requires that assumptions about pedagogy and learning goals be articulated and supported by all members of the team. The evidence to date indicates that the courses that oper-ate most effectively are those in which the faculty collaborate seri-ously and creatively. When the teaching team has committed to a collective strategy for the development and implementation of the course materials, the students have responded enthusiastically. Planning, communication, and compromise are critical to success in the new program. Although this process of investigation and con-sensus building has invariably proved to be time-consuming and challenging in ways that differ from the usual experience of con-ventional, independent course design, most faculty agree that the experience has been rewarding. In addition, faculty have profited from learning new pedagogical techniques from their colleagues.

Overwhelmingly, students are pleased to be able to study fewer works in much more depth, rather than having to devour a huge amount of material in a rushed and superficial way. Students inter-viewed in one focus group unanimously considered one of the highlights of the new program to be its focus on a few works, read in depth and analyzed from a variety of angles—an experience that they opposed to that of friends in the remaining CIV courses, in which the number of texts was not reduced. The limitation on the number of readings has helped to realize one important goal of the new legislation: it causes students to reread and study texts carefully rather than simply skim them. Eighty-eight percent of students in the two new fall IHUM courses reported that they reread the assigned texts.

These early returns suggest that the new program is already achieving many of its goals. Yet IHUM is only at the beginning of its trajectory. The enterprise is one in which everyone associated with Area One recognizes that the program and its courses must continue to evolve and improve. Written into the new legislation for IHUM are assurances that its courses will keep current with changes in the humanities. The legislation specifies that the whole program must be reexamined and redesigned in 2007. Presumably the echoes of past legislation and past debates on how to implement the humanities requirement will be heard again.

References

Bell, C. "The Ritual Body and the Dynamics of Ritual Power." *Journal of Ritual Studies,* 1990, *4*(2), 299–313.

Erickson, B., and D. Strommer. *Teaching College Freshmen.* San Francisco: Jossey-Bass, 1991.

Nussbaum, M. *Cultivating Humanity: A Classical Defense of Reform in Higher Education.* Cambridge, Mass.: Harvard University Press, 1997.

Schneider, A. "Stanford Revisits the Course That Set Off the Culture Wars." *Chronicle of Higher Education,* May 9, 1997, pp. A10–12.

Stanford University Committee on Undergraduate Studies. *Proposal Concerning the Area One Requirement: Cultures, Ideas and Values.* Stanford, Calif.: Stanford University, 1988.

Stanford University Committee on Undergraduate Studies. *Proposal Concerning the Area One Requirement: Introduction to the Humanities.* Stanford, Calif.: Stanford University, 1997.

Conclusion: What Now Shall We Teach?

Roger Shattuck

The Visiting Committee: A Parable

Sue Patterson, sixty-six years old, has just retired from the English department at a large southern university. Her book on Mary Wollstonecraft, published in the 1980s, was very well received. She has since been active in pedagogy and undergraduate teaching.

Andrew Spitz, forty-three, associate professor of classics at a western liberal arts college, recently published a book on the contemporaneity of Cicero's writings on education and moral philosophy.

The provost of McHugh University in Indiana, an undergraduate college of three thousand students plus graduate programs in social work and law, invited Patterson and Spitz to form the visiting team to evaluate the college's four-semester Humanities Program. The program is elected by about half the college's first- and second-year students. Humanities, popularly known as "Hums" dates back to the 1920s, was suspended for a decade beginning in the mid-1970s, and was reinstated in 1986.

Patterson and Spitz had never met before. Two months in advance they received ample materials on McHugh and on its Humanities Program, ranging from catalogue copy to faculty committee reports to student evaluations. They also, hastily, read each other's work.

Patterson and Spitz arrived on campus early Wednesday afternoon. From then until Friday night, their schedule carried them through a packed sequence of meetings with the responsible faculty committee, individual interviews with faculty members, students, and administrators (including the president with two trustees), visits to lectures and discussion sections, and social events. Sue and Andrew moved to a first-name basis almost immediately, but they barely had a chance to talk to each other until Saturday morning. That entire day was set aside for them to go over their notes and draft as much of their report as possible. Both had to leave Sunday morning.

They quickly established that, as stated in the catalogue, Hums is a straightforward great books sequence from *Gilgamesh,* the Old Testament, and Homer to (two years and four semesters later) Nietzsche and Dostoevsky. The syllabi are broken down into rough chronological divisions. In the first year students attend two lectures and one discussion session each week; in the second year, the proportion is reversed. All assigned works belong to what is conventionally called the Western tradition, with the exception of two weeks on Buddhism during the third semester. The program is generally well received by students and parents. Faculty members who teach in the program have mixed views about its purpose, the syllabi of readings, the contribution to their professional advancement, the absence of twentieth-century materials, and the near absence of non-Western materials.

On Saturday, working both together and separately with word processors, Sue and Andrew drafted the descriptive parts of their report. They laid it out as follows:

   I. History and Background of the Humanities Program
  II. Description of the Program
       A. Philosophy and purpose
       B. Direction and administration
       C. Faculty and budget
       D. Syllabi and readings: Major themes and questions addressed
       E. Structure and pedagogy: Lectures, discussion sections, written work, examinations
 III. Effectiveness of Lectures and Discussion Sections Visited
       A. First year
       B. Second year

IV. Responses to "Hums": Alumni, trustees, administrators, faculty, students

V. Conclusions and Recommendations

By the time they were due at the dean's house for dinner, Sue and Andrew had transformed their notes into prose through section IV. Andrew suggested that they meet at breakfast to discuss the last part, but because Sue's plane departed too early to permit that, they decided that each would draft a two-page sketch or summary of the conclusions and recommendations section and exchange these drafts in two weeks. Then they would combine and expand their ideas for the final document. Both believed this plan was practical and workable, and they congratulated themselves on accomplishing a great deal on that Saturday.

Sue and Andrew both met their deadline—barely. The following two documents virtually passed each other in cyberspace.

To: Andrew Spitz
From: Sue Patterson
Re: McHugh Humanities evaluation

Here's my draft for Part V—just in time.

Conclusions and Recommendations

The intermittent seventy-year history of McHugh University's Humanities Program provides a useful set of precedents on which to build. A great number of well-intentioned faculty members have created an intellectual space, genuinely important to many alumni, which constitutes a major part of the institution's identity and self-image. No one should be scornful of such an achievement. It deserves respect and continuation.

But this evaluation team must report frankly and firmly that the Humanities Program stands in need of radical reconstitution and reform if it hopes to survive and to be fully relevant to the educational needs of the new century. We suggest that revisions proceed along the lines laid out below.

1. The present syllabi of texts to be read, of lectures, and of topics to be covered in discussion sections set down in considerable

detail the sequence of all four semesters. In other words, you are asking both senior professors and junior faculty members trained in new approaches to accept a high degree of uniformity both in texts read and how to deal with them.

For the sake of both the faculty and the students, we urge you to introduce more choice and flexibility. You may want to have two tracks—one emphasizing historical junctures and contexts and the other emphasizing a small number of overarching philosophical questions. At a minimum, you should open up the second year by allowing professors to choose texts from an approved list, plus other texts not on the list. That way the lockstep of the first year would yield to a far greater diversity in the second year. The lectures could also be dropped in the second year.

2. Many of the faculty are already aware that "Hums" should be opened up both to non-Western texts and topics and to twentieth-century texts calling for nontraditional approaches. These concerns have established themselves incontrovertibly in the past thirty years. Feminism, postmodernist literary theory, "the prism of gender," and African American studies are nowhere mentioned in the current syllabi for the four courses forming Hums.

3. Two further questions tend to converge on a single solution. One is the need for an overall focus or emphasis in so extended and comprehensive a sequence of courses. The other is an adequate response to the claims of postmodernist literary theory that reason (or logical analysis) is patriarchal, oppressive, imperialist, and not suitable for women and minorities and non-Western peoples. We suggest that the combined response to these two different circumstances could be found in beginning the course with two weeks on philosophical method, critical thinking, and claims to objectivity and freedom from bias. No text presents these matters so dramatically as the Socratic dialogues. Thus critical reflection, careful reasoning, liberation from habits and customs, and the systematic questioning of stereotypes could become the leitmotif of everything that follows. Without such a guiding principle, Hums could easily remain a slack survey of great books simply because they are there.

A hundred other matters present themselves concerning faculty and student recruitment, budget, administration, and leadership. But the questions of curriculum and syllabus must be central for a program that contributes so much to the intellectual climate of McHugh University.

That's all for now. Sue

To: Sue Patterson

From: Andrew Spitz

Re: Part V. Conclusions and Recommendations

This is pretty rough and probably represents a personal view rather than a position that would result from a careful discussion between the two of us. Even so, I've said "we." See what you think.

Our close scrutiny of the Humanities Program at McHugh University, summarized in the earlier parts of this report, informs us that it is a surprisingly successful program in spite of strong criticism from a few faculty members and one dean, and in spite of (or because of?) its reemergence (after being eliminated for ten years) during a period of intense educational and intellectual debates. One could take the position: "If it works, don't fix it." But we believe that the time has come to inspect the foundations in order to determine how well they have held up. And it is important that a new generation of teachers participate in discussions about what stays in place and what needs revision. During their deliberations, the faculty should also listen to alumni of Hums in order to discover its potential meaning to students in their later years.

We are not sure that the Hums faculty needs outside advice about revisions in the program. But we may contribute by reporting back to them a synthesis of their remarks to us in interviews, of our observations at lectures and discussion sections, and of our combined experience with other comparable programs. Here are the major issues in our eyes—each accompanied by a question mark to indicate the complexity of these matters.

• The role of history? "Hums" is now taught for four semesters, following the chronological order of readings. The basic structure emerges as a succession of great books that increasingly begin to talk to one another across time. Each is given some historical background. But in this humanities course, history as a discipline based on the arrangement and interpretation of verifiable facts gets short shrift. History has grown up in the Western tradition as the essential complement to reason (not its opposite). Reason without history resembles a mill without grist. Ideas and propositions alone, without empirical observation and verification, take us back to Gulliver's Laputa.

Possibly Hums could arrange its readings more around major historical periods like the Renaissance and the French Revolution. Possibly a single-volume world history textbook could be used as collateral reading throughout the four semesters to tie everything together with the tidal movements of history. But does such a volume exist? Neither of us can name an existing one more recent than H. G. Wells's *The Outline of History.*

• Twentieth-century readings? At present the last semester of Heritage marches up to the twentieth century and stops short—with Nietzsche and Dostoevsky. Has the most pertinent and exciting part of this long march been omitted? We would remind the faculty that twentieth-century materials raise disputes that strain agreements reached about earlier writings, and that students are likely to read twentieth-century works in other courses. They need instruction most in noncontemporary writings. The current policy strikes us as reasonable and wise.

• Non-Western readings? Perhaps two weeks on Buddhism is not enough. We suggest that the rise and history of Islam, an importance force in Western history, be covered carefully at the appropriate moment. But the Qur'an, for structural and stylistic reasons, makes a poor choice for a major reading. Other works, such as the West African epic Sundiata, have considerable appeal. But we would recommend that the program of works read not flinch from the principle that Hums represents an attempt to bring to life the Western tradition or Western civilization. An immense diversity and ecumenism already awaits us there. Insofar as we have reasons to be ashamed or proud of that complex and multifarious tradition, we should bring out those considerations in the program.

• Uniformity and flexibility? One faculty member observed somewhat testily that he was being asked to teach this immensely varied program "in lock-step." It is true that compared to a multitrack core program, as at Stanford, incorporating extensive faculty and student choice, Hums offers only one path. But it is a broad, varied, intellectually challenging path. Uniformity in following a weak, poorly taught program obviously would compound the damage. On the other hand, reasonable uniformity in following a strong program contributes the marked advantage of commonality. Students in such a program can be moved to talk to one another outside class about the books and events and ideas that have enduring significance. And it is an advantage to have professors willing to teach courses based not on their specialty and their own approach, but on a larger scheme conveying a sense of our shared past. Perhaps there should be more flexibility toward the end of the program. But the merits of commonality also increase as the program goes on.

• A presiding narrative? We are wary of oversimplifications and reductionism. And no one would propose that we change the title "Humanities" to "The Triumph of the West" or something equally tendentious. For the West has not triumphed, and the costs of our dominance in the world have become all too real to us. But a program like Hums will probably gain in excitement and coherence if it adopts not one but a small number of overarching narratives, not as authoritative arrangements of the sequence but as hypotheses to be tried out and evaluated. The following examples could be helpful in grasping the marches and counter-marches in the program:

1. The top-down hierarchy of the great chain of being yielding to the bottom-up hierarchy of evolution and the survival of the fittest
2. Polytheism yielding to monotheism yielding to . . . ?
3. *Lex talionis,* justice as power, yielding to equal justice under law and supported by love and charity, challenged by a reversion to *lex talionis* (social Darwinism, Nietzsche, totalitarianism, ethnic cleansing)

Is all else secondary? No. The intelligence, preparation, dedication, imagination, and high standards of the professors teaching in the program and their willingness to discuss without rancor basic questions of structure and content count more than any other factor toward its success. But no report can accomplish much toward creating such a cadre of teachers. We can help most by encouraging existing teachers to reflect on their responsibilities.

I look forward to reading your draft, Sue. Where do we go from here? Andrew

After several weeks of exchanging e-mail messages and talking at length on the telephone, Sue Patterson and Andrew Spitz found that they could not satisfactorily combine their two drafts into a single document. They decided amicably to revise their own drafts of section V and submit both to the provost, who felt the report was better than satisfactory and passed it on to all concerned parties. The faculty committee chewed over the double report for more than a semester of meetings and made some changes in Hums, none of which seemed to arise directly from the report. Because a majority of professors believe in a strong core program, Hums is still very much alive at McHugh University.

Five Holistic Comments

The preceding account of Sue, Andrew, McHugh, and Hums is offered as a parable. As with all parables, it is meant to provoke comments. Five such comments follow.

1. We live in a profoundly adversarial society. Our market economy relies basically on competition among products and services. Our immensely glorified world of sports sets before us contestants whose wins and losses are magnified to heroic proportions by hyperbolic commentators. Democratic politics pits one candidate against another and one policy against another in a perpetual public process of polarized debate. And our system of equal justice under law defines itself and its elaborate court procedures as adversarial. One side engages the other in a two-sided struggle. Only one side can win.

Should education become adversarial too? Several years ago I wrote the following statement as a section of "Nineteen Theses on Literature":

> We have brought ourselves to a great perplexity about the
> basic role of education. Should education socialize the young
> within an existing culture and offer them the basic means to
> succeed in that culture? Or should education give the young the
> means to challenge and overthrow the existing culture,
> presumably in order to achieve a better life? Here I shall appeal
> to analogy.

Almost immediately after fertilization, the human embryo sets aside a few cells that are sheltered from the rest of the organism and the environment. These cells retain a special ability to divide by meiosis into haploid cells (that is, eggs and sperm) needed for sexual reproduction. Our gonads represent the most stable and protected element in the body and are usually able to pass on unchanged to the next generation segments of the genetic material we were born with. In this way the sins of the fathers and mothers during their lifetimes are not visited upon their children. Except for radiation and a few diseases, the life we live does not affect our gonads. Evolution has granted security to our germ line.

No such biological process is built into cultures. But all cultures have discovered something similar—an activity, sometimes developed into an institution, that we call education. By education we pass on to the young the customs, restrictions, discoveries, and wisdom that have afforded survival and development so far.

There is good reason to maintain that, unlike many other institutions—political, social, and artistic—which criticize and rebel against the status quo, education should remain primarily a conservative institution, like our gonads. We are overloading education when we ask it to reform society, redesign culture, and incorporate the avant-garde and bohemian into its precincts. In a free society, original and disaffected minds will always find a platform. Schools and colleges need not provide the principal home for political, social, and artistic dissidents. The primary mission of education is the transmission of a precious heritage. As the heritage is passed along at the higher levels, both teachers and students will increasingly test it and criticize it and seek to improve it. That healthy shift should not supplant the essential process of transmission. [Shattuck, 1994]

These mildly polemical remarks evoke the debate that lies latent in almost all discussions in education today. Should teaching serve to acculturate students by giving them the knowledge through which we have reached the present juncture? Or should we be teaching students above all to question culture and traditional knowledge? The extreme form of mechanical transmission is illustrated by a Qur'anic school in which children learn by heart to recite *surahs* in Arabic, often without understanding their meaning. The extreme form of education as liberation is illustrated by programs, starting sometimes before secondary school, to train students to challenge authority, including any claims that wisdom may be found in great books. The opposition between the two usually manifests itself not in the stark form of tradition versus subversion but in debates about what is to be learned.

On the one hand, schools may teach a standard curriculum of subjects in sequence, including literature, history and geography, mathematics, and science. On the other hand, schools may teach skills: reading, number skills, and critical thinking. In the former, the emphasis falls on a body of knowledge to be learned. In the latter, disdain for rote learning puts the emphasis on reasoning, asking, active learning projects, higher-order thinking, and approaches to knowledge. Education can become increasingly content free in the latter sequence, because the assumption is that we can teach the skills and the methods of rational inquiry to deal with any problem when it arises. In his account of going back to take the Lit. Hum. course at Columbia College, David Denby (1996) produces a sentence that embodies the adversarial approach to education: "What the books taught was not a stable body of knowledge or even consistent 'values' but critical habits of mind."

Denby has parroted a superficial and misleading half-truth because he employs the either-or formulation (in this case, stated as "not this, but that") instead of the nonexclusionary, nonadversarial both-and formulation. Is it not evident that one cannot exercise sound critical thinking about a subject—history, for example—until one has a considerable body of knowledge of it? One may, of course, dismiss history as a discipline. But the crux here lies in the order of events, not in the dismissal of any part of education. Basic knowledge of the events of history precedes the exercise of critical thinking about those events and their significance. Thereafter, knowledge and analytical interpretation continue together, alternatively and reciprocally.

Let me underscore this point. In some humanities courses today, one of the early claims made is that Socrates favors the primacy of reason and critical thinking over custom and traditional knowledge. I have heard some of my colleagues maintain that the Greek philosophers unanimously opposed anything resembling a great books curriculum. Except for some reservations about writing itself, the evidence points in the opposite direction. In *The*

Republic, Socrates displays intimate knowledge of Homer and Hesiod and a whole culture of traditional tales and wisdom about the history of gods and men. There is nothing content free about Socrates' training. As history moves on from Socrates and Plato, as we come to Aquinas, to the renewal of dialogue during the seventeenth and eighteenth centuries, and to the secular challenge of Diderot's *Encyclopedia,* knowledge of every aspect of life and respect for the past accompany the criticism of superstitions and unfounded traditions. Reason and critical thinking never become an alternative to knowledge and experience.

In our own day, a great number of authors have addressed the relations between tradition and innovation. In the nine pages of "Tradition and the Individual Talent," T. S. Eliot (1932) shuns the either-or approach and keeps the two terms in a reciprocal relation: "The past should be altered by the present as much as the present is directed by the past." The arrival of something new does not overthrow tradition. It brings about a readjustment "of the whole existing order [and a] conformity between the old and the new." Eliot's almost idyllic mood of reconciliation was already being undermined by forces of the avant-garde and radical experiment in the arts. Fifty years later, Lionel Trilling (1965) opened *Beyond Culture* with a deeply troubled meditation on "the disenchantment of our culture with culture itself" and on modern literature's "bitter line of hostility to civilization." Thus he recognized the adversarial intention of much modern literature. I submit that a similar adversarial intention has found its way into education on many levels, where it tends to destroy the essential and complementary relation between tradition and innovation, past and present. We need both knowledge (content) and rational method (skills), and in that order. Look askance at anyone who would try to sequester them or to promote one above the other.

2. Just as the basic unit of life is the cell, the basic unit of learning in our colleges and universities is the course. Ideally the course assembles and integrates certain continuities of subject matter, time, and method within a recognized area. The course presumably forms a coherent part of a larger unit of learning called a program or a discipline or a curriculum. Proficiency in an undergraduate field—civil engineering, Asian history, Arabic language

and literature, botany—entails completing a number of courses in the proper order. And the first two years of college, the "liberal education" segment in a college of arts and sciences, are used to require a certain number of courses, such as classical civilization, history of the world or of the West, survey of English literature, a laboratory science, a foreign language, history of philosophy. In some institutions, an integrated core curriculum was created to combine many of these fields.

Three major developments since World War II have modified this educational structure in which the courses a student followed in college were chosen primarily by the faculty according to the traditions of a liberal education and the development of the central academic fields. First, the elective system was reaffirmed, particularly by the establishment of highly flexible distribution requirements in the first two years. Second, the temporary wartime reduction of a course from a nine-month cumulative unit of learning to a one-semester, fourteen-week sequence of classes was made permanent. Third, in a shift that gained momentum in the 1970s and 1980s, the basic disciplines of the humanities (classics, history, literature and the modern languages, philosophy, and art history) came under increasing attack from ethnic minorities, theorists, feminists, and Marxists. By the late 1980s any agreed-on content for a freshman English course or a philosophy major had dwindled to a tenuous thread. An undergraduate, guided only by vague distribution requirements and a numerical minimum of courses in his or her major field, was called on to select between thirty-two and forty semester courses over a four-year period to constitute a degree out of a huge proliferation of offerings. In this way, a liberal education and a major became diluted and fragmented into an often incoherent set of semester courses without the focus and the final assessment of a set of comprehensive examinations at the end. An English major today may never have read Milton or Emerson or even Shakespeare with care. A history major may never have read Gibbon or Tocqueville. Methods and approaches and ideologies frequently take precedence over actual content.

The impulse among faculty members to reaffirm their responsibility not merely for individual courses, but also for coherent programs, has resurfaced in many programs of general education, core curricula, Western heritage, and great books. To those who find fault with these demanding programs by calling them "educational paternalism," I would answer that we have allowed college students to follow their fads and their bliss into educational capriciousness and confusion. There are some books everyone should read, some historic episodes everyone should study. Reconstituted core curricula reverse the trend toward the fragmentation of learning. Such programs restore to the faculty the responsibility of defining the shape and sequence of a field of study. And this attention to coherence may spread to the undergraduate major fields. Only a few highly enterprising and well-prepared students can benefit from designing their own undergraduate program. The vast majority will profit most if they learn the basic content and skills of a field, whose outlying regions they can later explore.

3. Since 1953 I have taught at four universities. At each one, under very different circumstances, I was drawn into a humanities program of some description for first- and second-year students. In one case (Plan II at the University of Texas, Austin), I participated in an already successful program. In three cases (Harvard University, University of Virginia, and Boston University), I helped to set up a core curriculum or a segment of such a curriculum. Out of these various experiences I offer the following report.

There are four principal ways of planning a core curriculum in the humanities—either a full-year course or two full-year courses, ideally combined with other courses covering other fields:

- *The great books.* Human achievement will reach us vividly and authentically in the words of authors and artists who have survived the test of time, along with the accompanying historical background. Such works include paintings, architecture, sculpture, and music, as well as books.
- *Major historical periods or junctures.* Examination of these periods will include an important role for works of literature and art and bring out the complex organization of society that underlies any major period.
- *Overarching themes, ideas, and motifs.* Here a philosophical outlook finds its pathway to the great works and the major periods of the past by beginning with probing and

encompassing questions concerning truth, religion, reason, social organization, the role of the individual, virtue, science, and art.

- *Ways of knowing.* The premise that different fields of inquiry and knowledge entail different kinds of thinking and analysis places the emphasis on methodologies more than on content. This is the most recent and least tested structure for a core curriculum and the furthest removed from a reliance on a sequence of great books or major periods.

I list these four ways of planning a core curriculum or general education program in the order of their effectiveness according to my experience. I remain skeptical about the empirical soundness and pedagogical usefulness of the "ways of knowing" approach. Harvard College's adoption of such a program was not based on convincing evidence and discussion and has not been particularly successful (Keller, 1982).

The chapters in this book on thirteen humanities programs around the country plus my own investigations tell me that the steadiest foundation of such programs lies in the central works that speak to us and to each other as vividly as they spoke to their own time. The list will not be everywhere the same. Nor will the variations be so enormous that there will not remain considerable overlap to represent a widespread sense of the core. When these works appear in the course, they often appeal to students apart from what teachers say in their presentations and discussions. And such works, better than abstract ideas and complex historical periods, lend themselves to classroom discussion and detailed scrutiny in writing assignments. All the evidence is there on the page to be examined, and everyone has the same evidence to deal with. We can too easily be led to forget that in teaching the humanities, the book remains the major pedagogical and cultural miracle.

Let me venture a schematic, albeit wildly oversimplified, diagram of a core program. The left-hand column in the list below represents the factors that set the scope of and give the shape to the prospective materials. (Kindly indulge the category error of grouping two active agents with an inert product of human thinking.) The right-hand column attempts to separate into basic categories the materials of such a program—both knowledge and ways of recording, analyzing, and transmitting that knowledge.

Shaping Factors	*Basic Organizing Categories*
Curriculum	*Supernatural or divine revelation,* especially
Teacher	scripture
Student	*Tradition,* including custom, common knowledge, common sense, institutions
	Works created by human beings: literature, architecture, painting, sculpture, music, dance
	History as a systematic critical discipline
	Discursive reason based on verifiable evidence and rules of logic

My justification for proposing so simplistic a scheme—beyond its heuristic value in provoking responses and objections—is that such an array of elements allows me to ask a difficult question: Where is bedrock? Which of these eight elements represents our principal concern and focus?

The passionate pedagogue will elect the last item in the left-hand column and opine that one must teach the student, not the subject. But such a slogan repeats the romantic error of rejecting knowledge in favor of self-fulfillment. The true religious believer will go to the top of the right-hand column and subsume everything else under divine revelation. The philosopher trained on Socrates and Aquinas and Kant will place the faculty of discursive reason at the center of the landscape. As a humanist devoted to literature and the arts, I would choose "works" as the sturdiest and most revealing category. For, like perfectly preserved fossil remains, they come to us whole, belonging both to their time and to our time, both mysterious and transparent, both general and particular. And with a little help, students can enter into direct communication with these works and come to know them as well as their own times and their own friends. Nothing exposes us so intimately and searingly to otherness and diversity as reading the works of the past.

But I have allowed myself to answer a question before questioning the question. Before the previous paragraph, the true critic should have intervened to point out the restrictive and unsatisfactory nature of the question. No reason has been advanced to establish that one element must take precedence over the others. No evidence has been given to disqualify the affirmation that it is the coordination and cooperation of all those elements in something approaching an organic process that finally produces a core curriculum in a humanities program. Not analysis but synthesis confers life.

4. The many descriptions and histories of humanities programs assembled in this book neglect one major consideration: how to extend such a program into foreign language study. Even in so completely integrated a curriculum as that of St. John's College, a foreign language is required and at the same time left dangling. Beyond its genuinely useful functions (including the teaching of grammar), can foreign language study contribute to the general mission of a core program? Must foreign language study remain an educational orphan?

Many years ago, as a young instructor, I was put in charge of about fifteen sections of the second-year French course at an institution that had also established a fairly rigorous general education program in the first two years. It entailed some choice by students among a set of courses in the humanities, social sciences, and sciences. Foreign language study through the fourth semester was included as a routine codicil to other requirements. As I saw it, the situation offered a remarkable opportunity. I drew up for inclusion in the third-semester French course a set of proverbs, counting rhymes, nursery rhymes, and simple short stories. My colleagues and graduate student teaching assistants helped design a workbook of questions testing comprehension and knowledge of grammar in these passages. During the fourth semester, we had another workbook using graded materials from well-known works to prepare the students for our three major authors in the original French. In science they read forty or so pages from Claude Bernard's *Introduction à la médecine expérimentale*. For the social sciences they read selections from Tocqueville's *De la démocratie en Amérique*. In the humanities they worked through Montaigne, Pascal, Voltaire, and Rousseau and then read Baudelaire as the principal author.

During the two years that we carried out this project in

second-year French, we learned a great deal about its advantages and shortcomings. The choice of readings linked the language course to general education courses persuasively enough to excite a few students and add intellectual substance to this level of language learning. Professors in charge of the general education program supported our endeavor with varying degrees of enthusiasm and skepticism. The principal resistance came from the graduate student teaching assistants, who taught all the sections other than mine. They complained about their lack of preparation to teach Claude Bernard on scientific method and Tocqueville on early American society and also about any change in the established textbook and an already familiar syllabus. On the other hand, two other language programs began to consider a parallel course whose readings would be integrated with the general education requirements. I feel certain that after a year or two of adjustments, including better preparation of the teaching assistants, the new readings would have given an augmented purpose to the language courses in French and perhaps in other languages. It was a genuinely promising, if modest, curriculum change that deserved a full tryout. But when I left for another position after two years, my replacement restored the previous textbook and syllabus.

Contemporary high school and college language teaching tends to emphasize oral work and conversation more than reading, a further obstacle to implementing a program based on reading mainline works. But some of us continue to believe that active reading (including accurate pronunciation in reading aloud) is the most useful skill at the college level. Courses based on this premise obviously lend themselves to a sequence of readings related to other parts of a student's liberal arts program. Language departments would do well to investigate their role in contributing to and taking advantage of humanities and general education programs during the first two years of college.

5. *Core* is an odd word. Here are three definitions culled and collated from several dictionaries:

"A central portion of something that is cut out and thrown away"

"A disease in sheep"

"The dry, horny capsule containing the seeds of apple, pear, etc."

The first definition confounds us—and reminds us of the unexpected games that language always plays with our expectations; that is not the right definition at all. The second provokes a laugh and misses the mark in a different direction. The third strikes home and returns to the metaphor of culture and its germ line perpetuated by education. This dry, horny capsule contains the kernels of knowledge that will germinate and grow into mature plants and trees. They in turn will nourish and clothe and shade us intellectually and emotionally for the rest of our lives. This core we shall not throw away. We shall keep it in order to plant its seeds.

References

Denby, D. *Great Books: My Adventures with Homer, Rousseau, Woolf, and Other Indestructible Writers of the Western World.* New York: Simon & Schuster, 1996.

Eliot, T. S. "Traditions and the Individual Talent." In T. S. Eliot, *Selected Essays, 1917–1932.* Orlando, Fla.: Harcourt Brace, 1932.

Keller, P. *Getting at the Core: Curriculum Reform at Harvard.* Cambridge, Mass.: Harvard University Press, 1982.

Shattuck, R. "XIX Theses on Literature." *Association of Literary Scholars and Critics Newsletter,* 1994, *1*(1).

Trilling, L. *Beyond Culture: Essays on Literature and Learning.* New York: Viking, 1965.

Index